The
Writings of Robert Grosseteste

The Writings of Robert Grosseteste

Bishop of Lincoln

1235–1253

by

S. HARRISON THOMSON
Professor of Medieval History, University of Colorado

Cambridge
AT THE UNIVERSITY PRESS
1940

CAMBRIDGE UNIVERSITY PRESS
Cambridge, New York, Melbourne, Madrid, Cape Town,
Singapore, São Paulo, Delhi, Mexico City

Cambridge University Press
The Edinburgh Building, Cambridge CB2 8RU, UK

Published in the United States of America by Cambridge University Press, New York

www.cambridge.org
Information on this title: www.cambridge.org/9781107668645

First published 1940
First paperback edition 2013

A catalogue record for this publication is available from the British Library

ISBN 978-1-107-66864-5 Paperback

To

ANDREW GEORGE LITTLE

CONTENTS

PHILOSOPHICAL AND SCIENTIFIC WORKS

PLATES

INTRODUCTION

THE present essay in medieval bibliography grew out of the writer's study of Wyclyf's philosophical treatises. Wyclyf held Grosseteste in high regard and quoted him with striking frequency. A study of the literary tradition concerning the Bishop of Lincoln made it clear that insufficient serious attention had been paid to his literary activity. There was need of an extensive study of Grosseteste's works based upon the original sources, that is upon the manuscripts scattered widely in the libraries of Europe. As a contribution to such a study, an effort has been made to see every known MS containing a work by Grosseteste, authentic or spurious. Over 140 libraries have been visited and approximately 2500 MSS consulted. Many of these MSS were examined without previous knowledge that they contained works of Grosseteste, but because of a hopeful suspicion that they might. The large number of times that such a fortuitous examination has yielded positive results makes it almost certain that much MS material has still escaped notice, and equally probable that other students will be able to make substantial additions and corrections to the work in its present form.

The nature of the material has, in large measure, determined the form which the catalogue has taken. The wideness of Grosseteste's interests and the versatility of his talents made necessary a division into categories of content. It has seemed convenient to classify his works in this way: Translations from the Greek, Commentaries, Philosophical Works (including Mathematics and Physics), Pastoral Works (except Sermons and *Dicta*), Miscellaneous Works, Anglo-Norman Works, Sermons, Letters, *Dicta* (distinguished from Pastoral Works and Sermons simply by reason of mass and tradition), Doubtful Works, Spurious Works, and Lost or Untraced Works. There is inevitably some overlapping in any such arbitrary classification. The considerable number of works noticed here for the first time will be evident from a perusal of the text. There undoubtedly remain some of Grosseteste's works of which no trace has been found in the course of these investigations.

The most important problem throughout has been that of authenticity. Where doubt has arisen, the burden of proof has fallen most reasonably on priority of MS ascription. The validity of such priority has then rested upon the paleographical criteria for the date of the MS or ascription involved. Such judgments of date, it must be emphasized, are always matters of some delicacy, where disagreements among specialists are sure to occur. Yet the study of dated MSS is doing much to make our judgments more reliable and to minimize the greater diversities of opinion. To anyone who has used printed catalogues of MSS it is hardly necessary to observe that the datings in the great majority—there are a few happy exceptions—of printed catalogues must be accepted with great reserve.

In consideration of these two factors, the necessary emphasis on the dating of MSS and the general unreliability of published datings, it has been imperative to pay particular attention to paleographical chronology. An endeavour has been made to date all the MSS seen, quite independently of all previous datings. *In primis*, it has often been overlooked, even by those who work continually with medieval MSS, that the provenance of a MS is most often to be decided before a definitive date is assigned. For example, there are certain characteristics of the gothic bookhand which mark the scribe as having learned to write somewhere along the upper Rhine; at the same time there may be other characteristics of his writing which, a half-century or more previously, had been common at Paris or Oxford but had since gone out of vogue. The general *ductus* of his script may easily lead to a considerable error until one realizes that it is not a French or an English, but a German, hand. An attempt has been made to ascribe a provenance to all the MSS listed, but with many more misgivings, it must be confessed, than the infrequent question-marks would indicate. The provenance of MSS now in England and not otherwise described may be accepted as English. The conclusions thus reached as to date are far from satisfactory, but it was felt that an effort to date the MSS should be made. Perhaps the fact that so many MSS were examined by one person, many of them more than once, within a relatively short time, having in view criteria of comparison empirically arrived at, may add something of consistency and reliability to the result. In general, more confidence is felt that the dates assigned to MSS of English, North French, and South German or Bohemian provenance are approximately correct than that those of Italian origin are at all accurately placed. Paleographical monstrosities were rife in Italy of the later Middle Ages and accurate criteria are not easily attainable. It should be noted that a suggested date is intended to allow approximately twenty years' latitude either way.

Although MS evidence has, as a general principle, been considered determinative for authenticity, other kinds of evidence have not been disregarded. Arguments from content, from style, from the testimony of contemporaries, from later literary characters, from the long line of bibliographers, have all been drawn upon. There are cases where internal evidence has been sufficient to cause the rejection of works apparently authenticated by MS ascription. The *Summa Philosophie* is a case of this kind. Although ascribed to Grosseteste in the MSS, this work contains references to events, such as the death of Simon de Montfort, which did not occur until after the death of Grosseteste. The *Tractatus de Lingua* and the *Summa Iusticie* (both by the same author) are rejected for a combination of internal reasons. Some works are listed among *Dubia* for no better reason than that the MS evidence is so late as to be quite suspect or that the content seems un-Grossetestian. The reasons for so classifying these works are given as simply and clearly as possible in each case.

The catalogue can lay no claim to add anything of consequence to our purely biographical knowledge of Grosseteste.* There is singularly little of an autobiographical nature in any of his works with the notable exception of his Letters. The editing of his writings will bring to light what scattered data there are in his various works. In spite of the temerity of the undertaking, dates have been suggested for the composition of many works. They have been based on a combination of internal and external evidence, such as information given by Matthew Paris, or the use in a contemporary MS of the title *episcopus*, or the use of Greek and untranslated works of the Greek Fathers, for we have good reason to believe that Grosseteste did not know Greek well enough to translate it until the episcopal period.†

* There is certainly need for a new biography of Grosseteste. An example of the sort of work that must be done, preliminary to a definitive biography, is a recent article by J. C. Russell in the *Harvard Theological Review*, XXVI (1933), 161–172, on the early years of Grosseteste and his *adiutores*. Russell has brought to light certain important errors in accepted tradition concerning Grosseteste's early ecclesiastical preferments. For possible confusion between several R. Grossetestes, in addition to those mentioned by Russell, see *Cartulary of Oseney Abbey*, I (ed. H. E. Salter, Oxford Historical Society, LXXXIX, Oxford, 1929), 217, among the witnesses of a confirmation, 1184–1189, a Magister Ricardus Grosseteste.

† But see below, p. 121 f., under the *De Cessacione Legalium*.

Professor Ezio Franceschini, Dr R. W. Hunt and Miss Ruth J. Dean have consented to collaborate with me in the laborious task of editing the principal *inedita* of Grosseteste. The first volume, *Opera Minora Philosophica*, is well under way, and, *deo volente*, may be expected to appear in 1940.

BIBLIOGRAPHERS OF GROSSETESTE

The history of the successive efforts of various scholars since the time of Grosseteste to list the Bishop's writings is, as would be expected, a story of cumulative borrowing, piecing out, and occasional original study. The merits of these cataloguers vary greatly. We have much information concerning different aspects of Grosseteste's literary activity from his contemporaries and from subsequent writers whose interest was doctrinal or political, or who desired to take advantage of the great authority of his name. References to these men can be found listed in the *Index Nominum* under Roger Bacon, Matthew Paris, Duns Scotus, Burley, Bradwardine, Hermannus Alemannus, Nicholas Trevet, William of Ware, Wyclyf,* etc. Baur† has given a summary of this history.

The first attempt to list Grosseteste's works was made by Boston of Bury (*fl.* 1400) who compiled a *Catalogus Scriptorum Ecclesie* printed in the *Praefatio* of Tanner's great work. Because of the relative rarity of Tanner's *Bibliotheca*, Boston's list of Grosseteste's works is here printed as in Tanner (p. xxxvii):

ROBERTUS LINCOLN. Episcopus, qui et Grosteste dicitur, floruit A.C. MCCL, et obiit A. MCCLIII, et scripsit multa, ‡in triplici lingua eruditus, Latina, Hebraica, et Graeca. Multa de glossis Hebraeorum extraxit, de Graeco multa transferri fecit; utpote libros Dionisii, quorum novam translationem perlucide commentavit.‡

Item in logica et astrologia et in cunctis liberalibus artibus excellenter erat eruditus. Ad papam Innocentium misit epistolam invectivam, satis tonantem pro eo quod ecclesias Angliae exactionibus indebitis vexare videretur. Hac

* Ludwig Baur, *Die philosophischen Werke des Robert Grosseteste Bischofs von Lincoln* (Münster i.W., 1912), Bd. IX of *Beiträge zur Geschichte der Philosophie des Mittelalters*), p. 7*, gives a partial list of Wyclyf's citations from Grosseteste. The list could be greatly increased from yet unpublished philosophical works of Wyclyf. See also Johann Loserth, "Johann von Wiclif und Robert Grosseteste" in *Sbte d. kais. Akad. d. Wissenschaften*, Phil.-hist. Kl. Bd. 186, 2. Abh. (1918).

† Baur, *op. cit.*, pp. 1*–14*.

‡—‡ Boston took this section *verbatim* from Nicholas Trevet's *Annales* (ed. Hog, London, 1845), p. 243. See also Baur, p. 5*.

de causa vocatus est ad curiam, et cum ibi molestaretur, appellavit constanter a curia papae Innocentii ad tribunal Christi, unde contigit, quod eodem Roberto in Anglia obeunte, audita est vox in curia papae, *Veni, miser, ad judicium*, et papa in crastino inventus est exanimis, quasi cuspide baculi in latere percussus. Hiis de causis licet perspicuus effulserit Robertus miracula transferri, tamen nec in sanctorum cathalogo poni non est a curia permissus: Scripsit Super Dionisium De Caelesti et ecclesiastica Ierarchia, lib. ii, De originali peccato, lib. i. Pr. *Quocirca*. Super Dionisium de divinis nominibus. De libero arbitrio quaestiones, lib. i. Pr. *Cum per*. Fin. *contrarium*. De sphaera, lib. i. Pr. *Intentio*. De astrolabio, lib. i. De compoto, lib. i. Super librum posteriorum. Pr. *Intentio*. Fin. *posteriorum*. Super libros physicorum notulas. Pr. *Cum scire*. Super Dionisium de mystica theologia. Super prologum Bibliae, expos. i. Exameron. Super Psalterium. Pr. *Beatus vir*. Super Epistolam ad Galathas. Pr. *Ut apostolus*. Fin. *quid docetur*. De x preceptis. Pr. *Sicut dicit*. Fin. *sex mandatis*. De cessatione legalium. Pr. *Fuerunt*. De confessione, tract. i. Pr. *Quum cogitabo*. Fin. *potentiam*. De cura pastorali. De eo quod oportuit Deum fieri hominem. De Veritate, serm. i. Pr. *Ego sum*. Fin. *in singulis*. De resurrectione, serm. i. De civitate Dei compendium. Super Job. De prima forma et forma omnium. Pr. *Rogavit*. Fin. *corripias*. 168. De luce. Pr. *Formam*. Fin. *temporibus*. De colore vel coloribus. Pr. *Color est*. Fin. *ostenduntur*. De potentia. Pr. *Omne quidem*. Fin. *ad effectum*. De Yride. Pr. *Et perspectim*. Fin. *variationis*. Secundum opus ejusdem De libero arbitrio. Pr. *Quia circa*. Fin. *dicenda*. De scientia Dei. Pr. *Quaeritur*. Fin. *recte*. De misericordia et justitia Dei. Pr. *Consequitur*. Fin. *per Dei gratiam*. De locali praesentia Dei. Pr. *Hic quaeritur*. Fin. *filius*. Summam de articulis fidei et de omnibus quae pertinent ad officium sacerdotale. Pr. *Templum*. Fin. *a servitute*. Dicta quaedam. Pr. *Amor*. Fin. *et misericordiae*. Item Testamenta xii patriarcharum de Graeco transtulit in Latinum, quae per multa tempora incognita et abscondita fuerunt per invidiam Judaeorum, nec ad notitiam Jeronimi vel alterius interpretis pervenerunt. Manifeste enim in eis de Salvatore prophetiae reperiuntur. Principium autem sic est. *Transcriptum*. Fin. *exi de terra*. 74. 168. 164. 154. Item Summam de septem vitiis capitalibus secundum quosdam. Pr. *Providendi*. Fin. *plangit*. 82. 1. Item transtulit de Graeco in Latinum librum, qui dicitur Suda, quem composuerunt viri sapientes sc. Eudemius Rhetor, Elladius, qui fuit tempore Theodosii juvenis, Eugenius Frigius, Zosimus, Gazeus, Caecilius, Siculus, Longinus, Casineus, Lupertus, Boritius, Justinus, Julius Sophista, Pacatus, Pamphilius, Zophirion, et Polion. Sermones. Pr. *Erunt signa*. Fin. *attemptatum*. De natura laminis et diafoni. Pr. *Considerandum*. Encheridion.

There can be little doubt that Boston had seen a not-inconsiderable number of MSS. In several cases, his evidence for authenticity is as good as or better than anything we now have: e.g. the two treatises *De Libero Arbitrio* (see below, p. 90 f.) and the *Questiones Theologice* (see below, p. 113 f.). His details in the case of the *Testamenta XII Patriarcharum* and *Suidas* were probably taken from the present B.M. Royal MS 4. D. vii, thought to have been partially written by

Matthew Paris. Several works which he lists are either spurious, unidentified, or lost (see below, p. 256, *Spurium* 36, and p. 267 f., *Spurium* 62). The importance of Boston for the literary history of Grosseteste lies in the fact that his list was taken over by succeeding bibliographers and merely successively expanded.

Thomas Gascoigne (1403–1458), several times Chancellor of Oxford University, made no effort to compile a list of Grosseteste's works, but has told* of seeing a number of MSS in Grosseteste's own hand in Oxford libraries. One MS, which was once in Gascoigne's possession and has many notes by him (Bodley 198), has copious marginal signs of which the key is in Lyons MS 414.† He speaks of Grosseteste's glosses on the epistles of Paul, a MS which has not yet come to light, the *Psalterium* which would most probably be Lincoln Cathedral MS 144, and the *De Cura Pastorali* (*Epistola* 127); notes on the letters of Jerome (Lincoln Coll. MS 117, p. 473[b]):‡ *Nota Lincolniensem in margine super* 20. *epistolam beati Ieronimi in libro epistolarum suarum. Registratur L. Ieronimus inter fratres minores*; separate sermons (MS *cit.* p. 403[a]): *Sermo Natis et educatis.... Vidi illud opus correctum manu sua propria*; *Epistole*; *De Luxuria*, which, if not lost beyond recall, might be one of several possible sermons; *Dicta*; and the *Super Angelicam Hierarchiam Sancti Dionysii*.

The next attempt to list the works of Grosseteste was that of John Leland whose work,§ though fragmentary, has for us the advantage that it represents first-hand examination of MS collections in monastic libraries previous to the dissolution under Henry VIII. But Leland's work was far less systematic than that of John Bale who, in several variously arranged works, ‖ compiled a list of well over a hundred works of Grosseteste, and gave many incipits. Bale has included many works in his long list in the *Catalogus* on suspicion; he has been misled on several occasions to include a single work several times under separate titles; he has listed sermons as separate

* *Loci e Libro Veritatum* (ed. J. E. Thorold Rogers, Oxford, 1881), pp. 103, 126, 129, etc.

† See below under *Concordancia Patrum*, p. 122 ff.

‡ For references from this Lincoln Coll. MS, I am indebted to Miss W. A. Pronger. See her article in *EHR*. LIII (1938), 606–626 and LIV (1939), 20–37.

§ *Commentarii de Scriptoribus Britannicis* (Oxford, 1709), and *De Rebus Britannicis Collectanea* (Oxford, 1715; ed. Hearne, 6 vols. 1744).

‖ *Illustrium Majoris Britanniae Scriptorum Summarium* (1548), thirty-one items; *Scriptorum Britanniae Catalogus* (Basel, 1557), pp. 304–307, 123 works listed; *Index Britanniae Scriptorum* (ed. Poole and Bateson, Oxford, 1902), pp. 371–379, a list of MSS in various English college and private libraries.

works; he has included a number of demonstrably spurious items. But the list remains a considerable monument to sixteenth-century scholarly interest and industry. References to Bale in this catalogue are to his longer list unless *Index* is specified.

The lists of Trithemius,* Gesner,† Sixtus Senensis,‡ Simler,§ and Poissevin|| were compilations at second hand and have little value for our purposes.

No great contribution to our knowledge of Grosseteste's literary activity was made in the two centuries after the publication of Bale's *Catalogus*. The labours of Bruno Ryves, Thomas Barlow, John Williams, and Samuel Knight¶ were so limited in purpose or fulfilment as to have added nothing of great moment. The list given by John Pits** (†1619) is nothing more than a repetition of most of Bale's list, mistakes included, though he may have seen several Cambridge MSS, among them Pembroke 7. Polycarp Leyser†† relied on Bale and Pits. Edward Brown published‡‡ a large number of the *Dicta* and some sermons. He used some of the Trinity College, Cambridge, MSS. His marginal notes in B. 15. 20 testify to his use and record his low opinion of the scribe.

Wharton§§ examined MS collections in London and Cambridge, but not exhaustively; his evidence adds little to that of Bale and Brown. Cave|||| reproduced the notices of Brown and Wharton, adding, however, a notice of the Christ Church, Canterbury, MS D. 16 (see below, p. 127 f.), which appears to have been his own discovery.

Too much praise could hardly be given to Tanner¶¶ for the thoroughness of his independent researches into the available MS

* *Catalogus Scriptorum Ecclesiasticorum* (Basel, 1531), f. 77[a].

† *Bibliotheca Universalis* (Tiguri, 1545), f. 588[D]; Appendix, *ibid.* (1555), p. 94.

‡ *Bibliotheca Sancta* (Venice, 1566).

§ *Bibliotheca Instituta* (Tiguri, 1574).

|| *Apparatus Sacer ad Scriptores Veteris et Novi Testamenti* (Venice, 1606).

¶ See Baur, pp. 10*–11*.

** *Relationum Historicarum de Rebus Anglicis Tomus Primus* (Paris, 1619), pp. 327–331.

†† *Historia Poetarum et Poematum Medii Aevi* (Magdeburg, 1721), pp. 996–998.

‡‡ *Fasciculus Rerum Expetendarum et Fugiendarum* (2 vols. London, 1690), a revised and expanded edition of a collection published by Ortwinus Gratius in 1535. Grosseteste's works appear in vol. II, pp. 250–415.

§§ *Anglia Sacra* (London, 1691), II, 344–348.

|||| *Scriptorum Ecclesiasticorum Historia Litteraria* (Cologne, 1720; Basel, 1745).

¶¶ T. Tanner, *Bibliotheca Britannica-Hibernica* (London, 1748).

collections of England for works of English writers. His bibliography of the works of Grosseteste alone would have earned our respect and gratitude. Considering the conditions of transportation and communication in the eighteenth century, we may well wonder how he compassed such a task. He added to colossal industry no mean critical sense, expressing occasionally genteel doubt of the authenticity of a given work. His indications have been of inestimable value, so far as they go, and have lightened not a little the labour involved in the compilation of the present catalogue. In several cases he has repeated works under different titles, particularly in the case of sermon collections which are likely to appear in many combinations. He has added, on Bale's authority, titles of works which he himself had not seen. Yet he must have seen some few MSS which have since disappeared or are unidentified. He had certainly examined more English MSS containing works of Grosseteste than anyone else, and his evidence, if rejected, must be accounted for. We have no reason to think that his examination of MSS was critical as to age, but it would be unjust to demand modern paleographical canons of an early eighteenth-century scholar.

The 28-page classified bibliography printed by Samuel Pegge in his *Life of Robert Grosseteste* (London, 1793, pp. 263–291) is avowedly a conflation of the lists of Boston of Bury, Leland, Bale, Brown, Cave, Wharton and Tanner. As a consequence there are a great number of repetitions and an equally great number of errors perpetuated. Pegge made no claim to acquaintance with more than very few MSS. The book is exceedingly rare, many copies having been destroyed by a fire in the printer's shop at the time of publication.

The more recent biography of Grosseteste by F. S. Stevenson* was relatively thorough on political, religious and cultural phases of Grosseteste's career. But Stevenson limited himself to a study of available printed sources, and as hardly more than one-tenth of Grosseteste's known output had appeared in print, a fair judgment of his place in medieval literary history would have been difficult to make.

The frequent references throughout the present catalogue to the edition of Grosseteste's physico-philosophical works by Professor Ludwig Baur will indicate in some measure the extent to which

* *Robert Grosseteste, Bishop of Lincoln* (London, 1899), hereafter designated "Stevenson".

this work is indebted to it. It has often been necessary to date MSS very differently from Baur, and there also occurs occasional disagreement with his conclusions as to authenticity: e.g. *De Anima* and *Summa in VIII Libros Physicorum*, but, in the latter case, on the basis of a reconsideration of the evidence, or indeed of new evidence. Baur's edition contains such valuable information, both on MSS and on accumulated bibliography, that it has been an indispensable aid in the present work.* He has prefixed, in his Introduction (pp. 15*–50*), a discussion of Grosseteste as a commentator, rich in bibliographical and MS detail; a section (pp. 120*–141*) on the *spuria*, where he has succeeded in identifying as works of other authors some treatises erroneously ascribed to Grosseteste; and a short section (pp. 141*–143*) on dubious or untraced works. An effort has been made in the present catalogue to supplement, correct or make more specific his conclusions in every case where it has been possible. The increase in the number of items catalogued here over that in Baur is considerable, even for works of translation from Greek, mathematical and philosophical treatises. Baur considers less than fifty works in all. He avoided theological, pastoral, mystical and vernacular works entirely, and these form a large portion of the total literary output of Grosseteste.

More recently E. Zinner has published a *Verzeichnis der astronomischen Handschriften des deutschen Kulturgebietes* (Munich, 1925) which lists some two score manuscripts containing works of Grosseteste, found in Germany, Austria and Czechoslovakia. The whole is a work of assiduous compilation which must have been going on for a number of years, but which should, in the case of the works of Grosseteste, be used with some caution. Zinner has perhaps not seen all the MSS which he lists. Not infrequently the MS does not contain what he specifies. Several works are listed as Grosseteste's for the authenticity of which no proof is known to exist. His dating of MSS must be taken with some reserve; he may have been guided by available catalogues. Yet the present catalogue is indebted to Zinner's work for the listing of some MSS which would otherwise not have been noticed.

* This is not the place to pronounce on the quality of the text as such. It has become the fashion to speak ill of it. With that I have no sympathy. An editor working with late and inferior copies has a thankless task. Textual emendation on any considerable scale only makes matters worse.

PRINCIPAL MANUSCRIPT COLLECTIONS OF GROSSETESTE'S WORKS

A number of MSS have peculiar value for our study because they seem to represent conscious efforts on the part of their scribes to build a canon of Grosseteste's works. Various phases of his literary activity have appealed to different compilers. A considerable number of these volumes contain largely philosophical treatises, others pastoral or theological works, a few have works of both kinds. These MSS will appear often throughout the catalogue. By reason of both their intrinsic interest and the weight of their evidence for the authenticity of the works contained, they deserve more detailed discussion than can be given in the summary and necessarily disjointed description in the body of the catalogue. To avoid unnecessary duplication of matter already in print, the reader is referred, for MSS containing philosophical works, to Baur's useful descriptions (pp. 144*–153*) and to his chapter on "Das Verwandtschaftsverhältnis der Handschriften untereinander" (pp. 154*–175*) which represents painstaking collation of the numerous MSS he used for his edition. Collections of sermons are listed below (p. 160 ff.), but MSS containing only sermons are not specially described here.

(1) *Oxford, Bodl., Digby* 98, a miscellaneous codex, contains, ff. 152^b–161^a on paper (*ca.* 1400) written by John Pertrich, *in domo scolarium de Merton*, as we are informed on f. 151^a, *De Luce, De Colore, De Iride, De Potencia et Actu, De Impressionibus Aeris* and *De Sphera* of Grosseteste, all ascribed. For other items in this codex, sometimes wrongly ascribed to Grosseteste, see below, *Spuria* 6 and 12 (pp. 243, 246).

(2) *Oxford, Bodl., Digby* 104, a miscellaneous codex with items from the late twelfth to the early fifteenth century, contains (*a*) ff. 1^A–19^D, Grosseteste's *De Anima* written *ca.* 1215 (see below, p. 89 f.), (*b*) ff. 19^D–20^B, in the same hand, what may be regarded as the beginning of Grosseteste's Commentary on the *De Celo et Mundo*, (*c*) ff. 109^D–110^D, in a hand of the second half of the fourteenth century, *De Luce, De Coloribus* and *De Iride*.

(3) *Oxford, Exeter Coll.* 21, written in the early decades of the fifteenth century, probably in Oxford, contains the *Dicta*, beginning in the middle of *Dictum* 51, and, in a different hand from that of the

Dicta, a collection of eighteen sermons, with a few letters and extracts intercalated, followed by Grosseteste's *De X Mandatis*, *mut. in fine*.

(4) *Oxford, Exeter Coll.* 28 is a miscellaneous folio codex, the work of three hands of the early fourteenth century. The third hand, ff. 285–307, *ca.* 1325, has written Grosseteste's *De Veritate*, *De Libero Arbitrio*, and the *Questiones Theologice* which we believe to be by Grosseteste (see below, p. 113 f.). According to the *contenta* on the flyleaf, there was once in this MS an item: *lincoln. de libero arbitrio aliter quam prius*, by which we may understand Recension 1 (see Baur, p. 107* ff.).

(5) *London, B.M., Cotton Otho* D. x. This codex was badly damaged by the fire of 1731, but it has been carefully reconstructed and is for the most part fairly usable. Large quarto, written about the middle of the fourteenth century, it is one of the oldest large collections of Grosseteste's works that we have. It consisted originally of 291 leaves, now reduced to 258. Its relative illegibility may have discouraged Baur from examining it closely enough to note its contents. It contains the spurious *De Oculo Morali*, unascribed, the *De Venenis*, also unascribed, a few minor works of Anselm and Augustine throughout the codex, Grosseteste's *De Finitate Motus et Temporis*, *De Sex Differenciis*, *De Intelligenciis*, *De Veritate*, *De Ordine Emanandi Causatorum a Deo*, *De Impressionibus Aeris*, *De Iride*, *De Statu Causarum*, *De Luce*, *De Colore*, *De Impressionibus Elementorum*, *De Motu Corporali*, *De Motu Supercelestium*, the 147 *Dicta*, *De Sphera* (the *De Cessacione Legalium* was, according to Smith's catalogue of 1702, at one time in this place in the codex, but had been cut out before the fire), *Hexameron*, *De X Mandatis*, *De Confessione I* (*Quoniam cogitacio*...), and fifteen sermons. Many of the works of Grosseteste are ascribed, though often the scribe gave simply the title of the work, and assumed that the reader would know that the whole was obviously a collection.

(6) *London, B.M., Royal* 6. E. v contains more Grosseteste material than any other single MS, save perhaps the damaged Cottonian MS Otho D. x. It is a large folio codex written by one scribe about the middle of the fourteenth century. It was once (XIV²) *Liber ecclesie sancte Marie de Merton*. It contains the following exclusively Grossetestian items: *Dicta*, thirty-eight sermons with a few letters and extracts intercalated, as in Exeter Coll. MS 28, excerpts from *Epistole* 2–89, the *Hexameron*, *De Cessacione Legalium*, *De Oculo*

Morali, ascribed to Grosseteste, *De X Mandatis, De Impressionibus Aeris, De Iride, De Statu Causarum, De Luce, De Colore, De Impressionibus Elementorum, De Motu Corporali, De Motu Supercelestium, De Sex Differenciis, De Forma Prima, De Intelligenciis, De Veritate, De Veritate Proposicionis, De Sciencia Dei, De Ordine Emanandi Causatorum a Deo*, and *De Sphera*.

(7) *London, B.M., Royal* 7. E. II is notable for the large number of sermons it contains, forty in number, with the intercalations and extracts from letters usual in the larger sermon collections; but it also contains, before the sermons, the 147 *Dicta*, complete with table. This codex, containing also works of Richard Rolle, is slightly later than the two preceding collections, say *ca.* 1375.

(8) *London, B.M., Royal* 7. F. II, the oldest of the sermon collections (apart from Royal 7. D. XV, which is largely *Dicta*), a large folio codex, was written about the middle of the fourteenth century, and formerly belonged to the library of Westminster monastery. It contains the *De Veneno* unascribed, forty sermons (of which one is repeated), the usual intercalated extracts and letters, the *De Cessacione Legalium*, and the *De X Mandatis*. There follow some anonymous sermons, written by the same scribe, which, from their tone and their place in the codex, might conceivably be by Grosseteste. They appear, however, in no other known Grosseteste collection, and have not been considered as compelling inclusion in the present catalogue.

(9) *London, Lambeth Palace* 499. A miscellaneous codex, written by various scribes of the second half of the thirteenth century and the first half of the fourteenth, this MS contains some minor works of Grosseteste not found elsewhere. They are of a sufficiently informal nature to lead us to conjecture that they were copied by someone who had been a member of his household. The chancery hand in which these opuscula were written, ff. 184ᵃ–188ᵃ, is to be dated *ca.* 1270–1280. The collection comprises *De Obsequiis Bene Dicendis, Oraciuncula post Prandium Gallice, De Penitencia David, De Confessione et Modo Confitendi*, into which has been incorporated the *Iniunccio Penitenti Gallice* and a short *Confessio Gallica*, and the *Oracio ad Sanctam Margaretam Gallice*. This same scribe has compiled a miscellaneous collection of patristic excerpts of which these short works of Grosseteste form a not-inconsiderable middle section.

(10) *Cambridge, Trinity Coll.* B. 15. 20. This is a double collection of exclusively pastoral treatises, the work of two scribes of the second

half of the fourteenth century. The MS was used by Edward Brown for his edition of selected *Dicta* in the *Fasciculus Rerum Expetendarum* (1690); he made occasional notes and comments throughout the codex. In a note on the flyleaf he remarked how incapable the scribe was and how illegibly he wrote. The pagination is not uniform. The numbering is by columns (four to a leaf) as far as col. 742, then by folia to 899^{B}, which is really f. 337^{B}. In the text of this catalogue the numbers are given as in the MS. The codex contains the 147 *Dicta*, misnumbered 148, sixteen sermons, the *Templum Domini*, the *De Confessione I* (*Quoniam cogitacio*...), the *De Eucharistia*, apparently unique in this MS, but which may yet be found to be an extract from a sermon or a *Dictum*, *Epistola* 128, which often appears separately, the *De Cessacione Legalium*, the *De X Mandatis*, slightly *mut. in fine*. At this point, f. 742 (=f. 186^{D}), the second collection begins. It contains twelve sermons, the 147 *Dicta*, seven folia of *excerpta notabilia* from *Epistole* 2–89, and, as an appendage, a fragment of Egidius Romanus' *De Regimine Principum*. From the fact that Brown has numbered some of the sermons as *Dicta*—the sermon *Beati pauperes*... he has numbered *Dictum* 152—we may infer that he was not quite certain of the nature of the collection of *Dicta*, or, it may be, had just begun his work of collation of Grosseteste's MSS and had not observed that the collection of 147 was usual.

(11) *Cambridge, Trinity Coll.* B. 15. 38. This is a miscellaneous codex, the work of several hands writing about the middle of the thirteenth century.* One hand has written ff. 1–145, which includes, *inter alia*, all the Grosseteste material in the MS: ff. 32^{a}–33^{a}, a considerable extract from Grosseteste's *De X Mandatis* (in *Mandatum* III =B.M., Royal 6. E. v, f. 230^{B-C}); f. 33^{b}, another short item, *De Triplici Rectitudine*, possibly an extract but so far unidentified as such, and a number of sermons, later known as *Dicta* 50, 21, 37, 38, 41, 35; then, after miscellaneous anonymous extracts and sermons, Grosseteste's translation of the *Testamenta XII Patriarcharum*, his *De Contemptu Mundi*, and the extract from Suidas on Ἰησοῦς. This is one of the oldest MSS containing these sermons; it is the oldest containing any part of the *De X Mandatis* and is unique in regard to the *De Triplici Rectitudine* and the *De Contemptu Mundi*.

(12) *Durham Cathedral* A. III. 12 is certainly one of the most

* See F. Pelster, "Eine Handschrift mit Predigten des Richard Fishacre O.P...." in *Zeitschrift für katholische Theologie*, LVII (1933), 614–616.

valuable of all Grosseteste MSS, by reason of both its age and its contents. It deserves much more space than can be given it here. See also below, p. 34 f. It is a folio codex, the work of at least a dozen hands, none of them later than the middle of the thirteenth century. A miscellaneous lot of folia of various sizes have been bound into one volume. We know that it was bound in its present shape before the year 1258 (though it was rebound in the eighteenth century) from the list of *contenta* on the verso of f. 1. The donor, Bertram of Middleton, died in that year. The *contenta*, written *ca.* 1260–1270, are as follows:

Liber sancti cuthberti ex dono Bertrami de Midiltona prioris Dunelmensis

1. Quedam notabilia super psalterium
2. Notabilia super misterio crucis cum quibusdam divisionibus de trinitate
3. Sentencie super psalterium
4. Quedam divisio virtutum
5. Quedam divisio oracionis
6. Tractatus de aversione a summo bono
7. Notabilia super quibusdam collectis
8. Quedam questio scripta in quodam rotulo
9. Sermo qui sic incipit: Omnipotens itaque
10. Libellus de scematibus
11. Duo sermones · scilicet Terra illa et Vidi
12. Quaternus de divisione VII. viciorum
13. Duo folia de notabilibus
14. Quidam sermones et notabilia
15. Sermones qui continent X. quaternos
16. Quidam quaternus de sentenciis super evangelium
17. Concordancie biblie per V. libros distincte
18. Sentencie super Ecclesiasticum et Exodum
19. Tractatus de sacramentis ecclesie
20. Quedam sentencie litterales.

The arabic numerals were added about the middle of the fifteenth century. It will be noticed that the scribe who compiled the *contenta* carefully avoided pronouncing upon the authorship of any of the treatises. Bertram of Middleton was Prior of Durham 1244–1258. The codex was presented in this form to the chapter library before his death, for it is *ex dono* and not *ex legato*, the usual phrase if left by bequest. But we have more exact information about almost the whole codex from a partially legible note in plummet at the bottom of f. 130^{A-B} which reads approximately as follows:

pe. p[s] omni die quo adiunxit diceret XXII *pater noster* propter VII horas VII propter septiformam deum spiritus sanctus [!] V in honore V vulnerum

Christi 3 in nomini patris et filii et spiritus sancti eodem modo L Ave Maria quolibet die tocius vite mee. Item quolibet anno dicam 20 psalteria in propria persona et non per alium. Item quolibet anno durante septennio abstinebo a carnibus tantum die mercurii et sabbato avis autem et caste et huius vescibus. Item quolibet anno durante septennio ieiunabo 20 dies veneris in pane et aqua. Item recipiam a septem durante VI [f. 130[B]] unam disciplinam a sacerdote vel a me ipso. Item pascam [one word illegible] pauperes per quemlibet annum dicuntur septem. Item abstinebo a carnibus per adventum totum sed si opus fuerit licebit bis comedi in die. Item providebo aliquod ornamentum ad honorem beate Marie, eodem modo ad honorem beati Thome et Keterine. Item dicam cotidie infra septem septem psalmos penitenciales vel quindecim pro benefactoribus meis. Hec penitencia iniuncta est mihi iiii Kalendas marc. [mart.] anno ab incarnacione domini M°CC°XXXI.

This note, like others of varying lengths throughout the codex, might, on paleographical grounds, be in the hand of Grosseteste. There are certain generally unmistakable peculiarities which could be easily understood on this supposition. At all events, the codex, or that part of it in which this plummet hand appears, is almost certain to have been written and assembled before 1231. The paleography of the sections affected will easily bear this date (see also below, p. 35). At the bottom of f. 122[a] in the same plummet hand is written approximately the following note:

Expensa pecunie... [illegible]...addwalader ad episcopum. Sequenti die in vino viii quod detulit secum ad opus episcopi apud...unde sextalis die sequenti in vino sextalis. In duobus aneis 4 d. In transitu aque ii d. apud london'; in transitu Tamisie ii d.; pro quibusdam literis decimarum iii d.; in husis xviii d.; in reditu suo apud Bristol' in vino viii quod detulit secum; apud Merthune ad opus episcopi die sequenti. Cum moram ibidem fecisset ad equos suos reccandos in vino viii d.; in reditu in transitu Savernie ii d.

At the foot of f. 137[C–D] is a list of *debita* in the same plummet hand:

teneor Joseph de precio VII pellis vitilis respondere. Item eidem de VIII pellis multonum. Item de rasura unius duodene. Item de ligacione Mathei et Marci. Debitum W. precio tenetur michi. Willelmus socius meus in v. soldis cremonensibus. Item in XIX den. parisiensibus Magister [here follows, cancelled in plummet: Willelmus socius meus tenetur michi in XVIII den. parisiensibus]. Helias Walensis tenetur michi in XII parisiensibus.

Hec debet W. precio [?] pro coclearibus xx soldos. Item in iudaismo XXX soldos parisienses super ystoriam scolasticam. Item magistro W. phisico VIII den. Ade mercatori castellorum 33 den. Magistro Ricardo de Sancto Yltuto II soldos. Item Domino Bricio socio meo v soldos parisienses.

If the hand by any chance should be Grosseteste's, we have interesting documents and suggestive details of his budgetary life. But the data demand more detailed study before we can feel sure that Grosseteste could have been the writer. A scribe using plummet would write differently from the way he would write with a *penna*, and my suspicion may be completely unjustifiable.

Ff. 2^A^–17^D^ contain, in an order found nowhere else, certain of the *Dicta* of Grosseteste which have been incorporated into his definitive *Commentarius in Psalmos I–C* (see below, p. 75 f.). Most of this section was, I believe, written by Grosseteste himself. See below, p. 35. It is significant that this collection begins with the section that appears as an introduction to the *Commentarius in Psalterium*. There are a few sections which do not appear either as *Dicta* or in the *Commentarius*, sometimes short citations from Church Fathers, sometimes brief definitions or etymologies. In view of the age of this MS we are probably safe in assuming that the collection of *Dicta* as such was based in part at least on this copy. On ff. 18^A^–34^D^, in another, contemporary, hand, is a running commentary on Pss. xlviii–lxxii. It may be by Grosseteste, yet I have found no correspondence with marginalia in Grosseteste's own hand in the *magnum Psalterium* in Lincoln Cathedral MS 144, with his definitive *Commentarius in Psalmos*, or with marginal notes in Bodley MS e Mus. 230 sufficiently clear to warrant more than a suspicion that these extensive collected glosses are by him. Another, still contemporary, hand has written, ff. 38^A^–48^D^, two works, *De Effectibus Virtutum* and *De Aversione a Summo Bono*, which have been placed, with some reluctance, among the *Dubia* (see below, p. 235 f.). They give every internal indication of being genuine, but the lack of an ascription or other external evidence compels us to regard them as doubtful. On ff. 42^C^–43^B^ there are several marginal notes in Grosseteste's hand. Ff. 49–58 are the work of various contemporary hands, of which one is possibly that of Bertram, who has filled the whole codex with minute marginal notes. As to the author or authors of the two following items, both sermons, I have no suggestion: ff. 59^A^–60^C^ *Terra illa multa facta est.... Cum quamlibet...*, and ff. 61^a^–63^b^ *Vidi et ecce super firmamentum.... Qui aurum effodiunt vel argentum....* They are written by two contemporary scribes whose hands do not appear elsewhere in the codex, and on leaves markedly smaller than the rest of the book. The author of the first sermon was intelligently interested in natural phenomena and betrays a considerable knowledge of climate and of marine matters. We know at least that he was

English and hardly before the twelfth century. He says (f. 59^A) *Nota quod normanni habitantes ultra mare multum solent....* There follows, ff. 64^a–69^b, a collection of patristic quotations, and several leaves still blank. The next gathering, ff. 70^A–77^D, is an incomplete anonymous collection of *sentencie*. The author regards Peter Lombard rather more highly than Grosseteste seems generally to have done. There is no real similarity between this author's treatment of *Iusticia et Misericordia Dei* (ff. 74^C–75^A) and Grosseteste's *questio* on the same subject (see below, p. 113 f.). The tone of the argument would fit the end of the twelfth century rather than the thirteenth. We can safely eliminate Grosseteste from the list of possible authors. For a detailed description of the remainder of this codex, containing a great amount of Grosseteste matter, see below, p. 182 ff.

This codex may be regarded as one of the most valuable of all Grosseteste MSS, but its value is partially hidden by anonymity and becomes evident only if studied with the text of other well-authenticated codices. We cannot be at all sure that all the Grosseteste matter present in the MS has been identified.

(13) *Assisi, Biblioteca Comunale* 138 is one of the earliest Grosseteste MSS, but as it contains only two works we can ascribe to him, it is sufficiently described under these items (see below, pp. 89 and 117). The same may be said of *Milan, Ambros.* E. 71 sup. which contains two unique ascriptions of translations of Aristotelian opuscula from the Greek. Its importance lies in its early date, XIII^m, and its South French provenance. As no ascriptions of these works have appeared in MSS of English provenance, the provenance and date of the Milan MS suggests that Grosseteste made these translations at the Council of Lyons in 1245 (see below, pp. 58 ff., 67 f.).

(14) *Florence, Biblioteca Marucelliana* C. 163. A short notice of this MS has previously appeared.* The codex contains other matter (Holcot, Burley, etc.); the Grosseteste items, occupying ff. 1^A–31^C, are on paper, written by an Italian scribe *ca.* 1400. This is the most complete collection of Grosseteste's *opera physica* which we have, containing twenty-three of the twenty-eight treatises (one in two recensions) edited by Baur and the unedited *De Accessu et Recessu Maris.* The scribe was either not extremely careful or his zeal was

* See S. H. Thomson, "The Text of Grosseteste's *De Cometis*" in *Isis*, XIX (1933), 19 ff. I then dated the codex "latter half of the fourteenth century". That judgment should now be revised to "*ca.* 1400"; and below, p. 94, n.

greater than his knowledge, for the text does not always make sense, but the importance of this extensive corpus testifying to the persistent Italian tradition can hardly be overemphasized. The following works appear in order, all ascribed: *De Luce*, *Quod homo sit minor mundus*, *De Artibus Liberalibus*, *De Generacione Formarum* (*Sonorum*), *De Calore Solis*, *De Generacione Stellarum*, *De Differenciis Localibus*, *De Unica Forma Omnium*, *De Intelligenciis*, *De Veritate*, *De Veritate Proposicionis*, *De Passionibus* (*Impressionibus*) *Elementorum*, *De Motu Corporali et Luce*, *De Finitate Motus et Temporis*, *De* (*Lineis*) *Angulis et Figuris*, *De Natura Locorum*, *De Accessu et Recessu Maris*, *De Fraccionibus Radiorum* (*De Iride*), *De Cometis et Causis Ipsarum*, *De Speciebus Cometarum et Significacionibus Earum* (*De Cometis*, Recension II), *De Predestinacione et Presciencia Dei* (*De Sciencia Dei*), *De Eternitate Divinarum Personarum* (*De Ordine Emanandi Causatorum*), *De Libero Arbitrio* (Recension I, incomplete). In the case of several of the treatises this codex offers desired substantiation of the hitherto weak evidence for authenticity furnished by the Venice MS. In general it is the most valuable single codex for the physico-philosophical works.

(15) *Modena, Biblioteca Estense* lat. 54 is a paper codex written by several Italian scribes in the first half of the fifteenth century. On ff. 1^{A}–48^{C} is the *Compendium regularum libri priorum per clarissimum linconiensem editum* (see below, p. 87), written in a clear italic script. There follow minor works of Thomas Aquinas and Boethius in another italic hand. On f. 73^{b} begins a copy of a few of the *opera physica*, the *Quod homo sit minor mundus*, *De Generacione Sonorum*, *De Veritate Proposicionis*, *De* (*Lineis*) *Angulis et Figuris*, *De Natura Locorum*, in the tradition of the Venice MS, but clearly, from mistakes and variants, not a copy of it.

(16) *Modena, Biblioteca Estense* lat. 649 is a paper codex in one neat italic hand, written *ca.* 1500, bearing the ex-libris *D. Grimani Cardinalis S. Marci* (cardinal 1493–†1523). It contains, ff. 2^{A}–28^{C}, the following ascribed *opera physica*: *De Inchoacione Formarum*, *Quod homo sit minor mundus*, *De Artibus Liberalibus*, *De Generacione Sonorum*, *De Calore Solis*, *De Generacione Stellarum*, *De Coloribus* (*Colore*), *De Statu Causarum*, *De Motu Supercelestium*, *De Differenciis Localibus*, *De Unica Forma Omnium*, *De Intelligenciis*, *De Veritate*, *De Veritate Proposicionis*, *De Impressionibus Elementorum*, *De Motu Corporali et Luce*, *De Finitate Motus et Temporis* (which ends incomplete ...*attingere non potuit* as the Venice and B.M., Cotton Otho D. x MSS = Baur,

p. 105, l. 35; the scribe has left a space blank, perhaps in the hope that he might yet find a perfect copy), *De Natura Locorum*. The treatises appear in the same order as the Venice and Florence (Marucelliana) MSS and the Venice 1514 print. The text is not taken from either the Venice or the Florence MSS nor from the printed edition, if we may judge from the textual variants. But these four together form a closely related group of which there must have been an archetype, and, in all likelihood, several other copies, from one or more of which these later MSS were directly taken.

(17) *Pavia, University* 69 is a small codex of 107 leaves written by various English scribes *ca.* 1225–1250. The stubby and ungraceful gothic script common to all the scribes is that found in the district between Cambridge and Lincoln in the first half of the thirteenth century. The first item, ff. 1^{A}–19^{A}, bears the title *Enchiridion penitentis ex summa Reymundi et ex distinccionibus W. Autissiodorensis et R. Lincolniensis et R. de Leycestria et cuiusdam doctoris parisiensis excerptus* (see below, *Spurium* 19); *Meditaciones Bernardi* occupy ff. 19^{A}–24^{D}; Grosseteste's *Templum Dei*, here called *Distincciones*, ff. 25^{a}–33^{b}; the *Summa* usually ascribed to William de Montibus but collected by Richard of Wetherstede,* ff. 34^{A}–84^{C}.† A section of this *Summa*,‡ ff. 47^{A}–66^{D}, is ascribed in a later hand, *ca.* 1300, *Tractatus de virtutibus et viciis venerabilis domini lincolniensis*. There follows, in another contemporary hand, ff. 85^{a}–88^{b}, a sermon *Restat agere de luxuria* (see below, Sermon 81), here described by an Italian scribe, *ca.* 1300, as *Sermo beati episcopi Lincolniensis Rengni Anglie aprobatus per eclexiam velud dicta beati Augustini*. The second *l* in *Lincolniensis* almost authenticates the ascription of itself. The scribe must have had before him an English archetype. The normal Italian spelling would have been almost anything else. Yet the *Restat* indicates that this sermon might have been part of a longer treatise. Ff. 89–91 are blank; the *Canon Misse* of Richard of Wedinghausen, ascribed in the *contenta* of this MS to Grosseteste (see below, p. 244, *Spurium* 8), is on ff. 92^{a}–95^{b}. The *R* for *Ricardus* may have deceived the copyist. The last considerable

* See B. Smalley and G. Lacombe, "The Lombard's Commentary on Isaias and other Fragments", in *New Scholasticism*, v (1931), 141 ff.

† For a marginal *oracio dominica in materna lingua* see my note "A XIIIth Century *Oure Fader* in a Pavia MS" in *Modern Language Notes*, April, 1934, pp. 235–237.

‡ In the above-mentioned note I accepted this erroneous early ascription to Grosseteste. Dr R. W. Hunt pointed out to me that it is a part of the *Summa* of Richard.

item in the codex is *Tractatus de canone Misse domini Innocencii pape tercii incompletus*. The early Italian owner (*ca.* 1300) has written the *contenta* on a small piece of parchment and pasted it to the back cover. Not all of his data are, however, correct, as may be seen from the above description. The *contenta*, with rather original grouping of subjects and titles, read as follows:

Encheridion penitencialis optimus. Item meditaciones beati Bernardi incomplete. Item distincciones valde preciose domini lincolniensis. Item tractatus de presbitero et prelato et que eis debentur. De articulis fidei || De oracione dominica || De septem donis spiritus sancti || De virtutibus et viciis et de septem sacramentis || de decem preceptis, de luxuria et peccato contra naturam. De canone misse supradicti domini lincolniensis. Item tractatus de canone misse domini Innocencii pape tercii incompletus.

(18) *Prague, University* 1990 (x. H. 12). This MS was described by Baur (p. 150*).* A miscellaneous codex on paper, it contains, ff. 34[b]–50[a], several of the *opera physica*. The codex is dated 1472 on f. 39[b] and belonged to the Augustinian chapter at Časlava. The Grosseteste items are: *De Eternitate Filii in Divinis* (*De Ordine Emanandi*), *De Sciencia Dei*, *De Veritate*, *De Intelligenciis*, *De Unica Forma Omnium*, *De Luce*, *De Veritate Contingencium Futurorum* (*Proposicionis*), *De Generacione Sonorum*, *De Erroribus Humanis* (*De Artibus Liberalibus*), and, some folia later, Grosseteste's translation of the spurious Ignatian correspondence. The textual value of the codex is not great.

(19) *Prague, National Museum* xii. E. 5† is a miscellaneous paper codex, the work of several fourteenth-century South German or Bohemian hands. The Grosseteste section, ff. 1[A]–88[A], by reason of its age and the variety of ascribed works it contains, ranks with B.M., Royal MS 6. E. v and Durham Cathedral MS A. iii. 12 as the most valuable of Grosseteste MSS. This section, written hardly later than the middle of the fourteenth century‡ by a scribe who throughout this catalogue has been labelled Bohemian,§ is in two columns of 90–110 lines to a column. The smallness of the script, not common

* See also J. Truhlář, *Catalogus codicum manu scriptorum Latinorum...in Bibl. publica et Universitatis Pragensis...*, ii (Prague, 1906), 109 ff.

† See F. M. Bartoš, *Soupis Rukopisů Narodního Musea...*, ii (Prague, 1927), 232.

‡ G. B. Phelan, "An unedited Text of Robert Grosseteste" in *Hommage... à M. De Wulf* (Louvain, 1934), p. 176, dates it "15th century".

§ The designation should be understood somewhat loosely and locationally. "South German" would perhaps be more satisfactory.

in paper codices, does not indicate carelessness, rather the contrary. Textually the transcription is probably the most satisfactory of all Grosseteste MSS.* The scribe was both interested and intelligent. He has copied out Grosseteste's *Hexameron, De Cessacione Legalium, De Veritate Contingencium Futurorum (Proposicionis), De Sciencia..., De Eternitate Divinarum Personarum (De Ordine Emanandi...), De Fraccionibus...vel de Angulis et Figuris, De Luce, Quod homo est minor mundus, De Liberalibus Artibus, De Generacione Sonorum, De Fraccionibus Radiorum (De Iride), De Accessu et Recessu Maris, De Calore Solis, De Generacione Stellarum, De Coloribus, De Statu Causarum, De Motu Supercelestium, De Differenciis Localibus, De Passionibus (Impressionibus) Elementorum, De Motu Corporali et Luce, De Finitate Motus* (as in Baur to p. 105, l. 29); and he has repeated this extract from Grosseteste's *Comm. in Physica*, prefixing to it a substantial paragraph from the *Commentarius* beginning *Perpetuitas motus i.e. carencia principii et finis*... (=Digby MS 220, f. 104^{A-B}) and giving to the whole a new title: *De Errore Philosophorum Ponencium Perpetuitatem Motus et Temporis*. The 147 *Dicta* follow immediately, with the *Tabula* appended, followed in turn by a collection of eighteen sermons.

(20) *Venice, San Marco* Cl. VI, Cod. 163. This codex, containing nineteen of the *opera physica* of Grosseteste, has been briefly described by Baur, p. 152* (see also J. Valentinelli, *Bibliotheca Manuscripta ad S. Marci Venetiarum*, Venice, 1868, I, 87–89). It is in two hands, but the Grosseteste matter, ff. 80^{A}–102^{D}, written by an Italian scribe toward the end of the fourteenth century, is on different paper from the preceding material (Thomas Aquinas). Like so many of the San Marco MSS, it was once (1448) the property of the collector Johannes Marchanova. The order of the works is the same as in the

* Dr Phelan has remarked *loc. cit.* that the text of the *De Cessacione Legalium* in this MS "is a combination of the other two mss. Sometimes a reading of several lines will be given from B.M. 6 E. v and then the corresponding lines in Q.C. 312 [i.e. Queen's Coll., Oxford, 312] will be added in the text." Dr Phelan would seem to contend that the scribe of the Prague MS made his copy from the two English MSS. We should then have to suppose that the English MSS were available to the Bohemian scribe, but there is no evidence that this geographical transposition took place. The reading of the text can hardly of itself be used to support such a contention. On paleographical grounds it is almost certain that the Prague copy was written before B.M., Royal 6. E. v. Textually it is impossible for it to have been a copy of the Queen's MS. The text is both fuller and different. All three MSS obviously go back to several previous copies, where scribal emendations had crept in and have been perpetuated.

Florence MS. The codex is *mutilus* at the beginning of the *De Natura Locorum*. We can only conclude that this MS once had all the works now found in the Florence MS, and, as the Florence MS is quite clearly—if we may judge from the nature of misreadings in the text—not a copy of the earlier Venice MS, we are led to posit the existence of an earlier corpus of Grosseteste's physico-philosophical works in Italy. Baur noticed the closeness of the Venice 1514 imprint to this MS, but also remarked that there were lacunae in the MS which were lacking in the printed edition. We must therefore add to our conclusions the necessary existence in Italy of a representative of the older tradition as late as the first quarter of the sixteenth century, and express the hope that it is not yet irrevocably lost.

GROSSETESTE'S HANDWRITING

As considerable attention will be paid to the handwriting of Grosseteste, and the authenticity of several items depends on it, some discussion of it is necessary. The identification of the hand in several places is beyond much doubt. All the evidence we have tends to identify his hand in Pembroke Coll., Cambridge, MS 7, the Cambridge Univ. Lib. MS Ff. i. 24, Greek *Testamenta XII Patriarcharum*, and Bodley MS 198, attested by Thomas Gascoigne, with signs corresponding to the *Tabula Magistri Roberti Grosseteste* in Lyons MS 414. The evidence is set forth in greater detail in the following pages. The identification of his hand in the remaining MSS is based on paleographical evidence, combined with sufficient study of the content to ascertain its Grossetestian character.

A cursory examination of the plates will show immediately that it is, for the early thirteenth century, decidedly an individual hand. Yet it is not so individual as not to have antecedents. A large number of the reproductions in Canon C. W. Foster's excellent edition of vol. I of the *Registrum Antiquissimum of the Cathedral Church of Lincoln* (Lincoln Record Society, XXVII, 1931) show that such a hand was in common use during most of the latter part of the twelfth century in the Lincoln episcopal chancery. Canon Foster has kindly shown me photographs of many others from the same period which he did not reproduce. At a rough estimate we could say that about half the episcopal documents during this half-century or more are written in this less formal chancery script; the other half in a more ornate and calligraphic hand. The two reproductions on Plate XXII

Cambridge Univ. MS Ff. i. 24, f. 42b

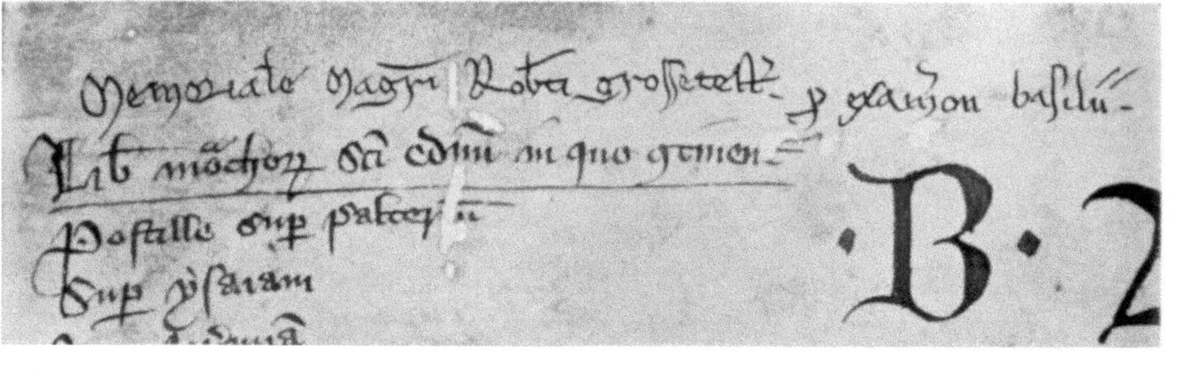

Pembroke Coll., Cambridge, MS 7, verso of flyleaf

(facing p. 262) of Canon Foster's edition, written within a few years of each other, well illustrate the difference in type of hand. It must be said that the scripts are essentially related: the less calligraphic has undoubtedly developed from the more calligraphic. Yet in appearance they are distinct. A few characteristics of the more cursive hand may be observed: the *a* with no ascender beyond the main loop; a *d* with the usually vertical stroke bending diagonally from the left, and curved to the right at the top; all letters with descenders below the line, including the developed Anglo-Saxon long *r*, curve to the left at the bottom; the top transverse member of the *s* and *f* is made with a heavy downward stroke, sometimes not even joining the vertical stroke; the Tironian sign for *et* is made like a 7, the horizontal stroke is curved, and there is a tendency to cross the vertical shaft, which goes below the line of writing, with a finishing stroke upward at about 45° from the vertical; in this early period the pen has been lifted at the bottom of the 7; finally a general heaviness and hurried appearance may be noted. The obvious parentage of Grosseteste's handwriting suggests that he may have learned to write at Lincoln or certainly under some master who was trained in the Lincoln chancery. This hand is not unknown elsewhere in England, but, so far as I am aware, it is nowhere else so dominant and persistent. It is, furthermore, almost unknown in MSS of literary content.

Grosseteste's hand maintains the general type throughout his life. He made some effort to learn the new gothic script, but was only partially successful. The portion written by Grosseteste (1215–1216) in Savile MS 21 has an occasional line which could be described as gothic, but it must have been done with much effort. The folia in Durham MS A. III. 12, written *ca.* 1230, which I believe to be in his hand (see below, p. 34 f.), indicate increased facility in the more calligraphic hand, but effort is evident, and unevenness is glaring. Most of his letters follow his early training, but there are some peculiarities which, though they may vary somewhat, may be said to be constant throughout his life. We have his writing in 1215, some which we must date *ca.* 1242, and some which we may reasonably suspect of being not before 1245, i.e. his ex-libris in Pembroke MS 7. Wherever he can, he puts the *e* of *de* at the top of the downward stroke of *d* by making a ^{2} to join on to the top of the *d*. This is done even in the middle of a word, e.g. *d*^{2}*mones*. The *e* is joined, where possible, to the following letter. The *g* is made in three strokes: two curves form the upper loop: the one on the right projects below the line, and the pen, lifted, moves slightly to the left and makes, from left to right, to join the projection, a slightly curved and almost horizontal line. The right minim of the *h* comes below the line and curves to the left, as does the final minim of the *m* and the *n*. The vertical stroke of the *h* and the *l* is a single line and quite straight. The direction of the pen movement is usually betrayed by a light line for a short distance before the heavier downward stroke is begun. The *l* is usually joined to the following letter. A final *i* extends below the line and curves to the left. The downward stroke of the *f* bends to the left at the bottom as in all his letters where the next stroke is part of a circular movement during part of which the pen is lifted, i.e. *f*, *q*, *r*, *s*. Grosseteste has, of course, two *r*'s: the forked or long *r* and the round or short *r* attached to a preceding loop, i.e. after *o* and *p*. The *et*-sign is often distinctive. The crossed ⁊ early came to be made by Grosseteste without lifting the pen from the page. The resultant lower loop ⁊ is so distinctive as to be, where it appears, almost determinative. This is more noticeable in his early writing, but he never completely lost it. It appears in Lincoln Cath. MS 144, though more often in the pencilled notes than in the ink where he used the crossed ⁊. It appears in the more carefully written section in Durham MS A. III. 12, in Shrewsbury School MS 1, again, slightly developed by age, in Corpus Christi, Oxford, MS 43, and in occasional notes in Pembroke, Cambridge, MS 7. This *et*-sign is also currently used as a verb-ending, e.g. *obtinet*, *posset*, *possidet*, *ardet*, *debet*, etc. The same movement is often used in the case of q̃ for *quam*, though more usually the pen has been lifted at the bottom of the stroke and only a simple diagonal transverse stroke shows. He generally has the old c̄ for *cum*, ·H· for *enim*, ꝙ for *quod* and ꝯ for *secundum*. The sign for *pro* is usually made in four movements: the downstroke, the loop, then, on a level with and to the left of the lower end of the descender, a reversed comma, finally a horizontal stroke joining this reversed comma to the descender. The separate strokes are usually distinguishable. No abbreviation or peculiarity of letter-formation is to be found without exception. A variant is likely to appear in the same line. Uniformity must not have appealed to Grosseteste as a cardinal virtue. Like St Paul and St Thomas Aquinas he would have had a short and ignominious career as a professional scribe.

SOME MANUSCRIPTS IN GROSSETESTE'S LIBRARY

In the course of examining so many MSS containing works of Grosseteste the hope has never been completely obscured that an autograph of one or more of his considerable works might appear. Though this hope has not been realized, it has been possible to reconstruct a small part of his private library by identification of his notes in MSS which he had used. Some of these MSS have been previously known to contain his handwriting. Dr M. R. James in his numerous and useful catalogues of Cambridge College libraries has noted a few MSS which he felt quite certain had been in Grosseteste's possession. It has been possible to make additions to this number, with one probable correction for Cambridge, and to draw attention to a few MSS hitherto unnoticed which are either unmistakably or probably to be traced to his library. Those who work with MSS will realize the difficulties of identifying a single scribe's hand, and in several cases I am not sure that my conjectures are well founded. But there are perhaps more where no hesitation is felt. The MSS are listed approximately in the order of logical consequence, those containing his signature, the Greek text we know him to have translated, the codex identified by Gascoigne as bearing Grosseteste's notations, the early mathematical autograph, the Lincoln *psalterium*, etc., with such paleographical and external evidence as is available. More codices will doubtless be identified as his when his very distinctive hand is better known.

Pembroke Coll., Cambridge, MS 7 contains a number of late twelfth-century and early thirteenth-century commentaries* on the books of Psalms, Isaiah, Jeremiah, Daniel, the Minor Prophets, and Mark. The whole codex was written by an English scribe at the beginning of the thirteenth century. There are no chapter-divisions throughout the MS. The *Postille in Psalterium* is the work of Stephen Langton† and some of the remaining postils may be his work. They are indistinguishable in method and manner from his authenticated works. What interests us about this codex is the fact that it once belonged to Grosseteste, and passed from his hands to the monks of Bury St Edmunds in return for a copy of the *Hexameron* of Basil.

* See M. R. James, *Catalogue of MSS...of Pembroke College, Cambridge* (Cambridge, 1905), p. 7, which corrects the description given in his *On the Abbey of S. Edmund at Bury* (Camb. Antiq. Soc. 1895), p. 50.

† See below, p. 254, *Spurium* 32.

That much we must infer from the note in Grosseteste's hand on the verso of the flyleaf: *Memoriale magistri Roberti Grosseteste pro exameron Basilii*, coupled with the fact that an early fourteenth-century Bury librarian wrote the *contenta* immediately below Grosseteste's note and the Bury signature B. 231. As MS copies of the *Hexameron* of Basil of this early date are rare in English libraries, it should not be a difficult task to find the copy which Grosseteste obtained, provided, of course, that it still exists. The transaction must have taken place shortly after 1240–1242.* His own *Hexameron* and the latter part of the *Commentarius in Psalmos* (see below, pp. 75 f., 100 f.) are the first considerable works in which the Greek fathers are quoted. This late date would accord with the obvious fact that the writing is that of an elderly if vigorous man. But Grosseteste has not only owned this codex: he has used it carefully. Marginal corrections in his hand are distinguishable in many places. Indeed at the beginning of the last item in the codex, the *Postilla in Evangelium Marci*, ff. 228^A–267^D,† we notice that the corrections are more than usually numerous, and suddenly cease altogether. Did Grosseteste find the text so bad that he gave up in disgust, and did he exchange this large and handsome but inferior codex without regret for a much smaller MS? Further examination of notes in his hand suggests that he must have had the book rebound. At the bottom of f. 1^a he has written κυατερνι 79 ·i· κθ and in numerous places he has written the *custos* at the bottom of the last page of a gathering, evidently to guide the binder in reassembling the codex. A note in another, perhaps earlier, hand that is almost contemporary with the writing of the codex, scratched through, reads: *Quaterni* 29 *sunt in universo glose baldewini Facies in introitu tabernaculi Swaph* [? *Steph'* ?] *Incipit liber ympnorum vel Soliloquiorum*,‡ and may indicate the name of a previous owner. At the end of the

* It would be possible to construct this case: his use of the MS had taken place about 1230, soon after we know him to have begun to be interested in theology; the rebinding took place after he had begun to learn Greek, *ca.* 1230–1235; he may have received the *Hexameron* from Bury *ca.* 1240–1242 as a gift. Then, toward the end of his life, in arranging for the disposition of his library, he excepted this volume from the general gift to the Oxford Franciscans, and remembered the Bury gift of some years before. *Memoriale* could well bear this construction, and most of the notes, though identical in detailed characteristics, would best be construed as written in the earlier years of the person who wrote the *Memoriale*, for the handwriting of this note shows a certain lack of dash and freedom.

† See below, p. 254, *Spurium* 32.

‡ Can this be the *Distincciones super Psalterium Petri Lombardi* of Pierre de Poitiers? See P. Glorieux, *Répertoire des Maîtres...*, 1 (Paris, 1933), 230, and P. S. Moore, *Works of Peter of Poitiers* (Notre Dame, 1936), 78 ff.

Oxford, Bodley MS 198, f. 139[B]

Oxford, Bodley Savile MS 21, f. 158[a]

Postilla in Psalterium, f. 132^B, is a collection of scripture quotations accompanied by leading remarks in nineteen lines, written by Grosseteste in a small hand in his usual black ink. The whole right half of the page is covered with plummet notes by Grosseteste of an exegetical character, but not continuously legible. The precise nature of these notes is therefore difficult to determine. At the foot of f. 228^B Grosseteste began to write the name of the author of the *Comm. in Marcum* in plummet, *Venerabilis Magistri*, but for some reason or other did not complete the ascription.

The use of Greek characters on f. 1^a, the nature of the contents, the probable date of the transaction (or the receipt of the *Hexameron* from them) with the monks of Bury St Edmunds, would lead us to believe that he owned this codex during his archidiaconate and through the early years of his episcopate, say *ca.* 1230–1242. Certainly he soon outgrew the painful glossarial type of exegesis beloved of Stephen Langton and his contemporaries.

Oxford, Bodley 198* is a large folio codex containing, ff. 1^A–106^A, Augustine's *De Civitate Dei*; ff. 107^A–298^D, Gregory's *Moralia in Job*; and, ff. 299^A–306^D, indexes to the two works. The text was written in a beautiful early English gothic bookhand *ca.* 1225. Thomas Gascoigne once owned the MS and has made numerous notes throughout the codex. He was aware that certain notes and strange signs in the margin were in Grosseteste's hand, though he was not quite sure of the exact significance of any given sign. His note at the foot of f. 107^a says:

> ...ubi est consimilis figura vel carecter ibi est consimilis materia. Exemplum de istis figuris in margine huius libri ∴ł ∴ł per quas datur intelligi quod in utroque loco illius figure est conformitas materie vel sentencie sicut est conformitas figure vel figure ad figuram. Hoc T. Gascoigne a° d^i 1433†... et nota quod omnes note et figure in margine istius libri fuerunt scripte propria manu sancte memorie Magistri Roberti Grosseteste episcopi Lincolniensis et istum librum dedit mihi sponte sub sigillo suo conventus fratrum minorum Oxonie....

* See *A Summary Catalogue of Western MSS in the Bodleian...*, II, pt. i (Oxford, 1922), p. 110 f., and S. H. Thomson, "Grosseteste's Topical Concordance of the Bible and the Fathers" in *Speculum*, IX (1934), 139–144. See also below, p. 122 ff.

† Another note on f. 298^D recites the story of his election to the rectorate of St Peter's de Cornhul in 1445, and his resignation, 21 Sept. of the same year, because of illness. Gascoigne possessed the book at least thirteen years. Rogers printed a facsimile of this note as a frontispiece to his *Loci e Libro Veritatum* (Oxford, 1881), and transcribed the note, p. 232.

The key to these signs is found in Lyons MS 414, ff. 17ᵃ–32ᵃ, which bears the rubric *Tabula Magistri Roberti lincolniensis episcopi cum addicione fratris Ade de Marisco...*,* from which we may infer that Grosseteste and Adam Marsh joined forces in compiling the concordance. The Lyons MS is not in Grosseteste's hand. We have three other MSS containing these signs. MSS 17 and 47 of St John's College, Cambridge, containing works of St Anselm and St Augustine, are copiously annotated, probably by Grosseteste, with these signs. These two MSS were originally bound in one codex. Lambeth MS 151 contains, ff. 51^{A}–114^{D}, some of these signs, but they were not made by Grosseteste. It is difficult to believe that, considering the great number of patristic and classical works referred to in the Lyons *tabula* in complete detail, many more MSS in which Grosseteste made these concordantial markings are not still in existence.

We find, in the Bodley MS, some Latin written in Greek characters in Grosseteste's hand. At the bottom of the right margin of f. 1^{A} we note: λινγυα ῑcυλτανc ῑ ιπcῦ α κυο δεφενδιτ' (that is: *lingua insultans in ipsum a quo defenditur*) facing Augustine's ...*quibus linguis usurpaverunt mendaciter ipsum nomen ut viverent vel quas linguas in locis*.... Again, in the left margin of f. 148^{A} he has written νεκορδια ÷ ινcιπιενκια (that is: *vecordia est insipiencia*) in Bk. VIII of Augustine's *De Civitate Dei* facing: *Hec vero ei sua vecordia placet interim sed non placebit, quia cum retribucionis*.... But Grosseteste was not restricted to using Greek characters for Latin words as here and in the Pembroke MS. We can be sure that he had access to a copy of the Septuagint which he quotes so frequently and so aptly in his *Hexameron*. On f. 289^{A}, in Bk. XVIII of Gregory's *Moralia*, facing the text: *Inter quos lucetis sicut luminaria in mundo. Quia enim sancta ecclesia lune appellacione exprimitur; propheta testatur dicens: "Elevatus est sol et luna stetit in ordine suo"* is a note in Grosseteste's hand:

abac' 3. secundum 70. ἐπηρθη ὁ
ἥλιος κ' ἡ cελήνη ἔcτη ἐν τῆ
τάξη† ἀυτῆc [Habak. iii. 11 *a*.]

In the left margin of f. 290^{A}, facing *Unde scriptum est*: *Dedit abyssus*

* See below, p. 122 ff.
† LXX, ed. Tischendorf, τάξει.

vocem suam ab altitudine phantasie sue, Grosseteste has written the Greek text of Habak. iii. 10*b*:

ἔδωκεν ἡ ἄυιcωc* φονην
ἀυτῆc ὕψοc φαντασιαc ἀυτῆc
abac' 3.

The LXX is the first Greek work to be cited by Grosseteste, *ca.* 1230 (see below, p. 73).

Cambridge, University Ff. i. 24 is a Greek MS of the late tenth century containing, ff. 1^{A}–103^{C}, 1 Chronicles in the LXX version;† ff. 104^{A}–198^{B}, the *Commonitorium* (*Yponosticon*) of Josephus Christianus, divided into 166 chapters; and, ff. 203^{A}–261^{B}, the *Testamenta XII Patriarcharum*. There is every reason to believe that this is one of the Greek MSS Grosseteste caused to be brought from Greece at the suggestion of John of Basingstoke.‡ Grosseteste has made notes throughout the codex and can be assumed to have read the whole book. He first obtained possession of this MS *ca.* 1241 and translated the *Testamenta*, with the aid of Nicholaus Grecus, in 1242. See below, p. 42 ff. We can thus consider his notes in this MS to have been written 1241–1242. Knowing that at this time Grosseteste was in his late sixties, we might be able to read into the script the characteristics of age, but the writing is certainly that of a strong, if perhaps nervous, person. The writing on the flyleaf of Pembroke MS 7, though evidently more carefully written, shows more of the indications of advanced age. Yet only a few years can have intervened between the writing in the two books. We know his health to have been increasingly delicate in the last years of his episcopate.

Gonville and Caius Coll., Cambridge, 403, a twelfth-century Greek MS of the four Gospels, has, in several places, e.g. f. 130^{b}, notes in Grosseteste's hand. The book was once the property of the Oxford Franciscans.§ Running titles in Grosseteste's hand have been mostly cut off in rebinding.

* LXX, ed. Tischendorf, ἄβυσσος.

† See *Catalogue of MSS...Cambridge University*, II (Cambridge, 1857), 313 ff. and R. H. Charles, *The Greek Versions of the Testaments of the Twelve Patriarchs* (Oxford, 1908), p. x.

‡ See Matthew Paris, *Chron. Maj.* (R.S.), IV, 232 and V, 285, and Stevenson, *Robert Grosseteste*, p. 227 ff.

§ See M. R. James, *Catalogue of MSS...of Gonville and Caius College, Cambridge*, II (Cambridge, 1908), 469 f. The "straggling hand" on p. 20 to which James refers is identical with that of some marginalia in Corpus Christi Coll., Cambridge, MS 480, but does not correspond to our known specimens of Grosseteste's hand.

Corpus Christi Coll., Cambridge, 480, is a small Greek *Psalterium* in which at least four different thirteenth- and early fourteenth-century hands have made marginal notes. Of these four, one has been believed to be Grosseteste's. But the looser "straggling" hand which has been taken for his* bears, on close comparison with known examples of his writing, no letter-for-letter similarity. All typical letters, *d*, *e*, *g*, *m*, *n*, *r*, *s*, are formed in a manner completely divergent from Grosseteste's. The signs for *est*, *et*, *-que* do not correspond to his. A third, early hand, small and more calligraphic than either of the "straggling" hands, is probably to be identified with that of ff. 321–325 of Merton Coll., Oxford, MS 14, which we have some reason to believe should be assigned to someone in the Grosseteste circle.† The latest hand in our MS 480 is that of Johannes Farley, who signs his name on f. 288[a] in Greek characters. ϰ (=*M*) Ιωαννες φαρλει. Dr James makes the suggestion that this codex also belonged to Grosseteste. There is no good reason to doubt it, but I do not believe any of the marginalia are in his hand.

Oxford, Bodl., Savile 21 is an extremely miscellaneous codex in numerous hands varying from *ca.* 1200 to *ca.* 1300. Annotations of various later owners until the beginning of the fifteenth century are found throughout the codex. The contents are almost exclusively astronomical and mathematical. A detailed description of the codex by Mr N. Denholm-Young is to appear in the next volume of the *Summary Catalogue*. Among the items is a considerable section (ff. 143[a]–160[a] and ff. 200[a]–201[a]) in Grosseteste's hand, which, so far as I am aware, is the largest single MS in his writing still extant. The matter which Grosseteste thought worth copying in 1215–1216 (see below) is of no small interest.

(*a*) ff. 143[a]–146[b]. *Algorismus Jordani tam in integris quam in fraccionibus demonstratus.*

This title is written in a neat chancery hand later (*ca.* 1250) than the text. The work begins *[F]igure numerorum sunt* IX *scilicet* 123456789 *et sunt prima unitatis, secunda binarii et sic deinceps*... and ends ...*et in se semel quod erat propositum.* This is not the *Algorismus Jordani* published by Schöner in 1534, whose authenticity is generally doubted, but the work consisting of

* See M. R. James, *Catalogue of MSS*...*of Corpus Christi College, Cambridge*, II (Cambridge, 1912), 422 ff.

† See S. H. Thomson, "The 'Notule' of Grosseteste on the *Nicomachean Ethics*" (*Proceedings of the British Academy*, XIX), p. 25 f.

34 propositions noted and analysed by G. Eneström in 1906.* Eneström's arguments for its authenticity were mainly internal; the only MS ascription he mentioned was that in the Berlin lat. 4° 510. The Savile copy is in all probability the earliest extant copy, and the early ascription places its authenticity beyond any reasonable doubt.

(*b*) ff. 146^b–150^a. *Jordanus de fraccionibus.*
This opusculum begins: *Quidlibet intellectum respectu partis aut parcium*... and ends ...*quesitam radicem efficienti per* 20^a et per 24^a.
This corresponds to the anonymous *Demonstracio de minuciis* noticed by Eneström (*op. cit.* p. 25, n. 5) as appearing in most of the MSS of the *Algorismus Jordani*. The Savile MS appears to be, if not the only, at least the earliest, ascribed copy. Eneström published extracts of this work from Berlin lat. 4° 510 in *Bibl. Math.* XIV (1913), 45 ff. He noted the Savile MS (p. 42), dating it "14. oder 15. Jahrh."

(*c*) ff. 150^b–151^a. *Thebith de proporcionibus.*
Begins: *Proporcio est rei ad rem determinata secundum*... and ends ...*non omnes pariter fiant triginta sex.*

(*d*) ff. 151^b–153^a. *Thebith de figura Catha.*
Begins: *Intellexi quod dixisti super figuram que nominatur Cata*... and ends ...*du gb quod oportuit ostendi.* The Latin translation is the work of Gerard of Cremona, *ca.* 1175. See Sarton, *Introduction*..., II, pt. i, p. 341. Of both (*d*) and (*e*) MSS in England are rather common, but this seems to be the earliest copy.

(*e*) ff. 153^b–155^b. *Tractatus patris Ascii Tebit filii Chore in motu accessionis et processionis.*
This rubric is in Grosseteste's hand. The work begins: *Imaginabor speram equatoris diei et micirculos*... and ends ...*motus accessionis et recessionis in eis.* The work was translated into Latin by Gerard of Cremona, *ca.* 1175. See Sarton, *Introduction*..., II, pt. i, p. 341. Edd. 1480, 1509, 1518.

(*f*) ff. 155^b–156^a contain three *tabulae* in Grosseteste's hand: *Aree numerorum anni expansi, Secessus tenebrarum in minuta eclipsi, Tabula ad cognoscendum in qua feria incipiat quilibet mensis Arabum.*

(*g*) ff. 156^b–158^a. *Ars inveniendi eclipsim solis et lune.* The rubric is in the hand that wrote the title of (*a*). The work begins: *Ars inveniendi eclipsim lune. Scias quod luna non obscurabitur nisi cum fuerit in opposito*... and ends ...*ascendens in puncto coniunccionis solis et lune quem in primis invenisti.*

(*h*) ff. 158^b–160^a contain numerous tables.
Tabula ad cognoscendum in qua feria incipit mensis Persarum.
Tabula ad cognoscendum in qua feria incipiat quilibet mensis antiquorum egipciacorum que arabice dicitur Repthie, preceded by a note on casting horoscopes.
Twelve tables: *equaciones* of the twelve zodiacal houses.

* "Ueber die 'Demonstratio Jordani de Algorismo'" in *Zft f. Gesch. d. Math. u. Physik*, VII (1906), 24–37. See also G. Sarton, *Introduction to History of Science*, II, pt. ii, pp. 613–616.

(*i*) f. 160[b]. Two square astrological diagrams. The first is labelled: *Hec figura anni* 611 *annis arabis*, 11 *mensibus et diebus* 40 *martis* 22 *die marcii die martis post meridiem hora jovis* (=A.D. 1215–1216). In the centre of this figure Grosseteste has written: *Coniunccio saturni et martis annis arabis perfectis* 612, *mensibus* 5, *die vicesimo primo sexti mensis in libra* 3° 50′.

The second figure has a label: *Hec est figura coniunccionis saturni et iovis annis arabis* 612 *perfectis*, *mensibus* 5, *diebus* 20 *hora aquarii*[?] 21 *minutis* 58.

The remainder of the codex, the *Massa Computi* of Alexander de Villa Dei, was in Grosseteste's possession, though none of his notes is to be found in the margins until, at the very end of the codex, we find two pages in his hand, now somewhat mutilated around the edges and much of the text so discoloured as to be illegible.

(*j*) f. 200[b], a paragraph describing persons born under the several planets. Almost an inch at the left is gone. The fragment begins: ...*tus ample faciei sub niē* [?] *iracundus et adinstar serpentis. Ad vindictam promtissimus lucentibus oculis palpebris pilosis*... and ends ...*contrarietate deprimitur solus et quietus et sine invidia esse probatur.*

This paragraph is followed by a longer section:

(*k*) *Si de qualitate futuri fiat tibi questio in hora solis talem esse scias*... ending on f. 201[a] ...*Si Aquarius quod querit accipiet, sed non per omnia que* [?] *vult* [?] *S*...*quesierit prosperabitur*....

The remainder of the page, part of which is illegible by reason of some discoloration and part of which has been torn away, contains two related paragraphs.

(*l*) *Posita halhidada** *in medio anguli quadrantis, locum capito summitatis*... ending ...*sunt quam est halhidada, caterus, linea vero orientalis basis.*

(*m*) *Si vis alicuius arboris aut columne aut aliquid talium in plano*..., the last three lines, so far as now remains, ending

...*tudine per singulos in descensu easdem proporciones*...
...*perveniat umbre de hinc halhidada*...
...*e per eos halhidada*...

This last paragraph is an extract from Gerbert's *Geometria*, chap. 1 (*Patr. Lat.* CXXXIX, col. 120), and appears separately in B.M., Royal MS 15. B. x, f. 60[b]. The preceding paragraph may conceivably come from the same source.

The importance of this MS for a judgment concerning the early interests and extent of knowledge of Arabian mathematicians of

* For the early use of this Arabic word in European mathematical works see M. Cantor, *Vorlesungen über d. Gesch. d. Math.* 1 (Leipzig, 1894), 812.

Grosseteste is difficult to exaggerate. On the assumption of a Paris stay, approximately 1209–1214, this would have been written soon after his return to Oxford. His familiarity with the scientific works of the Arabs might have been acquired, or at least increased, at Paris, yet the strongly scientific tradition connecting England with Arab centres in Spain goes back to the twelfth century, and it is quite possible that there are more MS copies of twelfth- and thirteenth-century scientific works in England than in Paris. If so, Grosseteste may have had to wait until he returned to England from Paris to continue his scientific studies. A not-inconsiderable part of his interests at Paris we can be sure centred upon theology and psychology. See below, p. 89 f.

Bodley, Laud Lat. 105* is a miscellaneous codex in several twelfth- and thirteenth-century hands. A note on f. 229ª, *Liber Sancte Marie Virginis in Ebberbach* and the date 1483 tell the location of at least the first 256 folia, and possibly of the whole codex at that time. The present binding is of the seventeenth century, and it is not now possible to say definitely that ff. 257–312, containing an incomplete copy of Priscian's *Institutio Grammatica*, were or were not at Ebberbach. The Priscian is written in a fine English hand of the first half of the twelfth century. The first leaf (f. 257) shows signs of wear, as if the MS had been used without a cover. At the top of the second leaf of the Priscian (f. 258ª) is, in writing which I take to be Grosseteste's, *Maius volumen Prisciani*. There are no other notations in the MS which are demonstrably in this same hand. Occasional early thirteenth-century notes in previous gatherings of the codex, from f. 205 to f. 255, are almost surely by an English scribe. The gothic book-hand of this part of the codex, however, might as readily be North French, Flemish or Burgundian as English. It is difficult to resist the impression that this part of the codex, ff. 205–312, has travelled from England, or from the possession of an English scholar, perhaps at Paris, to Germany, and has thence come back to England into the hands of Archbishop Laud by 1637.

Lincoln Cathedral 144 is a large folio codex of 279 leaves containing the commentary of Peter Lombard on the Psalms, written *ca.* 1175 by an English scribe.† The codex is *mutilus in initio*, beginning at the

* See H. O. Coxe, *Cat. Codd. MSS Bibl. Bodl.* II, pt. i (Oxford, 1858), p. 47.

† See R. M. Woolley, *Catalogue of MSS of Lincoln Cathedral Library* (Oxford, 1927), p. 100.

end of Ps. iv. The text of the Psalms is written down the centre of the page, and the commentary on both sides. Throughout the codex there are copious marginal notations and glosses in Grosseteste's hand. In many places long notes are in plummet; occasionally a plummet note has been recopied in ink.* The pen used in making these notes was less flexible than Grosseteste usually used: there is almost no shading at all in the formation of the letters. This is doubtless the volume referred to by Johannes de Sexton in a list of his own books now in Lincoln Cathedral MS 139 as *Psalterium magnum simplex quod fuit magistri Roberti*. The list was written about the middle of the thirteenth century.†

Shrewsbury School I contains the books of *Sapiencia* and *Ecclesiasticus*‡ with the *glossae communis* and *interlinearis*. As this codex was once in the possession of Alexander of Staneby (†1238)§ we may assume that it belonged to Grosseteste after Staneby's death. The writing in Grosseteste's hand throughout the codex is sufficiently crabbed and irregular for it to have been the work of his last years. There are times when the writing is less hurried and has some of the grace of the notes in Bodley 198, but for the most part it indicates great haste or carelessness. Both *et*-signs, i.e. the ⁊ and the ⁊, appear, and other characteristics of his hand.

The text itself was written very early in the century: there are no chapter-divisions. A neat sub-contemporary hand, probably that of Alexander, has made occasional glossarial notes in which chapters are specified. This would not have been likely much before he became Bishop of Lichfield and Coventry, 1224. An ex-libris on the verso of the flyleaf *Iste liber est fratrum predicatorum Cestrie* is sufficiently early to warrant the assumption that the Chester Dominicans possessed the book soon after Grosseteste's death.

Durham Cathedral A. III. 12 is one of the most important of all Grosseteste MSS.|| In the early part of the mixed collection of *Dicta* and parts of what was destined to become his *Commentarius in Psalmos*, occupying the first section of the codex, a change of hand

* See also below, p. 77 f.

† Woolley, *op. cit.* p. 98, dates the list "s. XIV". On paleographical evidence it could hardly be later than 1260, though we do not yet know who Sexton was.

‡ See below, p. 72.

§ See Russell, J. C., *Dict. of Writers of Thirteenth Century England* (London, 1936), p. 17 f.

|| See below, pp. 75 f., 121, and 182 ff.

occurs, the second hand beginning at the top of the second column of the verso of f. 4 and continuing to the middle of the first column of the recto of f. 15. This second hand, I feel sure, is that of Grosseteste. It is more calligraphic and gothic than the other and authentic examples of his writing, and this fact might justify some hesitation. But that he was not averse to trying to write the new gothic script is evident from the somewhat awkward occasional efforts in Savile 21. The Durham gothic is much more successful, but betrays a distinct uncertainty arising from conscious and even painful effort. The spacing of letters is irregular and may be seen to change several times in the course of a column. The size of the letters, the angle and length of the downward strokes, vary even from word to word. It is certainly not the writing of a professional scribe: his employment would have been worse than uncertain. Careful examination of separate letters reveals a striking similarity to known characteristics of Grosseteste's writing, and if we allow for the use of a sharper pen than was his custom, and for the effort to be a scribe, the conclusion that we have his own copy of this selection from his own *Dicta* is difficult to avoid. Most noticeable is Grosseteste's peculiar looped *et*-sign. The final *m* and *n* and the *h* have the last minim extending below the line and curving slightly to the left, a trait of Grosseteste's writing, though not uncommon elsewhere. The use of ÷ for *est* is somewhat general and of no particular significance, though almost habitual to Grosseteste. An occasional *r* has the downward stroke projected beyond the line and curved to the left. The downward stroke of the *d* is long and straight, diagonally from the left, a movement familiar to Grosseteste.

Oxford, Corpus Christi Coll. 43 contains, ff. 12^C–15^B, the *De Schematibus* of Bede written in a hand probably that of Grosseteste in his last years. The verso of the flyleaf, an alphabetical list of subjects from *Arcus* to *Vicium*, is in the same hand, which has also annotated other works in the codex. We have all the characteristics of Grosseteste's hand: the *d*; the *de* with *e* written at the top of the sloping down-stroke of *d*; the *e* with the upward finishing stroke; the *f* and *s* with juncture of the two strokes at the top showing clearly and an occasional leftward flourish at the bottom; the characteristic lower loop of the *g*; the leftward curve to the final stroke below the line of the *h*, *i*, *m* and *n*; the typical *et*-sign, though here the returning upward stroke completing the leftward loop is absent;

the use of this *et*-sign for a verb-ending, e.g. *solet*; the simple horizontal cross-stroke of the *s* for *secundum* and of *q* for *quod*; all combine with the general appearance of the script to put the case for Grosseteste as the scribe almost beyond doubt. The hand is, however, somewhat less free and vigorous than any of the other examples, though in only a slightly greater degree than the Shrewsbury MS. The scribe was obviously an old man. If we could suppose this to have been written *ca.* 1250, near the end of his life, the lack of firmness would be easily explained, and the persistence of basic movements in letter-formation is not less convincing.

In addition to the many MSS which we must suppose him to have had and annotated, judging by the formidable list of works in the *Concordancia Patrum*, we can assume that he had his own copy of the Greek works of Dionysius, those works of Johannes Damascenus which he translated, a Greek *Suidas*,* the Latin *paraphrasis* of the *Hexameron* of Basil mentioned in Pembroke, Cambridge, MS 7, a copy of the LXX which he used critically before writing his own *Hexameron* and from which he quoted in the margins of Bodley MS 198,† and a copy of Aristotle's *Ethics* in Greek, with the Greek commentators. It is possible that he may have had more than one copy of the Greek commentators. His optional renderings of some phrases would best be explained on this theory. From the fact that the only ascribed copy of the translation of the *De Lineis Indivisibilibus* and *De Virtute* is of South French provenance, it seems plausible to suggest that the work of translation was done at Lyons in 1245 or, less probably, 1250, and his original Greek copy may have been only borrowed. Concerning his translation of the spurious Ignatian correspondence, all the evidence we have (see below, p. 60) points to Lyons in 1245, and he may have borrowed this Greek original also. He possessed, at least for a time, a Greek copy of Basil's *Longer Rules*, as we must infer from his statements in *Epist.* 57 (see below, p. 203). For a summary of our information concerning MSS of Grosseteste noted by various writers to have been seen, for the most part in the Franciscan convent in Oxford, see A. G. Little, *Grey Friars*, p. 57 f.

* Dr James has supposed the Greek copy in Corpus Christi College, Oxford to be the one Grosseteste owned. It may be a copy of Grosseteste's, but these two MSS, 76 and 77, are of the fifteenth century.

† This copy may yet be found; its variant reading in Habakkuk iii might betray it (see above, p. 28 f.).

GROSSETESTE'S KNOWLEDGE OF HEBREW

It has long been assumed that Grosseteste knew Hebrew. Roger Bacon must be held responsible for the spread of this assumption. The obvious implication of his statement:

> Solus dominus Robertus propter longitudinem vite et vias mirabiles quibus usus est, pre aliis hominibus scivit sciencias; quia Grecum et Hebreum non scivit sufficienter ut per se transferret sed habuit multos adiutores...*

is that he did know Hebrew, even if not well enough to translate by himself. Nicholas Trevet is more specific. He remarks:

> ...multa de glossis Hebraeorum extraxit....†

John Tynmouth (*fl.* 1365) in his *Historia Aurea* (quoted by Wharton, II, 347) conflates Bacon and Trevet:

> Hic doctor in theologia, in triplici lingua eruditus, latina, hebrea et greca, multa de glossis hebreorum extraxit.

The assumption grew and, according to Cave‡ and Wood,§ Grosseteste was a profound Hebraist. More recently students have been less anxious to make a bald assertion that Grosseteste knew Hebrew. There are, however, exceptions to this counsel of reticence. L. I. Newman|| classes Grosseteste "among the distinguished English Hebraists of the thirteenth century". A. Kleinhans, O.F.M. says roundly:

> Ipse ordinis Fratrum Minorum fautor maximus Robertus Grossatesta linguae hebraicae et graecae peritus erat eorumque studium valde promovit.¶

Dr George Sarton has found evidence that Grosseteste "owned a copy of a literal Latin translation of the Old Testament with the Hebrew text".** Although no evidence is adduced in Sarton's book, there seems no good reason to doubt the truth of this tradition. In

* *R. Baconis Opera Inedita* (ed. Brewer, London, 1859, R.S.), pp. 91, 472.

† *Annales sex regum Angliae* (ed. T. Hog, London, 1845), p. 243.

‡ *Hist. Lit.* I (1694), 497 (ed. 1720, p. 629): ...*in linguarum Hebraicae, Graecae, Latinae scientia...eruditus.*

§ *Hist. and Antiquities of the Univ. of Oxford*, I (ed. Gutch, 1782), 193, 397. See also *Hist. litt. de la France*, XVIII (1835), 440: "Robert de Lincoln savait l'hébreu...."

|| *Jewish Influence on Christian Reform Movements* (New York, 1925), p. 81.

¶ "De Studio Sacrae Scripturae in Ordine Fratrum Minorum saeculo XIII" in *Antonianum*, VII (1932), 432.

** *Introduction to the History of Science*, II, pt. ii (Baltimore, 1931), 584.

passing, nevertheless, it is not unreasonable to distinguish between the possession of such a text and a knowledge of Hebrew. The case of Petrarch and his beloved MS of Homer comes to mind.

Without specifically asserting that Grosseteste knew Hebrew, J. C. Russell, in a recent illuminating article,* suggests that William of Arundel and William de Mara, both of whom are reputed to have known Hebrew, may have aided Grosseteste in matters of exegesis from Hebrew texts. As to William of Arundel, it may be said that even if the identification is admitted of a certain Robertus de Harundel, *in Hebreo...peritissimus*, whose obituary is recorded by Matthew Paris *s.a.* 1246,† with William of Arundel who was Archdeacon of Huntingdon in 1241, it is not necessary to claim that he cannot have been of assistance to Grosseteste. There is no positive evidence either for or against such a relationship. But as to the younger, William de Mara,‡ a Franciscan educated at Oxford, whose period of prominence came toward the end of the century, there seems no valid reason to try to force a connection with Grosseteste by relying on a possible identification of this William with an individual of the same name sufficiently old in 1250 to be *Magister...diaconus*, and instituted to a considerable church in Grosseteste's diocese.

The tradition that Grosseteste knew Hebrew seems not to rest on solid ground, but rather to be a later and apocryphal growth. There is room for uncertainty as to the meaning of the expression "to know Hebrew". It would be difficult to maintain the position that Grosseteste did not know, for example, the Hebrew alphabet, and, in the abstract, the principles of Hebrew syntax and morphology. It is quite likely that his curiosity, so evident in all things philological, would have led him to gather such general information. But as for any actual use of the language, it must be concluded that all available evidence is negative. I have found no evidence at all in his commentarial works that he knew a word of Hebrew which he could not have taken from the common *Interpretaciones nominum hebraicorum Jeronimi* appearing in so many twelfth- and thirteenth-century copies of the Vulgate. On the other hand, in cases where we should expect

* "The Preferments and 'Adiutores' of Robert Grosseteste" in *Harvard Theol. Rev.* XXVI (1933), 161–172.

† *Chron. Maj.* IV (R.S.), 553.

‡ See Little, *Grey Friars*, p. 215 f., and E. Longpré in *Dict. de théologie catholique*, VIII (Paris, 1909), cols. 2467–2469.

him to refer to the Hebrew text, as in the *Hexameron*, which we must date 1240–1245, he uses the LXX. There is no mention of an interest in Hebrew in any of his later letters. There is no reference, as far as I have been able to discover, in any of his sermons which could be construed as indicating any such interest or achievement. We have a considerable amount of writing of Greek characters in his own hand, but none of Hebrew.

Negative evidence always raises as many problems as it settles, perhaps more, and such is certainly the case in this matter. Grosseteste may have known Hebrew, or he may have begun the study of this language toward the end of his life, but we have no real proof of it, and, lacking positive evidence, it would be better to maintain a thorough-going scepticism on the subject.

* * * * *

In the course of collecting and compiling the material for the present work, a formidable indebtedness has been contracted which summary acknowledgment could ill discharge. The project of studying the manuscripts of Grosseteste's works at first hand was generously supported by the American Council of Learned Societies with the grant of a Travelling Fellowship for the year 1931–1932, later extended to a second year. Persistent demands have been made on the time and energy of hundreds of scholars and of those equally important folk, guardians of the scholar's hope-chest, the librarians and keepers of manuscripts. A glance at the list of manuscripts consulted and of libraries visited will reveal how dependent I have been on their courteous and often enthusiastic good-will. If only a few are thanked specifically it is only because their patience has been drawn upon more extensively.

The dedication of this volume to Dr A. G. Little cannot begin to measure its debt to him for encouragement, guidance and free access to his great store of knowledge. Prof. F. M. Powicke, Dr E. A. Lowe, and the late Mgr George Lacombe have generously responded to my frequent calls for help. Mgr Auguste Pelzer and Prof. F. Pelster, S.J., both of whom have made masterly contributions to our knowledge of the intellectual world of which Grosseteste was a part, have gladly given a labourer in the field needed encouragement and invaluable suggestions which have reduced sensibly the number of errors in the work. To Mr N. Denholm-Young and Dr R. W. Hunt

I am especially indebted: their exact knowledge of English MSS and literary history of the thirteenth century has been of immeasurable assistance.

My indebtedness to Prof. Ezio Franceschini of Padua is evident throughout the discussion of Grosseteste's translations. He has shared his discoveries with me in the truest spirit of scholarship. The volume could not have appeared as soon as it has were it not for the co-operation of Miss Ruth J. Dean, who has aided materially in the collation of notes and has brought to my notice several MSS and bibliographical details that would otherwise not have been included. She has undertaken the arduous task of editing the hitherto unpublished Anglo-Norman works of Grosseteste.

The staff of Duke Humphrey's Library in the Bodleian have made my prolonged labours there a keen pleasure. Mr H. W. Garrod, Librarian of Merton College, and Mr R. A. B. Mynors, Librarian of Balliol College, have been particularly interested and helpful. The courtesy and promptness of the staff of the Manuscript Students' Room in the British Museum are proverbial. Mr H. J. Pink of the Anderson Room in the Cambridge University Library, the late Mr A. L. Attwater, Librarian of Pembroke College, Mr H. Butterfield, Librarian of Peterhouse, Dr Z. N. Brooke, Librarian of Gonville and Caius College, Prof. C. W. Previté-Orton, sometime Librarian of St John's College, and the late Sir Edwyn Hoskyns, Bart., Librarian of Corpus Christi College, all made my brief visits to Cambridge more profitable than I had any right to expect. Preb. W. H. Kynaston, Librarian of Lincoln Cathedral, and the Rev. J. H. Srawley, Chancellor of Lincoln, were especially kind in allowing access to their beautiful library on days when it was ordinarily closed. The late Mr K. C. Bayley, Librarian of Durham Cathedral, made my short stay in Durham a delightful memory and placed me still further in his debt by allowing that precious codex, A. III. 12, to be deposited in Oxford for several months. The Librarian and Board of Governors of Shrewsbury School very generously permitted their MS 1 to be deposited at the Bodleian for a month. For various kindnesses I must thank Mr A. B. Emden, Principal of St Edmund's Hall, Miss Dorothy E. Sharp, Miss W. A. Pronger, Professor B. L. Ullman and Capt. R. B. Haselden.

On the Continent, more time was spent at the Vatican Library and at the University Library in Prague than anywhere else. His

Eminence, Cardinal E. Tisserant, now Prefect of the Vatican Library, extended me unmerited privileges. My repeated visits to Prague have inured Docent Dr Kleinschnitzová, in charge of MSS at the University Library, to the voracity of my appetite for MSS, and her charity has never failed. It was my happy experience to find unfailing courtesy in the many German and Austrian libraries visited. Often it was necessary to ask that the usual rules be waived governing advance application for permission to examine a codex. Such concessions were uniformly and cheerfully granted.

The three indexes, which are designed to make a very detailed and even confusing work more bearably useful, are the work of my wife. A scholar's wife could never adequately be thanked for enduring her lot, to say nothing of her *opera supererogatoria* of aiding and abetting his labours. But *caritas patiens est, benigna est, et omnia laete suffert.*

CATALOGUE OF AUTHENTIC WORKS OF GROSSETESTE

TRANSLATIONS FROM THE GREEK

1. *Testamenta XII Patriarcharum*

I. Inc.: Transcriptum testamenti Ruben: Quecunque mandavit filiis suis...

Expl.: ...usque ad diem exitus eorum ex terra Egipti.

II. The continued popularity of this christianized apocryphal work is attested by the frequency of its republication in the original Greek and in Latin translations. The first Latin edition was by Johannes Miller, Augsburg, 1520; thereafter Hagenau, 1532; Paris, 1549; Venice, 1604; Mainz, 1665; in *Magna Bibliotheca Patrum* (de la Bigne), various edd., Paris, 1575 etc.; with the Greek editions of Grabe, *Spicilegium SS. Patrum*, Oxford, 1698 and 1714; Fabricius, *Cod. Pseud. Vet. Test.*, 1713 and 1722–1723; Gallandi, *Bibl. Vet. Patrum*, 1675 ff.; Migne, *Patr. Gr.* II, 1025–1150.* For the numerous translations from Grosseteste's Latin into vernacular tongues see R. Sinker, *A Descriptive Catalogue of the Editions of the Printed Text of the Versions of the Testamenta XII Patriarcharum*, Cambridge, 1910, and below, note ‡.

III. Matthew Paris (*Hist. Maj., sub anno* 1242, R.S. v, 284 ff.) tells the story of John of Basingstoke, Archdeacon of Leicester, reporting to Grosseteste that he had heard of this work when in Athens. Grosseteste then commissioned him to procure a copy of the original Greek. Several of the early MSS of Grosseteste's translation have a colophon that gives in some detail the story of the translation, Grosseteste's conception of the Jewish origin of the work, the fact of the collaboration of Nicholaus Grecus, and the date of the translation, 1242. The tenth-century Greek MS, now Cambridge Univ. Ff. i. 24, bearing notes in Grosseteste's own hand, is in all probability the copy brought to England by Basingstoke. That Grosseteste was the translator was known to Salimbene who says simply *Hic...transtulit...Testamenta XII Patriarcharum et multos alios libros.*† Bonaventura mentions the Latin version (*In IV Sent.* IV (ed. Quaracchi, 1899), 703), but makes no reference to Grosseteste. The translation was known to all the bibliographers. Sinker, in the Introduction to his edition of the Greek *Testamenta* (Cambridge, 1869), listed thirty-one MSS of the Latin version, and added fifteen to this list in his *Appendix* (Cambridge, 1879).‡

* Baur, p. xi, lists the following editions which I have not seen: 1550, 1555, 1569, 1609, 1669, 1670, 1711, 1822.

† *MGH. SS.* XXXII (1905–1913), 233. See below, p. 48, under Damascenus, *De Fide Orthodoxa*.

‡ For a thirteenth-century Anglo-Norman translation of part of the *Testamenta* in Paris, B.N. n. a. fr. 10176, ff. 2–5, see Miss R. J. Dean's note in *PMLA.* LI (1936), 607–620. There are doubtless some further English translations not noticed by Sinker.

IV. MSS:

Oxford				
Add.	A. 21	ff. 145^{A}–170^{A}	XV^{m}	Unasc. So. Ger.
Bodl.	750	ff. 87^{A}–118^{C}	XIII^{m}	Asc. XV^{2}
Rawl.	C. 152	ff. 1^{a}–14^{b}	XIII^{m}	Unasc.
Selden	sup. 75	ff. 232^{a}–262^{a}	XIV^{m}	Unasc.*
C.C.C.	142	ff. 220^{A}–253^{D}	XIII^{2}	Asc.
Queen's	213	ff. 13^{b}–50^{b}	1449	Asc.†
	214	pp. 1–251	XVII	Asc.
London, B.M.				
Add.	18210	ff. 41^{A}–48^{B}	XIII^{m}	Asc. *mut. in init.*‡§
	32579	ff. 38^{A}–68^{C}	*ca.* 1300	Unasc.
Arundel	15	ff. 73^{A}–97^{C}	XIII^{m}	Unasc.
Egerton	2676	ff. 65^{a}–96^{b}	XIII^{m}	Unasc.§
Harley	876	ff. 1^{A}–15^{A}	XIII^{m}	Unasc.
	3853	ff. 83^{A}–114^{A}	XIV^{1}	Unasc. Ital.
	4725	ff. 10^{A}–19^{D}	XIII^{2}	Unasc. Abr.
	4736	ff. 129^{a}–165^{b}	XV^{1}	Asc.‡
Royal	4. D. VII	ff. 232^{C}–246^{C}, 248^{C}–249^{A}	XIII^{m}	Asc. w. *Suidas*‡
	13. D. I	ff. 225^{B}–236^{D}	1385	Unasc.
London, Gray's Inn	7	ff. 147^{b}–158^{b}	*ca.* 1300	Unasc.
Cambridge				
Univ.	Dd. i. 17	ff. 299^{A}–309^{A}	XIV^{2}	Unasc.
	Ee. ii. 29	ff. 238^{A}–255^{D}	XV^{2}	Unasc.
	Ee. vi. 10	ff. 129^{a}–160^{a}	XIII^{m}	Asc.
	Mm. vi. 4	ff. 123^{a}–159^{b}	*ca.* 1300	Asc.
C.C.C.	441	pp. 205^{a}–253^{a}	XIII^{2}	Asc. in *contenta*
Gonv. & Caius	402	ff. 349^{C}–359^{D}	XIV^{1}	Unasc. *mut. in fine*
	511	ff. 143^{a}–165^{a}	XV^{1}	Unasc.
Pembroke	229	ff. 157^{A}–174^{B}	XIV^{2}	Unasc.
St John's	184	ff. 347^{B}–365^{D}	XIII^{2}	Unasc. w. *Suidas*
Trinity	R. 5. 40	ff. 61^{A}–73^{B}	*ca.* 1300	Asc.‡
	O. 9. 28	ff. 59^{a}–77^{a}	XIV^{2}	Asc.‡§
Canterbury, Ch. Ch.	101	ff. 3^{a}–124^{a}	XIII^{2}	Asc.‖
Edinburgh, Univ.	67	ff. 1^{A}–17^{B}	XV^{1}	Asc. Ital.
Admont	462	ff. 38^{C}–51^{D}	XIV^{2}	Asc.¶
Avignon	4	ff. 354^{a}–358^{b}	XV	Asc.
Basel	A. III. 35			
Berlin	lat. 536	ff. 211^{a}–240^{a}	XV^{1}	Asc. Lowl.
Breslau	I. F. 118	ff. 1^{A}–15^{C}	XIII^{2}	Asc. Ital.
	I. F. 277	ff. 257^{B}–264^{B}	XV^{1}	Asc. Ger. Abr.**
Brussels	1108 (5138–41)	ff. 27^{a}–55^{a}	XIII	Unasc.
Erfurt, Amplon.	Q. 146	ff. 183^{a}–195^{b}	XV^{1}	Asc. Ger.
Graz, Univ.	577	ff. 22^{D}–44^{C}	XV^{1}	Asc. So. Ger.††
	978	ff. 128^{b}–172^{a}	1464	Unasc. So. Ger.

* The rubric reads: *secundum translacionem Johannis Crisostomi de hebreo in grecum.*

† On ff. 12^{b}–13^{a} is the *Testamentum Jacobi* from Gen. xlix, but in a different tradition from the Cambridge Univ. Ee. vi. 10, ff. 159^{b}–161^{a}.

‡ With long colophon. § With *Hist. Aseneth.* ‖ With long prologue.

¶ To *Methodus episcopus Linchoniensis*, followed, ff. 51^{D}–52^{A}, by *Testamentum Jacobi.*

** The manner and extent of the abridgment of the *Testamenta* arising in Germany in the early fifteenth century requires further study.

†† Written 1419–1432 in the Monastery of St Lamprecht in Bavaria.

Hamburg	Theol. 1028 fol.	pp. 3–46	XIV^{2}	Asc. Ger.
Klosterneuburg	322	ff. 167^{a}–182^{b}	XIV^{1}	Asc. Ger.
	752	ff. 154^{A}–185^{D}	XIV^{2}	Unasc. Ger.
	945	ff. 22^{a}–40^{a}	XIV^{1}	Asc. Ger.
Leipzig				
Stadtbibl.	lat. 875	ff. 2^{a}–24^{a}	XV	
Univ.	lat. 794	ff. 1^{A}–21^{C}	XIV^{1}	Asc. Ger.
Liége	184	p. 72 ff.*	XV	Asc.
Melk	494	ff. 205^{A}–226^{B}	1451	Asc. So. Ger.
Munich	Clm. 18656	ff. 14^{b}–15^{b}	XV^{1}	Asc. So. Ger.†
	Clm. 21573	ff. 11^{a}–43^{a}	XIV^{1}	Unasc. Ger.
Münster i. W.	18 (649)	ff. 59^{a}–96^{b}	XIV^{1}	Unasc. Ger.
Paris, B.N.	lat. 2042	f. 88^{B-D}, *frag.*	*ca.* 1310–20	Asc. Fr.
	lat. 3590	ff. 1^{a}–38^{a}	XIV^{m}	Unasc. Fr.
	lat. 3764	ff. 1^{a}–36^{a}	*ca.* 1300	Unasc. Rh.
	lat. 6041^{A}	ff. 160^{C}–178^{B}	XIV^{1}	Unasc. Ital.
Prague				
Univ.	51	ff. 153^{a}–168^{a}	1468	Unasc. Boh.
	822	ff. 99^{b}–115^{b}	*ca.* 1400	Unasc. Boh.
	876	ff. 1^{a}–24^{b}	1462–3	Unasc. Boh.
Metrop. Chap.	401	ff. 16^{a}–45^{a}	1432	Asc. Boh.
	1603	ff. 109^{a}–141^{b}	XV^{m}	Asc. Boh. *mut. in fine*
	1610	ff. 1^{a}–23^{b}	XV^{1}	Unasc. Boh.
San Marino, Huntington	1345	ff. 19^{C}–40^{A}	*ca.* 1300	Unasc. Engl.
St Florian	52	ff. 1^{a}–12^{b}, 19^{a}	*ca.* 1300	Asc. Ger.
	330	ff. 176^{a}–188^{b}	XIV^{2}	Asc. Ger.
Schlägl	24 Cpl. (823) 226	ff. 224^{a}–239^{b}	XIV^{1}	Unasc.‡
Utrecht	389	ff. 38^{A}–58^{b}	1458	Asc. Ital.
Vatican				
lat.	1807	ff. 70^{a}–114^{b}	XV^{2}	Unasc. Ital.
Pal. lat.	415	ff. 119^{A}–139^{D}	1450	Unasc. Ger.
Venice, S. Marco	VI. 81	ff. 162^{a}–193^{b}	XIV^{1}	Unasc. Ital.
Vienna, Nat. Bibl.	4620	ff. 79^{A}–84^{D}	XV^{m}	Asc. Ger. *mut. in fine*
	4739	ff. 258^{a}–289^{a}	XV^{m}	Asc. Ger.§
	13707	ff. 188^{A}–201^{A}	1472	Asc. So. Ger.
	14224	ff. 253^{A}–275^{A}	XV^{m}	Asc. Boh.
Weimar	O. 61	ff. 267^{a}–285^{a}	XV^{m}	Asc. Ger.
Wolfenbüttel	Helms. 185	ff. 230^{a}–236^{b}	XV^{2}	Unasc. Ger. Abr.
	Helms. 629‖	ff. 120^{a}–163^{b}	XV^{2}	Asc. Ger.¶
Würzburg	M. ch. q. 221	ff. 321^{A}–331^{A}	1468	Asc. Ger.**

* Dated in *Cat.* (1875), p. 120 f. "XII"; followed by *Hist. Aseneth.*

† Short extracts.

‡ By G. Vielhaber and G. Indra, *Cat. Codd. Plagensium...* (1918), p. 26 f., it is listed as *Excerpta*. It is probably the shorter version common in German copies.

§ The colophon reads: *Explicit libellus xii patriarcharum: doctrina sancti Basilii episcopi cesariensis ad religiosos carthusienses. Amen.*

‖ Helms. 630^{b} (cat. no. 679), ff. 244^{a}–245^{b} (XV^{2}) and Aug. 76. 25 (cat. no. 2749), ff. 258^{A}–263^{D} (XV^{1}) have so-called *Testamenta patrum*, but they have no connection with Grosseteste's translation.

¶ This copy has a free rendering of the long colophon, the only fifteenth-century copy to have preserved any of its details. The codex bears the signature of Matthias Flacius Illyricus.

** Sinker had in his own possession a fifteenth-century paper copy, bought in Leipzig in 1869. I have been unable to identify it. A copy was in Avignon in 1375. See F. Ehrle, *Hist. Bibl. Aven.* (Rome, 1890), p. 512.

2. *Opera Johannis Damasceni*

(i) *De Logica*

I. Inc.: Sanctissimo* et deo honorabili patri Cosme beatissimo episcopo Maiume
Johannes...Augustum quidem mentis et defectum...
Ens commune nomen est omnium encium. Hoc igitur ens dividitur...
Expl.: ...compositum est inconfusum et invertibile.

II. Unpubl. Greek text of Le Quien (1712) in Migne, *Patr. Gr.* XCIV, cols. 521–669 (through chapter 66 only).

III. The Latin corpus of the five works of Damascenus, *De Logica, De Centum Heresibus, De Fide Orthodoxa, Elementarium Dogmatum* and *De Hymno Trisagion*, must be treated as a unit. The translation, which we here ascribe to Grosseteste, has hitherto been attributed, without proof,† to Burgundio of Pisa, who was known to have translated the *De Fide Orthodoxa, ca.* 1150. No twelfth-century MS of any of the other four works in a Latin translation, nor any MS ascription of such translation to Burgundio, has been found. On the other hand, almost all the MS copies of Burgundio's translation of the *De Fide Orthodoxa* have approximately the same rubric: *Johannis presbiteri Damasceni qui Mansur liber incipit in quo est tradicio certa ortodoxe fidei capitulis centum divisa a Burgundione iudice cive pisano de greco in latinum domino Eugenio tercio bone memorie pape translatus.* As scribes were so careful in the case of this one work to give an elaborate inscription we might be justified in expecting the same translator to be mentioned in the rubrics of his other translations. But the translator of the other four works of Damascenus is not mentioned in the extant MSS. Furthermore, examination of the MSS containing some or all of these five works in the corpus we are considering reveals the suggestive fact that there existed a persistent tradition that these works belonged together, and the still more significant fact that, in five cases, the *De Fide Orthodoxa* in the authenticated translation of Grosseteste appears in the same codex, written by the same scribe as other works in this corpus. To these five we may add the four cases in which one or more works of the corpus (aside from the *De Fide*) appear with Grosseteste's authenticated *De Hymno Trisagion* (q.v.). We have additional evidence in the *Prologus Translatoris* which, in four MSS, precedes the *De Logica.* See below, p. 81. Chap. IX of this *Prologus* reads (Paris, B.N. lat. 2375, f. 390^{C-D}):

Quomodo composuit integrum librum ex tribus: logica scilicet et centum heresibus et sentenciis. Primum quidem ab ente incipiens eas que apud grecos optimas et utiles questiones exposuit. Consequenter autem scripsit hereticorum garrulitates ut mendacium cognoscentes veritati obediamus; posterius

* We have another translation of this dedicatory letter, ascribed to Burgundio and used as a prologue to a copy of his translation of the *De Fide Orthodoxa* in Bodley, Laud Misc. 268, f. 42^{C-D}, beginning: *Incipit prologus in libro theologie Johannis Damasceni. Dignissimo et divinitus honorabili patri Cosme episcopo Maiomaensi Johannes indignus. Attitudinem mentis et inopiam lingue mee dinoscens pigebat me o felix actractare*... and ending ...*credenti mandatis vestris et suscipienti obedienciam oracionum precium rependatis.*

† Le Quien in the preface to his edition (Paris, 1712) of the works of Damascenus, reprinted in Migne, *Patr. Gr.* XCIV, col. 67 f.

autem edidit tercium librum omnis sapiencie et intellectus et fidei pure inscriptum habentem veritatem. Deinde igitur conscriptores propter tercii libri magnitudinem et propter eam que in ipso fidei perfeccionem ex hoc scilicet: *Deum nemo vidit umquam*, inceperunt et testem fidelem factor libri nobis induxit dicens: *unigenitus filius qui in sinibus patris ipse nobis enarravit* et quis non admiretur sapientum libros ipsius pertranseuncium cum diligenti labore summam ipsius philosophiam et intellectus rectitudinem et puritatem, qualiter incepit insuper questiones.

This purports to be an introduction to the three books *De Logica, De Centum Heresibus* and *De Fide Orthodoxa*, but we notice that the *De Fide Orthodoxa* has already been translated. The first sure sign of Grosseteste's translation of the *De Fide* is the literal *in sinibus* for ἐν τοῖς κόλποις, where Burgundio's translation has *in sinu*. We find Grosseteste, therefore, in this translator's prologue, quoting from his own translation. We have additional evidence indicating that these three works were regarded as a quasi-unit in three of the oldest MSS (Magd. Coll. Oxford, 192; Cambridge Univ. Kk. iii. 19; Vatican, Chigi A. VIII. 245) where the colophon reads: *Explicit liber logices, heresum et sentenciarum Johannis Damasceni*. We can explain this colophon most simply by positing an archetype which had these three works in the above order, regarded as a trilogy, as the translator remarked in his prologue: *composuit integrum librum ex tribus*. The most reasonable deduction from the assembling of these facts is that Grosseteste was the translator of the three works mentioned in the *Prologus*. If we proceed on that assumption certain peculiarities in style, in appended glosses, both *ex greco* and original with the translator, become quite typical and comprehensible. The first three chapters of the Greek original of the *De Logica* are missing in the Latin and the text is divided differently from the Greek, with only fifty chapters, the last chapter corresponding to chapter 66 of the Le Quien (Migne) edition.

The principal MSS contain the Latin corpus of the five works of Damascenus in the following order:

	Magd. 192	Ashm. 1526	Canon., Pat. lat. 97	e Mus. 134	Laud Misc. 268	Merton 145	B.M. Add. 15608	Camb. Univ. Kk. iii. 19	Paris B.N. lat. 2155	Paris B.N lat. 2375	Vat. Chigi A. VIII. 245	Vienna N.B. 744
De Logica	1		1	1	3	2	1		2*	3		
De Centum Heres.	2		2		4		2				2	2
De Fide Orthod.	3	1				(1)†		1	1		1	
Element. Dogmat.	4	2		2	1	3		2		1	3	1
Trisagion	5	3		3	2	4				2		

* This MS is in some confusion. Both works are incomplete, and are by different hands. A copy of Burgundio's *De Fide* is in the codex, by a third hand.

† This is in Burgundio's translation, with the usual ascription, written by the same scribe as the remaining works, which bear no ascription.

As two of the five works are independently authenticated, the *De Fide* and the *Trisagion*, it is important to see how often each of the other three works appears with one or other of the genuine translations. In six out of eight cases the *De Logica* occurs with one or both of the authenticated works, the *De Centum Heresibus* in three out of six cases, and the *Elementarium Dogmatum* in eight out of nine cases.

IV. MSS:

Oxford				
Canon., Pat. lat.	97*	ff. 43A–53D	XIV1	Unasc. So. Fr.
e Museo	134	pp. 464a–492a	XIII2	Unasc.†
Laud Misc.	268	ff. 90D–99C	XIV1	Unasc. Lowl.
Magdalen	192	ff. 137A–146D	XIII2	Unasc.
Merton	145	ff. 50A–67D	XIII2	Unasc.
London, B.M.				
Add.	15608	ff. 91A–100A	XIIIm	Unasc. Fr.
Royal	5. C. IV	ff. 85B–92A	XIII2	Unasc.
Cambridge,				
Peterhouse	245	ff. 15A–28A	XIII2	Unasc.
Worcester Cath.	F. 142	ff. 1A–3D	XIII2	Unasc. *mut.*‡
Paris, B.N.	lat. 2155	ff. 173A–180B	XIIIm	Unasc. Fr.
	lat. 2375	ff. 391B–408D	XIII2	Unasc. Fr.
	lat. 14700	ff. 371A–388A	*ca.* 1300	Unasc. Fr.
	lat. 16598	ff. 34A–59D	XIII2	Unasc. Fr.

(ii) *De Centum Heresibus*

I. Inc.: Omnium heresum matres et primitive quatuor...
Barbarismus que heresis secundum seipsam est...
Expl.: ...deficiens recessit nichil opponens ad ipsum alterum.

II. Unpubl. Greek text in *Patr. Gr.* XCIV, cols. 677–780.

III. See under *De Logica*.

IV. MSS:

Oxford				
Canon., Pat. lat.	97	ff. 54C–63B	XIV1	Unasc. So. Fr.
Laud Misc.	268	ff. 100A–108A	XIV1	Unasc. Lowl.
Magdalen	192	ff. 146D–154D	XIII2	Unasc.
London, B.M., Add.	15608	ff. 100A–106D	XIIIm	Unasc.
Vatican, Chigi	A. VIII. 245	ff. 65D–76B	XIIIm	Unasc. Engl.
Vienna, Nat. Bibl.	744	ff. 174D–183B	XIII2	Unasc. Fr.

* Contains also, ff. 1A–42A, Burgundio's translation of the *De Fide*, in the same hand and, somewhat exceptionally, unascribed. This would seem to be the only case in which a scribe could be accused of confusing the two translations.

† Contains also, *a.m.*, pp. 367–454, XIIIm, Burgundio's translation of the *De Fide*.

‡ In this codex f. 1 had previously been pasted to the front cover. It is now the front flyleaf.

(iii) *De Fide Orthodoxa*

I. Inc.: Quam incomprehensibilis est deus... [beginning of *capitula*]
Deum nemo vidit unquam nisi unigenitus filius qui est in sinibus patris...
Expl.: ...et visi et indeficientem ab ipso leticiam fructificantes.

II. Unpubl. Greek text in *Patr. Gr.* XCIV, cols. 789–1228.

III. Two of the oldest MSS, and until now almost the only copies of Grosseteste's translation of the *De Fide* noticed, ascribe the translation to him. Bale says: *Damascenum annotavit lib.* 4. Tanner expands this notice to: *Annotationes in Librum Damasceni de Orthodoxa Fide.* Pits and Pegge also list the work; the latter may have seen a MS as he remarks (p. 291): "The work seems intended chiefly to correct the old version." More recently attention was first drawn to the translation by J. de Ghellinck in 1910* who had noticed frequent thirteenth-century references to a *translacio linconiensis* in Continental MSS. The first to notice the Pembroke MSS containing the actual translation, however, was E. Hocedez,† who showed, from a study of the texts, how slight were the alterations from the translation of Burgundio, and, collecting references from many different authors, pointed out how widely the revision was diffused by the end of the thirteenth century. Grosseteste's translation was known at least to Salimbene,‡ Bacon§ and Duns Scotus.‖

The colophon, found in almost identical form in the two Pembroke MSS, is informingly explicit. It is printed here from Pembroke MS 20, where it appears at the end of the *capitula*. In Pembroke MS 34 it appears at the beginning of the capitula.

Expliciunt capitula libri Johannis Damaceni numero centum et unum. Correxit autem dominus R. Grosseteste Lincolniensis episcopus veterem translacionem et inseruit eciam multa que transtulit ex greco exemplari que in veteri translacione non habentur. Intitulatur autem liber iste sic: Johannis Damaceni vocatur Masur edicio diligens de orthodoxa fide. Incipit liber Johannis Damaceni secundum correctam translacionem domini R. Lincolniensis episcopi.

The insertions to which the scribe makes reference appear, in general, in the English copies, and are wanting in copies of Continental origin. There are, at a maximum, about twenty considerable insertions introduced by *ex greco*,

* "Les œuvres de Jean de Damas en Occident au XIIe siècle" in *Rev. d. Questions Historiques* (1910), pp. 149–160. See also his *Le mouvement théologique du XII Siècle* (1914), p. 245 ff.

† "Les trois premières traductions du *De Orthodoxa Fide* de S. Jean Damascène" in *Musée Belge*, XVII (1913), 109–123; "La diffusion de la *Translacio Lincolniensis* du *De Orthodoxa Fide* de S. Jean Damascène" in *Bull. d'anc. litt. et d'archéologie chrétienne*, III (1913), 189–198. See also H. Dausend in *Theol. Quartalschr.* CXIX (1937), 173–192.

‡ *Hic secundo post Burgundionem...transtulit Damascenum. MGH. SS.* XXXII (1905–1913), 233.

§ *Opus Maius* (ed. Bridges, 1900) I, 70; III, 84, etc.

‖ *Opus Oxoniense*, III, dist. 21, no. 4 (ed. Wadding, Lyons, 1639), VII, 435: *dicit enim sic in translacione Lincolniensis.*

indented into the text like the scholia of Maximus Confessor in the works of the Pseudo-Dionysius (see below, p. 52 ff.). There are, in addition, in the English copies, numerous marginal variants introduced by *seu*... or *aliud exemplar habet*... and occasionally a longer *notula*, obviously the work of Grosseteste, beginning in some way already familiar to us from his *Notule in Ethica* (see below, p. 85 f.) as *aliqui libri latini habent*..., *quod nos dicimus*...*grecus dicit*..., or *in alio codice*. Indeed four of the longer of these marginalia are ascribed to *episcopus* in Pembroke MS 20: f. 2[D], *Non sicud aliqui latini posuerunt*...*non impossibile sed impassibile*; f. 10[A], *nomen grecum unde sumptum est adiectivum*... *omnibus vitam participantibus*; f. 17[B], *commentum episcopi: hec particula*...*comproporcionalia*; f. 24[A], *sciendum quod de ymaginibus*...*honor legitur et intelligitur*. The variant readings referred to above are not from Burgundio's translation; they may be translations of variants in his Greek originals, or they may be, save when he says *aliud exemplar* or *alius liber*, his own alternative suggestions. His method of translating and editing would bear further study than even Franceschini has given it.

It is hardly realized how literal his translation was. It might even be of value for the reconstruction of the Greek text in cases of doubtful reading. Two sections taken almost at random will illustrate the extreme literalness of his work. The Greek text is from *Patr. Gr.* XCIV and the Latin from Ashmole MS 1526, in each case in the exact order of the text.

Bk. II, chap. II (col. 792):

Χρὴ οὖν τὸν περὶ θεοῦ λέγειν ἢ ἀκούειν βουλόμενον σαφῶς
Oportet igitur eum qui de deo dicere vel audire vult manifeste
εἰδέναι ὡς οὐδὲ πάντα ἄρρητα ....
scire quod neque omnia ineffabilia....

Bk. IV, chap. I (col. 1101):

Μετὰ δὲ τὴν ἐκ νεκρῶν ἀνάστασιν πάντα μὲν τὰ πάθη
Post eam autem que ex mortuis resurreccionem omnes quidem passiones
ἀπέθετο φθοράν λέγω πεινάν τε καὶ....
deposuit corrupcionem dico et esuriem et ....

We have thus far no absolute criteria for dating this translation, but several indirect indications point toward a period early in the episcopate. There is as yet no known recorded intimation that he had begun to do any work of translation in the pre-episcopal period, and, fortified by Roger Bacon's statement that Grosseteste's knowledge of Greek came only toward the end of his life, we would place the *terminus a quo* at 1235. On the other hand, because the translation of the *De Fide* is quoted in the *Prologus translatoris* to the *De Logica*, we know that the translation of the former work antedates that of the *De Logica*. Furthermore, as both are noticeably rougher translations than the *Testamenta*, completed in 1242, an earlier date is indicated. The *De Fide* is avowedly only a corrected translation. If Grosseteste had already made one or more successful translations he would hardly have been satisfied with a mere correction. It seems reasonable to regard this work as most probably his maiden effort as a translator from the Greek.*

* For his use of the LXX *ca.* 1230 see below, p. 73, under *Comm. in Ep. ad Galathas*.

IV. MSS:

Oxford				
Ashmole	1526	ff. 121^{A}–169^{C}	XIII^{m}	Unasc.
Magdalen	192	ff. 155^{A}–200^{A}	XIII^{2}	Unasc.
London, Lambeth	151	ff. 180^{A}–204^{D}	XIII^{m}	Unasc.*
Cambridge				
Univ.	Kk. iii. 19	ff. 199^{A}–228^{B}	XIII^{2}	Unasc.
Pembroke	20	ff. 1^{A}–28^{B}	XIII^{m}	Asc.
	34	ff. 211^{D}–235^{B}	XIII^{m}	Asc.
Admont	593	ff. 66^{a}–132^{a}	XIII^{m}	Unasc. Ger.
Breslau, Univ.	I. F. 220	ff. 216^{C}–253^{D}	*ca.* 1300	Unasc. No. Fr.
Milan, Ambros.	C. 108 inf.	ff. 1^{A}–41^{D}	XIII^{2}	Unasc. Fr.†
Paris, B.N.	lat. 2155	ff. 127^{A}–138^{D}	XIII^{m}	Unasc. Fr. *mut.*
Vatican, Chigi	A. VIII. 245	ff. 1^{A}–65^{C}	XIII^{m}	Unasc. Engl.

(iv) *Elementarium Dogmatum* (*Introduccio Dogmatum*)

I. Inc.: In nomine patris et filii et spiritus sancti unius trisypostate et adorate deitatis...

Expl.: ...Fiat autem nos ipsius sequentis vestigia semper cum ipso esse...in secula seculorum.

II. Unpubl. Greek text in *Patr. Gr.* xcv, cols. 100–112. See below, III.

III. In the Ashmole, Magdalen, Cambridge Univ. and Chigi MSS are found the marginalia *in greco habetur...*, *pro eo quod nos dicimus...*, etc., which are typical of Grosseteste's method. The Latin translation includes as part of the *Elementarium* the *De Una Natura et Duabus Voluntatibus* which, in the Greek, forms a separate treatise (*Patr. Gr.* xcv, cols. 112–185). The translation is done in the literal style we have remarked upon as typical of Grosseteste's earlier efforts.

Patr. Gr. xcv, col. 100, and Chigi MS, f. 76^{C}:

Περὶ τούτων οὖν καὶ τῶν τοιούτων σκοπὸς ἡμῖν ἐστι εἰπεῖν περὶ ὧν καὶ
De hiis igitur et talibus intencio nobis est dicere de quibus et

ὑμετέρα συγκαταβατικῶς ἠρώτησεν ὁσιότης. Ἀρχόμενοι τοίνυν λέγομεν οὕτως.
vestra condecensione interrogavit sanctitas. Incipientes igitur dicimus sic.

IV. MSS:

Oxford				
Ashmole	1526	ff. 169^{D}–180^{D}	XIII^{m}	Unasc.
e Museo	134	pp. 492^{b}–516^{a}	XIII^{2}	Unasc.
Laud Misc.	268	ff. 79^{A}–85^{B}	XIV^{1}	Unasc. Lowl.
Magdalen	192	ff. 200^{A}–209^{D}	XIII^{2}	Unasc.
Merton	145	ff. 68^{A}–80^{A}	XIII^{2}	Unasc.
Cambridge, Univ.	Kk. iii. 19	ff. 228^{C}–236^{A}	XIII^{2}	Unasc.
Paris, B.N.	lat. 2375	ff. 367^{A}–380^{C}	XIII^{2}	Unasc. Fr.
Vatican, Chigi	A. VIII. 245	ff. 76^{C}–88^{C}	XIII^{m}	Unasc. Engl.
Vienna, Nat. Bibl.	744	ff. 164^{B}–174^{D}	XIII^{2}	Unasc. Fr.

* Ends: ...*deflexum resuscitabit rursus volens*, omitting last paragraph.

† Marginalia by an Italian hand *ca.* 1300.

(v) *De Hymno Trisagion*

I. Inc.: Dei honorato et zelo divino ornato domino Jordano archimandrite Johannes...
Eius qui ad te mei desiderii...
Expl.: ...lege amicicie adimplebitis indesinenter pro nobis orantes.

II. Unpubl. Greek text in *Patr. Gr.* XCV, cols. 21–61.

III. Grosseteste refers to his translation of this hymn in his comment on the *De Celesti Hierarchia* of the Pseudo-Dionysius, chap. VII:*

De hac autem ymnologia, Sanctus, sanctus, sanctus, etc., sufficienter tractat Johannes Damascenus in epistula quadam, quam de hoc scripsit ad Jordanem archimandritam, quam, quia nuper in latinum transtulimus, ad illam epistulam qui de hac ymnologia plenius scire satagit, recurrat.

This translation must therefore be placed before that of the Pseudo-Dionysius' *De Cel. Hier.*, but just how much time the *nuper* may measure we cannot know. Yet it is not without interest that Franceschini found a note in Grosseteste's *Comm. in Cel. Hier.*, chap. XIII, which mentions the *Sentencie* (i.e. the *De Fide Orthodoxa*). From this reference Franceschini inferred that the Pseudo-Dionysian works were translated and commented upon after the translation of the two works of the Damascene corpus (the only two known to Franceschini) was completed. I should concur in this inference, including, of course, the other three works of the Damascene corpus.

In chap. III of the *De Hymno* there is a typically Grossetestian scholium (Ashmole MS 1526, f. 182^A–B^) to the words *per ey diptongum* in the text:

posuimus hic dicciones grecas scilicet treys per ei diptongum, quod est latine tres, et tris per *i* solum, quod est ter et sumitur aliquando pro multociens, quia si pro eis posuissemus dicciones latinas non esset consonancia in sensu litere.

The translation is in the same literal manner as the other works of this early period.

IV. MSS:

Oxford				
Ashmole	1526	ff. 181^A–185^C	XIII^m	Unasc. *mut. in fine*
e Museo	134	pp. 516^a–528^a	XIII²	Unasc.
Laud Misc.	268	ff. 85^C–89^A	XIV¹	Unasc. Lowl.
Magdalen	192	ff. 210^A–215^B	XIII²	Unasc.
Merton	145	ff. 80^A–87^B	XIII²	Unasc.
Paris, B.N.	lat. 2375	ff. 380^C–387^D	XIII²	Unasc. Fr.

3. *Prologus Maximi Confessoris in Opera Pseudo-Dionysii*

I. Inc.: Nobilitatem quidem et preclarum in diviciis beatissimi Dionysii...
Expl.: ...sermones quos nunc in meas venire accidit manus.

II. Unpubl. Greek text in *Patr. Gr.* IV, cols. 16–21.

* This is the discovery of Franceschini. See his *Roberto Grossatesta*..., p. 42 f. He had found no MS of the *De Hymno*.

III. Franceschini suggests* that Grosseteste translated the *Prologus* of Maximus that is found in most of the copies of the *De Cel. Hier.* in Grosseteste's translation. This prologue is said by Grabmann to have been translated in the twelfth century,† but he adduced no evidence for so early a date. In its Latin form the work is not a complete translation of the Greek text, and the translator has added an appendix‡ containing a short exposition of his principles of transliteration from the Greek. This appendix, on internal grounds, is almost surely the work of Grosseteste. Failing specific contrary evidence, an acceptance of Grosseteste's authorship of the whole translation is almost obligatory. The painful literalness is certainly Grossetestian. There usually accompany this *Prologus*, written in the margin, *notule*,§ obviously by Grosseteste, concerning the authorship of the prologue and scholia. The first of these *notule* reads:

Non inveni in exemplari greco nomen auctoris prescriptum huic prologo. Conicio tamen quod Dyonisius archiepiscopus Alexandrie hunc prologum scripsit. Inveni enim post finem epistolarum decem huius Dyonisii Ariopagite sic scriptum grece: Sciendum quoniam alter Dyonisius archiepiscopus Alexandrie qui unus rethorum conscripsit scholia sancti Dyonisii. Auctor autem huius prologi, ut patet in prologo, scholia super hunc librum conscripsit.

IV. MSS:

See below, p. 55 f., under *De Cel. Hier.*, and p. 80, *Notule in Opera Ps.-Dionysii.*

The *Prologus* is wanting in the Paris Mazarine MS and in the Melk, Munich and Vienna MSS, which contain only excerpts of the commentary.

4. *Scholia Maximi Confessoris in Opera Pseudo-Dionysii*

I. The first scholium to the text of the *De Cel. Hier.* begins: Ex greco. Quoniam presbiteri nomen et episcopum demonstrat sicut quoniam presbiter.... The last scholium to this work ends: ...deificis superadventibus, hoc est deos facientibus et perficientibus.

The first scholium to the *De Eccl. Hier.* reads: Ex greco. Quoniam dominus operatur et perficit que ynanis ierarchia.

The last scholium to this wotk reads: Ex greco. Uniformes ait magis ad unum et simplex et divinum proprie habentes.

The first scholium to the *De Div. Nom.* begins: Ex greco. Signa quoniam alterum negocium elaboratum est ab isto patre....

The last scholium to this work ends: ...capitulum eius qui de mistica theologia sermonis.

* "Grosseteste's Translation of the ΠΡΟΛΟΓΟΣ and ΣΧΟΛΙΑ of Maximus to the Writings of the Pseudo-Dionysius Areopagita" in *JTS.* XXXIV (1933), 362 f. See further his *Roberto Grossatesta*..., pp. 26–39, for a brilliant study of Grosseteste's work with the Pseudo-Dionysian corpus.

† *Mittelalterliches Geistesleben*, I (Munich, 1926), 462.

‡ Printed by Grabmann, *op. cit.* p. 465 f.

§ In the Lincoln Coll. MS these *notule* are incorporated into the text.

II. Unpubl. The Greek *Scholia Maximi* publ. in *Patr. Gr.* IV, cols. 16–432.

III. Though no specific MS ascription of this translation has yet been noted, Franceschini argues* for Grosseteste as translator of the scholia of Maximus to the four principal works of the Pseudo-Dionysius. The scholia† in this translation appear only in MSS containing Grosseteste's translation of the text with his commentaries. The strongest proof available to Franceschini was a statement in Grosseteste's commentary on chap. VIII of the *De Cel. Hier.*: *Sed grecus qui ponit notas in greco quas nos in margine scribimus.* But the problem of the authorship of the translation remains complicated and not so simply solved. A gloss on the word *capitulacius* near the end of the *Prologus Maximi*, in the left margin of f. 1c of Cesena, Malatest. MS Pl. XII, dext. 1, of English provenance, XIIIm, reads:

> Capitulacius, id est compendiosius et brevius et magis comprehensive secundum ordinem processus huius libri apposui per scholia, id est studiosas de obscurioribus interpretaciones. Manifesta mihi etc. Scholia autem que apposuit iste sunt interpretaciones obscuriorum verborum quas ex greco sumptas apposuimus e directo textus in margine.

In this case Grosseteste has added a short explanatory note to the translated scholium. It would not yet appear certain, at least from these two passages, that Grosseteste has explicitly told us that he was the translator of the scholia. He does not elsewhere generally use *sumere*, *transferre*, and *scribere* as synonymous, and we have not yet found him to have used *transferre* in referring to the Latin version of these scholia. An early, *ca.* 1325, note in the margin of f. 41b, Dublin, Trin. Coll. MS B. 2. 11 (on part 10 of chap. VII of the *De Cel. Hier.*) raises the question of Grosseteste's authorship in a more urgent form:

> (*a*) Ex isto haberi potest quod lincolniensis non transtulit de greco hec scolia sed inscripsit libro suo hec ab alio translata puta Anastasio.

This refers to the text of the commentary:

> (*b*) Igitur prima celestium intellectum ierarchia ab ipsa celetarchia ierarchizata in ad ipsum immediate extendi castissima purgacione multo lumine preperfecta perfeccionis.

In the right margin is the scholium, corresponding to a *renvoi* to *multo* in the text of the commentary:

> (*c*) Ex greco: apletou magnum et multum. Ubi hic in latino ponitur multo in greco habetur apletoy quod glosat qui scribit hec scolia per magnum et multum.

* In "Grosseteste's Translation of the ΠΡΟΛΟΓΟΣ and ΣΧΟΛΙΑ of Maximus..." in *JTS.* XXXIV (1933), 355–363, reproduced in shorter form in his *Roberto Grossatesta...*, pp. 35–39.

† They were previously translated by Anastasius Bibliothecarius for Pope Nicholas I in 865, but, as Franceschini observes, *art. cit.* p. 357 n., we have no evidence that Grosseteste knew this translation. A comparison of the two translations would indicate that, if he knew the earlier work, he studiously avoided using any of the locutions of Anastasius. The latter's translation is found in St John's Coll., Oxford, MS 128 (X–XI), Brussels, Bibl. Royale, II, 1983 (XIII1) and Munich, Clm. 23456 (XIII1).

It is evident that the scribe of (*a*) based his conclusion that Grosseteste did not translate these scholia on the, to him, obvious fact that the first element in (*c*) was already a Latin version of a Greek scholium* to which Grosseteste thought it necessary to add an explanatory note, *Ubi*...*multum*. The whole problem remains somewhat confused, owing to the absence of a specific statement from Grosseteste that he translated the scholia from the Greek. But a compromise solution suggests itself.

(i) It is quite clear from the text of Grosseteste's commentaries that he knew and used the Greek original of the scholia. See Franceschini, *art. cit.* p. 360 f.

(ii) We must, I believe, conclude that Grosseteste had before him a Latin translation of these scholia other than that of Anastasius: from his apparently careful avoidance of the usual word for translating—*transferre*; from a possible intimated reference to a previous Latin translation of a gloss in (*c*) above†; and from a passage in his commentary on the *De Eccl. Hier.* quoted by Franceschini, *art. cit.* p. 361: Ex glosa autem marginali videtur debere esse *ex sacerdotalibus*, ubi nos posuimus *ex ierarchicis* quod aliquod exemplar habet. The marginal gloss reads: Ex greco. Quoniam sacerdotalem scienciam ex tradicionibus accepit.

If Grosseteste had translated the Greek scholium,‡ παραδόσεων ὅτι τὴν ἱεραρχικὴν ἐπιστήμην ἐκ παραδόσεως παρέλαβεν, using *sacerdotalis* for ἱεραρχικός, it would seem hardly comprehensible that he should be so sure that *ierarchicus* was the proper translation of the same Greek adjective in the text. It is not likely that he translated the scholia before translating the text, and then thought his own previous translation needed correction or apology. He must have been referring to a previous translation which used *sacerdotalis* for ἱεραρχικός. His own usual translation is *ierarchicus*.

(iii) But it is equally, or perhaps more, clear that he has translated afresh many of the scholia or emended the translation of whatever scholia he had available in Latin with some freedom, basing his corrections on the Greek text he had before him.

(iv) The MS tradition of these scholia in Latin is uneven; some MSS have a more complete tradition than others. From the more complete copies, the Merton, Paris B.N. 1620 and Cesena MSS, we discover that he added many original *notule* in the same way we found him to have annotated his translation of the *Ethics* and the Greek commentators (see below, p. 68 f.). The first such *notula* is the *Non inveni in exemplari greco* in which he discusses the authorship of the prologue to the *De Cel. Hier.* See below, p. 78 f.

IV. MSS:

Merton 86, Paris B.N. lat. 1620 and Cesena, Malatest. Pl. XII, dext. 1 alone contain the *Scholia in De Cel. Hier.* Franceschini had not noted any MSS containing these scholia (*Roberto Grossatesta*..., p. 36, n. 3).

* *Patr. Gr.* IV, col. 72: Ἀπλέτου φωτός. Ἄπλετον τὸ μέγα καὶ πολύ.

† It is obvious that this argument, by itself, is weak. The scribe who wrote the note in the Dublin MS, not knowing what the Greek scholium was, was confused by the gloss of Grosseteste, which depends, for clarity, on a construction of the verbs in the sentence.

‡ *Patr. Gr.* IV, col. 116A.

The Merton, Paris, Cesena, two Florence and Vatican, Chigi MSS contain the *Scholia in De Eccles. Hier.* See below, p. 56 f.

The Merton and Florence Laur. Pl. XIII, codd. dext. I and III contain the *Scholia in De Div. Nom.*

5. *Opera Pseudo-Dionysii Areopagite*

(i) *De Celesti Hierarchia*

I. Inc.: Omne datum bonum et omne donum perfectum desursum est descendens a patre luminum. Sed et omnis a patre mote...

Expl.: ...et super nos occultacionem silencio honorantes.

Incipits and explicits of the commentaries will be given below, p. 78 f.

II. Unpubl. Greek text in *Patr. Gr.* III, cols. 120–369.

III. That Grosseteste translated and commented on the four principal works of the Pseudo-Dionysius has never been seriously doubted. The tradition was known and accepted by Roger Bacon,* Nicholas Trevet,† Boston of Bury,‡ and Wyclyf.§ All the bibliographers since the sixteenth century, Trithemius, Bale, Pits, Tanner, Pegge and Stevenson, have accepted the tradition without question. Grabmann found (1926)|| a late fourteenth-century MS in Vienna (Nat. Bibl. 790) which mentioned both translation and commentary as the work of Grosseteste; but an actual early MS ascription of the text proper was not noted until 1932.¶

More often than not the four books are grouped together, with Grosseteste's commentaries intercalated in the text. There are numerous cross-references in each of the four commentaries that show that one person is responsible for the whole.**

IV. MSS (unless otherwise specified, the folia given indicate the beginning and ending of the complete work, prologue, text and commentary):

Oxford				
Lincoln	101	ff. 51^a–94^a	XV^1	Unasc.††
Merton	86	ff. 1^A–85^D	XIII^2	Unasc.
Dublin, Trinity	163	ff. 2^A–151^A	XIII^m	Unasc.
	164	ff. 1^a–84^a	XIII^2	Asc.‡‡

* *Comp. Studii Phil.* (ed. Brewer), cap. VIII, p. 474. For complete literature and discussion see Franceschini, *Roberto Grossatesta...*, p. 26 ff.

† *Annales sex regum Angliae* (ed. T. Hog, London, 1845), p. 243.

‡ *Apud* Tanner, p. xxxvii; he mentions three commentaries: *De Eccles. Hier. De Cel. Hier.* and *De Div. Nom.* See above, Introd. p. 5.

§ *De Ecclesia*, ed. J. Loserth (London, 1886), p. 350.

|| *Mittelalterliches Geistesleben*, I (Munich, 1926), 463 f.

¶ S. H. Thomson, "A Note on Grosseteste's Work of Translation" in *JTS.* XXXIV (Jan. 1933), 48 ff. The ascription in Dublin, Trinity MS 164 should be added. See below under *De Div. Nom.*

** See Baur, *Werke...*, p. 31* ff.

†† An abbreviated text, omitting much of Grosseteste's etymological and linguistic discussion.

‡‡ On f. 41^a a marginal note (XIV^1) in the lower left corner reads: *ex isto haberi potest quod lincolniensis non transtulit hec scolia sed inscripsit libro suo hec ab alio translato puta Anastasio.* For ascription see under *De Div. Nom.*

Cesena, Malatest.	Pl. XII, dext. I	ff. 1^{A}–82^{A}	XIII^{m}	Unasc. Engl.
Cusa, Hospital	44	ff. 141^{a}–235^{a}	XV^{1}	Unasc.
	45	ff. 59^{b}–68^{a}	XV^{1}	Asc. Ital.
Erfurt, Amplon.	O. 30	ff. 20^{A}–23^{C}	XIV^{m}	Asc. Ger. *frag.*
Florence, Laur.	Pl. XIII, dext. II	ff. 1^{A}–168^{D}	XIII^{2}	Asc. Engl.
	Pl. XIII, dext. V	ff. 1^{A}–36^{D}	XIII^{2}	Unasc. Fr. *mut.*
Melk	363	ff. 99^{a}–100^{a}	1456 in Melk	Asc. Excerpts
Munich	Clm. 18210	ff. 71^{D}–81^{D}	XV^{m}	Asc. Excerpts Ger.
Paris				
B.N.	lat. 1620	ff. 68^{B}–115^{A}	XIII^{2}	Asc. flyleaf *ca.* 1300. Fr.
Mazarine	787	ff. 1^{A}–38^{D}	*ca.* 1300	Asc. *contenta* XIV^{1}. Fr.*
Utrecht, Univ.	281	ff. 1^{A}–144^{D}	1407	Asc. Lowlands†
Vatican, Chigi	A. V. 129	ff. 209^{A}–263^{C}	XIII^{2}	Unasc. Fr.‡
Vienna, Nat. Bibl.	4525	ff. 202^{b}–216^{b}	*ca.* 1400	Asc. Excerpts So. Ger.

(ii) *De Ecclesiastica Hierarchia*

I. Inc.: Quoniam quidem que secundum nos hierarchia puerorum sanctorum sacratissime in deo manentis et divine est...
Expl.: ...divini ignis accendam scintillas.

II. Unpubl. Greek text in *Patr. Gr.* III, cols. 369–584.

III. See above under *De Cel. Hier.*

IV. MSS:

Oxford				
Lincoln	101	ff. 94^{a}–130^{b}	XV^{1}	Unasc.§
Merton	86	ff. 85^{D}–165^{A}	XIII^{2}	Unasc.
Dublin, Trinity	163	ff. 151^{B}–265^{D}	XIII^{m}	Unasc.
	164	ff. 84^{a}–155^{b}	XIII^{2}	Unasc.‖

* This codex belonged to the *libraria Carmelitarum Parisius*, according to a note on the flyleaf, where we also read *Mgr Petrus Orla*. This may be Petrus Aureolus (†1322).

† On the verso of the front flyleaf is written: *lynconiensis super angelicam ierarchiam pertinet ad carthusienses prope traiectum.* At the bottom of the page the hand of the text has written:

Habemus terciam translacionem librorum dyonisii cuius prologus incipit Cum in libris magni dyonisii ariopagite

Item dominum lynconiensem super angelicam ierarchiam (per se in presenti volumine)

Item eundem super divina nomina (in uno volumine

Item eundem super mysticam theologiam (et translacionem vercellensis cum aliis quibusdam simul in uno volumine.

Item super ecclesiasticam ierarchiam (per se in uno volumine.

The words after the parenthesis are probably by the same hand, but are added in blacker ink.

There remain two of the four volumes of Grosseteste's translation: the *Angelica Hierarchia* (MS 281) and the *De Myst. Theol.* (MS 79).

‡ For further description of this MS see my note in *JTS.* as above.

§ At end: *sed partim abbreviatum.*

‖ For ascription in this MS see under *De Div. Nom.*

Cesena, Malatest.	Pl. XII, dext. I	ff. 82A–157D	XIIIm	Unasc. Engl.
Cusa, Hospital	44	ff. 235a–321b	XVm	Unasc.
Erfurt, Amplon.	O. 30	ff. 61C–66B	XIVm	Asc. Excerpts Ger.
Florence, Laur.	Pl. XIII, dext. I	ff. 1A–142	XIII2	Unasc. Engl.
Paris				
B.N.	lat. 1620	ff. 115A–153D	XIII2	Asc. Fr.
Mazarine	787	ff. 39A–70D	*ca.* 1300	Asc. Fr.
Vatican, Chigi	A. v. 129	ff. 133A–207D	XIII2	Asc. Fr.

(iii) *De Divinis Nominibus*

I. Inc.: Nunc o beate post theologicas subfiguraciones ad divinorum nominum reseracionem...
Expl. ...Ad simbolicam autem theologiam duce deo transibimus.

II. Publ. from Paris B.N. 1620 in *Dionysiaca*, I (Paris, 1937), 5–561, with the Greek text and other translations. Greek text in *Patr. Gr.* III, cols. 585–996.

III. See under *De Cel. Hier.* The *De Div. Nom.* is quoted *secundum translacionem lincolniensem* by William of Nottingham (†1254) in *Super IIII Evangelia*, MS Laud Misc. 165, f. 13A.

IV. MSS:

Oxford				
Lincoln	101	ff. 25a–41a	XV1	Asc.*
Merton	86	ff. 170A–276D	XIII2	Unasc.
Dublin, Trinity	164	ff. 161a–262a	XIII2	Asc.†
Cesena, Malatest.	Pl. XII, dext. I	ff. 169D–298D	XIIIm	Unasc. Engl.
Cusa, Hospital	44	ff. 2a–130a	XVm	Unasc.
Erfurt, Amplon.	O. 30	ff. 66C–107B	XIVm	Unasc. Ger.
Florence, Laur.	Pl. XIII, dext. III	ff. 13A–247D	XIII2	Unasc. Engl.
	Pl. XIII, dext. IV	ff. 1B–100B	XIII2	Unasc. No. Fr.
Paris				
B.N.	lat. 1620	ff. 1A–63B	XIII2	Asc. Fr.
Mazarine	787	ff. 71A–119B	*ca.* 1300	Asc. XIV1 Fr.
Vatican, Chigi	A. v. 129	ff. 278B–385B	XIII2	Unasc. Fr.‡

(iv) *De Mystica Theologia*

I. Inc.: Trinitas supersubstancialis et superdea et superbona eiusque christianorum inspectrix divine sapiencie dirige nos...
Expl.: ...superexcellencia ab omnibus simpliciter absoluti et ultra universa.

* In a seventeenth-century hand. Text occurs here without commentary.
† On f. 262a, left margin in plummet: *Expl. L. de di. no.*
‡ But see *De Eccl. Hier.* for ascription in this MS.

II. Publ. Strasbourg, 1502–1503, with *Opera Dionysii* in translation of Johannes Sarracenus as well as in that of Grosseteste. The latter's translation and commentary, ff. 264^{b}–271^{b}. Also in *Dionysiaca*, I (Paris, 1937), 565–669, from Paris B.N. 1620. Greek text in *Patr. Gr.* III, 997–1064.

III. See under *De Cel. Hier.*

IV. MSS:

Oxford				
Lincoln	101	ff. 14^{a}–22^{a}	XV^{1}	Unasc.
Merton	86	ff. 276^{D}–285^{C}	XIII^{2}	Unasc.
Cambridge, Univ.	Kk. iv. 4	ff. 44^{A}–48^{B}	XV^{m}	Asc.*
Basel	A. x. 128	ff. 52^{a}–53^{a}	*ca.* 1400	Unasc. Ger.†
Cesena, Malatest.	Pl. XII, dext. I	ff. 298^{D}–309^{B}	XIII^{m}	Unasc. Engl.
Cusa, Hospital	45	ff. 68^{b}–79^{a}	XV^{m}	Asc. Ital.
Erfurt, Amplon.	O. 30	ff. 3^{C}–19^{D}	XIV^{m}	Asc. Ger. Excerpts
Florence, Laur.	Pl. XIII, dext. II	ff. 169^{A}–183^{D}	XIII^{2}	Unasc. Engl.
Melk	56	ff. 231^{a}–247^{b}	1456	Asc. So. Ger.
	363	ff. 88^{a}–97^{a}	1456 in Melk	Asc.
Munich	Clm. 18210	ff. 82^{A}–94^{C}	XV^{m}	Asc. Ger.
Paris				
B.N.	lat. 1620	ff. 63^{C}–68^{B}	XIII^{2}	Asc. Fr.‡
Mazarine	787	ff. 119^{C}–123^{B}	*ca.* 1300	Asc. Fr.
Subiaco, Abbazia	288	ff. 32^{b}–39^{b}	XV	Asc.
Utrecht	79	pp. 267–300	*ca.* 1400	Asc. Lowl.§
Vatican, Chigi	A. v. 129	ff. 265^{a}–273^{b}	XIII^{2}	Unasc. Fr.‖
Vienna				
Nat. Bibl.	4525	ff. 182^{b}–185^{a} ff. 202^{b}–216^{b}	*ca.* 1400	Asc. Excerpts¶
Schottenkloster	29	ff. 144^{a}–150^{b}	XV^{m}	Asc. Ger.

6. *Epistole Ignacii Martiris et Beate Virginis Marie*

I. (i) Inc.: Johanni sancto seniori Ignacius et qui cum eo sunt fratres. De tua...

Expl.: ...Tu autem diligenti modo disponas condesiderio meo et valeas.

(ii) Inc.: Johanni sancto seniori suus Ignacius. Si licitum est mihi...

Expl.: ...Bone preceptor propone me. Iubeas et valeas.

* There is no direct ascription of the translation. At the end of the first section of the text we read: *Sequitur commentum domini lincolniensis.*

† Text only.

‡ Asc. on flyleaf, perhaps slightly later than text.

§ By the same hand as MS 281, dated 1407.

‖ The *De Eccl. Hier.* (q.v.) in this MS is ascribed.

¶ The text is by itself, and followed by the *Comm.*; see below, p. 79 f.

(iii) Inc.: Christifere Marie suus Ignacius. Me neophytum Johannisque...
Expl.: ...et conneophiti qui mecum sunt ex te et per te et in te confortentur.

(iv) Inc.: Ignacio dilecto condiscipulo humilis ancilla Christi Ihesu. De Ihesu...
Expl.: ...et exultet spiritus tuus in deo salutari tuo.

II. Publ. Lübeck, 1478; Paris, 1495; Amsterdam, 1724; by Fabricius in *Cod. Pseudepigraph. Vet. Test.*, 1713 and 1722–1723; London, 1852; etc. See below, III.

III. Since Archbishop Ussher's edition of the letters of Ignatius* it has generally been accepted, on his suggestion, that Grosseteste was the author of the Latin translation of the "middle" recension. Ussher's argument was based on chronological probability. As Grosseteste was the first to quote Ignatius in this translation, Ussher reasoned, he must, given his knowledge of Greek and interest in the Greek fathers, have been the translator. Bishop Lightfoot accepted Ussher's conclusion,† and confirmed it by referring to an early MS in the Bibliothèque Municipale at Tours in which the translation was ascribed to Grosseteste. He argued from the ascription found at the beginning of the group of four letters of which the incipits are given above—the only letters in this codex—that the remaining Ignatian epistles had been in the archetype from which the Tours MS was copied, in the order in which they appear in the MS *Caiensis* (now Gonville and Caius 395) and *Montacutianus* (lost since the seventeenth century, but seen by Ussher and Pearson). Lightfoot further suggested that the ascription which now precedes the four epistles referred, in the archetype, to the supposed preceding genuine epistles. It is difficult to see the cogency of this argument.

It must, furthermore, be remarked that such evidence as Ussher based his conclusion upon is quite indecisive. The short passage from Grosseteste's *Comm. in De Eccl. Hier.* in which Ignatius is quoted (Ussher, *op. cit.* p. xv) is so short as to raise the question of possible fortuitous coincidence of translation or—which is equally probable—the existence of a translation perhaps contemporary with but independent of Grosseteste. It is of some significance that Grosseteste does not often quote his own translation. He frequently paraphrases the Greek afresh when he quotes.

* *Polycarpi et Ignatii Epistulae una cum vetere vulgata interpretatione...* (Oxford, 1644). The appendix bears the title: *Epistolarum Ignatii vetus Latina versio, ex duobus MSS in Anglia repertis nunc primum in lucem edita*, dated 1642.

† *Apostolic Fathers*, 2nd ed. (London, 1889), I, 76 ff. For a more recent discussion, see A. Hilgenfeld, *Ignatii Antiocheni et Polycarpi Smyrnaei Epistulae et Martyria* (Berlin, 1902), pp. xv–xvii. The Latin text in an improved form is printed on pp. 71–105. J. de Ghellinck accepts Lightfoot's arguments without question in his article "Patristique et argument de tradition au bas moyen-âge" in the Grabmann *Festschrift* (*Beiträge*, Münster i. W. 1935), p. 410 ff. Franceschini, *Roberto Grossatesta...*, p. 21 ff., also accepts the ascription, remarking erroneously that the Tours MS contains the same letters as the Cambridge MS.

There is no MS authority for ascribing the translation of the "middle" recension to Grosseteste. The oldest MS of these letters now extant is the work of Walter Crome (Gonv. and Caius 395, ff. 164–181), and was written in the second quarter of the fifteenth century. The two seventeenth-century copies (Gonv. and Caius 445 and Dublin, Trin. Coll. D. 3. 11) are of only secondary interest, inasmuch as they are known to be copies of either the Crome copy or the *Montacutianus*, now lost. Of this latter we know nothing save that it was written on parchment, and might, therefore, quite well have been written late in the fifteenth century, and be of no more intrinsic value than the Crome MS.

On the other hand, if Grosseteste did translate the middle recension of the Ignatian correspondence, we should properly assume that he did so before composing the work in which he quotes from these letters, i.e. the *Comm. in Eccles. Hier.*, written probably *ca.* 1240 (q.v.). But, so far as I am aware, this is the only quotation from the Ignatian correspondence that has thus far been noticed. If he were sufficiently interested in Ignatius to translate his letters, we might reasonably expect him to cite them occasionally. Funk* remarked on the fact that the style and manner of translating were not at all identical with Grosseteste's authenticated translations. Though arguments from style are not in themselves determinative, yet they may be strongly corroborative.

While we have no grounds for ascribing the genuine Ignatian epistles to Grosseteste, we are in an entirely different position with regard to the four spurious letters. We have a contemporary and explicit MS ascription, and are not dependent on conjectures. But we are confronted by the difficulty that there seems to be no copy of the Greek original† from which the translation could have been made. It has, indeed, usually been assumed that the four letters were a purely Latin forgery.‡ Lightfoot reports Cotelier's (1624) assertion that he had seen "in a catalogue of MSS belonging to the Church of St Peter at Beauvais the entry 'Epistolae duae aut tres B. Ignatii martyris ad B. Mariam Virginem et ad S. Johannem Evangelistam quae inventae sunt Lugduni, tempore concilii Innocentii Papae IV, et de Graeco in Latinum conversae.'" It is not without significance that the only ascribed copy of this translation is of the middle of the thirteenth century and of Southern French provenance, and that Grosseteste was at the Council of Lyons in 1245. The Beauvais MS seen by Cotelier may still be extant. We need not assume confusion between the Tours and the Beauvais copies, as there is every indication that the Tours MS has been in its present home for more than three centuries. The details which Cotelier furnishes are not the same as are given in the Tours rubric, while it is hardly likely that he would have omitted such a point as the name of the translator had it been given in the MS he saw.

Because of the weight attached to Lightfoot's explanation of the rubric in

* F. X. Funk, *Die Echtheit der Ignatianischen Briefe* (Tübingen, 1883), p. 142 ff.

† Gesner published the letters in Greek in 1560, with a Latin translation.

‡ See Lightfoot, *op. cit.* I, 235. He connects the "forgery with the outburst of Mariolatry which marked the eleventh and following centuries". MSS earlier than the thirteenth century are not known. Lightfoot eliminates St Bernard's support for these *spuria*.

the Tours MS, and his conclusion that it refers, not to the letters which follow, but to the supposed "middle" recension that should have preceded, had the scribe but known it, it seems proper to describe the MS more fully.* It is a small octavo codex of 513 folia and flyleaves, containing opuscula and excerpts from Greek and Latin fathers. The whole codex is the work of one very careful scribe, who has rubricked every work he has transcribed, and foliated the whole. The scribe was clearly of the old school in his theological preferences. Augustine, John Damascene, Anselm, Hugh and Richard of St Victor figure most prominently in the MS. The item immediately preceding the *Epistole Ignacii* is rubricked *Excepta de oracionibus Anselmi*, ff. 479^{A}–482^{D}, and is clearly intended to be complete. The next page, numbered by the original scribe 483 (in red) has the running title *Epl'e Beati Ignacij* (in red) by the same scribe, and the rubric in the first column, written in red and underlined in black, after which the letters come in the order given above (I)

> Has epl'as tñ̄stulit de greco in latinum Mgr̄
> Robert' grossa testa linconiensis epc̄
> Johannis sc̄o seniori Jgnacius et qui cum eo sunt....

This rubric gives no indication that the scribe was misled as to the intent of the rubric he was copying, but seems to be quite explicit. In fine we must regard the cumulative impression of the evidence available to us as final in favour of Grosseteste's authorship of the translation of these spurious letters, and find the suspicion of Ussher, accepted generally since his time,† that Grosseteste translated the "middle" recension of the Ignatian epistles, as unsubstantiated.

The following list of MSS must necessarily be incomplete. In many catalogues, published and still in MS, such a short item may go unnoticed. The order in which the letters appear is noted. When such a note is wanting, I have not seen the MS. All MSS are unascribed, save Tours 247.

IV. MSS:

Oxford				
Canon., lat. class.	93	f. 3^{b}	*ca.* 1500	Ital. 234
Canon., Misc.	32	ff. 69^{b}–70^{a}	XV^{2}	Ital. 1234
Lincoln	101	ff. 48^{b}–49^{a}	XV^{1}	3412
Magdalen	76	f. 213^{a-b}	XV^{2}	Ital. 1234
London, B.M.				
Add.	21065	f. 78^{a-b}	*ca.* 1300	Ital. 1234
	22767	f. 75^{a-b}	XV^{m}	Ital. 34
	29984	f. 161^{a}	XV^{m}	Ger. 234
Harley	232	f. 7^{b}	*ca.* 1325	1234
Cambridge, Gonv. & Caius	395	f. 180^{b}	1441	1234‡
	445		1631	1234§

* See also A. Dorange, *Catalogue...des Manuscrits de la Bibliothèque de Tours* (Tours, 1875), p. 137 ff.

† See M. R. James, *Catalogue of MSS...of Gonville and Caius College, Cambridge*, II (Cambridge, 1907 f.), p. 461 f.

‡ See James, *ubi supra*, and Lightfoot, *op. cit.* p. 81 f.

§ See Lightfoot, *ubi cit.*

Dublin, Trinity	D. 3. 11			XVII^{1}	1234
Bologna, Archig.	A. 24	f.	116^{a}	XV^{1}	Ger. 34
Brunswick	157	ff.	56^{b}–57^{a}	*ca.* 1400	Ger. 12
Brussels, Bibl. Roy.	905 (20132)	ff.	25^{b}–26^{a}	XVI	1234
	1387 (12014–41)	f.	289^{C-D}	*ca.* 1300	Lowl. 3412
	1387 (20026–27)	f.	107^{b}	XIII^{m}	Lowl. 34
Darmstadt	768	ff.	129^{D}–130^{A}	XV^{m}	Ger. 1234
Florence					
Laur.	Pl. XV, dext. XII	f.	8^{A-D}	*ca.* 1300	Ital. 3412
	Pl. XXIII, 20				
Strozzi	4	ff.	27^{B}–28^{A}	XV^{1}	Ital. 34
	18	ff.	140^{b}–141^{a}	XV^{m}	Ital. 1234
Klosterneuburg	205	f.	1^{A}	XV^{m}	So. Ger. 34
Leipzig, Univ.	lat. 379	f.	154^{C-D}	XIII^{m}	Ger. 1234
Melk	77	pp.	85–86	XV^{2}	Ger. 34
	163	pp.	28^{b}–29^{a}	XV^{m}	So. Ger. 3412
	406	p.	360	XV^{2}	So. Ger. 34
	416	p.	393	XV	So. Ger. 34
	730	f.	126	XV	Ger.
Milan, Ambros.	E. 69 sup.	ff.	108^{b}–110^{a}	XIV^{m}	Ital. 234
Munich	Clm. 468^{B}	f.	96^{b}	XV^{m}	Ger. 341
	Clm. 616	ff.	267^{a}–268^{a}	1560	Ger. 3412
	Clm. 7547	f.	67^{B-D}	XV^{1}	Ger. 3412
	Clm. 7666	f.	229^{a}	XV^{1}	Ger. 34
	Clm. 7981	f.	159^{B-D}	XIII^{2}	Ger. 3412
Padua, Univ.	1108	ff.	190^{b}–191^{a}	1572	Ital. 34
	1305	ff.	89^{b}–90^{a}	XIV^{2}	Ital. 3412
	1473	ff.	140^{b}–141^{a}	XV^{1}	Ital. 1234
Paris, B.N.	lat. 1150	f.	45^{b}	XV^{2}	Ital. 34
	lat. 3522^{A}	ff.	90^{b}–91^{b}	*ca.* 1300	Lowl. 342
Prague					
Univ.	1990	f.	73^{a-b}	1472	Boh. 123
Metrop. Chap.	1054	ff.	23^{b}–24^{a}	XV^{1}	Boh. 1234
			69^{b}–70^{a}	XV^{1}	Boh. 1234
Salzburg, S. Peter	a. VI. 34	f.	58^{a-b}	XIV^{m}	Ital. 1234
St Florian	126	f.	6^{a-b}	XIV^{2}	Ger. 1234
Tours, Bibl. Mun.	247	f.	483^{A-B}	XIII^{m}	So. Fr. 1234
Vatican					
lat.	524	ff.	155^{a}–156^{a}	*ca.* 1500	Ger. 1234
	672	f.	50^{A-B}	XIII^{m}	Fr. 1234
Pal. lat.	1262	f.	214^{a-b}	XV^{m}	Ger. 12
Vienna					
Nat. Bibl.	695	f.	87^{D}	1344	Ger. 3412
	812	ff.	103^{D}–104^{C}	XIII^{m}	Ger. 1234
	930	ff.	216^{a}–217^{a}	1488	Ger. 3412
Schottenkloster	290	f.	12^{b}	1464	Ger. 1234
Würzburg	M. ch. q. 156	ff.	270^{a}–271^{a}	XV^{m}	Ger. 3412

7. *Lexicon Suida*

There does not seem to be a complete copy of the seventy-one articles from the *Lexicon* of Suidas translated by Grosseteste. But we do have a list of the seventy-one and, from two MSS, a majority of the seventy-one in actual Latin text. The first leaf of the B.M., Royal 8. B. IV, XV¹, has the following list:*

[recto] Liber qui vocatur Suda continet 71 capitula, qui sic incipit ex libro interpretatorio parcium oracionis grecarum qui grece vocant Suda. Primum capitulum sic incipit: Deus etc., secundum Temporibus, 3ᵐ Adam, 4ᵐ Seth, 5ᵐ Lamech, 6 Abraham, 7 Seruth, 8 Johannes, 9 Pafinicius, 10 Leoncius, 11 [*cod.* 12] Mares, 12ᵐ Diodorus, 13 Sancto Confessori, 14 Grisogonus, 15 Helena, 16 Aidesia, 17 Antiope, 18 Semiramis, 19 Justinianus, 20 Traianus, 21 Marcellinus, 22 Brachman, 23 Alexander, 24 Augustus, 25 Efestus, 26 Thulis, 27 Oidepous, 28 Gaius, 29 Johannes, 30 Johannes Grammaticus, 31 Spado, 32 Hunc fecit, 33 Hermen, 34 Orpheus, 35 Plato, 36 Anaxagoras, 37 Anaximandrus, 38 Protagoras, 39 Apolonius, 40 [numbered 41] Iustinus, [41 Prometheus],† 42 Porphirius, 43 Sophocles, 44 [Athenes]† iste, 45 Ibicus, 46 Palamedis, 47 Tholomeus, 48 Thelephus, 49 Legum, 50 Contempnentibus, 51 Nonius, 52 Pelidonius, 53 Glaucus, 54 Liberius, 55 Euchinius, 56 Shiapodes, 57 Latini, 58 Senatores, 59 Canopus, 60 Gaius, 61 Medusa, 62 Sirenas, 63 Skytale, [verso] 64 Piladium, 65 Jovis, 66 Huius, 67 Echo, 68 Nomos, 69 Kosmos, 70 Pan, 71 Hoc nomen passio. ffinis libri thimos autem ira principatus.

Of these seventy-one, the second article, on Ἰησοῦς or *De Probacione Virginitatis Beate Marie*, appears almost always as a separate ascribed translation (see following item). Of the remaining seventy the Royal MS contains, ff. 75ᵃ–80ᵃ (XIVᵐ), in order, items 2, 6, 3, 24, 33, 23, 10, 34. At the end of this selection, which ends ...*et malorum operum et ad vivere miserabiliter dispositum*, is written in the same hand which composed the list of seventy-one: ***Non plus habetur apud Leniam sed residuum est Oxonie. Non continet in toto unum psalterium.***

In the Bodleian Library Digby MS 11‡ contains, ff. 33ᵃ–43ᵇ (XIV¹), slightly over half the seventy-one items (32½–71 inclusive). It begins *mut.* in the middle of item 32: *Aliunde dixit suaderi ipsum saciari altero viro*. The separate items are called *capitula*, and the numbers and incipits correspond to the list given in the Royal MS with enough variation in detail to show that

* It has been suggested by M. R. James in "A Greco-Latin Lexicon of the XIIIth Century" in *Mélanges...Chatelain* (Paris, 1910), p. 399 f., that this list was written by Boston of Bury. But Boston died in 1410, and this list can hardly have been written so early. The text of the eight items in this codex is considerably earlier and might be Boston's work, though I am not aware that we have any of his autographs. The codex was at Bury St Edmunds long before the end of the fourteenth century, from the signature on f. 74ᵇ. The same *librarius* has written the *contenta* who wrote in Pembroke, Cambridge, MS 7. See above, Introd. p. 25 f. See also V. Rose, "Suidas Lateinisch" in *Hermes* v (1871), 155 ff.

† Wanting, supplied from Digby 11.

‡ Not noticed by Franceschini, *Roberto Grossatesta*..., p. 63 ff.

the latter is not derived from the former.* There is no reference to Grosseteste in the fragmentary Digby MS. Of the seventy-one *capitula* or items known to have been translated by Grosseteste, we have 45½, many of which include more than a single item from Suidas' *Lexicon*.

The ascription at the top of f. 73^{a}, written by the scribe of the text, reads: *Narracio Libri de Suda quem Robertus episcopus Lincolniensis de greco transtulit in latinum*. The prologue begins: *Narracio ex libro qui grece dicitur Suda quem composuerunt viri sapientes isti....* The first item, on *Deus*, is wanting. The last *capitulum*, 71, in the Digby MS ends: ...*invida et insidiativa. Tymos autem sua litera principativa. Explicit liber Suda.* It was this explicit that the scribe of the Royal MS was trying to give at the end of his list.

Both Rose and Pelzer have remarked that some of Grosseteste's glosses on the *Ethics* presuppose a knowledge of the *Lexicon* of Suidas. As a matter of fact the number of such *notule* in which the *Lexicon* has obviously been drawn upon is considerably larger than has hitherto been supposed.† M. R. James was of the opinion‡ that we have in MSS 76 and 77 of Corpus Christi Coll., Oxford, a Greek text of the *Lexicon* which was probably a transcript of Grosseteste's original. They are both of the fifteenth century, and have Oxford connections.

8. *Suidas on* Ἰησοῦς (*De Probacione Virginitatis Beate Marie*)

I. Inc.: Quedam narracio ex libro qui vocatur Suda...
Temporibus piissimi imperatoris Justiniani...
Expl.: ...apud Judeos abscondit secretum propalavit.

II. Unpubl.

III. The popularity of this one article out of the seventy-one which Grosseteste translated from the *Lexicon* of Suidas is attested by the large number of early copies extant. A thirteenth-century Anglo-Norman translation of Grosseteste's Latin has been discovered by Miss R. J. Dean§ in Paris, B.N., n. a. fr. 10176, ff. 1^{a}–2^{a}. There is no indication that the vernacular version is the work of Grosseteste.

IV. MSS (of this article alone; for the seventy-one articles see preceding item):

Oxford, Douce	88	ff. 126^{b}–129^{b}	XIII^{2}	Unasc.
London, B.M.				
Add.	18210	ff. 48^{B}–49^{D}	XIII^{m}	Asc.
Arundel	52	ff. 72^{B}–73^{C}	XIV^{1}	Unasc.‖
Royal	4. D. VII	ff. 246^{D}–248^{B}	XIII^{m}	Asc.
	8. A. IV	ff. 203^{b}–205^{b}	XV^{m}	Unasc.
	8. B. IV	ff. 73^{a}–75^{a}	XIV^{1}	Asc.

* H. H. E. Craster has suggested (*Bodl. Quart. Record*, III (1920), 51) that the Digby fragment might well be the remnant of the *residuum*...*Oxonie* to which the scribe of the Royal list referred. It seems an acceptable suggestion. Contrary to Craster's remark that only one of the later chapters (33) occurs in both MSS, chapters 33 and 34 occur in both copies.

† See below, p. 85 f., under *Notule in Ethica*....

‡ *Art. cit.* p. 400.

§ *PMLA*. LI (1936), 607–620.

‖ With *Templum Dei*.

Cambridge				
C.C.C.	179	ff. 21^{b}–24^{a}	XV^{m}	Asc.
St John's	184	ff. 345^{C}–347^{B}	XIII^{2}	Unasc.*
Trinity	B. 15. 38	ff. 79^{b}–80^{b}	XIII^{m}	Asc.†
Canterbury, Ch. Ch.	101	ff. 124^{b}–136^{a}	*ca.* 1300	Unasc.*
Dublin, Trinity	E. 1. 29	ff. 93^{C}–94^{D}	XV^{1}	Asc.
Vatican, lat.	693	f. 125^{a-b}	XV^{m}	Unasc. Ital.

9. *Aristotelis Ethica Nicomachea*

I. Inc.: Omnis ars et omnis doctrina similiter autem et actus et eleccio...

Expl.: ...legibus et consuetudinibus utens, dicamus igitur incipientes.

II. The text has been repeatedly published with the commentaries of Thomas Aquinas, Albertus Magnus, Walter Burley *et al.* It was separately printed in 1516.

III. The discussion of the question of Grosseteste's translation of the *Nicomachean Ethics* from Greek into Latin has a long history. Hermannus Alemannus in 1254 said quite definitely that Grosseteste had translated the text of Aristotle and that of his Greek commentators, and had added his own *notule.*‡ A. Jourdain, V. Rose, C. Marchesi, Baur, Grabmann, P. Minges, Pelzer, Powicke and Franceschini have all made contributions to the solution of the question, with the result that no serious student now doubts the fact that Grosseteste made the translation. The most conclusive argument was that brought forward by Baur in 1912 in a few lines§ when he noted the two early ascribed MSS, Vat. Ottobon. 2214 and St Omer 598. Since Baur wrote, four other thirteenth-century MSS of the combined work, i.e. the text of the *Ethics* and the Greek commentators, bearing ascriptions to Grosseteste have been noticed: Oxford, All Souls Coll. 84; Peterhouse, Cambridge, 116; Naples, B.N. VIII. G. 4||; Toledo, Cabildo, Fol. 95. 14, and Eton Coll. 117 (XV^{1}).

The date of the translation of this work is bound up with that of the Greek commentators (see below, p. 68 f.). The whole must be before 1244, and may be before 1242. See below, p. 209, under Letter 106, and p. 69, *Commentatores Greci...*, n. ‡.

IV. Due to the fact that a complete list of MSS of this translation is given

* With *Testamenta*, q.v. † To *Sanctus Robertus.*

‡ *Et postmodum reverendus pater magister Robertus grossi capitis sed subtilis intellectus Lincolniensis episcopus ex primo fonte unde emanaverat greco videlicet ipsum est complecius interpretatus et grecorum commentis proprias annectens notulas commentatus*, from B.N. lat. 16673 (Sorbonne 1779), first quoted by A. Jourdain, *op. cit.* pp. 139–141, corrected by M. Luquet, *Hermann l'Allemand*, p. 409, n. 2; also in Baur, p. 25*, in the uncorrected form; corrected by Pelzer, "Les versions latines..." *Rev. Néo-Scolastique*, XXIII (1921), 378; by Powicke, *Robert Grosseteste...*, p. 6.

§ *Werke...*, p. 27*.

|| See below, pp. 68 ff., 85 f. and 88, *Commentatores Greci...*, *Summa in Ethica*, *Notule in Ethica...*, and literature there given.

in the inventory of Aristotle MSS, compiled under the direction of the late Mgr. George Lacombe, only the three ascribed MSS are listed here. See also below, p. 69, *Commentatores Greci...* and p. 85 f., *Notule in Ethica....*

MSS:

Naples, B.N.	VIII. G. 4	(combined text)	XIII^{m}	Asc. Engl.*
St Omer	598	ff. 259^{a}–315^{a}	XIII^{2}	Asc. Fr.†
Vatican, Ottobon.	2214	ff. 1^{a}–88^{a}	XIII^{2}	Asc. Engl.‡

10. *Aristotelis De Celo et Mundo*

I. No complete MS of Grosseteste's translation has as yet been identified. Leland (*Collectanea*, IV, 53), Bale, Tanner, Pegge and Stevenson (p. 346, n. 1) all list a commentary on the *De Celo et Mundo*, but the earliest (Leland's) attribution is so vague that it would appear to be founded on no definite data. Baur (p. 45*) remarked that there was no MS evidence for such a commentary.§ But there is no doubt that Grosseteste did make a translation of most, if not all, of the *De Celo et Mundo*. Vatican MS Pal. lat. 2088, an English codex of the middle of the thirteenth century, has numerous marginal notes|| in a neat English chancery hand, contemporary with the text, 69 of which are ascribed ·*l*· or *linc*'. Some are more specific, e.g. (f. 7^{a}) *alia translacio non lincolniensis*, or (f. 18^{b}) *translacio lincolniensis habet hoc plus*.¶ Several of the additions are long enough to raise the question of the nature of the Greek original which Grosseteste was using or of possible interpolation by him in the manner we know him to have used in his translation of the Greek commentators of Aristotle's *Ethics*. The work of translation was either never completed or the annotator of this MS had an imperfect copy before him. In the right margin of f. 22^{a}, two-thirds through Bk. III, the scribe of the

* I am indebted to Prof. Franceschini for the decipherment of the almost obliterated rubric of the *Summa in Ethica* in the Naples MS, which reads: *Primus liber morum Aristotelis est de fine virtutis qui dicitur felicitas et secundum translatorem scilicet dominum linc. continet* 19 *capitula*.

† Franceschini, *op. cit.* p. 53, taking his reference from Grabmann, *Uebersetzungen*, p. 253, reads *Lincolniensis* in the colophon. The tell-tale second *l*, however, is not in the MS. It is consequently not of English provenance. The codex has generally been dated "XIV". There are many marginalia, always more indicative of date than a calligraphic text-hand, that could hardly be dated later than 1280. The first part of the codex, to f. 137, should be dated *ca.* 1300.

‡ From the library of the Cambridge Franciscans. See H. M. Bannister, *Collectanea Franciscana*, I (Brit. Soc. of Franciscan Studies, V, Aberdeen, 1914), p. 136. Dated by Baur "XIII–XIV". A more likely date is *ca.* 1275. Its certain English provenance allows us to judge the handwriting more satisfactorily.

§ See below, p. 86, under *Questiones in De Celo et Mundo*.

|| Mgr. George Lacombe first drew my attention to these notes as Grosseteste's glosses. Closer examination revealed their great importance.

¶ See further my note "The *De Anima* of Grosseteste", in *New Scholasticism*, VII (1933), 218 ff., and G. Lacombe, *Compte Rendu de la XIIIe Session annuelle du Comité* (Union Acad. Internationale, Brussels, 1933).

text has written *Hucusque d. R.* (i.e. dominus Robertus). There are none of the chancery-hand marginalia beyond this point. It is indeed quite probable that the gothic text and the chancery notes are the work of the same scribe.

It is difficult to suggest a date for this translation. The use of *linc.* would point to the episcopal period, and this suggestion is confirmed by the fact that we have no evidence for any translating activity prior to that time. So far as we know the first group of translations included only Damascenus and the Pseudo-Dionysian writings. The *Ethics* and the Greek commentators must have occupied the early years of the 1240's. We know of a revival of Grosseteste's interest in the *compotus*, from his revision of his own earlier work in 1244. This very slight clue might justify a conjecture of a date around 1245, before or more probably after his visit to the Council at Lyons.

First ascribed variant, f. 5ᵃ to text *Adhuc autem si et dĕscripta sunt*. The three dots are repeated in the margin, followed by: *linc' dilaterata*.

Last ascribed variant, f. 21ᵇ to text ... *quod preter ŏmne non est*. The two dots repeated in the margin are followed by: *aut omnino non est. l.*

Franceschini has discussed the translation and published several of the more significant variants and explanatory glosses.*

IV. MS:

Vatican, Pal. lat.	2088	ff. 1ᵃ–32ᵃ	XIIIᵐ	Asc. Engl.

11. *Pseudo-Aristotelis De Lineis Indivisibilibus*

I. Inc.: Utrum sunt indivisibiles linee et totaliter in omnibus quantis...
Expl.: ...amplius lapidis articulis non est neque habet, puncta autem habet.

II. Unpubl.

III. A contemporary ascription in the same valuable Ambrosian MS, and in the same hand that revealed that Grosseteste translated the *De Virtute*, attributes the translation of this pseudo-Aristotelian work to him. The ascription at the top of f. 156ᴬ reads: *Aristotelis de lineis indivisibilibus liber incipit translatus ab episcopo linconiensi de greco in latinum*. This fact was not known until 1930. The first to publish it was M. Ussani,† whose article has been reprinted twice subsequently; the discovery was also noted by Franceschini in 1932.‡ Before I knew of these reports I had published the ascription in a brief note.§ So far as is known at the present time, this is the only MS in which the ascription occurs. This work, like the *De Virtute*, is probably to be dated *ca.* 1245, and for the same reason, that the only ascription appears in a MS of southern French provenance, and a connection with Grosseteste's attendance at the Council of Lyons in 1245 is quite likely. Franceschini lists thirteen MSS in Italian libraries in his *Roberto Grossatesta*.... There are at

* *Roberto Grossatesta*..., pp. 57–60.

† In *Relazione dell' anno accademico* 1930–1931 (Rome, 1931), p. 15.

‡ In *Studî Trentini XIII* (1932), p. 122. See also his *Roberto Grossatesta*..., p. 62 f.

§ "A Note on Grosseteste's Work of Translation", *JTS.* XXXIV (Jan. 1933), 51 f.

least twenty-five more in German, Bohemian and Austrian libraries, most of which I have examined. The total number of copies of this work might amount to over sixty, but the inventory of Aristotle MSS compiled by Lacombe should be consulted. The single ascribed copy only is listed here.

IV. MS:

Milan, Ambros.	E. 71 sup.	ff. 156^{A}–158^{B}	XIII^{m}	Asc. So. Fr.

12. *Aristotelis De Virtute*

I. Inc.: Laudabilia quidem sunt bona, vituperabilia autem turpia...
Expl.: ...Omnia autem que malicie et consequencia ipsi vituperabilium sunt.

II. Unpubl.

III. The first to notice the ascription of the translation of this work to Grosseteste was Pelzer in his "Les versions latines..." (1921).* It is in the same hand in the same codex as the ascribed translation of the *De Lineis Indivisibilibus* (see preceding item). For the same reasons we would ascribe the translation to the period of Grosseteste's stay at the Council of Lyons, 1245. This then is the third work we believe to have been translated at the Council, the first being the pseudo-Ignatian correspondence (see above, p. 60). In the case of the *De Virtute*, we have the additional fact that the work appears in the Peterhouse MS 116, following Grosseteste's translation of the Greek commentators to the *Ethics*, which was done before 1244.

IV. MSS (this list is avowedly incomplete; see the inventory compiled by Lacombe):

Cambridge, Peterhouse	116	ff. 241^{A}–242^{B}	XIII^{2}	Unasc.
Florence, Laur., Gaddiana	Pl. LXXXIX sup. 39	p. 26	(from Pelzer)	Unasc.
Milan, Ambros.	E. 71 sup.	ff. 1^{A}–2^{B}	XIII^{m}	Asc. So. Fr.
Vatican, Urbinat. lat.	541	f. 34	(from Pelzer)	Unasc.
Venice, S. Marco	x. 179	ff. 38–40	(from Pelzer)	Unasc.

13. *Commentatores Greci in Ethica Nicomachea Aristotelis*

I. Inc.: Prologue: Philosophia in duas partes divisa dico in theoricam et practicam...
Text: Consuete Aristoteles universale preordinat in presenti doctrina...
Expl.: ...in semper animabus bonum amantibus et deiformissimis.

II. The Latin translation of the Greek commentators was printed at Venice, 1536. C. Heylbut edited most of the Greek text in vols. XIX and XX (Berlin, 1889, 1892) of *Commentaria in Aristotelem Graeca*. Hayduck edited the remainder, the commentary of Michael of Ephesus on Bk. V, in the same series, vol. XXII, pt. 3 (1901).

* *Art. cit.* p. 319 ff.; see also Franceschini, *Roberto Grossatesta...*, p. 60 f.

III. Hermannus Alemannus is our only contemporary witness for Grosseteste as translator of the Greek commentators (see above, p. 65) of whom there were at least four: Eustratius of Nicea, Bks. I and VI; Aspasius, Bk. VIII; Michael of Ephesus on Bks. V, IX, and X, and the Anonymous on Bks. II–IV and VII. There is some authority for ascribing the comment on Bks. II–IV to Aspasius. The translation was used by Thomas of York between 1250 and 1260 and by Albertus Magnus by 1252,* although neither mentions any author of the translation. Our MS evidence for Grosseteste's authorship is conclusive. The Peterhouse MS, containing the complete text of the *Ethics* and the commentators,† has, in the left margin of f. 40[A], facing one of Grosseteste's additions to the text of Bk. I beginning *Ubi autem nos posuimus "omnino omnimode" in greco habetur pantH pantos...*, this note, written by the scribe of the text: *dominus lincolniensis translator*. The ascription in the rubric of the Naples MS (see above, p. 66, n. *) might conceivably refer only to the text of the *Ethics*. But a marginal note in the Eton Coll. MS, f. 41[D], *hic errat commentator sicut dicit episcopus qui hunc librum transtulit apud l.*, is more explicit. Finally, the Toledo MS, containing the combined work in an early (XIII²) Spanish hand, has this rubric (f. 1[A]): *Incipit commentum Eustracii archiepiscopi in Nikomachiam Aristotelis editum ab eo in greco et translatum a magistro Roberto Grosseteste episcopo linkoniensi in latinum.* It is noteworthy that most of the MSS of the combined text are older than the texts of the *Ethics* alone. This fact leaves small room for doubt that Grosseteste translated the *Ethics* and the commentators together.‡ We may even conclude from a marginal note in the Eton MS, f. 106[C] (Bk. VI, cap. 4): *in libro episcopi sic in contrarium cadit ipsis; unde secundum ipsum ordina sic...* that there was an acknowledged *liber episcopi* containing a combined text which, in all probability, was the original with which Grosseteste worked.

IV. MSS:

Oxford				
All Souls	84	ff. 10[C]–240[A]	XIII[m]	Unasc.
Balliol	116	ff. 1[A]–266[D]	XIII²	Unasc.
Cambridge, Peterhouse	116	ff. 13[A]–241[A]	XIII²	Asc.
Dublin, Trinity	C. 2. 8	ff. 1[A]–72[D]	XIII[m]	Unasc.§
Eton Coll.	122	ff. 1[A]–221[B]	XIII²	Asc.
Florence				
Laur.	Pl. LXXIX, 13	ff. 1[A]–377[D]	XIII[m]	Unasc. No. Fr.?
B.N.	I. V. 21	ff. 1[A]–224[C]	XIII²	Unasc. Engl.‖

* See P. Minges, *Phil. Jhbh.* XXXII (1919), "Robert Grosseteste Uebersetzer der Ethica Nicomachea", p. 241; and in general V. Rose in *Hermes*, v (1871), 61 ff.; Grabmann, *Uebersetzungen*, p. 251 ff. and Pelzer, "Les versions latines...".

† See Pelzer, *art. cit.* p. 387 ff. and S. H. Thomson, "The 'Notule' of Grosseteste on the 'Nicomachean Ethics'" (*Proceedings of the British Academy*, XIX, London, 1934), p. 12 f.

‡ Franceschini has found, *op. cit.* p. 54, one reference to the *Ethics* in the *Comm. in De Div. Nom.* chap. VIII: *sicut determinat philosophus in quinto moralium ad Nicomachum.* The *Ethics* was therefore wholly or partially translated by the time of composition of the commentaries on the pseudo-Dionysian works. See above, p. 51.

§ A fragment: Bk. VII, chap. 8; Bk. VII, chap. 14–Bk. X, chap. 15.

‖ Once the property of Coluccio Salutati, whose signature is legible on f. 229[A].

Monteprandone, S. Giacomo	(Comunale) 15			
Naples, B.N.	VIII. G. 4	ff. 9^C–227^D	XIII^m	Asc. Engl.
Olomouc, Chap.			*ca.* 1300	
Paris				
B.N.	lat. 6458	ff. 1^A–291^D	XIV^m	Unasc. Ital.*
	lat. 16582	ff. 1^A–329^C	XIV^1	Unasc. Fr.
	lat. 17832	ff. 1^A–273^A	*ca.* 1300	Unasc. Engl.?
Arsenal	698	ff. 3^A–155^D	XIII^2	Unasc. Fr.
Mazarine	3473	ff. 159^D–161^C	XIII^2, *frag.* Bk. I	Unasc. Fr.
Reims	876	ff. 1^A–165^C	*ca.* 1300	Unasc. Fr.
Seville, Colomb.	82. 1. 5	ff. 1^a–92^a	*ca.* 1300	Unasc. Sp. & Ital.†
Toledo, Cabildo	Fol. 95. 14	ff. 1^A–239^B	XIII^2	Asc. Sp.
Vatican				
lat.	2171	ff. 1^A–211^D	XIII^2	Unasc. Engl.
Urbinat. lat.	222	ff. 1^A–223^a	1481	Unasc. Ital.
Venice, S. Marco	VI. 122	ff. 1^A–204^A	XIII^2	Unasc. No. Fr.?
Vienna, Nat. Bibl.	2327	ff. 1^A–105^D	*ca.* 1300	Unasc. Lowl. *mut. in fine* ‡

14. *De Vita Monachorum*

Baur drew attention (p. 42*) to a letter (ed. Luard, *Epist.* LVII, pp. 173–178) which Grosseteste wrote to the Abbot and Convent of Bury. He relates how

> Quiescens hac septimana proxima paululum ab exteriorum tumultu, quadam eiusdem septimane die, leccioni parumper vacans, incidi in quandam conscripcionem de vita monachorum que eam decenter extollit, et quia vestro studio credidi gratum fore, si quod ibidem intelligere potui vobiscum communicarem, non verba que ibidem inveni, quia alterius quam latine sunt lingue, sed extractum pro modulo meo verborum sensum, adiectis alicubi paucis ad dilucidacionem in hanc paginam redigens, vobis destinare curavi.

Baur suggested that it was a translation of Ὁ βίος τῶν μοναχῶν of Basil the Great and referred to *Patr. Gr.* XXXI, col. 619 ff. But such a title is not found among Basil's works,§ and the subject-matter of Grosseteste's letter is certainly not found in the Ἀσκητικὴ προδιατύπωσις at the place suggested by Baur. Franceschini has further clearly shown that a part of the letter comes from chap. VI of the *De Eccl. Hier.* of the pseudo-Dionysius (*Patr. Gr.* III, col. 532 f.). He suggests therefore that the work which Grosseteste translated or paraphrased was posterior to the sixth century, in order to account for the incorporation of a passage from the pseudo-Dionysius. But such an hypothesis may be regarded as unnecessary. The pseudo-Dionysian passage

* This codex once belonged to Petrarch. See P. de Nolhac, *Pétrarque et l'humanisme*, 2nd ed. (Paris, 1907), II, 150–152, who has found numerous notes in Petrarch's own hand. De Nolhac read *priorum* where the MS has *primum*, and *Incipit liber primus* where the MS has *parvus*. See also Sandys, *Hist. of Classical Scholarship*, II (Cambridge, 1908), 10.

† Wanting the commentary on Bks. VI–IX.

‡ A copy of *Eticas cum comento Eustachii* was at Avignon in 1369. See F. Ehrle, *Hist. Bibl. Aven.* (Rome, 1890), p. 323.

§ See Franceschini, *Roberto Grossatesta...*, p. 46 ff.

begins: *Est enim vita monastica, ut aiunt, omnium perfectorum*.... The *ut aiunt* seems to indicate a break with what precedes. When translating or paraphrasing, Grosseteste refers to his source as *conscripcio*. The brief section which precedes the *ut aiunt*:

> Monstrat igitur prefata conscripcio, quod monachi sunt viri philosophantes circa regulas vite in excellencia sanctitatis agende: adhuc in carne viventes, per carnis maceracionem mortificare, et sobria quadam insania presencia bona deserentes transire semper de bonis veris ad meliora usque quo attigerint summa,

is best understood as a summary of the Προοίμιον of the Ὅροι κατὰ πλάτος of St Basil (*Patr. Gr.* xxxi, cols. 889–1052). The remaining sections of Grosseteste's letter that are not etymological in character—he never consciously avoids an opportunity to discuss etymology if it can be brought in—are in all probability taken from chaps. vi–viii of this work which treat of the need for retirement from the world. It may be added that the Latin does not read at all like the usual Latin of Grosseteste's translations; it is, as a matter of fact, rather good thirteenth-century Latin. When he translates, the result, as Latin, is uniformly bad, a fact of which he was quite aware.

We are led to the conclusion that the letter is a paraphrase of sections from the Longer Rules of St Basil, freely interpolated with Grosseteste's etymologies and a short section from the *De Eccl. Hier.*, upon the translation and commentary of which he may recently have been working. Franceschini's suggestion that it was written early in the episcopate is quite acceptable, say 1238–1240.

This letter is not known to exist apart from the collections of letters. See below, no. 57, p. 203.

COMMENTARIES

A. BIBLICAL

15. *Prohemium et Glose in Libros Sapiencie et Ecclesiastici*

I. Proh. in Sapienciam inc.: Liber iste recte post librum cantici legendus. Occurit solum...

Proh. expl.: ...se iudicandum pocius quam iudicatur in qua sciret... [incomplete]

First gloss in Sap.: [f. 2B] Humiliter et catholice non contempnendo facilia...

Last gloss in Sap.: [f. 45b, interlinear] ...serpencium ignatorum *over* corruptibilium animalium [XIX, 20].

First gloss in Eccl.: [f. 46a] Nota quod de hoc libro legitur in ecclesia...

Last gloss in Eccl.: [f. 133b, LI, 32] Duo importat hoc verbum siciunt, scil. appetitum et defectum; hic unum, scil. defectum.

II. Unpubl.

III. These glosses are in Grosseteste's own hand in Shrewsbury MS 1, a codex containing the two books of *Sapiencia* and *Ecclesiasticus*, with the two glosses, *communis*, usually associated with the name of Walafrid Strabo, and *interlinearis*, of which Anselm of Laon was most probably the author. Grosseteste wrote a short introduction to *Sapiencia* on the verso of the flyleaf and annotated the text and glosses throughout the codex. His glosses would indicate that he had compared this text with a more exact or more copious copy, as he adds occasional parts to a gloss from Rabanus, or indicates the source of an unascribed gloss. A careful comparison of these glosses with some of his sermons on texts from these two books would probably help in dating the sermons, as we know (see above, Introd. p. 34) that the codex came into his possession after 1238. The book was the property of Alexander Staneby, Bishop of Lichfield and Coventry, 1224–1238. A note at the top of f. 2a reads: *Ecclesiasticus et liber Sapiencie Magistri Alexandri de Staneby*, in a hand, probably Alexander's, that has added occasional notes in the margins of the text. The Dominicans of Chester owned the book after Grosseteste. At the top of f. 1b is the ex-libris: *Iste liber est fratrum predicatorum Cestrie* in a hand of the second half of the thirteenth century. The text itself was written in the first quarter of the thirteenth century by an English scribe.

IV. MS:

Shrewsbury School	1	ff. 1b–134b (text, ff. 2a–134a)	XIII1

16. *Commentarius in Epistolam Pauli ad Galathas*

I. Inc.: Ut Apostolus revocaret Galathas ad doctrinam evangelicam...
Expl.: ...adhuc dei invisibilia sicut ipse testatur [*mut. in fine cap.* VI].

II. Unpubl.

III. Thus far only one late MS of this commentary has come to light. The scribe of this codex, however, was in no doubt as to Grosseteste's authorship, as he has written a specific ascription in the upper right corner of each recto.* A close reading of the text reveals clearly Grossetestian characteristics. Frequent citations from Chrysostom, Jerome—copiously on exegetical points—Augustine, perhaps less than usual, *Glose Lombardi*, Avicenna's *De Anima* and the *De Fide Orthodoxa* of John Damascene, long a favourite of Grosseteste's, are noticeable. There are several other noteworthy authorities: the author appeals often to LXX *interpretes*, to *codex grecus* and *codices greci*. The phrase *de cessacione legalium* occurs several times in the comment on chap. v, and suggests that the idea of the longer and more *ad hoc* treatise of that name may have occurred to Grosseteste as he was composing this commentary. Such a suggestion is rendered more plausible when we find that he refers to this commentary in the *De Cessacione Legalium* (q.v.) which we know him to have written *ca.* 1231. In the earliest copy of the latter work, Lincoln Coll., Oxford, MS 54, f. 12^{D}, we read:

> Verba quoque predicti loci epistole ad Galathas convenienter possunt resonare et quod sensit Jeronimus et quod sensit Augustinus, quod eciam nos pro modulo nostro ostendimus in exposicione parvula quam super eandem epistolam scripsimus.

We are able thus to date this commentary 1231 or earlier, and at the same time ascertain that he had made sufficient progress in his study of Greek to be able to use for exegetical purposes Greek MSS of the LXX and of the New Testament as well. To that extent we can modify substantially Roger Bacon's statement that Grosseteste could not use Greek until the end of his life. But we have as yet no information which would lead us to say that he had begun any serious work of translation so early.

The existence of such a commentary has been known to all the bibliographers since Bale.

IV. MS:

Oxford, Magdalen	57	ff. 1^{a}–32^{b}	XV^{1}	Asc.

* Gascoigne's inclusive statement that Grosseteste wrote *exposicionem suam propriam...super epistolas beatissimi Pauli apostoli* is too vague to be satisfactorily applicable to this commentary or to this codex. See *Loci e Libro Veritatum* (ed. J. E. T. Rogers, Oxford, 1881), p. 142.

17. *Commentarius in Epistolam Pauli ad Romanos V–XVI*

I. Inc.: *Iustificati ex fide*, scilicet, que est causa formalis iustificacionis. Contra, supra 3. iustificati gracia ipsius. Augustinus: si ex fide quomodo gratis et non ex meritis? Respondeo: fides est ipsa gracia, fidem enim non precedit meritum, et cum in fide sit gracie infusio ut bonum cogitemus, secundo ut cogitatum velimus, tercio ut volitum perficiamus, patet quod primum est ita ex gracia quod sine nobis, secundum et tercium ex gracia ita quod ex nostri cooperacione. Unde Bernardus...

Expl.: ...quo autem fine subdit: ad obedicionem fidei in omnibus gentibus.

II. Unpubl.

III. This commentary, in the unique MS, follows immediately after Grosseteste's *De Humilitate Contemplativorum* (see below, p. 133). As in the latter work, there are copious marginal notes around the text on three sides, of patristic excerpts or simple additional comment. The only ascription in the commentary is a *Lincoln'* in the left margin of f. 58^b. There seems no reason to doubt that it refers to the whole work. It cannot logically refer to the marginal note below which it is written, as the note is continued at the top of f. 59^a. An ascription of such a single note would normally come at the end of it. There is nothing in the text opposite the *Lincoln'* to which it could reasonably be attached to the exclusion of the rest of the text. The ascription was written by the scribe of the text, and the marginal note by another, though perhaps contemporary, scribe who had to finish his note on the next page because the *Lincoln'* prevented his continuing in the margin of f. 58^b.

That Grosseteste was deeply interested in the epistles of St Paul we know from his constant use of them. Gascoigne tells of having seen (1450) a copy of the epistles, accompanied by the *glosa communis* which Grosseteste had annotated in his own hand:

> Habet idem doctor dominus Lynconiensis, doctor Robertus Grosseteste, predictam explanacionem in exposicione sua propria scripta super epistolas beatissimi Pauli apostoli et virginis et doctoris orbis et est illud scriptum domini Linconiensis de manu sua propria inter fratres Oxonie; in illo libro scribitur in margine illius libri et ibi exposuit certos textus beati Pauli apostoli, sed non omnes, et eciam glose communis seu exposicionis communis.*

This manner of annotation seemed to be customary with Grosseteste. We have his *magnum psalterium* and the books of *Sapiencia* and *Ecclesiasticus* annotated in his own hand (see pp. 33 f., 72 and 77 f.). This MS, however, is not in Grosseteste's distinctive hand, though his own notes can quite well have been the source of this collection. On the other hand both the age of the MS and the organization of the material would justify us in regarding the whole as taken down from *lecciones*. On f. 61^a the scribe of the text has

* *Loci e Libro Veritatum* (ed. J. E. T. Rogers, Oxford, 1881), p. 142.

written *Dominica quarta post pentecosten* which, coming in the middle of the commentary on chap. VIII, would have no significance unless to date the *leccio*. Further on in the codex, f. 71^a, almost immediately following the commentary, begins a sermon on *Non potest arbor bona* (Mt. vii. 18) which is rubricked by the original hand *Sermo dominica septima post pentecosten*. The natural conclusion would be that the intervening matter had been "read" in the preceding three weeks.

The commentary is largely made up of scriptural and patristic quotations. Augustine, Jerome, Gregory, Anselm, Remigius, Rabanus, and Bernard furnish most of the citations. There is one short quotation from Damascenus, though whether from Grosseteste's own translation or from the current version of Burgundio of Pisa I cannot determine. The Greek fathers, so common in his last works, do not yet appear.

A note in the margins of ff. 63^b–64^a: *In vita beati Francisci: clamat una de ovibus nocte quadam, quiescentibus ceteris...illud factum noveritis*, would suggest that the scribe was a Franciscan. It is possible to identify the hand of the *librarius* of Bury St Edmunds who, not later than *ca.* 1350, wrote the *contenta* on the flyleaf of Pembroke, Cambridge, MS 7, in occasional notes in the margins of our commentary.

IV. MS:

Cambridge, Gonv. & Caius	439	ff. 57^B–70^b	XIII^1

18. *Commentarius in Psalmos I–C*

I. Inc.: Psalmorum liber grece psalterium ebrayce nablo, latine organum dicitur...

Expl.: ...ab iniusticia consistit conversacio perfecta.

II. Unpubl.

III. The Bologna MS, known to Tanner, was written by an English scribe early in the fourteenth century. It has the following informative colophon (f. 173^D): *Explicit lincolniensis super psalterium quem reperitur ipsum fecisse secundum exemplar librorum librarie Oxonie. Amen.* The exemplar here referred to, doubtless the one Gascoigne saw,* has disappeared. There remain but two copies of the definitive work. That this commentary had a checkered career is evident from the constitution of the text. James noticed† that a sharp break in manner of treatment occurs at the end of Psalm lxxix. From Psalm lxxx to Psalm c‡ a thorough knowledge of Greek and Greek exegesis,

* *Et psalterium, expositum et scriptum manu sua propria, registratur Oxonie* [sc. Grosseteste] *inter fratres minores. Episcopus Lincoln. d: et Psalterium suum, quod non scribitur manu propria domini Lincolniensis, registratur ibidem. Episcopus Lincoln. ff.* The second copy may be either the Bologna or the Eton MS, more probably the former, as the Eton copy was contemporary with Gascoigne. See *Loci e Libro Veritatum*, p. 177.

† "Robert Grosseteste on the Psalms", in *JTS*. XXIII (1922), 181–185.

‡ *Chronicon de Lanercost* (1839), p. 43, *Nam et Psalterium legendo postillavit usque ad medium nec ulterius licuit propter vitae terminum.*

hitherto not at all evident, is prominent. We now know, as is made clear below in the discussion of the *Dicta*, that much of Grosseteste's *Comm. in Psalmos* is nothing but a collection of more or less related *Dicta*. That these were composed early in his ecclesiastical career is shown by their presence in a MS (Durham Cath. A. III. 12) which we must date 1231 or earlier. In this early MS, furthermore, they are preceded by the introductory section later incorporated into the commentary.

Grosseteste's interest in the Psalms was unflagging. In addition to the lost autograph MS of the commentary we have the Lincoln Cath. MS 144, with his copious marginal notations (see next item), and Bodley e Museo 15 which contains the introductory section and notes to Peter Lombard's commentary on the Psalms (see next item). Further examination and comparison of these various texts is necessary. I am not at all sure that a simple theory of successive drafts or reworking of his material satisfies the complicated conditions of the problem.

The following *Dicta* appear in the commentary: 17, 41–43, 45, 50, 53–54, 58, 64, 71, 73, 77–79, 81–82, 88, 94, 97–100, 102–106, 112, 117, 119, 121–122, 125, 128, 140, 147. See below under *Dicta*.

Though the authenticity of the whole is beyond doubt, it is extremely doubtful if Grosseteste would have consented to call this almost amorphous collection a commentary. It is more likely that some student or member of his household has made a selection of his unorganized pronouncements on separate passages of the Psalms and put them in as consecutive an order as possible. Many Psalms are not even mentioned.

IV. MSS:

Oxford, e Museo	15	f. 1^{A-B}	XIII[1]	Unasc.*
Durham Cath.	A. III. 12	ff. 2^{A}–13^{C}	*ca.* 1230	Unasc.†
Eton Coll.	8	ff. 1^{A}–203^{D} (Index, ff. 205^{A}–216^{B})	XV[1]	Unasc.
Bologna, Arch.	A. 893	ff. 1^{A}–173^{D}	*ca.* 1325	Asc.‡

* This MS has the prologue as found in the Bologna MS, f. 1^{A-D}, but adds the *Regule Tyconii* (ed. F. C. Burkitt in *Texts and Studies*, III, 1, Cambridge, 1894), greatly abridged. A marginal note, f. 1^{B}, reads: *Regule Tyconii que habentur in tercio libro de doctrina christiana versus finem et possunt notari super illam partem proemii que incipit sic: Modus tractandi etc.*

† Has the prologue as the Bodley MS, with the *Regule Tyconii*, f. 2^{B-C}, but begins the comment on Psalm i on f. 2^{C}, and proceeds approximately as the Eton and Bologna texts, with a few omissions, as far as f. 13^{C}. See below under *Dicta*, p. 214ff., and Sermons, pp. 180, 182ff. The first *Dictum* to appear is on Psalm i. 3 and it becomes *Dictum* 98 in the collection.

‡ A trembling hand (XIV[2]) has marked sections for reading, *feria ii*[a] or *sabbato*, etc. from the beginning as far as f. 80, then begins again at f. 160 and goes to the end.

19. *Notule in Psalterium seu in Commentarium Petri Lombardi in Psalmos*

In addition to the organized material on the Psalms represented by the commentary just described, there is a mass of glossarial matter hitherto unnoticed. Lincoln Cath. MS 144 (see Introd. p. 33 f.) contains the commentary of Peter the Lombard on the Psalms, beginning at the end of Psalm iv (almost the whole first gathering lost or destroyed). Throughout the codex the margins are filled with marginalia in Grosseteste's hand, *notule* and glosses to the Lombard as well as to the text of the Psalms. The glosses are replete with scripture references and quotations from patristic and classical authors: Augustine, Jerome, Ambrose, Symmachus, Gregory, Basil, Boethius, Anselm, Bernard, Seneca, Ovid and at least one reference to the *Topica* of Aristotle. There are some Greek etymologies, but they are rare and do not give evidence of first-hand knowledge of Greek.

Bodley MS e Museo 15, written in the first half of the thirteenth century, contains, ff. 2[A]–205[D], the *Comm. in Psalmos* of Peter the Lombard. The text is written in neat early gothic. Throughout the codex several early scribes have copiously annotated the text, marginally and interlinearly. The earliest of these scribes, contemporary with the text,* has written on the recto of f. 1 the introduction of Grosseteste's *Comm. in Psalmos* as it is found in Durham A. III. 12, with the *Regule Tyconii*. On the verso of f. 1 he has begun what can only be called a gloss on the *Prefatio* of Peter the Lombard to his *Comm. in Psalmos*. It begins (f. 1[C]):

> *Cum omnes prophetas.* Ista prefacio magistri dividitur in duo. In prima manifestat ea que sunt precognoscenda ad totam doctrinam sequentem. In secunda parte manifestat ea que precognoscenda quo ad primum psalmum. Ibi *De primo itaque psalmo videamus* etc. Prior harum in duas iterum partes dividitur....

There are points of correspondence in detail between the notes of this scribe and those found in both the Lincoln and Durham MSS, but for the most part it must be said that the Bodley MS presents a separate body of glosses. Though the problem calls for more careful investigation, a tentative suggestion may not be out of place: that the Bodley MS contains a student's notes taken from Grosseteste's lectures, which, though based on his own notes in the Lincoln MS, must have been given partially *ex tempore*. Occasional short notes, jotted down without order in the Bodley MS, would indicate hurried and *in situ* annotation, taken directly from informal lectures. At the top of f. 1[b], where the scribe has copied the short gloss of Grosseteste to the *Prefatio* of the Lombard, is written: *Non est bonum in proemio effluere et*

* This may have been the MS seen by Gascoigne, as this note-hand has many similarities with Grosseteste's writing. Detailed comparison, however, forces us to conclude that it is not his. The codex belonged to Alexander Fetherston, Vicar of Wolverton (Bucks), Prebendary of Lichfield, in 1680. It gives no indication of belonging to the Franciscans at any time. A note at the end, f. 206[b], *ca.* 1275, reads: *Istud psalterium legavi, quando feci testamentum meum, domino Johanni nepoti, me capellano coram domino R. de Meleburn' can. Derk* [Derl? = Darley] *qui ibi fuit presens.*

in tractatu succingi, which, in addition to having a Grossetestian flavour, would seem to connect the introduction of Grosseteste to what was to follow. Another note, f. 2^C^, *puto dicit falsum*, might be by the scribe himself. There are, however, many such notes which indicate selective transcription from dictation. It is impossible, on paleographical grounds alone, to decide which of these three groups of *notule* is the earliest. The Bodley copy can easily be as early as *ca.* 1230, the *terminus ad quem* of the Durham MS. The text of the Lincoln codex is earlier, but the notes in Grosseteste's hand could have been written at any time in the prime of his life, i.e. 1215–1240, though the absence of any demonstrably original use of Greek would put the composition in the pre-episcopal period. We would have to count as more than a possibility the repetition and consequent reworking of the whole. The loss or destruction of the first leaves of the Lincoln MS is the more to be regretted in that they may have contained material which would have solved our complex problem.

B. PHILOSOPHICAL

20. *Commentarii in Opera Pseudo-Dionysii*

(i) *De Celesti Hierarchia*

I. Inc.: Eorum qui hunc librum de greco in latinum transtulerunt...
Expl.: ...et humilitas nobis inpetret indulgenciam.

II. Unpubl.

III. The tradition of the commentary is bound up with that of the translation (q.v. above, p. 55). References to this commentary occur in the thirteenth century, and Grosseteste was sufficiently well known as its author to be occasionally described simply as *commentator* or *expositor*. Roger Bacon in his *Greek Grammar** says: *dominus Robertus...exposuit in suis commentariis super libros Dionisii et corrigit ceteros translatores.* Thomas of York says, in his *Sapienciale* (MS Vatican lat. 6771, f. 90^A^): *Amplius sicut dicit angelica ierarchia, cap.* 4, *totum quod sunt lux sunt, super quod expositor: totum quod est vita sunt et eorum spirituales.* William of Ware (*fl.* 1290) says in his *In IV Sent.* (MS Vatican lat. 1115, f. 64^a^): *comentum super* 2. *capitulum angelice ierarchie dicit quod amoris mocio in divina terminum non habet.* Roger Marston (*fl.* 1270) in his *Questiones Disputate* (Quaracchi, 1932) makes frequent references to Grosseteste's commentary, e.g. pp. 159, 296, *dicit commentator super angelicam hierarchiam*; p. 298, *ubi subdit commentator.* An early (XIII^m^) Bodley MS, Greaves 53,† which contains (ff. 26^A^–31^C^) extracts from various patristic and classical writers, has two short quotations, ff. 27^D^ and 28^D^, *Impuritas est commixtio que...* and *Laus communiter dictarum...* ascribed *ex commento Lincolniensis super angelicam ierarchiam*, on the third and fourth chapters respectively. Wyclyf makes frequent use of the commentaries on all four works, e.g. *De Apostasia*, pp. 62–64, 181.

* Ed. E. Nolan and S. A. Hirsch (Cambridge, 1902), p. 118.
† I am indebted to Dr R. W. Hunt for this reference.

IV. MSS:

See above, p. 55 f., under Grosseteste's translation of the *De Cel. Hier.* MS 209 of the Bibl. Comunale of Cortona has, ff. 141–146, according to the catalogue of G. Mancini, *I manoscritti della libreria del comune e dell' Accademia Etrusca di Cortona* (Cortona, 1884), p. 65, *Liconius super libros S. Dionisii episcopi Athenarum.* I suspect, without having seen the MS, that it is a catena of extracts from Grosseteste's commentaries. Erfurt MS O. 30 contains only the commentary to the *De Myst. Theol.* and the beginning of the commentary on the *De Cel. Hier.*

(ii) *De Ecclesiastica Hierarchia*

I. Inc.: Liber de angelica hierarchia huic libro de ierarchia ecclesiastica preponitur...

Expl.: ...quod in fine exposicionis prioris libri supplicavi.

II. Unpubl.

III. See above, under *Comm. in De Cel. Hier.* p. 78. This commentary is also quoted in the Greaves MS, f. 28ᴮ, and by Uhtred of Bolton (*fl.* 1375), Cambridge, C.C.C. MS 103, p. 311ᵇ.

IV. MSS: see above under translation of *De Eccl. Hier.*, p. 56 f.

(iii) *De Divinis Nominibus*

I. Inc.: Scripturus iste pater beatus Dionysius de divinis nominibus qui labor...

Expl.: ...sed caritative mee compaciatur insufficiencie.

II. Unpubl.

III. See above, p. 78, *Comm. in De Cel. Hier.* This work was perhaps better known than the work on the *De Eccl. Hier.*, particularly to the Franciscans of the Augustinian tradition. William of Ware (MS Vatican lat. 1115, f. 19ᵇ): *Item Lincolniensis super Dyonisii de divinis nominibus partem 4 cap. 2 dicit quod sicud omnia non in sole sed in quadam superfusione luminis illa omnia non videntur in deo sed in perfeccione divini luminis*; William in a *questio determinata* (MS Bibl. Angelica, Rome, 1017, XIV[1], f. 108ᵇ): *Item Lincolniensis de divinis nominibus cap. 4. parte prima dividens seculum dicit sic: nomen grecum quod transferunt in hoc nomen seculum.* William of Nottingham, O.F.M. (†1254) quotes from this commentary in his *In Sent.* II, dist. 1, qu. 3.*

IV. MSS: see above, p. 57, under translation of *De Div. Nom.*

(iv) *De Mystica Theologia*

I. Inc.: Mystica theologia est secretissima et non iam per speculum et per imagines...

Expl.: ...nimirum dictorum defectus a perfectis benevole suppleri.

* M. Schmaus, in "Guillelmi de Nottingham O.F.M. doctrina de aeternitate mundi" in *Antonianum*, VII (1932), 161. In the index one is surprised to find *Robertus de Grossatesta O.F.M.*, and the *de* in a note on p. 161.

II. Publ. Strasbourg, 1502–1503. See above, p. 57.

III. See above, p. 78, under *Comm. in De Cel. Hier.* This commentary was used and ascribed to Grosseteste by Roger Marston, *op. cit.* p. 334 ff.

IV. In addition to the MSS noted above, p. 58, under the translation of the text, the commentary appears separately in Munich, Clm. 280[B], ff. 282[a]–295[b], *ca.* 1500, Asc. Ger., and Trèves, MS 713, ff. 63–71, XV. I have not seen the Trèves MS, and the work may not be complete, or it might conceivably be the text alone.

21. *Notule in Opera Pseudo-Dionysii*

See above, p. 52. The first of these *notule* begins: *Non inveni in exemplari greco nomen auctoris prescriptum huic prologo....* The total of these *notule*, interspersed with Grosseteste's translation of the Scholia of Maximus (q.v.), limited for the most part to the *De Cel. Hier.*, would not be great. Further investigation is needed to make clear the nature and extent of these *notule*. The Merton; Dublin 163; Cesena; Paris, B.N. lat. 1620; Florence, Laur. Pl. XIII, dext. 1; Vatican, Chigi MSS have varying numbers of these *notule*. Their authenticity is beyond any doubt. They are often quite personal and explicitly connected with the translating of the text.

22. *Notula super Epistolam Johannis Damasceni De Trisagion*

I. Inc.: Sentencia grecorum est quod spiritus sanctus est spiritus filii...
Expl.: ...pateret contrariorum verborum non discors sentencia.

II. Quoted entire by Duns Scotus in his *Opus Oxoniense*, ed. Wadding, v, 858, and ed. Venice, 1612, p. 259 f.

III. In addition to the authority of Duns Scotus for this *notula* we have it ascribed in the Magdalen MS which contains several translations by Grosseteste of works of John Damascene (see above, p. 45 ff.). In the right margin of f. 215[B] of this codex a second hand, XIII[2], has written: *nota verba lincolniensis*. The presence of the *notula* in the later Grosseteste canons is corroborative of this early attribution.

IV. MSS:

Oxford, Magdalen	192	f. 215[B]	XIII[2]	Asc.
London, B.M.				
Lans.	458	f. 175[C]	XV[1]	Asc.
Royal	7. E. II	f. 341[A–B]	XIV[2]	Asc.
	7. F. II	ff. 72[D]–73[A]	XIV[m]	Asc.
York Cath.	XVI. A. 6	f. 113[a]	*ca.* 1500	Asc.

23. *Prologus in Librum Johannis Damasceni De Logica*

I. Inc.: Quemadmodum dulce philocosmis existit sensibilium paradisorum...

Expl.: ...dei gloriam aspiciens et ineffabili gaudio astans.

II. Unpubl.

III. This prologue, usually rubricked *Prologus Translatoris*, is connected, in the MS tradition, with the works of Damascenus which Grosseteste translated, though it appears as an introduction to the *De Logica* alone. The importance of chap. IX of this prologue for our ascription of the translation to Grosseteste has been pointed out above, p. 45 f., q.v. It is probable that he had before him, when writing this prologue, the letter of Damascenus to Cosmas Majumae (*Patr. Gr.* IV, cols. 517–518), as some of the facts concerning the writing of the works given by Grosseteste are almost translations of parts of this letter. Most of the prologue, however, is Grosseteste's own.

The prologue was certainly written after the translation of the *De Fide*, as it quotes from this translation. It is likely that it was written after the other two works, the *De Centum Heresibus* and the *De Logica*, were translated. In any case it was written in the late 1230's.

IV. MSS:

Oxford				
e Museo	134	pp. 459ᵃ–464ᵃ	XIII²	Unasc.
Laud Misc.	268	ff. 89ᴬ–90ᴰ	XIV¹	Unasc. Lowl.
Magdalen	192	ff. 135ᴬ–136ᶜ	XIII²	Unasc.
Paris, B.N.	lat. 2375	ff. 387ᴰ–391ᴮ	XIII²	Unasc. Fr.

24. *Commentarius in Sophisticos Elenchos Aristotelis*

I. Inc.: De sophisticis autem elenchis et de hiis que videntur elenchi, cum dubium sit utrum sit eiusdem continuitatis liber iste...

Expl.: ...indulgeant inventis autem multas referant grate[s].

II. Unpubl.

III. The early ascription in the unique Merton MS is sufficient for the authenticity of this commentary. Bale,* who lists *Questiones Elenchorum*, may have seen this MS. Tanner and Pegge probably take their note of this work from him. Tanner adds a Bodleian MS, e Museo 22 (now e Museo 133) but, as Baur pointed out (p. 30*), the treatises are quite distinct. The Bodleian MS is quite short (ff. 146ᴬ–150ᴰ) and, though early (XIII²), gives no indication of authorship, either as to content, which is severely non-committal, or ascription, as the work is anonymous. It does not seem probable that we have here an instance of a first and a second redaction. There is not sufficient similarity on any point.

As to the date of composition, we are not without clues. The unique MS is, of course, a copy, but a scrupulous scribe has left us a significant detail. The colophon says the work was *datus a magistro Roberto Grostest*. The title

* *Index* (ed. Poole and Bateson), p. 378.

magister puts the work in the pre-episcopal period. Because we know that from the time of his lectureship to the Franciscans, 1229, his interests were mostly theological and pastoral, we are safe in suggesting as broad limits the period 1215–1229, and perhaps the earlier part of this period.

IV. MS:

Oxford, Merton	280	ff. 3^{A}–37^{C}	*ca.* 1300	Asc.*

25. *Commentarius in VIII Libros Physicorum Aristotelis*

I. Inc.: Cum scire et intelligere adquirantur ex principiis ut sciantur...
Expl.: ...motus et tempus cum cessabit hominum generacio.

II. Unpubl.

III. The earliest MS of this commentary is of the beginning of the fourteenth century, and the ascription is contemporary. The bibliographers from Boston of Bury to Pegge have all attributed a commentary on the *Physics* to Grosseteste, but only Bale and Tanner gave the incipit of the commentary. Tanner had obviously not examined the printed editions of the *Summa in Physica* (q.v. below, p. 83), as he gave the incipit of the *Commentarius* and asserted that it had been printed, 1504, 1506 *Venetiis*. The commentary and the *Summa* have long been confused. Burley, in his commentary *In VIII Libros Physicorum*, frequently quotes this work of Grosseteste—e.g. in Burley, ed. Venice, 1501, the quotation of f. 6^{C} = Digby MS 220, f. 84^{A}, l. 4 ff.; Burley, f. 150^{B} = Digby, f. 99^{A}, ll. 7–11, etc. Wyclyf makes an extensive quotation in his *De Ente Primo* from *Lincolniensis in prologo primo Physicorum*.†

The short tractate *De Finitate Motus et Temporis* (q.v. below, p. 98) is the last section of the commentary. Its appearance as a separate work in several fourteenth-century MSS, and the fact, pointed out by Baur (p. 93*), that it comes from a tradition independent of any of which we know, adds weight to the other early ascriptions. Grosseteste uses the Greek-Latin translation current at the beginning of the century. We have no precise data as to the date of composition of this commentary, but it is quite unlikely to have been done at any time after *ca.* 1229, when we know that his interests focussed almost entirely on theology and ecclesiastical concerns.

IV. MSS:

Oxford				
Digby	220	ff. 84^{A}–105^{A}	XV^{1}	Asc.
Merton	295	ff. 120^{A}–145^{A}	*ca.* 1325	Asc. *a. m. coeva.*
Venice, S. Marco	VI. 222	ff. 2^{A}–30^{C}	XIV^{1}	Asc. Ital.‡

* Both in *contenta* in contemporary hand and in colophon by original scribe: *Explicit narratus super librum elenchorum datus a magistro Roberto Grostest* [*de Lyncolnia* added *a.m.p.* XIV^{m}]. Powicke, *Merton Books*, p. 115 f., tells how the codex came to Merton *ca.* 1325–1345 as a gift from William Ingge, Archdeacon of Surrey (†1347).

† *De Ente*, ed. S. H. Thomson (Oxford, 1930), p. 104, l. 19, beginning *omne agens* to p. 105, l. 6, ending ...*manus propinquiores*, substantially as found in Digby MS 220, f. 84^{A-B}.

‡ MS Bibl. Angelica, Rome, 127, ff. 7^{a}–19^{a}, has an incipit like this commentary, but it is in reality the *Summa in Physica* which has suffered confused

26. *Summa in VIII Libros Physicorum Aristotelis*

I. Inc.: In primo libro physicorum cuius subiectum est corpus mobile...

Expl.: ...immobile, infatigabile, nullam habens magnitudinem.

II. Publ. 1498, 1500, 1506, 1515, 1535, 1551, 1583, 1586, 1637.

III. Baur (p. 19* ff.) argued against the genuineness of this work on the grounds that (*a*) the extant MSS were not earlier than the fifteenth century;* (*b*) the "Terminologie und Sprache" differ greatly from those of known works of Grosseteste; (*c*) the thought content is that of a period much later than Grosseteste.† As to (*a*), it may be pointed out that one MS of the work, not noticed by Baur, of English provenance, written *ca.* 1325, lacks the first leaf. This MS is as early as the earliest known copy of the *Commentarius*. As to (*b*), it is sufficient to observe that we do not have here a commentary at all, but a paraphrase (*abreviacio*), probably intended as a handbook for students. There is every indication that the author scrupulously avoided putting any of his own thought into the work. The difference in "Terminologie und Sprache" which Baur discovers is not apparent. As to (*c*), it need only be remarked that the thought content is strictly that of Aristotle, and can hardly have been characteristic of any particular century.‡

Finally the MS evidence is of itself conclusive. Eight MSS are now known to exist, written by scribes in England, Spain, Italy, France and Germany. One, the English copy, lacks the first leaf. Of the remaining seven, six ascribe the work to Grosseteste and the seventh bears no ascription. Such unanimity of ascription is rare.§

IV. MSS:

Cambridge				
Peterhouse	188	ff. 119^D–127^C	1450	Asc.
Trinity	O. 2. 11	ff. 1^a–16^b	*ca.* 1325‖	
Berlin	lat. 975	ff. 163^a–170^b	1426	Asc. Ger.
Munich	Clm. 402	ff. 104^a–110^a	1458	Asc. Ger.
	Clm. 8950	ff. 278^a–290^b	1420	Asc. Ger.
	Clm. 26889	ff. 21^a–30^b	*ca.* 1400	Unasc. Ger.
Rome, Angelica	127	ff. 7^a–19^a	1470	Asc. Ital.
Tours	704	ff. 68^a–87^a	1426 in Valencia	Asc. Sp.

Bodl. MS e Museo 230, ff. 1^a–19^b (XV^1), mentioned by Baur, is a different work. See below, p. 258, under *Spuria* 39–43.

scribal redaction. See S. H. Thomson, "The Summa in VIII Physicorum of Grosseteste" in *Isis*, XXII (1933), 12–18. In Bodl. MS e Museo 230, ff. 1^a–19^b, XV^1, a commentary on the *Physics* is ascribed to Grosseteste. See below, p. 258, *Spuria* 39–43.

* By contrast with the *Comm. in VIII Libros Physicorum*, of which there is an early fourteenth-century copy.

† Steinschneider, *Hebräische Uebersetzungen* (Berlin, 1893), p. 476, notes a translation of this *Summa* into Hebrew by Elias ben Joseph of Nola in 1537. See also G. Sarton, *Introduction to History of Science*, II, pt. ii (Baltimore, 1931), 585.

‡ There are three quotations from Averroës, but they are brief and rendered necessary by the unsatisfactory nature of the Latin translation of the *Physics*.

§ I have discussed this *Summa* more at length in *Isis*, XXII (1933), 12–18.

‖ The first folium has been cut out. The colophon bears no ascription.

27. *Commentarius in Libros Analyticorum Posteriorum Aristotelis*

I. Inc.: Intencio Aristotelis in hoc libro est investigare et manifestare...

Expl.: ...et demonstracione in omni sillogismo se habente.

II. Publ. Venice, 1494, 1497 (asc. to *Robertus episcopus Parisiensis*), 1499, 1504 (the author has become *archiepiscopus Parisiensis*), 1514, 1521, 1537, 1552 (again *archiepiscopus*).*

III. Most of the thirteenth-century MSS ascribe the commentary to Grosseteste. Its popularity is evidenced by the comparatively large number of extant MSS, and sustained interest in it is shown by the large number of early imprints. The Vendôme MS, though containing but two columns of the commentary, has, ff. 144ᵃ–165ᵇ, the text of the *Posteriora* with copious marginalia citing or explicitly quoting from *linconiensis*. Robert Carew (*fl.* 1280)† begins his commentary on the *Posteriora*: *Testante Lincolniensi in primo Posteriorum.*‡ Duns Scotus quotes Grosseteste's commentary frequently.§ Walter Burley refers to *lincolniensis in Posteriora*, e.g. in *Super Artem Veterem* (Venice, 1519), f. 3ᴰ, and in his own *Comm. in Posteriora* (Oxford, 1517), in chap. III, near the end, and in chap. IV. Bradwardine quotes our commentary in his *De Causa Dei* (London, 1618), p. 160 f. Wyclyf quotes the work in his *De Universalibus* (Gonv. and Caius, Cambridge, MS 337, f. 45ᵇ). It was generally known to the bibliographers.||

IV. MSS:

Oxford				
Digby	207	ff. 29ᴬ–40ᴰ	XIIIᵐ	Asc.
Balliol	173ᴬ	ff. 1ᵃ–40ᵃ	XIII²	Asc.
Merton	280	ff. 107ᴬ–130ᶜ	XIV¹	Asc. *contenta*
	289	ff. 101ᴬ–124ᴮ	XIV¹	Asc.
	292	ff. 157ᴬ–184ᶜ	*ca.* 1300	Asc. XIV¹
	295	ff. 92ᴬ–119ᴰ	*ca.* 1325	Asc.
London, B.M., Add.	28873	ff. 1ᴬ–59ᶜ	1468	Asc. Ital.
Chicago, Ricketts	35	ff. 1ᵃ–61ᵃ	XVᵐ	Asc. Ital.
Erfurt, Amplon.	Q. 268	ff. 9ᴬ–34ᴰ	XIV¹	Asc. Ger.
	Q. 270	ff. 118ᵃ–159ᵃ	1390	Asc. Ger.
Florence, B.N.	I. iii. 6	ff. 39ᴬ–50ᴰ	1318	Asc. Ital.
Leipzig, Univ.	lat. 1363	ff. 1ᴬ–18ᴰ	1322	Asc. Ger., Univ.
	lat. 1365	ff. 1ᴬ–22ᴮ	*ca.* 1325	Asc. Ger.
Los Angeles, Univ. So. Cal.		ff. 1ᵃ–60ᵃ	XVᵐ	Asc. Engl.

* G. Sarton, *op. cit.* p. 585, lists an ed. "1475?" I do not know of so early an edition.

† See Powicke, *Merton Books*, p. 97 n.

‡ Bale, *Index* (ed. Poole and Bateson), p. 382.

§ See P. Minges in *Phil. Jhbh.* XXXII (1919), 242 f.

|| C. Prantl, *Gesch. d. Logik im Abendlande*, III (1867), 85, noticed that Grosseteste had used translations other than the current one of Boethius, and the commentary of Themistius on the *Posteriora*. See further the illuminating chap. XI, "Versions of Aristotle's Posterior Analytics" in C. H. Haskins' *Mediaeval Science* (Cambridge, Mass. 1927), p. 223 ff., and particularly p. 239.

Paris				
B.N.	lat. 12992	ff. 187^{B}–209^{A}	XIII^{2}	Asc. Fr.
	lat. 13204	ff. 1^{A}–8^{D}	XIV^{1}	Unasc. Fr. *mut. in fine*
	lat. 14704	ff. 1^{A}–28^{A}	XIII^{2}	Asc. Fr.
	n. a. l. 573	ff. 1^{a}–131^{b}	*ca.* 1500	Asc. Ital.
Mazarine	3473	ff. 1^{A}–14^{C}	XIII^{2}	Unasc. Fr.
Prague, Univ.	2569	ff. 1^{a}–86^{b}	XV^{1}	Asc. Boh. *mut. in fine*
Turin, B.N.	702	ff. 1^{A}–31^{C}	*ca.* 1300	Asc. Fr.
Vatican, Borghese	127	ff. 135^{A}–159^{D}	XIII^{2}	Asc.
Vendôme	171	f. 143^{C-D}	XIII^{2}	Asc. Fr.
Venice, S. Marco	VI. 150	ff. 53^{A}–63^{C}, 65^{A}–71^{D}	*ca.* 1300	Asc. So. Fr.
	VI. 222	ff. 30^{D}–81^{D}	XIV^{1}	Asc. XIV^{2} Ital.*

28. *Notule in Ethica Nicomachea et in Commentatores Grecos in eadem*

I. The first known *notula* begins: Policeia dicitur a polis quod est civitas pro quo translatores ponunt hoc nomen urbanitas...†
The last known *notula* ends ...istud ut ex altero ut quod sequitur.

II. Unpubl. as such, but a large number of these *notule* appear in Burley's *Comm. in Ethica* (Venice, 1519), ascribed to *Lincolniensis.*

III. A few of these glosses appear, in variant forms, in almost all the MSS of Grosseteste's translation of the Greek commentators of the *Nicomachean Ethics*. The glosses are sometimes incorporated into the text of the comment, sometimes appear as ascribed or unascribed marginalia. Our earliest literary authority for their existence is Hermannus Alemannus, whose remark ...*et grecorum commentis proprias annectens notulas commentatus* passed unobserved until Rose drew attention to the intercalations in the text of the Latin translations of the Greek commentators and connected them with the quotations made by Burley from Grosseteste. Grabmann (1916) remarked again upon Burley's long quotations, and Pelzer (1921) studied more closely the actual text of the Latin translation. Powicke studied (1930) Merton MS 14, a collection of some of these glosses and intercalations, but had found no MS containing anything like a complete collection of Grosseteste's *notule*. Such a MS, however, does exist, and contains almost all of the quotations found in Burley, and many which he does not cite. Unstudied before 1933, All Souls, Oxford, MS 84 is by far the most valuable of the MSS of Grosseteste's translation of the Greek commentators. It is a large codex with wide margins, copiously annotated in several early hands. The earliest of these note-hands is a small, neat chancery hand of the third quarter of the thirteenth century, a second is a neat modified chancery hand of *ca.* 1300. There may be distinguished two other note-hands of the fourteenth and early fifteenth

* See F. Ehrle, *Hist. Bibl. Aven.* (Rome, 1890), p. 337 for a copy at Avignon in 1369.

† This first *notula* appears as a gloss on the words *Quatuor partes urbanitatis* (τέτταρα δὲ πάντα τῆς πολιτείας τὰ μέρη, Heylbut, p. 3, l. 10) in the introduction of Eustratius. The first *notula* after the beginning of the text of the *Ethics* begins: *Nostri vocant primam philosophiam metaphysicam....*

centuries. The earliest hand has written, throughout the whole codex, over 300 notes varying in length from a simple gloss to a long discursive paragraph. Over 100 of these *notule* are preceded by *Epc̄* (*Episcopus*). About thirty of these 100 correspond to citations from *Lincolniensis* in Burley's *Comm. in Ethica* to which Rose, Grabmann, Pelzer and Powicke have drawn attention. There are several ascribed *notule* in Peterhouse 116 and more in the Eton MS. Many of the same *notule* appear in the Naples, Paris Arsenal MSS, in both the Florence copies and a few in the Monteprandone MS. The Balliol, Dublin, three Paris B.N., Urbino (Vatican) and Venice copies contain, so far as I have been able to discover, none of these *notule*. The Vatican lat. MS has very few. It is significant that only MSS of English provenance contain any of these *notule*. All the MSS thus far mentioned contain the combined text of the *Ethics* and the commentators. But there is one copy of the *Ethics* alone which contains a number of these *notule*, of which about a dozen are ascribed *Episcopus*. This is Worcester Cath. MS F. 63 (XIII²), ff. 1^{A}–47^{A}. In addition to the approximately 125 of these *notule* which are ascribed to Grosseteste either in one of the MSS or by Burley, we must certainly include those in the earliest note-hand in the All Souls MS and those notes in the other English MSS which are obviously of the same sort. This inclusion would make our estimate of 300 a moderate one. None of the scribes was more than casual about ascription, and many *notule* may be ascribed in one MS and not in another. We may still hope to find the *liber episcopi* which the scribe of the Eton MS had before him (f. 106^{C}).*

IV. MSS: see above, p. 69 f., under *Commentatores Greci in Ethica.*

29. *Questiones in De Celo et Mundo Aristotelis*

I. Inc.: Dubitatur hic si sciencia naturalis non transcendit...
Expl.: ...Omnia corpora tam celestia quam inferiora naturalia sunt.

II. Publ. by S. H. Thomson in *New Scholasticism*, VII (1933), 218 f.

III. The authenticity of this fragment is bound up with that of Grosseteste's *De Anima* (see below, p. 89 f.). Written by the same scribe with a break of only one line in the earliest of Grosseteste MSS, Digby 104, it pursues the same method as the *De Anima* and exhibits the same viewpoint we find Grosseteste adhering to in his other physical and cosmological works. He uses the Arab-Latin text of the *Metaphysics*, and this fact may be of some consequence in strengthening the ascription of this translation to Gerard of Cremona in preference to Michael Scot,† because of the early date which we feel must be assigned to this work, *ca.* 1215.

IV. MS:

Oxford, Digby	104	ff. 19^{D}–20^{B}	*ca.* 1215‡

* See above, p. 68 ff., for literature. I have discussed these *notule* more in detail in "The 'Notule' of Grosseteste on the 'Nicomachean Ethics'".

† See Haskins, *Mediaeval Science* (Cambridge, Mass. 1927), p. 273.

‡ For ascription see below, p. 90, under *De Anima*.

30. *Regule Libri Priorum Analyticorum Aristotelis*

I. Inc.: [prologue] Precibus tuis inductus, carissime, presumpsi facere quod rogasti...
[text] Incipiendum enim est a primis principiis materialibus per ordinem...
Expl.: ...per aliquod commune repertum in ipso.

II. Unpubl.

III. The tradition that Grosseteste was the author of some kind of commentary on the *Prior Analytics* goes back at least to the Erfurt Amplonian (1412) catalogue.* While Boston of Bury seems not to have known of it, Bale gives two titles, *Questiones Priorum lib.* 2 and *In Priora Aris. lib.* 2, beginning: *Cum omnis sciencia veri inquisitiva est.* Pits repeated the former, and Tanner, followed by Pegge, took over the latter, possibly judging the two to be the same work. Baur pointed out (p. 45*) that this work was Kilwardby's commentary on the *Prior Analytics*, well authenticated by a number of early ascribed MSS.† But Bale's *Questiones Priorum* and the item in the Amplonian catalogue remain.‡ As to the latter it is possible that Amplonius may have been misled by an ascription *Magistri Roberti* into attributing a copy of Kilwardby's work to Grosseteste. It is, furthermore, not impossible that Bale may have been in error, as we know him to have been in several cases.§ Yet we have in the Modena MS an explicit ascription of a work on the *Prior Analytics* to Grosseteste. The MS is late, yet this work is accompanied by other and authentic works in a different but contemporary hand. We have already in several places had occasion to remark how well established and authentic the Italian tradition of the philosophical works of Grosseteste proves to be. In the case of this work we may even go so far as to suggest that this unique copy is based upon an English original. There occurs repeatedly *a^ca*, which is a typical English abbreviation for *aliqua*, limited on the Continent, so far as I am aware, to copies of English MSS.

The present tractate shows no such characteristic as the citation of works posterior to Grosseteste, which render the *Summa Philosophie* unmistakably spurious, and the latinity and manner of exposition are distinctly Grossetestian. Failing better contrary evidence we are constrained to accept the attribution of the MS.

IV. MS:

Modena, Estense	lat. 54 (α. O. 7. 17)	ff. 1^{A}–48^{C}	XV^{1}	Asc. Ital.

* See F. M. Powicke, *Merton Books*, p. 116; P. Lehmann, *Mittelalterliche Bibliothekskataloge Deutschlands...*, II (Munich, 1928), 159, 218: *Exposicio librorum priorum Aristotelis Roberti Anglici*, Erfurt. Most probably Robert Kilwardby is meant. The spelling of his name caused continental scribes no little trouble. *Anglicus* was simpler.

† Add to Baur's list Bologna Univ. MS 846 (1626), ff. 1^{A}–56^{C}, XIII^{2}, asc., written in a north Italian hand. See also under *Spuria*, no. 48, p. 260.

‡ W. Schum, *Verzeichnis d. Amplon. Hss.* (Berlin, 1887), pp. 563, 795.

§ E.g. in ascribing Ockham's *Difficilia naturalis sciencie* to Grosseteste. See below, p. 247.

31. *Summa in Ethica Nicomachea*

I. Inc.: Primum capitulum de eo quod est aliquis finis perfectissimus...
Expl.: ...et qualiter ordinata et quibus legibus et consuetudinibus utens.

II. Publ. Venice, 1483, with Averroës' commentary on the *Ethics* (Hain, 1660), and Lyons, 1542.

III. This *Summa* or *abbreviacio* is often found preceding Grosseteste's translation of the Greek commentators of the *Nicomachean Ethics*. Bale identified the work as *Commentarii in Ethica Lib.* 10,* and lists another work *Questiones Ethicorum Lib.* 10. Leland claims to have seen a *Questiones Ethicorum Lib.* 10 among the MSS of Grosseteste in *bibliotheca Carmelitarum* in London. Pits, Tanner and Pegge mention a *Summa in Ethica*. Pelzer ("Les versions latines...", p. 337 ff.) cleared up the confusion introduced into the question by Baur's misunderstanding (p. 24* ff.) of the tradition. Pelzer furthermore found the Vendôme MS, which Baur had supposed, as MS 104, to be lost, to be in reality MS 105. Powicke corrected the erroneous transcription of the *secundum R.* in Coxe's catalogue description of the Merton MS.

IV. MSS:

Oxford				
All Souls	84	ff. 1^{A}–10^{A}	XIII^{m}	Unasc.†
Merton	14	ff. 326^{A}–329^{D}	XIII^{m}	Asc.
Cambridge, Peterhouse	116	ff. 1^{A}–11^{C}	XIII^{2}	Unasc.
Berlin	lat. 8° 142	ff. 131^{A}–154^{D}	1325	Asc. Ger.‡
Florence, Laur.	Pl. VI dext. v	f. 119^{a} ff.	XIII^{2}	Asc. Engl.§
Naples, B.N.	VIII. G. 4	ff. 1^{A}–9^{B}	XIII^{m}	Asc. Engl.
Paris, B.N.	lat. 17811	ff. 1^{A}–11^{C}	*ca.* 1300	Unasc. Engl.
	lat. 17832	ff. 283^{a}–299^{a}	*ca.* 1300	Unasc. Engl.
Reims	876	ff. 165^{C}–175^{C}	*ca.* 1300	Unasc. Fr.
Vatican, Urbinat. lat.	221	ff. 188^{a}–242^{a}	1483	Unasc. Ital.
Vendôme	105	ff. 93^{A}–98^{D}	XIII^{2}	Asc. Fr.

* *Index* (ed. Poole and Bateson), p. 372.

† Not noticed in Coxe's catalogue.

‡ The rubric reads: *Incipit sentencia ethicorum Aristotelis abreviata a domino Lynconiensi qui et ipsa transtulit de greco in latinum de eo quod est....* The colophon reads: ...*Sentencia libri ethicorum Aristotelis abreviata a domino Roperto Lynconiense grossi capitis scripta Parisius per manus Conradi de Saxonia a. d. MCCCXXV° sequenti die b. Andree apostoli.* See P. Lehmann, "Mittheilungen aus Hss. IV." *Sbte d. Bayer. Akad.* (Munich, 1933, Abhg 9), p. 27 ff.

§ See Pelzer, *op. cit.* p. 338.

PHILOSOPHICAL AND SCIENTIFIC WORKS

32. *De Accessu et Recessu Maris* (*De Fluxu et Refluxu Maris*)

I. Inc.: Intendentes de accessione et recessione maris, intendendum est...
Expl.: ...via secundum magis et minus.

II. Unpubl.

III. Unnoticed by any of the bibliographers, and apparently unquoted by any of Grosseteste's contemporaries, this short *questio* was discovered by Pelster in Assisi MS 138 in 1926.* The early ascription (*ca.* 1225): *De fluxu et refluxu maris a magistro Roberto Exonie*† *in scolis suis determinata*, fixes at least the *terminus ad quem*. The use of the title *magister* shows that the work was composed before the episcopal period. The expression *in scolis suis* would, furthermore, point to a time before the lectureship to the Franciscans, i.e. before 1229. See also below, p. 117, under *De Subsistencia Rei*, in the same MS.

IV. MSS:

Assisi, Comun.	138	ff. 261^{D}–262^{B}	*ca.* 1225	Asc. Engl.‡
Florence, Marucell.	C. 163	ff. 18^{A}–19^{C}	*ca.* 1400	Asc. Ital.
Prague, Nat. Mus.	XII. E. 5	ff. 41^{C}–42^{A}	XIV^{m}	Asc. Boh.
Vatican, Barb. lat.	165	ff. 402^{D}–403^{B}	1288	Unasc. Ger.§

33. *De Anima*

I. Inc.: Multi circa animam erraverunt. Quidam posuerunt...
Expl.: ...aut diminutive voluntatem imperfectam.

II. Publ. by Baur, pp. 242–274, as a *dubium*.

III. Leland‖ was the first bibliographer to ascribe a tractate *De Anima* to Grosseteste, and gave the incipit of this tractate. He had, no doubt, seen this unique MS when it was at Fountains Abbey. William of Ware (*fl.* 1280) quotes our treatise explicitly in his *Comm. in IV Sent.* (Vatican MS lat. 1115, f. 24^{a}) from a passage found in Baur's ed. on p. 253, ll. 10–12. Wyclyf,

* See *Scholastik*, I, 576 f.

† *Exonia* is occasionally found, even in English MSS of the thirteenth century, for *Oxonia*.

‡ The hand of this part of the codex may be French, but it was probably written in Oxford, to judge from the presence in the codex of other Oxford *questiones*. The last part of the codex, ff. 286–291, is clearly in an English hand.

§ Rubric reads: *Incipit tractatus de fluxu maris Boecii.* Only first half of work, ending ...*ut patet ultima proposicione de speculis*, followed immediately by the *De Iride*, q.v., p. 105.

‖ See *Collectanea*, IV (Oxford, 1715), 45.

in his *Trialogus* (ed. Lechler, Oxford, 1869, p. 113), cites the *De Anima* of Grosseteste in a clear reference to the argument on p. 254 of Baur's ed. Some confusion has arisen because an early copy (Digby 172, ff. 1^{A}–6^{B}, *ca.* 1325) of Walter Burley's unpublished *De Potenciis Anime* (Inc.: *Sicut dicit philosophus 2° de Anima...*) is ascribed in a hand of the first half of the fourteenth century to *lincolniensis*. But in addition to unanimity of ascription to Burley in the other MSS of this work, it quotes works of Albertus Magnus that were not written until after Grosseteste's death. The ascription in our MS of the *De Anima* is of the third quarter of the thirteenth century, *ca.* 1260–1270; it reads: *Tractatus beati Roberti Grosteste episcopi de Anima*. The internal evidence is strongly corroborative.* Father Leo Keeler pointed out, in a recent discussion of this work,† that it is most probable that the *De Anima* is a *reportacio* of lectures of Philip the Chancellor of Paris, delivered in the years 1208–1210. But Keeler also remarks that there is no inconsiderable amount of original matter, more strongly Augustinian than the thought of the Chancellor, and a frequent re-ordering of the subjects treated. The suggestion of Englhardt that the *De Anima* is dependent upon the *Summa* of Philip‡ is rejected by Keeler. The *Summa* was not edited until about 1230, and the unique MS of the *De Anima* could under no conditions have been written so late. Keeler adds corroboration from internal grounds. The work is undoubtedly one of the earliest of Grosseteste's works, only partially his own, written at Paris *ca.* 1208–1210.

IV. MS:

Oxford, Digby	104	ff. 1^{A}–19^{D}	*ca.* 1215	Asc. *ca.* 1260

34. *De Libero Arbitrio I*

I. Inc.: Quia circa rerum esse potest esse dubitacio, questionum...
Expl.: ...hoc ideo quia diu de hac materia disputavimus.

II. Publ. by Baur, pp. 150–241.

III. That Grosseteste wrote a treatise with this title has been known to all the bibliographers from Boston of Bury to Baur, who lists all their citations. The work was frequently cited by Bradwardine in his *De Causa Dei* (ed. London, 1618);§ by his contemporary, Thomas of Buckingham (†1350), in his *Questiones Contra Errores Pelagii* (MSS Merton 143, f. 8^{B}, and New College 134, f. 329^{C}); and at least once by Wyclyf (*De Ente Predicamentali*, p. 73). The early Laurentian MS, of English provenance, has the colophon: *Expliciunt questiones magistri Roberti Grossetet*. The simple *magister* in the

* I have discussed the authenticity and date of this work more fully in "The *De Anima* of Robert Grosseteste" in *New Scholasticism*, VII (1933), 201–221, with a reduced reproduction of the first page of the MS.

† "The Dependence of R. Grosseteste's *De Anima* on the *Summa* of Philip the Chancellor" in *New Scholasticism*, XI (1937), 197–219.

‡ *Die Entwicklung d. Glaubenspsychologie in d. mittelalterlichen Scholastik...* (*Beiträge*, 1933), pp. 200–201. See also Dom Lottin in *Rech. de Théol. anc. et méd.*, Bulletin, Oct. 1934, p. 366, Dom Pouillon, *ibid.*, Bulletin, Oct. 1937, p. 167 ff., and F. Pelster in *Scholastik*, XIII (1938), 441.

§ For numerous quotations see Baur's ed., p. 152 *et passim*.

colophon and the whole tenor of the work require an early date. I suggest *ca.* 1225.

IV. MSS:

Worcester Cath.	F. 152	ff. 1A–10D	XIV²	Asc.
Florence				
Laur.	Pl. XVIII dext. VII	ff. 249B–265A	XIII^m	Asc. Engl.
Marucell.	C. 163	ff. 22D–31C	*ca.* 1400	Asc. Ital. *mut. in fine*

According to the *contenta* (XIV^m) in Exeter Coll., Oxford, MS 28, this work was originally in that codex as well as Recension II. It is described as *lincolniensis de libero arbitrio aliter quam prius.* Bale may have seen this MS since he cites the incipit of this recension as in this MS. See *Index*, p. 377.

35. *De Libero Arbitrio II*

I. Inc.: Cum per arbitrii libertatem dignior sit homo ceteris...
Expl.: ...cui accidit esse divine voluntati contrarium.

II. Publ. by Baur, pp. 150–226, as Recension II.

III. The authenticity is assured by the valuable Exeter Coll. MS and the fact that the work is indubitably a recension of the preceding item, q.v. Baur's manner of printing the two works shows the great amount of common material. See Baur, p. 107* ff. for Bradwardine's use of this shorter recension. This work was known to Boston of Bury, Wharton, Cave, Bale and Tanner.

IV. MSS:

Oxford				
Jones	15	pp. 1–85	XVII²	Asc.*
Exeter	28	ff. 296B–305B	*ca.* 1325	Asc.
Dublin, Marsh's Lib.	3. 6. 20	pp. 1–70	XVII^m	Unasc.†

Tanner had noted this work in what is now B.M. Cotton Otho D. x before the fire of 1731 which seriously damaged the codex. A large part of the MS is completely gone, and much of what is left is shrivelled beyond recognition. There is no reason to doubt the evidence of Tanner. This MS is slightly later than the Exeter copy.

36. *De Artibus Liberalibus* (*De Utilitate Arcium*)

I. Inc.: In operibus humanis triplici de causa ingerit se error...
Expl.: ...duracione et quantitate preparacio medicine.

II. Publ. Venice, 1514, f. 2A–D; Baur, pp. 1–7.

* A copy of the Exeter MS.

† Mr Newport B. White, Librarian of Marsh's Library, kindly informs me that a note on p. 1 reads: *E Mss^to Bibliothece Coll. Exon. apud Oxon.*, and that the shelf-mark would suggest that the codex was among Archbishop Marsh's own MSS.

III. There seems to be no specific external reference to this treatise before the Venice edition. Bale (*Index*, p. 377) cites a C.C.C., Oxford, MS which appears now to be lost. Yet his notice has value, particularly when combined with that of Leland who (*Collectanea*, IV, 21) cites a MS in Gonv. and Caius, Cambridge, and another in the Bodleian, neither of which is known at present. Baur, writing in 1912, remarked (p. 56*) that the tradition was not older than the fifteenth century. One of our MSS, however, is of the middle of the fourteenth century, and the presence of this work in five of the physical collections assures its genuineness. It is known to the later bibliographers from the Venice edition and Anthony à Wood.

It is the polished work of a man who is sure of his ground and, though covering a considerable range in a short compass—the seven arts—shows the pre-episcopal Grosseteste at his best. Baur remarks on the similarity of style and thought to the *Hexameron* (see below, p. 100 f.) and *Dictum* 1, but it is certainly much less theological than the *Dictum*, and less philosophical than the *Hexameron*. From the nature of the subject-matter it seems reasonable to place the work in the early years of Grosseteste's chancellorship and to regard it as an attempted formulation of the aims of the study of the *artes liberales*.

IV. MSS:

Florence, Marucell.	C. 163	ff. 2^{C}–3^{D}	*ca.* 1400	Asc. Ital.
Modena, Estense	lat. 649	ff. 4^{B}–6^{A}	*ca.* 1500	Asc. Ital.
Prague				
Univ.	1990	ff. 48^{a}–50^{a}	1472	Asc. Boh.★
Nat. Mus.	XII. E. 5	ff. 40^{D}–41^{A}	XIV^{m}	Asc. Boh.★
Venice, S. Marco	VI. 163	ff. 82^{A}–83^{D}	XIV^{2}	Asc. Ital.

In Dresden, Landesbibliothek, MS N. 100, f. 304^{b} (written in Cracow, 1487–1488) is a short extract *Linconiensis in tractatu de erroribus humanis* beginning: *Nulla enim aut reata est operacio que nature sit et nostra....* It is a rather free variant of a paragraph of the *De Art. Lib.* (ed. Baur, p. 4, l. 19 ff.) and the title suggests some connection with the Prague Museum MS.

37. *De Calore Questio*

I. Inc.: Calor qualitas sensibilis passio est et accidens...
Expl.: ...frigidior terra. Ita solvunt. Vos discutite.

II. Unpubl.

III. This paragraph appears in only one MS, Madrid B.N. 3314, between Grosseteste's *De Calore Solis* and the longer, hitherto unnoticed, recension of the *De Cometis*. Other Grosseteste items follow, the *De Iride* and *De Colore*. The tone of the *questio* is typical of Grosseteste's "Lichtmetaphysik", and its presence among other unascribed genuine works gives it the same authenticity. It seems not to have been noticed before. It would probably best be assigned to the period preceding the lectureship to the Franciscans, say 1220–1225.

★ Entitled *Tractatus de Erroribus Humanis*.

IV. MS:

Madrid, B.N.	3314	ff. 89^{D}–90^{A}	XIII^{m}	Unasc. Engl.

38. *De Calore Solis*

I. Inc.: Cum principalis intencio nostra sit de calore solis...
Expl.: ...et propterea maior disgregacio et calor.

II. Publ. Venice, 1514, ff. 3^{D}–4^{A}; Baur, pp. 79–84, using only the Venice edition and the Venice MS.

III. The presence of this work in the valuable Madrid MS and in four of the Continental physical collections places its genuineness beyond doubt. It is most probable that this is the work to which Roger Bacon referred in the *Opus Maius* (ed. Bridges, I, 108 and 167) under the title *De Generacione Caloris*. Tanner and Pegge mention the treatise by name without indicating any MS, most probably from the Venice edition.

IV. MSS:

Florence, Marucell.	C. 163	ff. 4^{B}–5^{B}	*ca.* 1400	Asc. Ital.
Madrid, B.N.	3314	f. 89^{C-D}	XIII^{m}	Unasc. Engl.
Modena, Estense	lat. 649	ff. 7^{A}–8^{B}	*ca.* 1500	Asc. Ital.
Prague, Nat. Mus.	XII. E. 5	f. 42^{B}	XIV^{m}	Asc. Boh.
Venice, S. Marco	VI. 163	ff. 84^{C}–85^{D}	XIV^{2}	Asc. Ital.

39. *De Colore (De Coloribus)*

I. Inc.: Color est lux incorporata perspicuo. Perspicui vero due sunt...
Expl.: ...omnes modos colorum, quos voluerint ostendere possunt.

II. Publ. Venice, 1514, f. 4^{C-D}; Baur, p. 78 f.

III. This work was known to Bartholomeus Anglicus (†1250 or 1275),* who quotes it in his *De Proprietatibus Rerum* (Bk. XIX, chap. 7) without, however, naming the author.† It is ascribed to Grosseteste by Boston of Bury, Leland, Bale, Pits, Wood, Tanner and Pegge. A number of MSS cited by some of these bibliographers appear to be lost. The work is found in the principal physical collections and elsewhere, ascribed or with an ascribed work. The use of this work by Bartholomeus might help us to date its composition, but, beyond the fact that the *De Proprietatibus* was begun in Paris after 1230, we cannot be sure of our data. This work of Grosseteste falls in the group on which his early fame was founded. A date shortly before 1220 seems likely.

IV. MSS:

Oxford, Digby	98	f. 154^{a}	*ca.* 1400	Asc.
	104	f. 110^{D}	XIV^{1}	Unasc. Engl.‡
	190	ff. 199^{b}–200^{a}	XIII^{m}	Unasc.§
	220	f. 107^{C-D}	XV^{1}	Asc.

* See Ueberweg-Geyer, *Die patristische und scholastische Zeit* (Berlin, 1928), p. 379, for literature. A long-standing confusion with the later Bartholomeus de Glanvilla has rendered investigation of his *cursus vitae* difficult.

† See Baur, p. 85*.

‡ With *De Luce* and *De Iride*. § With asc. *De Iride*.

London, B.M.				
Cotton	Otho D. x	f. 61^b	XIV^m	Asc.
Royal	6. E. v	f. 243^C	XIV^m	Asc.
Florence, Marucell.	C. 163	ff. 5^D–6^A	*ca.* 1400	Asc. Ital.
Madrid, B.N.	3314	f. 91^A	XIII^m	Unasc. Engl.
Modena, Estense	lat. 396	f. 9^{B-D}	*ca.* 1500	Asc. Ital.
Prague, Nat. Mus.	XII. E. 5	f. 42^{B-C}	XIV^m	Asc. Boh.
Venice, S. Marco	VI. 163	ff. 86^D–87^A	XIV^2	Asc. Ital.

40. *De Cometis et Causis Ipsarum*

I. Inc.: Occasione comete que nuper apparuit...
Expl.: ...vel stella alia de natura planete.

II. Publ. by S. H. Thomson in *Isis*, XIX (April, 1933), 21–25.

III. Roger Bacon (*Comp. Stud. Phil.* chap. 8; ed. Brewer, p. 469) mentions a tractate *De Cometis* by Grosseteste. The two recensions that have appeared, ascribed in late MSS to Grosseteste and edited by Baur, pp. 36–41, are really two separate treatises: the first an awkward abridged rearrangement of the real *De Cometis*, and the second an abstract on the nine comets from Ptolemy's *Almagest*. See below, p. 112. Leland, Bale, Pits and Tanner list a *De Cometis*, but the MSS they cite do not offer the text at all. Our text, found in the Riccardiana MS, unascribed, but with some works of Roger Bacon, was ascribed to Bacon by A. G. Little (*Roger Bacon Essays*, Oxford, 1914, p. 379, item 12).*

IV. MSS:

(*a*) Baltimore, Garrett	95	ff. 17^a–18^b	XV^1	Asc. Engl.
Florence				
Marucell.	C. 163	ff. 20^D–21^B	*ca.* 1400	Asc. Ital.
Riccard.	885	ff. 213^a–214^b	XIII^2	Unasc. Engl.?

The text is also found, with variants so considerable as almost to warrant calling it a longer recension or a reworking, in Madrid, B.N. MS 3314, f. 90^{A-B}, XIII^m, Engl., unasc., but with other Grosseteste opuscula. See above, p. 92 f., and below, pp. 105 f. and 110 f.

(*b*) Abridged rearrangement, ed. Baur, pp. 36–41:
Inc.: Relictis opinionibus de natura tricarum...
Expl.: ...destruitur et veritas assumatur, ut patet supra.

MS: Berlin	lat. 963	ff. 129^B–130^A	XV^m	Asc. Ger.

41. *Compotus I* (fourteen chapters)

I. Inc.: Multiplex est annus, scilicet solaris et lunaris, quia secundum cursum...
Expl.: ...quod mora. Unde Boecius: Quid tempus ab evo ire iubes.

II. Unpubl.

* See further S. H. Thomson, "The Text of Grosseteste's *De Cometis*", *Isis*, XIX (1933), 19 ff., and corrections to the text by E. Franceschini, "Intorno ad alcune opere di Roberto Grossatesta, Vescovo di Lincoln" in *Aevum, Rivista di Scienze Storiche Linguistiche e Filologiche*, VIII (1934), 529–533.

III. This *Compotus*, not noticed by any bibliographer, appears to exist in a single MS. Its authenticity is assured by the early (XIII^1) ascription. The whole text should be compared with the *Compotus Correctorius* (see next item), but it would appear that the present work antedates the *Kalendarium*, which, in turn, is corrected by the *Compotus Correctorius*, and that some years later (1244) Grosseteste found it necessary to bring his calculations again up to date (see below, p. 97, *Compotus Minor*). In view of his interest in the reckoning of time and Arabic mathematics as early as 1215 (see Introd. p. 30 ff.), a date of composition before 1220 would seem to be indicated. The chapter headings are as follows: 1. *De duplici anno*, 2. *De septimana*, 3. *De mense*, 4. *De anno etc.*, 5. *De concurrentibus*, 6. *De regulari solari*, 7. *De bissexto quid sit*, 8. *De ciclo solari*, 9. *De divisione anni in quattuor partes*, 10. *De anno lunari*, 11. *De epactis et regularibus*, 12. *De regulari lunari*, 13. *De saltu lune*, 14. *De festis mobilibus*.

IV. MSS:

Oxford, Bodl.	679	ff. 65^a–75^a	XIII^1	Asc.*

42. *Compotus Correctorius* (twelve chapters)

I. Inc.: Capitulum primum de causa bissexti... [*Summa Capitulorum* often prefixed]

Compotus est sciencia numeracionis et divisionis temporum...

Expl.: ...Ut ieiunemus nos admonet atque Matheus. [Some MSS have a short epilogue ending ...*consuetudinibus est permissa*]

II. Publ. Venice, 1518; by R. Steele as appendix, pp. 212–267, to Roger Bacon's *Compotus* (Oxford, 1928), from B.M. Add. MS 27589 with variants from Harley MS 3735.

III. Many of the thirteenth-century MSS are ascribed. Roger Bacon used this *Compotus* (ed. Steele, p. 40)† as did Campanus (†1267) in his *Compendium* (Venice, 1518). The large number of early MSS testifies to its popularity until the beginning of the fourteenth century. But the relative absence of later copies would indicate that other *compoti* superseded it. The bibliographical tradition is specific from Boston of Bury onwards.

Steele dates the work (*ed. cit.* p. xxi) as contemporary with the *Compotus* of Sacro Bosco (i.e. 1232), but remarks that Grosseteste appears to be more familiar than Sacro Bosco with Arabic astronomy. But as we know that Grosseteste was interested in Arabic mathematics at least as early as 1215 (see Introd. p. 30 ff.), we are not obliged to consider so late a date. Certainly as early as 1229, and until after 1240, his interests were almost exclusively theological and pastoral, including, of course, in that category his translations from the Greek. We have no known evidence for his pursuit of any purely

* For other important items in this valuable codex see my note "Eine ältere und vollständigere Hs. von Gundissalinus 'De divisione scientiarum'" in *Scholastik*, VIII (1933), 240–242.

† See Baur, p. 42*.

scientific subject between these two approximate dates. As this *Compotus* was written professedly to correct (*ed. cit.* pp. 212, 214 *et passim*) the *Kalendarium*, and the early *Compotus* (see preceding item) must also be accounted for, we have three similar or related works which we should place between the years 1215 and 1229 in this order: *Compotus I*, *Kalendarium*, *Compotus Correctorius*. Duhem made the mistake of regarding the *Compotus* and the *Kalendarium* as the same work.* He further asserted, because Grosseteste used the Paris meridian for his computations, that the work was written "au début de sa carrière, lorsqu'il enseignait à l'université de Paris". This might conceivably be true, but it is neither demonstrable nor necessary.†

IV. MSS:

Oxford				
Digby	17	ff. 41^a–68^a	XVI^1	Asc.
	28	ff. 86^a–97^b	XIV^1	Asc.‡
	191	ff. 103^a–124^b	XIII^1	Asc.
	228	ff. 20^A–27^B	*ca.* 1325	Asc.
Laud. Misc.	644	ff. 147^D–162^C	1277	Asc.§
Savile	21	ff. 127^a–141^a	XIII^2	Asc.
C.C.C.	260	pp. 11–81	XVII^1	Asc.
Univ. Coll.	41	ff. 3^a–9^a	*ca.* 1300	Asc. XIV^m
London, B.M.				
Add.	27589	ff. 77^A–100^D	XIII^m	Asc.‖
Harley	3735	ff. 82^C–105^B	XIII^2	Asc. Fr.
	4350	ff. 68^a–111^a	XIII^m	Unasc. Fr.
Cambridge				
Univ.	Kk. i. 1	ff. 178^a–191^a	XIII^m	Unasc.
C.C.C.	439	ff. 2^A–13^D	XV^1	Asc.
Gonv. & Caius	141	ff. 57^a–90^b	XIV^1	Asc.
Pembroke	278	ff. 1^a–24^b	1299	Asc.
St John's	162	ff. 1^A–29^C	XIII^1	Asc.§
Dublin, Trinity	441 (D. 4. 27)	ff. 100^b–121^a	*ca.* 1300	Asc.
Berlin	lat. 957	ff. 1^A–12^D	XIII^2	Unasc. Rh.
Erfurt, Amplon.	O. 82	ff. 122^A–156^B	XIII^2	Asc. Fr.
Florence				
Laur.	Pl. XI, dext. III	ff. 124^A–139^B	XIII^2	Unasc. Fr.§
Riccard.	885	ff. 224^A–248^B	XIII^2	Unasc. Engl.?§
Munich	Clm. 14448	ff. 54^b–69^b	XIII^2	Asc. Fr.¶
Paris, B.N.	lat. 7195	ff. 93^A–115^D	*ca.* 1300	Asc. Engl.
	lat. 7255	ff. 147^b–155^a	XIII^m	Asc. Engl.
	lat. 7298	ff. 89^C–107^B	*ca.* 1300	Asc. So. Fr.
	lat. 7374^A	ff. 59^a–76^a	XIII^2	Asc. Engl.§
Toledo, Cabildo	8°. 98. 28	ff. 82^a–120^a	XIII^m	Asc. Engl.§
Vatican				
Pal. lat.	1414	ff. 44^A–61^B	XIII^2	Asc. Lowl.
Urbinat. lat.	1428	ff. 117^a–174^b	XIII^m	Asc. Fr.

* *Système du Monde*, III (Paris, 1915), 280 ff.

† For the influence of this work on Bacon's thought, see Baur, "Einfluss d. Grossetestes..." in *Bacon Essays*, p. 44.

‡ Ends in chap. XI. § With epilogue.

‖ In the rubric: *factus ad correccionem kalendarii nostri.*

¶ With anonymous commentary.

43. *Compotus Minor*

I. Inc.: Que vel dimissa sunt in alio tractatu compoti vel minus lucide...
Expl.: ...et dicitur evum ad quod mora. Unde Boecius qui tempus ab evo ire iubes.

II. Unpubl.

III. The authenticity of this previously unnoticed *compotus* is clearly indicated in the Dublin MS. The opening sentence mentions the writer's *alius tractatus compoti*. The work is conveniently dated for us, f. 107[b], *sed nativitate Domini elapsi sunt* 1200 *anni et eo scilicet* 44 *amplius, in quo numero sunt decies centum et decies* 20. There is a further reference, f. 108[a], to his *Kalendarium* (q.v. below, p. 106 f.). Much of the *Compotus Correctorius* reappears.

IV. MS:

Dublin, Trinity	441 (D. 4. 27)	ff. 104[b]–111[a]	*ca.* 1325	Asc.*

44. *De Differenciis Localibus* (*De Sex Differenciis*)

I. Inc.: Differenciarum idem genus condividencium nulla...
Expl.: ...corrupcionis habent, sicut satis notum est.

II. Publ. Venice, 1514, f. 14[A–B]; Baur, pp. 84–87.

III. Tanner and Wharton mention the two MSS now in the B.M. There has not been noticed, thus far, any external evidence for the use of this short work that would antedate the Venice edition. The presence of the treatise in the seven physical collections would guarantee its authenticity, which is strongly confirmed both by the style and by the physical theory. Its composition is most probably to be placed in the period when he was *in scolis* (see above, p. 89). The method is scholastic; the only quotations are from the *Physics* and the *De Celo et Mundo*.

IV. MSS:

London, B.M.				
Cotton	Otho D. x	f. 52[a–b]	XIV[m]	Asc.†
Royal	6. E. v	f. 245[B–C]	XIV[m]	Asc.
Baltimore, Garrett	95	ff. 20[b]–21[a]	XV[1]	Asc. Engl.
Florence, Marucell.	C. 163	ff. 8[D]–9[B]	*ca.* 1400	Asc. Ital.
Modena, Estense	lat. 649	ff. 14[D]–15[C]	*ca.* 1500	Asc. Ital.
Prague, Nat. Mus.	XII. E. 5	f. 43[B]	XIV[m]	Asc. Boh.
Venice, S. Marco	VI. 163	ff. 90[D]–91[B]	XIV[2]	Asc. Ital.

* Asc. in the *contenta a.m. coeva*. See below, p. 234, under *Ars Algorismi* (*dubium*).

† Baur asserts that this MS is lost (p. 88*).

45. *De Finitate Motus et Temporis*

I. Inc.: Primum argumentum quod ponit Aristoteles ad probandum...
Expl.: ...et tempus cum cessabit hominum generacio.

II. Publ. Venice, 1514, ff. 9^{D}–10^{B}; Baur, pp. 101–106.

III. Baur has pointed out (pp. 93*–95*) that this work is really the concluding section of Grosseteste's *Comm. in Physica Aristotelis*, very slightly abridged. He has further remarked on parallels with passages in the *Hexameron*. The separate appearance of this section, ascribed to Grosseteste, in five of the physical collections supports, therefore, the early ascription of the complete commentary. How or by whom this section came to be separated from the body of the commentary we do not yet know. But that such separation took place quite early is evident from the fact that it appears in three separate traditions: the Cotton MS, of English tradition; in three Italian collections, whose prototype we suspect of being an early English MS; and the Prague copy, of an independent but excellent tradition. In this last codex the work* has as a prologue the preceding paragraph of the commentary, indicating probably an earlier attempt at excerpting from the commentary subject-matter which would make a satisfactory and coherent short treatise on the non-eternity of the world.

IV. MSS (only MSS of this excerpt are noted; for the complete *Commentarius* see above, p. 82):

London, B.M., Cotton	Otho D. x	ff. 49^{b}–51^{a}	XIV^{m}	Asc.
Florence, Marucell.	C. 163	f. 15^{A-D}	*ca.* 1400	Asc. Ital.
Modena, Estense	lat. 649	f. 24^{A-B}	*ca.* 1500	Asc. Ital.
Prague, Nat. Mus.	XII. E. 5	ff. 43^{C}–44^{A}	XIV^{m}	Asc. Boh.
Venice, S. Marco	VI. 163	ff. 99^{B}–100^{A}	XIV^{2}	Asc. Ital.

46. *De Forma Prima Omnium (De Unica Forma Omnium)*

I. Inc.: Dilecto sibi in Christo magistro Ade Rufo Robertus...
Rogavit me dulciflua dileccio tua, quatenus scriberem tibi...
Expl.: ...perfecte et ei ex omni parte simile fingere.

II. Publ. Venice, 1514, f. 6^{A-B}; Luard, *Epistolae*, pp. 1–7; Baur, pp. 106–111.

III. Appearing in the earliest MSS as a separate treatise, this work is *Epistola* 1 in the collection of Grosseteste's letters which must go back to *ca.* 1300 (see below, p. 192). Apart from the salutation and an occasional lapse into a conversational manner, it maintains the character of a purely metaphysical disquisition. Our oldest copy is the work of an Italian scribe. Luard (p. xcix) dated it before 1210 on the ground that the salutation does not indicate that Grosseteste had any preferment at the time of writing. But in many of his pre-episcopal works and references to himself the simple title

* It is entitled *Tractatus de errore philosophorum ponencium perpetuitatem motus et temporis eiusdem d. l.* and begins *Perpetuitas motus i. e. carencia principii et finis*. The *Primum argumentum Aristotelis* begins about one third way down the column.

magister is all that appears. Though we may doubt the specific date, it must be reckoned among his early works. There are many striking parallels between this work,* with its appendage, *De Intelligenciis* (q.v.) and the *De Anima* (q.v.), which we have dated *ca.* 1215. Pecham refers to it in one of his letters (*Epistola* DCLXI in *Registrum Epistt. Fr. Joh. Peckham*, III (ed. C. T. Martin, London, 1885), 923); Wyclyf quotes it extensively (*De Apostasia*, p. 135; *De Ente Predicamentali*, pp. 147–149; *De Materia et Forma*, in *Misc. Phil.* I, 171; *De Veritate Sacre Scripture*, I, 38).† The work is mentioned by all the bibliographers, without, however, separating it from the *De Intelligenciis*.

IV. MSS:

Oxford				
Bodl.	312	f. 126^{A-D}	XIV^{2}	Asc.‡
Digby	220	f. 81^{A-D}	XV^{1}	Unasc.§
Queen's	312	ff. 1^{A-C}	XIV^{m}	Asc.‡
London, B.M.				
Cotton	Otho D. x	ff. 52^{b}–53^{b}	XIV^{m}	Asc.‡
Royal	6. E. v	ff. 245^{C}–246^{B}	XIV^{m}	Asc.
Cambridge				
C.C.C.	123	f. 64^{a-b}	1456	Asc.
	453	ff. 1^{a}–3^{a}	*ca.* 1400	Asc.
Sid. Suss.	92, pt. ii	p. 1 ff.	XVII	Asc.‖
Florence, Marucell.	C. 163	ff. 9^{B}–10^{B}	*ca.* 1400	Asc. Ital.
Modena, Estense	lat. 396	ff. 15^{C}–16^{D}	*ca.* 1500	Asc. Ital.
Prague				
Univ.	763	ff. 1^{a}–3^{b}	*ca.* 1410	Asc. Boh.‡
	1990	ff. 42^{a}–43^{b}	1472	Asc. Boh.
Metrop. Chap.	272	ff. 2^{a}–4^{b}	*ca.* 1425	Asc. Boh.‡
	509	ff. 175^{A}–176^{D}	XV^{1}	Asc. Boh.‡
	1572	ff. 1^{a}–3^{a}	XV^{1}	Asc. Boh.‡
Venice, S. Marco	VI. 163	ff. 91^{B}–92^{D}	XIV^{2}	Asc. Ital.
Vercelli, Capit.	72	front flyleaf	XIII^{2}	Asc. Ital.‡

47. *De Generacione Sonorum*

I. Inc.: Cum sonativum percutitur violenter, partes ipsius...
Expl.: ...formandas consonantes sicut inclinaciones accidentales.

II. Publ. Venice, 1514, ff. 2^{D}–3^{B}; Baur, pp. 7–10.

III. Baur used but two MSS for his edition, the Venice and the Prague Univ. copies. As he pointed out (p. 58* f.) there are verbal parallels between this work, the *De Artibus Liberalibus* and Grosseteste's *Comm. in Post. Anal.*,

* P. Duhem, *Système du Monde*, V (Paris, 1917), 351 ff., translates parts of the work.

† Baur mentions a reference to this letter in the *Questiones logice et philosophice*, published with the *De Ente Predicamentali*, p. 261. These *questiones* are not by Wyclyf, but by later Bohemians. See S. H. Thomson, "Some Latin Works..." in *Speculum*, III (1928), 382–391.

‡ Appears in this MS with *De Intelligenciis*.

§ *Mut. in init.* Begins *quosdam versus*..., i.e. ed. Baur, p. 107, l. 11. With *De Intelligenciis*.

‖ A note on the flyleaf tells that it was copied from *libro imperfecto in biblioteca dunelmi*.

and he argued that the present work was a first draft of matter later incorporated into the commentary. The texts might bear that interpretation. It is, however, more likely that the *De Gen. Son.*, longer than the corresponding section in the commentary, is a later reworking of matter which seemed to demand fuller treatment than the natural limits of a commentary had previously warranted. In any case the three treatises are closely connected. The *De Gen. Son.* is not mentioned by any bibliographer before Tanner, in spite of its publication in the 1514 Venice edition.

IV. MSS:

Baltimore, Garrett	95	ff. 1^a–2^b	XV^1	Asc. Engl.*
Florence, Marucell.	C. 163	ff. 3^D–4^B	*ca.* 1400	Asc. Ital.
Modena, Estense	lat. 54	ff. 73^b–74^a	XV^m	Asc. Ital.
	lat. 649	ff. 6^A–7^A	*ca.* 1500	Asc. Ital.
Prague				
Univ.	1990	ff. 47^a–48^a	1472	Asc. Boh.
Nat. Mus.	XII. E. 5	f. 41^{A-B}	XIV^m	Asc. Boh.
Venice, S. Marco	VI. 163	ff. 83^D–84^C	XIV^2	Asc. Ital.

48. *De Generacione Stellarum*

I. Inc.: Res eiusdem nature eiusdem operacionis secundum naturam...
Expl.: ...corruptibile quam corruptibile fieri incorruptibile.

II. Publ. Venice, 1514, f. 4^{A-C}; Baur, pp. 32–36.

III. The tract is found in four of the continental collections of Grosseteste's works, of which only one, the Venice copy, was known to Baur. Wyclyf quotes it in his *De Actibus Anime* (*Misc. Phil.* I, 76). Although printed in the early Venice edition, it is not mentioned by any bibliographer until Tanner, and, from Tanner, by Pegge.

IV. MSS:

Florence, Marucell.	C. 163	f. 5^{B-D}	*ca.* 1400	Asc. Ital.
Modena, Estense	lat. 649	ff. 8^B–9^B	*ca.* 1500	Asc. Ital.
Prague, Nat. Mus.	XII. E. 5	f. 42^B	XIV^m	Asc. Boh.
Venice, S. Marco	VI. 163	ff. 85^D–86^D	XIV^2	Asc. Ital.

49. *Hexameron*

I. Inc.: [prologue] Frater Ambrosius etc. Hanc epistolam prepositam...
[text] Omnis sciencia et omnis sapiencia materiam habet et...
Expl.: ...iustificacionem nobis concedat universorum conditor.

II. Unpubl. Miss Sharp printed extracts of sections on cosmology from the Royal MS.† Part of the introductory chapter was printed by Dr G. B. Phelan in 1934,‡ and an edition of the whole is promised.

* This MS contains other Grosseteste items, but the description in the De Ricci-Wilson *Census*, I (1935), 883 is confusing rather than helpful.

† *Franciscan Philosophy*..., p. 15 ff.

‡ "An unedited Text of Robert Grosseteste..." in *Hommage...à M. De Wulf* (Louvain, 1934), p. 172 ff.

III. All the extant MSS ascribe the work to Grosseteste. The whole manner of argument and exposition, the copious use of the Greek fathers, Gregory of Nyssa, Gregory of Nazianzus, Basil, John Damascene and Chrysostom, extensive use of the LXX and frequent employment of Greek exegesis, the almost verbal accord of the cosmology with what we have in other authentic works, all combine to make the *Hexameron* a typical Grosseteste *opus* of the early episcopal period. The literary and linguistic content would point to a date *ca.* 1240, hardly before.

Duns Scotus refers to this work several times, e.g. *Opus Oxoniense*, III, prol. art. 1 (ed. Venice, 1612, p. 18).* Wyclyf quotes it frequently, e.g. *De Benedicta Incarnacione* (ed. Harris), pp. 88, 128, 177. Bale† and Leland and all the subsequent bibliographers cite it.

IV. MSS:

Oxford, Queen's	312	ff. 38^{A}–102^{D}	XIV^{m}	Asc.‡
London, B.M.				
Cotton	Otho D. x	ff. 156^{a}–212^{b}	XIV^{m}	Asc.
Royal	6. E. v	ff. 136^{A}–184^{D}	XIV^{m}	Asc.
Cambridge, Univ.	Kk. ii. 1	f. 310^{A-D}	XV^{m}	Asc.§
Prague, Nat. Mus.	XII. E. 5	ff. 1^{A}–26^{D}	XIV^{m}	Asc. Boh.

50. *Grammatica*

I. Inc.: Sciencia est ordinacio depicta in anima unitatis et diversitatis...

Expl.: ...et que figure et quare non plures erunt in libro figurarum.

II. Unpubl.

III. This grammar seems to have escaped the earlier bibliographers. It was noticed by Little in his "Roger Bacon" (*Proceedings of the British Academy*, XIV (1928), 15), where he cites two MSS and quotes Bacon's unfavourable judgment of the work. Bacon proves‖ that Aristotle, or any Greek for that matter, could not have been either the author or the translator, in spite of a common opinion that such was the case. His point is well taken. The text is quite obviously the work of a scholastic. Almost the whole corpus of Aristotle's works is cited as forming part of the quadrivium (MS Arundel 165, f. 1^{B}). It is significant that Bacon says some rather harsh things about the author, which, had he thought Grosseteste had written the work, he would probably not have said. The colophon in the early Arundel MS is sufficiently explicit to warrant us in not allowing Bacon's ignorance or

* See P. Minges in *Phil. Jhbh.* XXXII (1919), 243.

† Bale lists also an *Exposicio in Genesim*, probably a duplication of title.

‡ Wanting prologue.

§ A single leaf at beginning.

‖ *The Greek Grammar of Roger Bacon* (edd. E. Nolan and S. A. Hirsch, Cambridge, 1902), p. 57 f. See also L. Thorndike, *Magic and Experimental Science*, II (New York, 1923), 248 and n. 4; Franceschini, *Roberto Grossatesta*..., p. 67. V. Rose in *Aristoteles Pseudepigraphus* (Leipzig, 1863), p. 605, and *Hermes*, v (1871), 155, showed it to be no translation, but possibly by Grosseteste.

strictures to influence our judgment too strongly. It may be observed, furthermore, that Bacon's explicit criticisms of the work are not exactly apposite. We may even doubt if he read the work through. It does not pretend to be a grammar of the Greek language, in spite of the elaborate colophon in the Arundel MS. It is rather an introductory treatise on language: the relation of language to knowledge, comparative phonetics, the eight parts of speech and the relations between them, all with apt illustrations from Latin or Greek or both, as the case may demand. Although the statement of the Arundel scribe regarding Aristotle is clearly wrong, there is no reason to doubt the connection with Grosseteste on internal evidence. The work is worthy of him and represents adequately his linguistic interests.

A statement of Matthew Paris (R.S. v, 268) makes the problem of authorship slightly more complex. He tells of the translation into Latin of a Greek grammar by John of Basingstoke:

Memoratus insuper magister Johannes quoddam scriptum transtulit de greco in latinum, in quo artificiose et compendiose tota vis grammatice continetur, quod idem magister Donatum Grecorum appellavit.

It is barely possible that this notice may refer to our *Grammatica*, but several facts lead us to suspect that Matthew is guilty of some hopeful embellishment. We have no other evidence that John translated any such work as Matthew ascribes to him. The chronicler follows this notice with a second that is surely erroneous, that Basingstoke was the author of the *Templum Domini* (see below, p. 138). If Matthew refers to our *Grammatica*, he is in error, because the work is not a translation.

Balancing what unsatisfactory positive evidence we have against what evidence is lacking, it is with some reserve that we include this work among the authentic writings of Grosseteste.

IV. MSS:

Oxford, Digby	55	ff. 158A–178A	XIII²	Unasc.
London, B.M., Arundel	165	ff. 92A–100C	*ca.* 1300	Asc.*
Paris, B.N.	lat. 11277	ff. 88A–102D	XIII²	Unasc. Fr. *mut. in fine*

51. *Quod homo sit minor mundus*

I. Inc.: Magnus deus in semetipso ad semetipsum hominem fecit...
Expl.: ...arida sicut terra sive sicca sicut terra.

II. Publ. Venice, 1514, f. 12D; Baur, p. 59.

III. This short paragraph, occupying only thirteen lines in Baur's edition, can hardly be called a treatise. Baur suggests (p. 78*), perhaps correctly, that a marginal notation may have been independently perpetuated. But its appearance as a separate opusculum in eight physical collections would

* The colophon reads: *Explicit tractatus gramatice editus ab Aristotile prout aliqui opinantur quem magister Robertus Grosseteste lincolniensis episcopus de greco n latinum transtulisse dicitur.*

indicate that its independence was established very early in the history of the Grosseteste canon. Tanner lists the work from the Venice edition. It may yet be possible to trace its source in a larger work, but its authenticity is beyond question.

IV. MSS:

London, B.M.				
Add.	31046	f. 23^{a}	XV^{1}	Asc.
Cotton	Otho D. x	f. 59^{b}	XIV^{m}	Asc.
Royal	6. E. v	f. 241^{D}	XIV^{m}	Asc.
Baltimore, Garrett	95	f. 20^{a}	XV^{1}	Asc. Engl.
Florence, Marucell.	C. 163	f. 2^{C}	*ca.* 1400	Asc. Ital.*
Modena, Estense	lat. 54	f. 73^{b}	XV^{m}	Asc. Ital.
	lat. 649	f. 4^{A-B}	*ca.* 1500	Asc. Ital.
Prague, Nat. Mus.	XII. E. 5	f. 40^{D}	XIV^{m}	Asc. Boh.
Venice, S. Marco	VI. 163	f. 82^{A}	XIV^{2}	Asc. Ital.

52. *De Impressionibus Aeris (De Prognosticacione)*

I. Inc.: Ad precognoscendum aeris diversam disposicionem futuram...
Expl.: ...se aspexerint planete humide in signis aquosis.

II. Publ. by Baur, pp. 41–51.

III. Although the work is unascribed in the earliest MSS it usually appears with one or more other works of Grosseteste. The earliest explicit ascription occurs about the middle of the fourteenth century. The work was known to Bacon, who paraphrases Grosseteste's exposition of the *dignitates planetarum* without acknowledgment of the source,† to Bale, Pits, Tanner and Pegge. It was written before July, 1249, as is evident from a passage near the end (Baur, p. 50): *Cum sol in anno gracie* 1249 *mense Julii fuerit in leone et sic in domo sua, erit Mars eodem tempore*....‡

IV. MSS:

Oxford				
Bodl.	464	ff. 122^{b}–125^{b}	XIII^{2}	Unasc.
Digby	48	ff. 182^{a}–188^{a}	XV^{2}	Asc.
	98	ff. 156^{a}–157^{b}	*ca.* 1400	Asc.
Laud Misc.	594	ff. 159^{D}–160^{B}	*ca.* 1300	Unasc.
Savile	17	ff. 46^{a}–49^{b}	*ca.* 1300	Unasc.
	25	ff. 200^{a}–201^{b}	XIV^{m}	Asc.
Univ. Coll.	41	ff. 33^{a}–34^{b}	*ca.* 1300	Asc. XIV^{m}
London, B.M.				
Cotton	Otho D. x	ff. 57^{b}–58^{b}	XIV^{m}	Asc.
Royal	6. E. v	ff. 240^{A}–241^{A}	XIV^{m}	Asc.
	12. E. xxv	ff. 166^{b}–169^{b}	XIII^{m}	Asc. XIV^{2}

* The four Italian copies are in the tradition of the Venice print, all beginning: *Magnus mundus*, but there are substantial variants which preclude the possibility that we yet have the MS used as a basis for the edition.

† *Secreta Secretorum*, ed. Steele, p. 20; cf. Baur, p. 42 f.; cf. also Bacon in *Opus Maius*, I, 261, and on *Metaphysics*, ed. Steele, p. 49.

‡ See Duhem, *Système du Monde*, III (Paris, 1915), 278 f.

Cambridge				
Univ.	Gg. vi. 3	ff. 134ᵇ–137ᵇ	XIV¹	Unasc.
C.C.C.	424	ff. 20ᵇ–21ᵃ	XV¹	Asc.
Baltimore, Garrett	95	ff. 131ᵃ–134ᵇ	XV¹	Asc. Engl.
Paris, B.N.	lat. 7413, pt. ii	ff. 44ᴮ–48ᴮ	XIIIᵐ	Unasc. Fr.*
Vatican, Pal. lat.	1414	ff. 216ᶜ–220ᴬ	XIII²	Unasc. Lowl.
Vienna, Nat. Bibl.	5239–5239*	ff. 56ᵇ–58ᵇ	*ca.* 1400	Unasc. Ger.
	5508	ff. 202ᴬ–204ᴬ	*ca.* 1300	Ger.†

From the *contenta* in Munich, Clm. 11067 (written 1445–1448) we learn that an ascribed copy of this work was once in that codex. A gathering is now missing, between present ff. 84 and 85, where the treatise should be.

53. *De Impressionibus Elementorum*

I. Inc.: Ut testatur Jacobus in canonica sua, omne datum...
Expl.: ...prima a nube sicut differt pluvia a rore.

II. Publ. Venice, 1514, f. 9ᴮ⁻ᶜ; Baur, pp. 87–89.

III. This work is ascribed to Grosseteste in six physical collections. Roger Bacon refers to it in his *Opus Maius* (ed. Bridges, I, 108; cf. *Roger Bacon Essays*, p. 164). Baur has (p. 89* f.) remarked on the confusion among the bibliographers and particularly in Tanner resulting from the similarity of title between this tractate and the *De Impressionibus Aeris* (q.v.).

IV. MSS:

London, B.M.				
Cotton	Otho D. x.	ff. 61ᵇ–62ᵃ	XIVᵐ	Asc.
Royal	6. E. v	ff. 243ᶜ–244ᴬ	XIVᵐ	Asc.
Baltimore, Garrett	95	ff. 18ᵇ–20ᵃ	XV¹	Asc. Engl.
Florence, Marucell.	C. 163	f. 14ᴮ⁻ᴰ	*ca.* 1400	Asc. Ital.
Modena, Estense	lat. 396	ff. 22ᴰ–23ᶜ	*ca.* 1500	Asc. Ital.
Prague, Nat. Mus.	XII. E. 5	f. 43ᴮ	XIVᵐ	Asc. Boh.
Venice, S. Marco	VI. 163	f. 98ᴬ⁻ᶜ	XIV²	Asc. Ital.

54. *De Intelligenciis*

I. Inc.: Voluisti insuper scire a me quid senciam...
Expl.: ...invenias rescribendo errorem meum corrigas.

II. Publ. Venice, 1514, ff. 6ᴰ–7ᴰ; Luard, *Epistolae*, pp. 8–19, as second part of *Epistola* 1; Baur, pp. 112–119.

III. This work is the second part of the letter to Adam Rufus, of which the first part appears as the *De Forma Prima Omnium* (q.v.). It is the argument of this tractate that Wyclyf paraphrases in his *De Logica*, III, 138. Bale and Pits list a *De Natura Intellectus*, without doubt an alternative title for this treatise.

* With *De Sphera*; a variant text, with an additional paragraph.

† *Incipit liber hali de disposicione aeris*. The colophon repeats the *hali*. The text differs substantially from the best tradition.

IV. MSS:

Oxford				
Bodl.	312	ff. 126^D–127^D	XIV^2	Asc.
Digby	220	ff. 81^D–83^B	XV^1	Unasc.*
Queen's	312	ff. 1^C–3^A	XIV^m	Asc.†
London, B.M.				
Cotton	Otho D. x	ff. 53^b–54^b	XIV^m	Asc.‡
Royal	6. E. v	ff. 246^B–247^B	XIV^m	Asc.‡
Cambridge				
C.C.C.	123	ff. 64^b–66^a	1456	Asc.†
	453	ff. 3^a–6^a	*ca.* 1400	Asc.†
Sid. Suss.	92, pt. ii	p. 1 ff.	XVII	Asc.
Florence, Marucell.	C. 163	f. 10^B	*ca.* 1400	Asc. Ital.‡
Modena, Estense	lat. 649	ff. 16^D–18^D	*ca.* 1500	Asc. Ital.
Prague				
Univ.	763	ff. 3^b–7^a	*ca.* 1410	Asc. Boh.
	1990	ff. 39^b–42^a	1472	Asc. Boh.§
Metrop. Chap.	272	ff. 4^b–8^a	*ca.* 1425	Asc. Boh.
	509	ff. 176^D–179^C	XV^1	Asc. Boh.
	1572	ff. 3^a–6^a	XV^1	Asc. Boh.
Venice, S. Marco	VI. 163	ff. 92^D–94^C	XIV^2	Asc. Ital.
Vercelli, Capit.	72	flyleaf^{C-D}	XIII^2	Asc. Ital.

55. *De Iride (De Fraccionibus Radiorum)*

I. Inc.: Et (ut) perspectivi et physici est speculacio de iride...
Expl.: ...colores omnes arcus varii variaciones.

II. Publ. by Baur, pp. 72–78.

III. The earliest ascription of this work to Grosseteste is in plummet (XIII^m) in Digby 190. The work is also found in five of the physical collections and in the early and important Madrid copy. Roger Bacon refers to it in the *Comp. Studii Phil.* chap. 8 (ed. Brewer, p. 468) and the *Opus Maius* (ed. Bridges, I, 108). Duns Scotus mentions *Lincolniensis in tractatu de radiis* in his *Questiones in I et II Posteriorum.*|| This *De Radiis* is obviously the *De Iride*, as the title *De Fraccionibus Radiorum* appears in the excellent Florence and Prague MSS. The work was known to Bale, Pits, Tanner, Wharton and Pegge.

* In T. Allen's 1622 catalogue of Digby MSS Fol. 9 contained *R. Linc. de Intelligentiis.* This MS seems now to be lost. See W. D. Macray, *Cat.... Bodl. pars nona* (Oxford, 1883), col. 249.

† Used by Luard.

‡ Separate from *De Forma.*

§ The scribe has reversed the order of the two parts of the letter, and has then corrected his mistake in the colophon to the *De Forma*, f. 43^b: *Sequitur immediate post hoc tractatus de intelligenciis ante istum scriptum scilicet Voluisti insuper a me scire etc.*

|| See P. Minges, "Robert Grosseteste Uebersetzer..." in *Phil. Jhbh.* XXXII (1919), 243, who notes this reference, but, as Baur had not given the alternative title, was unable to identify the work.

IV. MSS:

Oxford				
Digby	98	ff. 154ᵃ–155ᵃ	*ca.* 1400	Asc.
	104	f. 110ᵇ	XIV²	Asc.
	190	ff. 197ᵇ–199ᵇ	XIIIᵐ	Asc.
Merton	306	f. 118ᵃ, *frag.**	XIV²	Asc.
London, B.M.				
Cotton	Otho D. x	ff. 58ᵇ–59ᵇ	XIVᵐ	Asc.
Royal	6. E. v	f. 241ᴬ⁻ᴰ	XIVᵐ	Asc.
Baltimore, Garrett	95	ff. 61ᵃ–63ᵇ	XV¹	Asc. Engl.
Florence, Marucell.	C. 163	ff. 19ᶜ–20ᶜ	*ca.* 1400	Asc. Ital.
Groningen	103	ff. 124–127	XVI¹	Asc.
Madrid, B.N.	3314	ff. 90ᴮ–91ᴬ	XIIIᵐ	Unasc. Engl.
Prague, Nat. Mus.	xii. E. 5	f. 41ᴮ⁻ᶜ	XIVᵐ	Asc. Boh.
Vatican, Barb. lat.	165	f. 403ᴮ⁻ᴰ	1288	Unasc. Ger.†

56. *Kalendarium*

I. Inc.: Ad noticiam istius kalendarii (habendam) primo sciendum quod...

Expl.: ...5 hore et 48 minuta, et habebis semper propositum.

II. Publ. by A. Lindhagen in *Arkiv för Matematik, Astronomi och Fysik*, II, item 2 (1916), 15–41.

III. There are many ascribed thirteenth-century copies. It is referred to both in the *Compotus Correctorius* and in the later (1244) *Compotus Minor* (qq.v.). The numerous early MSS bear witness to its popularity, but other *Kalendaria* would seem soon to have superseded this work. The calendar is calculated on the Paris meridian (see Baur, p. 65*). We have given (see above, pp. 30 ff. and 95 f.) reasons for dating this work not later than *ca.* 1225. A marginal note (*ca.* 1300, in a French hand) in Harley MS 3735, f. 6ᵃ, reads: ...*cav*[endum] *tamen quod hunc kalendarium fecit anno domini* 1260 *vel circiter*.... There is no reason to suppose that this scribe was registering more than a general warning that the computations of a scholar dead approximately half a century should be read with care.

IV. MSS:

Oxford, Laud Misc.	644	ff. 1ᴬ–7ᴬ	XIII¹	Unasc.
London, B.M.				
Add.	25031	ff. 14ᵃ–16ᵇ	XIII¹	Unasc.
Harley	3735	ff. 6ᵃ–12ᵃ	XIII¹	Asc. Fr.
	7402	ff. 102ᵃ–104ᵇ	XIII¹	Asc.
Cambridge				
Univ.	Ii. i. 15	ff. 43ᵇ–46ᵇ	XIII¹	Asc.
	Ii. i. 17	ff. 16ᵇ–22ᵃ	*ca.* 1300	Unasc.
Gonv. & Caius	137	pp. 2ᵇ–14	XIII¹	Unasc.‡

* In Baur's ed. p. 75, l. 33 to p. 76, l. 34.

† The rubric reads: *Incipit tractatus de yride Boecii.* See above, p. 89, under *De Accessu et Recessu Maris.*

‡ With asc. *De Sphera.*

Basel	O. II. 7	ff. 43^A–49^b	*ca.* 1300	Asc. No. Fr.*
Berlin	lat. 957	ff. 13^A–21^a	XIII²	Unasc. Rh.
Bruges	522	ff. 3^a–9^a	*ca.* 1300	Unasc.†
Darmstadt	2661	ff. 193^a–199^a	XIII²	Unasc. Engl.
Erfurt, Amplon.	O. 82	ff. 94^a–99^b	XIII²	Asc. Fr.
El Escorial	O. ii. 10	ff. 4^a–10^a	XIII^m	Unasc. Engl.
Lilienfeld†	144	ff. 14^b–27^b+ 29–31	XIII	
New York, Pub. Lib.	69	ff. 1^a–8^b, 13^D	*ca.* 1300	Unasc. Engl.
Prague, Univ.	1298	ff. 87^b–94^a	XV¹	Unasc. Boh.
Reun†	3‡	ff. 66^a–71^b	1260	
Stams†	12§	ff. 39^a–41^b	XV	
Stockholm	A. XII		XIII²	
Toledo, Cabildo	8°. 98. 28	ff. 222^b–228^b	XIII^m	Unasc. Engl.
Vatican, Reg. lat.	1312	ff. 1^a–6^b	XIII²	Asc. Fr.‖
Vienna, Nat. Bibl.	2367	ff. 1^A–7^a	1294	Unasc. Fr.
	5508	f. 205^B	*ca.* 1300	Asc. Ger. *fragm.*

57. *De Lineis, Angulis et Figuris*

I. Inc.: Utilitas consideracionis linearum, angularum et figurarum...
Expl.: ...forciores essent in contrarium que predicte sunt.

II. Publ. Nürnberg, 1503; Venice, 1514, ff. 10^D–11^A; *Bibl. Math.* I (1900), 54 ff., by M. Curtze (from Munich MS, rather badly; see Baur, p. 78*, and also G. Hellmann in *Bibl. Math.* II (1901), 443); Baur, pp. 59–65.

III. A number of early MSS contain this treatise ascribed to Grosseteste. It was almost certainly used by Bacon (see *Opus Maius*, I (ed. Bridges), 211, and cf. ed. Baur, p. 60, etc.; cf. Baur pp. 78*–81*). Because of a passage which refers to other cognate works: *Cum ergo in aliis dictum sit de his que pertinent ad totum universum et partes eius absolute et de aliis que motum rectum et circularem sequuntur*, Baur concludes, probably correctly, that the *De Sphera*, *De Motu Corporali* and *De Motu Supercelestium* were written before this work, The suggestion of Hellmann (*Bibl. Math.* II, 144) that this work formed part of a larger work on optics, with the *De Luce*, *De Colore* and *De Iride*, may be valid, but there is no evidence, either in the MSS or in external literary tradition, to support it. A large work such as that would have had to be could hardly have escaped notice by Bacon, who knew Grosseteste's scientific works so well. Although we may reject Hellmann's suggestion, we have good MS evidence for regarding the *De Natura Locorum* and the *De Lineis* as organically connected. Baur noticed (pp. 81*–

* On f. 42^{a-b} are the *contratabula deserviens tabule Gerlandi et linconiensis* and the *tabula linconiensis principalis*.

† From Zinner, *Verzeichnis d. astronomischen Hss*....

‡ From Zinner. Without having seen the MS, I doubt if it is Grosseteste's. The catalogue (*Xenia Bernardina*, II, pt. i (Vienna, 1891), 8) indicates that the calendar begins with the year 1255.

§ From Zinner, but this must be an error for MS 13. See *Xenia Bernardina*, II, pt. ii (Vienna, 1891), 470.

‖ Rubricked *Introduccio in kalendarium Roberti linc. Archiepiscopi philosophi astrologi.*

83*) this connection. The Munich and Prague MSS, both of excellent tradition, have in common as the last sentence of the *De Lineis* the opening sentence of the *De Natura*. It is even more evident in the Florence B.N. and the Laud copies, the two oldest MSS, *ca.* 1275, where the two tractates are copied and rubricked as one. It is therefore possible that they were originally but a single treatise and that the division into two is the work of a later editor. The bibliographers from Bale onwards have known of the work, though Tanner, followed by Pegge, Felten and Stevenson, laboured under some confusion, making two works out of the one.

IV. MSS:

Oxford, Laud Misc.	644	ff. 207^{C}–208^{D}	XIII^{2}	Asc.
Baltimore, Garrett	95	ff. 63^{b}–66^{a}	XV^{1}	Asc. Engl.
Basel	F. IV. 18	ff. 25^{A}–26^{C}	XIII^{2}	Asc. Ger.
Florence				
B.N.	I. V. 18	f. 71^{A-D}	XIII^{2}	Asc. Fr.
Marucell.	C. 163	ff. 15^{D}–16^{D}	*ca.* 1400	Asc. Ital.
Groningen	103	f. 124 ff.	XVI^{1}	Asc. Ger.
Modena, Estense	lat. 54	ff. 74^{b}–77^{a}	XV^{1}	Asc. Ital.
	lat. 396	ff. 25^{A}–26^{D}	*ca.* 1500	Asc. Ital.
Munich	Clm. 534	ff. 25^{C}–26^{C}	XIII^{2}	Asc. Ger.*
Prague, Nat. Mus.	XII. E. 5	f. 40^{A-B}	XIV^{m}	Asc. Boh.
Venice, S. Marco	VI. 163	ff. 100^{B}–101^{C}	XIV^{2}	Asc. Ital.
Vienna, Nat. Bibl.	5508	ff. 158^{a}–161^{a}	1462	Unasc. So. Ger.

58. *De Luce* (*De Inchoacione Formarum*)

I. Inc.: Formam primam corporalem quam quidam corporeitatem vocant...

Expl.: ...modulacionibus, gesticulacionibus et rythmicis temporibus.

II. Publ. Venice, 1514, ff. 11^{D}–12^{D}; Baur, pp. 51–59.

III. This work appears in seven of the physical collections and the important early fourteenth-century Merton MS 295. It was known to Boston of Bury, and, from the Venice edition, to successive bibliographers. It is of considerable importance in view of the marked leaning of Oxford speculation after the time of Grosseteste toward a "Lichtmetaphysik".

IV. MSS:

Oxford				
Digby	98	ff. 152^{b}–153^{b}	*ca.* 1400	Asc.
	104	ff. 109^{D}–110^{D}	XIV^{2}	Asc.
	220	ff. 106^{B}–107^{C}	XV^{1}	Asc.
Merton	295	ff. 145^{D}–147^{A}	*ca.* 1325	Asc.
London, B.M.				
Cotton	Otho D. x	ff. 60^{b}–61^{b}	XIV^{m}	Asc.
Royal	6. E. v	ff. 242^{C}–243^{C}	XIV^{m}	Asc.
Baltimore, Garrett	95	ff. 66^{a}–68^{b}	XV^{1}	Asc. Engl.
El Escorial	g. iii. 17	ff. 98^{a}–99^{b}	XIII^{2}	Unasc. Engl.
Florence, Marucell.	C. 163	ff. 1^{A}–2^{C}	*ca.* 1400	Asc. Ital.†
Modena, Estense	lat. 396	ff. 2^{A}–4^{A}	*ca.* 1500	Asc. Ital.

* Rubricked *Tractatus linconiensis de fraccionibus et reflexionibus radiorum.*

† Beginning: *Quidam corporeitatem vocant.*

Prague				
Univ.	1990	ff. 44^{a}–46^{a}	XV^{2}	Asc. Boh.
Nat. Mus.	XII. E. 5	f. 40^{B-D}	XIV^{m}	Asc. Boh.
Venice, S. Marco	VI. 163	ff. 80^{A}–82^{A}	XIV^{2}	Asc. Ital.

59. *De Motu Corporali et Luce*

I. Inc.: Unum inquantum unum solum efficiens est...
Expl.: ...est appetitus corporalis et naturalis.

II. Publ. Venice, 1514, f. 9^{C-D}; Baur, pp. 90–92.

III. This short work appears in six physical collections. Its authenticity is corroborated by the doctrine of *lux* as the *prima forma corporalis*, characteristically Grossetestian. The argument of the tractate is closely connected with that of the *De Luce*, and both, because of parallels with the *De Anima*, should be placed early in his career, say 1215–1220.*

IV. MSS:

London, B.M.				
Cotton	Otho D. x	f. 62^{a-b}	XIV^{m}	Asc.
Royal	6. E. v	f. 244^{A-B}	XIV^{m}	Asc.
Florence, Marucell.	C. 163	ff. 14^{D}–15^{A}	*ca.* 1400	Asc. Ital.
Modena, Estense	lat. 396	ff. 23^{C}–24^{A}	*ca.* 1500	Asc. Ital.
Prague, Nat. Mus.	XII. E. 5	f. 43^{B-C}	XIV^{m}	Asc. Boh.
Venice, S. Marco	VI. 163	ff. 98^{C}–99^{B}	XIV^{2}	Asc. Ital.

60. *De Motu Supercelestium* (*De Motu Circulari* or *De Disposicione Motoris*)

I. Inc.: Quoniam motus simplex aut est circularis...
Expl.: ...ponit Alpetragius de ipsis ad presens supersedemus.

II. Publ. Venice, 1514, ff. 13^{A}–14^{A}; Baur, pp. 92–100. P. Duhem, *Système du Monde*, v (Paris, 1917), 354 f. translates a few sections.

III. This work appears in the same six collections as the *De Motu Corporali*. Baur has pointed out (p. 92*) that there is a reference to Grosseteste's *De Angulis et Figuris* (his ed. p. 60) which probably refers to this work, and further that Bacon may be referring to this work in his *Opus Maius* (ed. Bridges, I, 108) when he speaks of Grosseteste's *De Celestibus*; but Baur rejects the suggestion that the treatise meant by Bacon might be the *De Sphera*. The MSS of the *De Sphera* do not vary as to title. The work was known to Tanner, Wharton, Cave and Pegge, most probably from the Venice edition, though Tanner and Wharton cite the Cotton MS.

IV. MSS:

London, B.M.				
Cotton	Otho D. x	ff. 62^{b}–63^{b}	XIV^{m}	Asc.†
Royal	6. E. v	ff. 244^{B}–245^{B}	XIV^{m}	Asc.†
Florence, Marucell.	C. 163	ff. 7^{B}–8^{D}	*ca.* 1400	Asc. Ital.
Modena, Estense	lat. 396	ff. 11^{C}–14^{D}	*ca.* 1500	Asc. Ital.
Prague, Nat. Mus.	XII. E. 5	ff. 42^{D}–43^{A}	XIV^{m}	Asc. Boh.
Venice, S. Marco	VI. 163	ff. 88^{D}–90^{D}	XIV^{2}	Asc. Ital.

* Cf., e.g., Baur, p. 92, l. 7 ff. (*De Motu*) and p. 258 f. (*De Anima*).

† Rubricked *De disposicione motoris et moti in motu circulari.*

61. *De Natura Locorum*

I. Inc.: His igitur regulis et radicibus et fundamentis datis ex potestate...

Expl.: ...densitas aeris, quod vivere nullatenus possemus.

II. Publ. Venice, 1514, f. 11^{A-D}; Baur, pp. 65–72.

III. Though printed in 1514, this work was not cited by Bale, Leland or Pits. Tanner, however, followed by Pegge and Stevenson, listed the work from the early printed edition. Baur has pointed out that Bacon, having incorporated whole sections of it into his *Opus Maius*, certainly knew it. For its connection with the *De Lineis, Angulis et Figuris*, see above p. 107 f.

IV. MSS:

Oxford, Laud Misc.	644	ff. 208^{D}–210^{B}	XIII^{2}	Asc.
Florence				
B.N.	I. V. 18	ff. 71^{A}–72^{D}	XIII^{2}	Asc. Fr.
Marucell.	C. 163	ff. 16^{D}–18^{A}	*ca.* 1400	Asc. Ital.
Groningen	103		XVI^{1}	Asc.
Modena, Estense	lat. 54	ff. 77^{a}–79^{b}	XV^{m}	Asc. Ital.
	lat. 396	ff. 26^{D}–28^{C}	*ca.* 1500	Asc. Ital.
Prague, Nat. Mus.	XII. E. 5	f. 40^{B}	XIV^{m}	Asc. Boh.*
Venice, S. Marco	VI. 163	ff. 101^{D}–102^{D}	XIV^{2}	Asc. Ital.

62. *De Operacionibus Solis*

I. Inc.: Altitudinis firmamentum pulcritudo eius....Ecclus. xliii. Altitudo simpliciter dictum celum...

Expl.: ...non inmerito dicitur in sermonibus eius festinavit iter.

II. Unpubl.

III. This work appears, so far as is yet known, only in Madrid B.N. 3314, an English MS of the middle of the thirteenth century. It follows, without rubric, in the same hand, Grosseteste's *De Colore* and, like that and the other Grosseteste works by this same scribe (see pp. 92 ff., 105 f.), bears no ascription. The next item, a hitherto unnoticed work of Roger Bacon,† bears an ascription *D. Bacun* in the original hand in the right margin. We should naturally infer that the scribe intended to make clear that he was conscious of a different authorship, and, by his uniform treatment of the preceding works, assumed them to be by the same author, Grosseteste. This work is striking in at least one regard. It is an exposition of Ecclus. xliii. 1–5, with only one reference to any non-Christian work, the *Meteora* of Aristotle, f. 91^{D}. This is extraordinary in Grosseteste's physico-philosophical works, where he is usually generous in quotations from Aristotle, Euclid, Ptolemy and the Arabians. But the reader is immediately struck by the thought that the whole is a kind of *tour de force*, whereby the writer is trying to show that there is nothing unchristian about his physics, but that, on the contrary, it

* The opening sentence of this tractate, all that appears in this MS, is appended to the *De Lineis, Angulis et Figuris*.

† Ed. S. H. Thomson in *Isis*, XXIII (1937), 219–224.

accords perfectly with express statements to be found in the Scriptures. Someone may have reproached Grosseteste with too great dependence on pagan philosophers. There is no doubt about the pure Grossetestian character of the doctrine, which a few random examples will show.

[f. 91[B]] Aliter autem naturaliter sol esse in conspectu dei, quia forte lux eius [f. 91[C]] est lux prima visibilis manifestans visui species omnes colorum, et cum sit lux incorporata, que propter incorporacionem non movet se ad visum, nisi cum lux superfunditur, manifestum est quod color connativus est luci invisibili. Si igitur lucis visibilis oculis nostris radix est in sole omnis color habet in sui substanciam de luce solari, cui lux superfusa se unit, ut faciat colorem actu visibilem et ita quicquid est conspectibile per naturam et vas conspectibile....

Cf. the *De Colore*, *De Calore Solis* and *De Luce*.

[f. 92[A] (on Ecclus. xliii. 4)] Forte eciam sol dicitur tripliciter exurere montes, quia effeccior est tripliciter cause urentis. Est enim fons caloris et fons luminis quod congregacione radiorum ascendit, et est causa motus qui parcium disgregacione ascendit, nec sunt plures cause accendentes et urentes nisi calor et radiorum luminosorum multiplicacio et per motum disgregacio....

We should not expect to, and indeed do not, find more than occasional verbal parallels, but the physical theory, the style and the general presentment are unmistakably by the same person that wrote the other short treatises on light and heat. How distinctively Grosseteste treats these subjects appears if we compare, e.g., relevant sections of Roger Bacon's *Liber Communium Naturalium* (ed. Steele, 1911, pp. 268–274). The treatise should not be dated before *ca.* 1225. Stephen Langton's chapter-divisions are used.

IV. MS:

Madrid, B.N.	3314	ff. 91[B]–92[D]	XIII[m]	Unasc. Engl.

63. *De Ordine Emanandi Causatorum a Deo* (*De Eternitate Filii in Divinis*)

I. Inc.: Multum coangustat mentes indissertas et corporalium...
Expl.: ...apud imaginacionem ponentem spacium extra mundum.

II. Publ. Baur, pp. 147–150.

III. This work is closely related to the *De Veritate*, *De Veritate Proposicionis* and *De Sciencia Dei*, both as to subject-matter and as to manner of argument. It was listed by Wharton, Cave, Tanner and Pegge. Wharton had seen the Cotton MS before the fire of 1731. Baur knew and used only the Royal and Prague Univ. MSS.

IV. MSS:

London, B.M.				
Cotton	Otho D. x	f. 57[a–b]	XIV[m]	Asc.
Royal	6. E. v	f. 249[A–C]	XIV[m]	Asc.
Florence, Marucell.	C. 163	f. 22[D]	*ca.* 1400	Asc. Ital.*
Prague				
Univ.	1990	ff. 34[b]–35[b]	1472	Asc. Boh.†
Nat. Mus.	XII. E. 5	ff. 39[D]–40[A]	XIV[m]	Asc. Boh.

* The rubric reads *Linconiensis de eternitate divinarum personarum.*
† The rubric reads *De eternitate filii in divinis.*

64. *De Potencia et Actu*

I. Inc.: Omne quod est aut est ens actu aut ens in potencia...
Expl.: ...in potencia de potencia ad effectum.

II. Publ. Baur, pp. 126–129.

III. This tractate is preserved in but three MSS, none earlier than the first quarter of the fourteenth century. But it is ascribed in two of the three, and an ascription should be assumed in the third, a valuable Grosseteste codex. The work was known to Boston of Bury. Bale was at one point confused (*De Scriptoribus*, p. 305) by a false attribution to Grosseteste, in the *contenta* (XIV[1]) of Digby 172, of Walter Burley's *De Potenciis Anime* (see above, p. 90), but he gives the correct incipit in his *Index*, though the error was repeated by Tanner and Pegge. Pits quotes the incipit of our tractate. Baur distinguished (p. 101*) between the two tractates of Grosseteste and Burley.

In spite of the shortness of the work and the fact that it contains no quotation at all, the influence of the *Physics* of Aristotle is strikingly evident in phraseology and method, but there are persistent Neo-Platonic conceptions of the precedence of act over potency. *Omnem autem potenciam precedit actus naturaliter* (Baur, p. 129).

IV. MSS:

Oxford				
Digby	98	ff. 155^{b}–156^{a}	*ca.* 1400	Asc.
Merton	295	f. 145^{A-D}	*ca.* 1325	Unasc.*
Cambridge, Univ.	Ii. i. 19	ff. 211^{C}–212^{A}	XIV[1]	Asc.

65. *Ptolomeus de Novem Planetis*

I. Inc.: Ptolomeus in hoc loco seu libro tricas et tricarum nomina ponit. Sunt...†
Expl.: ...qualitas rei future cuius est signum.

II. Publ. by Baur, pp. 36–40, from the Erfurt MS.

III. The three known MSS ascribe the abstract to Grosseteste. Considering Grosseteste's interest in the general subject, there is no reason to doubt the definite attribution. The additional fact that the three copies are of different provenances and traditions would necessitate the positing of an early copy on the Continent from which these derive.‡

IV. MSS:

Erfurt, Amplon.	Q. 361	f. 126^{B-D}	XIV[m]	Asc. No. Ger.
Florence, Marucell.	C. 163	f. 21^{B-D}	*ca.* 1400	Asc. Ital.
Munich	Clm. 588	ff. 112^{C}–113^{B}	1340	Asc. Fr.

* Between Grosseteste's *Commentarius in Physica* and the *De Luce*, the latter ascribed. All three works written by the same scribe.

† This is the incipit of the Erfurt and Munich MSS. The Florence copy is of an independent tradition: *Ptholomeus in libro quidem centiloquium tricas et tricarum nomina significacionum vero effectus. Sunt igitur....* See A. Pelzer, "Une source inconnue de Roger Bacon, Alfred Sareshel" in *Arch. Franc. Hist.* XII (1919), 44–67, particularly p. 59, n. 1.

‡ See above, p. 94, under *De Cometis*.

66. *De Quadratura Circuli*

I. Inc.: Quadratura circuli per linulas hoc modo est: ponatur...
Expl.: ...et toti circulo. Hec est ergo quadratura per linulas.

II. Unpubl.

III. Wood, Tanner and Pegge mention Digby MS 153 in ascribing this short work to Grosseteste. Stevenson was inclined to accept it as genuine. Baur (p. 142*) regarded it as doubtful. The early ascription is confirmed by the presence of the treatise in early codices, most of which contain other mathematical and physical works of Grosseteste.

IV. MSS:

Oxford				
Digby	153	f. 184^a	*ca.* 1325	Asc.
	190	f. 87^b	XIII^m	Unasc.
e Museo	125	f. 116^a	XIII^m	Unasc.
London, B.M., Royal	12. E. xxv	f. 150^b	XIII^2	Unasc.
Dresden	Db. 86	f. 213^a	XIII^2	Unasc. Fr.
Erfurt, Amplon.	Q. 234	f. 113^a	*ca.* 1325	Unasc. Engl.?
	Q. 385	f. 207^a	XIV^m	Unasc. Ger.
Florence, B.N.	I. v. 18	f. 33^A	XIII^2	Unasc. Fr.

Almost all the copies have the same two diagrams.
Baur's reference (p. 142*) to Univ. Coll., Oxford, MS 41, ff. 36^b–40^b, is a slip. This work does not appear in the codex.

67. *V Questiones Theologice*

I. (i) Inc.: Queritur de sciencia dei quomodo scit singularia...
Expl.: ...ea que contingunt a casu vel a libera voluntate.
We shall call this *De Sciencia Dei II*. See below, p. 115, *De Sciencia Dei I*.

(ii) Inc.: Consequenter queritur qualiter deus scit ea que contingunt...
Expl.: ...quia vult, sed ipsa gracia est eam volendi recte.

(iii) Inc.: Consequenter queritur de voluntate dei que distinguitur...
Expl.: ...ad voluntatem dei dicendum posterius in secundo, ubi dicetur de peccato.

(iv) Inc.: Consequenter autem dicto de voluntate dicendum de misericordia et iusticia...
Expl.: ...retribuendo et puniendo posterius dicetur in quarto per dei graciam.

(v) Inc.: Hic queritur de locali presencia creatoris utrum sit ubique...
Expl.: ...quod sic nascitur ex eo cuius est verbum in eo quod seipsam dicit generat pater et generatur filius.

II. Unpubl.

III. The matter of the authenticity of these *questiones* is complicated by the confusion in the information given us by the bibliographers. Boston of Bury lists: *De Sciencia Dei*. Pr. *Queritur*. Fin. *recte*. *De misericordia et justitia Dei*. Pr. *Consequitur*. Fin. *per Dei gratiam*. *De locali praesentia Dei*. Pr. *Hic quaeritur*. Fin. *filius*. His list accounts for *questiones* (i) and (ii) (combined as one *questio*), (iv) and (v). Tanner, probably following Bale, lists *questio* (i) with a more complete incipit than that given by Boston, and, separately, *questiones* (iv) and (v) from "MS Br. Twin 8 133". Twyne MS 22* bears this mark, but p. 133 has nothing about any Grosseteste material. Yet there can be no doubt that Tanner saw a MS containing these *questiones* probably ascribed, or that Twyne had recorded the correct incipits of the *questiones*. It seems difficult to avoid the conclusion that whoever saw and recorded these items must have examined a MS other than Exeter Coll. 28. In this MS the *questiones* are distinctly separated. Boston gives as the explicit of the first *questio* the explicit of *questio* (ii) in the Exeter MS, as if the MS or MSS from which he had obtained his data included the first two items as one. No bibliographer mentions *questio* (iii), which, in our Exeter codex, is quite separate from *questiones* (ii) and (iv), and could hardly have escaped even the most cursory examination. It is possible that Tanner includes it with *questiones* (i) and (ii) in his title *De scientia et voluntate* lib. i. The explicit which he gives for *questio* (iv) is substantially different from that in our MS, a fact which would again lead us to posit the existence of a MS, now lost or unknown, which must be supposed to bear an ascription of these *questiones* to Grosseteste. Otherwise we find ourselves unable to explain the independence of Tanner's tradition from that of Boston of Bury, as we should likewise be unable to explain Boston's original attribution. The presence of these *questiones* in a codex which contains, immediately preceding and in the same hand, Grosseteste's *De Libero Arbitrio* in what Baur has called Recension II, and, immediately following, without so much as a vacant line to indicate a break in subject-matter or authorship, the beginning of Grosseteste's *De Statu Causarum* (see below, p. 117), and which, furthermore, once contained, according to the *contenta* (XIV[2]), *lincolniensis de libero arbitrio aliter quam prius*, i.e. Recension I, is strong external evidence of their authenticity.

Internal evidence is corroborative. The noticeable reliance upon Augustine, the doctrine of illumination, the characteristic use of chap. 13 of Bk. I of John Damascene's *De Fide Orthodoxa*, accord with the dominant features of Grosseteste's method. What precisely is meant by *retribucio...posterius dicetur in quarto per dei graciam* is not, at the moment, clear, but an indexed edition of his works might solve the question. A fairly early date suggests itself, because of the academic method and the quasi-philosophical subject-matter, say *ca.* 1220–1225. It certainly belongs in the period before the lectureship to the Franciscans, i.e. before 1229, when he was still *in scolis suis*. See above, p. 89.

IV. MS:

Oxford, Exeter	28	(i) f. 306[A–B]; (ii) f. 306[B–C]; (iii) ff. 306[C]–307[B]; (iv) f. 307[B–C]; (v) f. 307[C–D]	*ca.* 1325	Unasc.

* See *Wood's Life and Times*, ed. A. Clark (Oxford, 1895), pp. 204–226, for an account of the Twyne MSS.

68. *De Sciencia Dei I* (II is *Questio Theologica I*)

I. Inc.: Si deus scit antichristum esse vel fuisse vel fore...
Expl.: ...secundum illud "qui tempus ab evo ire iubes".

II. Publ. Baur, pp. 145–147.

III. The work is ascribed to Grosseteste in all the extant MSS. Four of the five known copies are among the best canons of his works that we have. Internal evidence, as Baur has shown (p. 105*), is corroborative. There are verbal parallels with chap. v of *De Libero Arbitrio II* (Baur, pp. 163–166). For *De Sciencia Dei II* see above, *V Questiones Theologice* (i).

IV. MSS:

London, B.M.				
Cotton	Otho D. x	ff. 56^b^–57^a^	XIV^m^	Asc.
Royal	6. E. v	f. 249^A^	XIV^m^	Asc.
Florence, Marucell.	C. 163	ff. 21^D^–22^B^	*ca.* 1400	Asc. Ital.
Prague				
Univ.	1990	ff. 35^b^–36^a^	1472	Asc. Boh.
Metrop. Chap.	1446	f. 267^a–b^ (*bis*)	XV^m^	Asc. Boh.

69. *De Sphera*

I. Inc.: Intencio nostra in hoc tractatu est describere figuram machine...
Expl.: ...duorum semidiametrorum scilicet solis et lune.

II. Publ. Venice, 1508, 1513, 1518 (twice), 1531; Baur, pp. 10–32, from eleven MSS.

III. The great number of early MSS of this work, many of which are ascribed, bear witness to its wide diffusion. It was probably known to Roger Bacon as *De Celestibus*, to Nicholas Trevet, *Annales*, *s.a.* 1253, to Boston of Bury and to all subsequent bibliographers, though not without some confusion with homonymous works. There was, indeed, early confusion in MS ascriptions, some copies of Sacro Bosco's *De Sphera* being ascribed to Grosseteste.* Many copies have been copiously glossed and there have been several abridgments. Though there are many more copies of this work than of either the *Compotus* or the *Kalendarium*, the three works are often found in the same MS. Baur argues briefly for a date of composition (1215–1230) earlier than that of Sacro Bosco's work (1236). Sarton holds† that Grosseteste's work was derived from Sacro Bosco. But, in view of Grosseteste's advanced scientific knowledge as early as 1215,‡ it is imperative that we recognize the possibility of his independence of Sacro Bosco. Indeed, it might even be plausibly argued that Sacro Bosco could well have gained some of his information from Grosseteste. A closer study of the respective

* Cf. Baur, pp. 60*–64*, who gives a fairly complete list of MSS. See also P. Duhem, *Système du Monde*, III (Paris, 1915), 279 f.

† *Introduction to the History of Science*, II, pt. ii (Baltimore, 1931), 584.

‡ See above, Introd. p. 30 ff.

texts is needed than has hitherto been made. See also below, p. 118 f., *De Universitatis Machina*.

IV. MSS:

Oxford				
Bodl.	676	ff. 229^{a}–241^{a}	XV^{m}	Asc.
Digby	98	ff. 158^{a}–161^{a}	*ca.* 1400	Asc.*
	147	ff. 69^{b}–76^{a}	XV^{1}	Asc.
	191	ff. 125^{a}–131^{b}	XIII^{2}	Asc. *mut.*
Laud Misc.	644	ff. 143^{A}–147^{D}	XIII^{2}	Asc.
C.C.C.	41	ff. 144^{b}–152^{a}	XIV^{1}	Asc.
Merton	35	ff. 239^{C}–245^{D}	XIV^{1}	Unasc.
London, B.M.				
Add.	27589	ff. 69^{A}–76^{B}	XIII^{m}	Asc.
Cotton	Otho D. x	ff. 147^{a}–149^{b}, *frag.*	XIV^{m}	Asc.
Egerton	843	ff. 15^{a}–22^{a}	XIII^{2}	Asc.
	847	ff. 57^{a}–62^{b}	XV^{1}	Asc.
Harley	321	ff. 30^{a}–33^{b}	*ca.* 1400	Unasc.†
	3735	ff. 74^{A}–82^{C}	XIII^{2}	Asc. Fr.
	4350	ff. 4^{a}–15^{a}	XIII^{m}	Asc. Fr.
Royal	6. E. v	ff. 249^{C}–251^{D}	XIV^{m}	Asc.
London, Goldschmidt	Cat. 21, no. 5	ff. 101^{C}–106^{A}	*ca.* 1300	Unasc. So. Ger.
Cambridge				
Univ.	Ff. vi. 13	ff. 11^{a}–17^{a}	XIII^{m}	Asc.
	Gg. vi. 3	ff. 200^{b}–205^{b}	XIV^{1}	Asc.
	Ii. i. 13	ff. 36^{a}–39^{b}	XIV^{1}	Asc.
	Mm. iii. 11	ff. 144^{A}–149^{B}	XIV^{2}	Asc.
Gonv. & Caius	137	pp. 15^{a}–24^{a}	XIII^{2}	Unasc.‡
Baltimore, Garrett	95	ff. 111^{a}–120^{b}	XV^{1}	Asc. Engl.
Bologna, Univ.	957	ff. 101^{A}–106^{A}	XIII^{2}	Asc. Fr.
Erfurt, Amplon.	Q. 351	ff. 46^{A}–49^{D}	XIII^{2}	Asc. Engl.
	Q. 355	ff. 1^{A}–5^{D}	XIII^{2}	Unasc. Engl.
El Escorial	&. iv. 19	ff. 79^{a}–86^{b}	XV^{2}	Asc. Ital.
Florence, Riccard.	885	ff. 1^{A}–7^{D}	XIII^{2}	Asc. Engl.?§
Munich	Clm. 14448	ff. 50^{a}–54^{a}	XIII^{2}	Asc. Fr.
Paris, B.N.	lat. 7195	ff. 67^{D}–74^{A}	*ca.* 1300	Asc. Engl.
	lat. 7298	ff. 31^{A}–36^{C}	*ca.* 1300	Asc. So. Fr.
	lat. 7413, pt. ii	ff. 37^{A}–44^{A}	XIII^{m}	Asc. Fr.
Utrecht, Univ.	772	ff. 90^{a}–94^{b}	XIV^{1}	Asc. No. Ger.
Vatican				
Pal. lat.	1414	ff. 34^{D}–41^{A}	XIII^{2}	Asc. Lowl.
Urbinat. lat.	1428	ff. 180^{A}–186^{A}	XIII^{m}	Unasc. Fr.
Verdun	25	item 4	XIII	Asc. Engl.
Vienna, Nat. Bibl.	5239–5239*	ff. 83^{a}–88^{b}	*ca.* 1400	Asc. Ger.
	5508	ff. 205^{C}–207^{D}	*ca.* 1300	Asc. Ger.‖
Wolfenbüttel	Helms. 696	ff. 112^{b}–114^{b}	XV^{2}	Asc. Ger.¶

* See Introd. p. 10.

† Harley 941, ff. 30^{a}–49^{b}, XV^{1}, contains Sacro Bosco's *De Sphera* ascribed to Grosseteste.

‡ Zinner, *Verzeichnis*, no. 3856, cites Basel F. IV. 18, but this MS contains, ff. 2^{A}–17^{D}, the *Commentum Roberti Anglici* on the *De Sphera* of Sacro Bosco, composed in Paris in 1271 according to the colophon. See below, p. 261, *Spurium* 53.

§ *Mut. in init.* ‖ *Mut. in fine.* ¶ Excerpts only.

70. *De Statu Causarum* (*De Causis*)

I. Inc.: Aristoteles in secundo prime philosophie sue supponens...
Expl.: ...remotissima est yle scilicet materia prima.

II. Publ. Venice, 1514, ff. 4–5; Baur, pp. 120–126.

III. This work has been known under several titles. Bale calls it *De Sufficientia Causarum*, Wood and Tanner *De Statu Causarum*, followed by Wharton and Pegge. In one MS (Rawl. C. 677) it appears as *De Causis*, in another (Royal 6. E. v) the colophon gives the title *De statu, sufficiencia et ordine causarum*, but usually it appears as *De Statu Causarum*. It is found in six of the physical collections. In two MSS (the Royal and Cotton copies), the small work *Quod homo sit minor mundus* precedes as an integral part of our *De Statu*. In an early tradition it may have formed a sort of prologue, but the subject-matter is not cognate.

IV. MSS:

Oxford				
Digby	220	ff. 105^{B}–106^{A}	XV^{1}	Asc.
Rawl.	C. 677	ff. 77^{B}–78^{C}	*ca.* 1400	Asc.
Exeter	28	f. 307^{D}	*ca.* 1325	Unasc.*
London, B.M.				
Cotton	Otho D. x	ff. 59^{b}–60^{b}	XIV^{m}	Asc.
Royal	6. E. v	ff. 241^{D}–242^{C}	XIV^{m}	Asc.
Florence, Marucell.	C. 163	ff. 6^{B}–7^{B}	*ca.* 1400	Asc. Ital.
Modena, Estense	lat. 396	ff. 9^{D}–11^{C}	*ca.* 1500	Asc. Ital.
Prague, Nat. Mus.	XII. E. 5	f. 42^{C-D}	XIV^{m}	Asc. Boh.
Venice, S. Marco	VI. 163	ff. 87^{A}–88^{D}	XIV^{2}	Asc. Ital.

71. *De Subsistencia Rei*

I. Inc.: Tribus modis res subsistere habent, in actu sive in seipsis...
Expl.: ...idem a multis participatur et est de subsistencia participancium.

II. Unpubl.

III. This short work was first noticed by Fr. Pelster in the unique Assisi MS in 1926.† The ascription is in the original hand. In all likelihood the work was composed at about the same time as the *De Accessu et Recessu Maris* (q.v., p. 89), while Grosseteste was still *in scolis suis*. Here he is called simply *Magister R. Grosseteste*. There are two whole gatherings at the end of the codex in an unmistakably English hand, different from, but contemporary with, the hand of our text. In two places, f. 232^{C} and f. 286^{A}, is found written in plummet, XIII^{2}, *frīs bonaventure*, which suggests that the codex may have belonged to Bonaventura. Its early connection with Assisi, attested by the typical Assisi quire-marks, lends some colour to this conjecture.

IV. MS:

Assisi, Comunale	138	f. 262^{B-C}	*ca.* 1225	Asc. Engl.

* A fragment of ten lines. See above, p. 113 f., *V Questiones Theologice*.
† *Scholastik*, I (1926), 572 f.

72. *Theorica Planetarum*

I. Inc.: Quia in causa [natura? creacione?]...
ad inveniendum medietates [?]...
betur motus...
endum est enim quod sol...circulum...
a centro terre per totum...
Expl.: ...epicicli existente in auge differre tunc ambe staciones distant ab auge radio epicicli.

II. Unpubl.

III. In the printed catalogue of the MSS of the Bibliothèque Communale of Cambrai the statement is made* that the first two works in MS 1330 (1180), as listed in the *contenta*, are gone. The catalogue may have been compiled before the various parts of this badly mutilated codex were reassembled, but, in any case, the first item in the *contenta*, *Linconiensis theorica planetarum*, is now in its proper place at the beginning of the codex. The whole twelve folia have suffered from exposure or some chemical action in such a way that the parchment, in the shape of a long triangle with a two-inch base at the top of the page, is completely eaten away. Some of the later folia contain large sections that are fairly legible. On f. 4[C], e.g., a section begins:

Compositores tabularum scripserunt tabulas medii motus lune in eadem forma ut in medio motus solis...; [and again on f. 5[C]] Sequitur nunc de tribus superioribus planetis, scilicet Saturno, Iove et Marte, qui unam doctrinam habent in circulis...; [and on f. 6[A]] Ut melius et facilius possimus intelligere motum istorum planetarum, videamus primo quid sit medius motus in epiciclo....

There are numerous tables and several diagrams. It is not easy to determine exactly where this treatise ends. It may end at the bottom of f. 12[D], as above, or it may go to f. 13[B] ending ...*esse prius* [?] *in signo cancri est*. The rubric, in red, at the top of f. 1[A], in the original No. Fr.-Lowl. hand of the first quarter of the fourteenth century reads: *Incipit theo...linc'...nsis*. The *contenta* on f. 77, in a XIV[2] hand, reads 1[9] *Theorica linconiensis de planetis a folio* 1° *ad* 13[m]. Without older contradictory evidence we must be prepared to accept the early ascription. There is no discernible relation between this treatise and the recension of the current *Theorica Planetarum* ascribed to him in the Cambridge Univ. MS. See under *Dubia*, below, p. 238 f.

73. *De Universitatis Machina*

I. Inc.: Universitatis machina in duo divisa est, in elementarem...
Expl.: ...equaliter temperantes. Hec in tres partes divisa est, scil. Asiam, Affricam et Europam.

II. Unpubl.

* *Catalogue général des départements*, XVII (Paris, 1891), 487.

III. This work was first listed by Baur in his description (p. 151*) of Cambridge Univ. MS Ff. vi. 13 without comment as to its genuineness. The one MS contains two copies of the treatise, the first, somewhat longer and with substantial variants from the second, which alone is ascribed. On cursory examination it would appear that we have an earlier or perhaps original draft of the *De Sphera*, but the text needs further examination. Of the genuineness of the second copy in the codex the early ascription (XIII^{m}) does not allow us to doubt. The unascribed copy may be Grosseteste's reworking, or indeed that of a pupil. It follows immediately an early copy of the *De Sphera*. Certain similarities of text suggest comparison with portions of Sacro Bosco's *De Sphera*, e.g. the paragraph following the introduction of Sacro Bosco's work begins: *Universalis autem mundi machina in duo dividitur, in ethereum scil. et elementarem regionem. Elementaris quidem alteracioni continue pervia*.... This suggests a re-examination of the chronology of the literary activity of Sacro Bosco in the light of the possibility of larger borrowing from Grosseteste than has hitherto been considered.

IV. MS:

Cambridge, Univ.	Ff. vi. 13	ff. 17^{b}–26^{a}	XIII^{m}	Unasc.
		ff. 37^{b}–43^{b}	XIII^{m}	Asc.

This text seems to be the source of the work in Digby 98, ff. 168^{A}–171^{A}, beginning: *Cum de composicione machine mundane que sperica est sit presens intencio, primo videndum est*... and ending ...*planete quinque dicuntur erratice. Explicit tractatus de spera secundum episcopum lincolliensem* [*ca.* 1300]. A later hand, XIV^{2}, has added *sed abreviatus*.

74. *De Veritate*

I. Inc.: Ego sum via, veritas et vita. Hic ipsa veritas dicit se...
Expl.: ...per appropriacionem diversificata in angulis.

II. Publ. Venice, 1514, ff. 7^{B}–9^{B}; Baur, pp. 130–143; Engl. translation by R. McKeon, *Selections from Medieval Philosophers*, I (New York, 1929), 263–281.

III. This tractate is found in six physical collections. The oldest extant MS, Lincoln Coll. 54, bears an ascription to Grosseteste in the hand of Thomas Gascoigne.* In view of Gascoigne's repeated assertion, certainly well founded, that he had seen many MSS in Grosseteste's own hand,† we must allow great corroborative weight to this ascription. The next oldest MS, Exeter Coll. 28, written *ca.* 1325, is ascribed in a contemporary hand. Boston of Bury, Leland, Bale, Tanner, Wharton, Pits and Pegge (the last-named twice) mention the work. Wyclyf cites the work several times: *De Actibus Anime*, ed. Dziewicki, in *Misc. Phil.* I (London, 1902), 96, and *Sermones*, III (ed. Loserth, London, 1888), 190. The treatise is connected with both recensions of the *De Libero Arbitrio*.‡

* Cf. Baur, p. 148*. † See Introd. p. 6.
‡ Cf. Baur, p. 104*.

IV. MSS:

Oxford				
Exeter	28	ff. 294^{C}–295^{D}	*ca.* 1325	Asc.
Lincoln	54	ff. 15^{D}–17^{C}	XIII^{1}	Asc. XV^{1}
London, B.M.				
Cotton	Otho D. x	ff. 54^{b}–56^{b}	XIV^{m}	Asc.
Royal	6. E. v	ff. 247^{B}–248^{D}	XIV^{m}	Asc.
Florence, Marucell.	C. 163	ff. 11^{C}–13^{D}	*ca.* 1400	Asc. Ital.
Modena, Estense	lat. 649	ff. 19^{A}–22^{B}	*ca.* 1500	Asc. Ital.
Prague, Univ.	1990	ff. 36^{a}–39^{b}	1472	Asc. Boh.
Venice, S. Marco	VI. 163	ff. 94^{C}–97^{C}	XIV^{2}	Asc. Ital.

75. *De Veritate Proposicionis* (*De Veritate Futurorum Contingencium*)

I. Inc.: Rem que partim est vel fuit et partim futura est...
Expl.: ...Primo modo est necessarium, sed secundo modo non est necessarium.

II. Publ. Venice, 1514, ff. 5^{D}–6^{A}; Baur, pp. 143–145.

III. This short work appears in nine Grosseteste collections. It is obviously connected as to content with the *De Veritate* and the *De Libero Arbitrio I*, and may safely be assumed to belong to the same period of Grosseteste's life. It is cited by Wharton, Tanner and Pegge. Wyclyf must have known and used this work; there are striking parallels with some of Grosseteste's expressions in many of the reformer's works, though thus far no explicit quotations from it have been found in any of his published works. Baur has pointed out (p. 108*) that Bradwardine was familiar with the *De Libero Arbitrio*; a study of his yet unpublished works, considerable in number, might well reveal an acquaintance with this shorter work in the same vein.

IV. MSS:

London, B.M.				
Cotton	Otho D. x	f. 56^{b}	XIV^{m}	Asc.
Royal	6. E. v	ff. 248^{D}–249^{A}	XIV^{m}	Asc.
Florence, Marucell.	C. 163	ff. 13^{D}–14^{B}	*ca.* 1400	Asc. Ital.
Modena, Estense	lat. 54	f. 74^{a-b}	*ca.* 1500	Asc. Ital.
	lat. 649	f. 22^{B-D}	*ca.* 1500	Asc. Ital.
Prague				
Univ.	1990	ff. 46^{b}–47^{a}	1472	Asc. Boh.
Metrop. Chap.	1446	f. 267^{a} (*bis*)	XV^{m}	Asc. Boh.
Nat. Mus.	XII. E. 5	f. 39^{D}	XIV^{m}	Asc. Boh.
Venice, S. Marco	VI. 163	ff. 97^{C}–98^{A}	XIV^{2}	Asc. Ital.

PASTORAL AND DEVOTIONAL WORKS

76. *Ars Predicandi*

I. Inc.: Cum appropinquasset Ihesus Iherico etc. Si linguis hominum loquar...
Expl.: ...quis resistet? et alibi regni eius non erit finis. Explicit ars predicandi.

II. Unpubl.

III. This treatise is embedded in the collection of *Dicta* and sermons in the Durham MS A. III. 12 between items 22 and 24, as listed below, p. 185. Eight classes of people are designated: *milites, iudices, principes terrarum, claustrales, sacerdotes, sponsati, vidue, virgines.* For each class Grosseteste points out scriptural injunctions that apply to it.

IV. MS:

Durham Cath.	A. III. 12	ff. 83C–84D	*ca.* 1230

77. *De Cessacione Legalium*

I. Inc.: Fuerunt plurimi in primitiva ecclesia qui...
Expl.: ...quasi doloris languoris et infirmitatis medicinam.

II. Part I (of four parts) was published in London, 1658.* See Brown, *Fasc. Rer. Expet.* II, 246 f. for abstract of whole work.

III. The treatise was quite clearly intended to be the complement of the *De X Mandatis*, and appears along with it in many MSS. Wyclyf used the work *passim* in his *De Veritate Sacre Scripture* (ed. R. Buddensieg, London, 1901–1904), but particularly in chap. XXII. Boston of Bury mentions the work, and all the bibliographers since have listed it. The composition is to be dated *ca.* 1231 as connected with the projected conversion of the Jews.†

Grosseteste's knowledge of Hebrew chronology and his thorough familiarity with the text of the LXX, noted in his *Comm. in Galathas* (see above, p. 73), are convincingly displayed. Of the results in conversions of Jews we have no direct information.‡

* Wharton, II, 345, lists under *Edita*: *Prodiit Londini 1652 4° sed mutilus.* Stevenson, p. 104, says "Lyons". I have been unable to trace any 1652 edition; Lyons would seem to be a mistake due to a confusion between *Londini* and *Lugduni*.

† See Stevenson, p. 99 ff. and Matthew Paris, *Chron. Maj.* v (R.S.), 516 ff.

‡ See L. M. Friedman, *Robert Grosseteste and the Jews* (Cambridge, Mass. 1934), p. 21 ff. Friedman relies principally on Stevenson.

IV. MSS:

Library	Shelfmark	Folios	Date	Notes
Oxford				
Arch. Seld.	B. 8	ff. 304–314	XVII^1	Asc.*
Lincoln	54	ff. 1^A–15^D	XIII^1	Unasc.
Magdalen	3	ff. 1^a–103^b	XV^1	Asc.
Merton	82	ff. 106^A–150^D	XIV^2	Unasc.
Queen's	312	ff. 3^A–38^A	XIV^m	Asc.
London, B.M.				
Cotton	Otho D. x†			
Royal	5. C. III	ff. 264^A–267^C	XV^1	Asc.‡
	6. E. v	ff. 185^A–211^A	XIV^m	Asc.
	7. F. II	ff. 121^A–167^C	XIV^m	Asc.
Sloane	683	ff. 22^b–26^b	XIV^2	Excerpts
Cambridge				
Univ.	Kk. iv. 4	ff. 1^A–20^D	XV^1	Asc.§
Pembroke	244	ff. 1^A–49^B	XIV^1	Asc.
Trinity	B. 15. 20	cols. 527–674	XIV^2	Asc.
Eton Coll.	117, vol. II	pp. 1^a–85^a	XV^1	Asc.
Lincoln Cath.	180	ff. 89^A–120^B	XIV^2	Unasc.
Worcester Cath.	F. 152	ff. 39^A–49^C	XIV^m	Unasc.‖
Cambridge, Mass. U.S.A.	L. M. Friedman (*olim* Phillipps 6907)	ff. 1^A–30^C	XIV^m	Asc. Engl.¶
Prague, Nat. Mus.	XII. E. 5	ff. 27^A–39^C	XIV^m	Asc. Boh.

78. *Concordancia Patrum*

In Lyons MS 414, ff. 17^a–32^a, is to be found a topical concordance of the Bible and the fathers.** This probably unique copy is the work of an English scribe writing between 1235 and 1250. The use of the title *episcopus* determines the earlier date and the *terminus ad quem* is set on paleographical grounds. The title in red in the upper right corner of f. 17^a reads: *Incipit tabula Magistri Roberti lincolniensis episcopi cum addicione fratris Ade de Marisco, et sunt distincciones* IX *quarum hec prima est de deo*. The first four pages of the concordance are taken up by a table of signs, in three columns of about thirty-five signs each, making a total of around 400 signs, each followed by its subject, e.g. ⊗ *De eternitate*. Beyond a few elementary and obvious signs, there seems no system by which the various subjects are represented. Mathematical figures, conjoined conventional signs, and additional dots, strokes and curves, are pressed into service. This *index signorum* ends in the first column of f. 19^a and is followed by a list of parts of the body and human ailments, this in turn followed, in the third column, by another more

* Part I only. Probably the MS from which the 1658 ed. was printed.

† The tractate was in this codex, between present ff. 149 and 150, before the fire of 1731. See Smith's Catalogue *in loco*.

‡ Excerpts from Parts I, II and IV.

§ Some folia gone between present ff. 1 and 2.

‖ Incomplete, ending near beginning of Part II.

¶ Once belonged to Peter Le Neve and Pegge. Purchased from Goldschmidt, London, in 1933.

** See S. H. Thomson, "Grosseteste's Topical Concordance of the Bible and the Fathers" in *Speculum*, IX (1934), 139–144.

general list of topics omitted in the original *tabula*, but without corresponding signs. On f. 19[b] the concordance proper begins; it ends on f. 32[a]. On each page there are from five to ten subjects, allowing under each sign and its corresponding subject space for citations from the Bible and fathers of the Church. Wherever Grosseteste has not listed references from either one of these sources, the space is left blank. It is reasonable to suppose that the concordance was constantly growing. The wideness of his reading as well as its depth is well shown by the catholicity of his citation. Yet he remains Augustinian in his preferences. The first subject under *Distinccio* 1 is as follows:

8T An deus sit
Gen. 1 a
Aug. Contra adversarios legum et prophetarum lib. 1. De Trin. 12. De lib. arb. lib. 1. De vera relig. Epis. 38. De Civ. Dei lib. 8. 10. 11. Greg. Dial. lib. 4. 27; 10. 13. Damascenus Sentenciarum lib. 1. cap. 3. 41. Anselmus Proslog. cap. 2. 3 Monologion,

and in the right margin: *Aristotelis Metaphysice lib.* 7.

The nine distinctions into which the concordance is divided are: (i) *De Deo*; (ii) *De Verbo*; (iii) *De Creaturis* (but mostly man); (iv) *De Ecclesia*; (v) *De Sacra Scriptura*; (vi) *De Viciis*; (vii) a further catalogue of vices; (viii) *De Futuris* (including also the elements and the lower animals); (ix) *De Anima et Virtutibus eius.*

The whole Augustinian corpus is used, Ambrose, Jerome, Bede, Rabanus Maurus, John Damascene, *Omelia* as well as the *De Fide Orthodoxa*, Isidore, Bernard of Clairvaux, Chrysostom and, sparingly, the Pseudo-Dionysius, Hugh of St Victor, the *Hexameron* of Basil. The right margin of each page has additional references. These prove to be almost exclusively from Boethius' *De Consolatione*, Seneca's *Epistolae*, *De Naturalibus Questionibus* and *De Beneficiis*, with occasional references to Prudentius, Sedulius, the letters of Horace, Cicero's *De Natura Deorum*, the *Prohemium Almagesti*, Algazel's *Metaphysics* and, of Aristotle, the *De Animalibus* in nineteen Books,* *De Sompno et Vigilia*, *De Vegetabilibus* and the *Metaphysica* (in eleven Books).

There are some omissions which are of considerable interest. There are no citations from Aristotle's *Ethics*, which, considering the appositeness of the subject-matter, and Grosseteste's own translation of it, we should expect to find if he had already begun the work of translation. We may therefore safely infer that his concordance was compiled before 1240–1243, the period of his translation of the *Ethics* and the Greek commentators (see above, pp. 65, 68 f.). But we may go even farther in using significant omissions to aid us in dating the compilation. His citations from John Damascene and the Pseudo-Dionysius are not nearly so numerous as to indicate any degree of preoccupation with these two authors. We have pointed out (see above, p. 49) that it is most reasonable to suppose that the *opera Damasceni*, at least, were his earliest works of translation, and the fact that he pays almost no attention to them in this concordance immediately suggests that the

* This would be the Arab-Latin translation of Michael Scot, *ca.* 1220.

concordance may have been compiled before he entered seriously upon his work as a translator. There are, furthermore, no citations from Gregory of Nazianzus or Gregory of Nyssa, whom we know him to have been familiar with later in the episcopate.* Taking all these factors into consideration, we would seem to be justified in placing the compilation of the concordance at the beginning of the episcopate. I should like to suggest the possibility that the actual work of compilation began even before the episcopate. From 1232, when he resigned his preferments because of illness, until his election as bishop in 1235, he may be assumed to have had more time than either before or after those dates. He would have needed a good deal of time to do the reading necessary to collect the thousands of references given in this concordance.

Florilegia were abundant in the Middle Ages, but these citations made by Grosseteste are too detailed, too well classified according to his own system, to allow us to suspect him of having depended upon any such second-hand source. We are, furthermore, in a position to verify the carefulness of his reading. There are known to be at least four codices which contain the signs in his *index signorum*, indicating painstaking and systematic reading of the texts. The works in these four MSS account for only a small proportion of the works Grosseteste cites, but it is likely that other such marked MSS will come to light as soon as the nature of these signs is more widely known. MS Bodley 198 is a large codex containing the *De Civitate Dei* of Augustine and the *Moralia in Job* of Gregory, written in the first quarter of the thirteenth century in a beautiful gothic hand. It was once in Grosseteste's possession, and was left by him to the Franciscans in Oxford. Later it was owned by Thomas Gascoigne who has written numerous notes, at various places in the codex, concerning the marginal signs and notes that are in Grosseteste's hand on almost every page throughout the 308 folia. If a reader knew the signs he could, by rapidly turning the leaves, find proof-texts for any given subject (see Introd. p. 27 f.). MSS 17 and 47 of St John's Coll., Cambridge, were originally bound together as one codex.† MS 17 contains various works of Anselm. Our concordantial signs are found in profusion on ff. 1^A^–91^A^, in the heavy black ink characteristic of Grosseteste. MS 47 contains works of Augustine, and the concordantial signs are found throughout the codex, fols. 146. In neither codex is there any writing, apart from these signs, in Grosseteste's hand. MS 151 of Lambeth Palace, London, a miscellaneous codex (XIII^{1-2}) which was once the property of the Franciscans in Gloucester, contains, ff. 51^A–114^D, the *De Genesi ad Litteram* and the *Enchiridion* of Augustine. The margins have frequent signs found in our concordance, but in a hand that is probably not Grosseteste's. It may be hoped that other MSS containing these signs will be found, which will enable us to reconstruct a larger portion of Grosseteste's library, and judge more accurately his biblical, patristic and classical reading. Of his ingenuity there can be no doubt.

* See above, pp. 75 n.† and 100 f., under *Comm. in Ps.* and *Hexameron*.

† See M. R. James, *Catalogue of MSS...St John's College, Cambridge* (Cambridge, 1913), pp. 22–24, 67 f.

79. *De Confessione I*

See Sermon 15: *Quoniam cogitacio....*

80. *De Confessione II*

Inc.: Deus est quo nichil melius excogitari potest...
Expl.: ...quo nichil melius cogitari potest.

See below, Sermon 32. A common rubric of this work is: *Quomodo examinandus est penitens cum venit ad confessionem.* It should, perhaps, be listed as a separate tractate, but as it always occurs with other sermons it has been so grouped. In Lambeth MS 523 an extract is given, f. 123^{a-b} (*ca.* 1400), and at the end is described: *Hec lincolniensis in sermone qui sic incipit: Deus est quo nichil melius cogitari potest.*

81. *De Confessione III*

I. Inc.: Perambulavit Judas quinque civitates et perdidit impios...
Expl.: ...vel iuramentum vel fidem falso dedisti.

II. Unpubl.

III. This short work seems to be a sermon or an extract from a longer work. The lateness of the single known ascription and the summary character of the argument raise some doubt as to its genuineness, certainly in this form, and it is included among the authentic works with some reserve. It has distinct resemblances to the doubtful but often ascribed *De Venenis.* See below, p. 268 f.

IV. MSS:

Oxford, Laud Misc.	527	ff. 257^{a}–262^{b}	XIII^{2}	Unasc.
Dublin, Trinity	E. 1. 29	ff. 63^{A}–66^{C}	*ca.* 1425	Asc.

82. *De Confessione et Modo Confitendi Peccata*

I. Inc.: Natus in Judea Deus. Judea interpretatur confessio...
Expl.: ...sed ita dicat anglica vel gallica lingua.

II. Unpubl.

III. Apparently unknown to earlier bibliographers, this treatise on confession was first noticed by James and Jenkins in their *Catalogue of the MSS in the Library of Lambeth Palace* (London, 1932).* It is ascribed in the original hand, like the *Oraciuncula post Prandium Gallice* (see below, p. 158) and the *De Penitencia David* (see below, p. 137) with a simple *Idem* before the title. It is a manual for confessors. The *Iniunccio gallice* (see below, p. 155) follows immediately after the explicit of this *De Confessione.* The work was written

* For other items in this MS see pp. 135, 137, 155, 157 f.

after 1250, as may be gathered from a reference at the bottom of f. 186^b to *epistola ad curiam romanam, scilicet Dominus noster Jesus Christus*. There are frequent references to the use of the vernacular, but mostly *gallica* is specified.

IV. MS:

London, Lambeth	499	ff. 186^a–187^b	XIII^2	Asc.

83. *De Modo Confitendi* (*Canones Penitenciales*)

I. Inc.: Primo (Nunc) dicat sacerdos confitenti: Frater, venisti ad me causa...

Expl.: ...erat, in quadruplum restitue et xx dies peniteas.

II. Unpubl.

III. This work is listed by Bale as *Penitenciale quoddam* beginning: *Ad primum dicat*.... Tanner mentions the Lambeth MS under the title *Canones Penitenciales*. Pegge makes one tractate out of Tanner's notice and another out of the St John's MS. The rubric in the three earliest MSS reads:

> Incipiunt diversi tractatus penitencie in unum redacti secundum magistrum Robertum Grosseteste. In principio istius libelli admonet quod nullus sacerdos ex proprio sensu alicui iniungat penitenciam, quia si aliquis sacerdos per ignoranciam grossam vel negligenciam secundum graciam aliquam vel fautorem ad arbitrium tantum et libitum non canonici...generacionem et institucionem antiquorum patrum salvus eris.

The B.M. MS calls it *Penitencias a sanctis patribus traditas ex diversis libris*.... It is distinctly a work of compilation, and, from the simple *magistrum*, instead of an explicit *episcopus*, is most probably to be assigned to the archidiaconal period.

IV. MSS:

Oxford, Bodl.	828	ff. 211^a–215^b	XIV^2	Asc.
London, B.M., Add.	6716	ff. 63^A–67^B	XV^m	Asc.
London, Lambeth	144	ff. 138^A–140^B	XIII^2	Asc.
Cambridge, St John's	62	ff. 114^D–116^D	XIII^m	Asc.
Canterbury, Ch. Ch.	37	ff. 1^a–2^b	*ca.* 1300	Asc.

84. *Constituciones* (*Epistola 52**)

I. Inc.: Debentes de vobis racionem reddere...

Expl.: ...adiuvante domino Ihesu Christo canonice punituros.

II. Publ. Wilkins, *Concilia*, III, 59–61 (as *Acta Synodi Eliensis*, 1364, of Simon Langham, Bishop of Ely); E. Brown, *Fasc. Rer. Expet.* II, 410–413, and summary, p. 414; Luard, *Epistolae*, pp. 154–164.

III. This work was known to Bale as *Constitutiones Synodales*, to Leland and Tanner as *Decreta Synodalia*. Their promulgation should be dated early in the episcopate, perhaps even before the "1238?" suggested by Luard. A second edition of the *Constituciones* has an added paragraph, adapting them to use by the archdeacons of the diocese. A summary of the *Constituciones*, beginning *Sciant sacerdotes decalogum, septem criminalia*... and ending ... *Quod excommunicaciones oxonienses concilii singulis annis innoventur*, is added to most of the MSS, but appears separately in Gonv. and Caius MS 33, f. 123ᵃ, XIIIᵐ, Asc. Printed by Luard, pp. 164–166.

IV. MSS (see also under Letters, no. 52*, p. 202):

Oxford				
Ashmole	1146	ff. 80ᵃ–82ᵇ	XIVᵐ*	
Barlow	49	ff. 4ᴬ–5ᶜ	XV¹	Asc.
Bodl.	424	ff. 157ᵇ–159ᵇ	XV¹	Unasc.
Laud Misc.	439	ff. 81ᴬ–82ᴬ	XIIIᵐ	Asc.
Rawl.	C. 301	ff. 80ᵃ–84ᵇ	XV¹	Unasc.
Magdalen	104	ff. 153ᴰ–155ᶜ	*ca.* 1400	Unasc.†
St John's	136	ff. 109ᵃ–111ᵇ	XIIIᵐ	Asc.
London, B.M.				
Add.	6158	ff. 134ᶜ–136ᶜ	XIV²	Asc.
Cotton	Nero D. II	f. 266ᴬ⁻ᴰ	*ca.* 1400	Asc.
Royal	7. A. IX	f. 115ᴬ⁻ᴮ	XIII²	Unasc.‡
	9. A. XIV	ff. 193ᴬ–196ᴬ	XIII²	Unasc.
	11. B. X	ff. 176ᴮ–178ᴬ	XIVᵐ	Asc.§
Cambridge				
Univ.	Ii. ii. 7	ff. 147ᶜ–149ᴮ	XIV²	Unasc.
C.C.C.	255	ff. 209ᴰ–211ᴰ	1385	Unasc.§
Emmanuel	27	ff. 79ᴬ–80ᴰ	XIIIᵐ	Unasc.
Gonv. & Caius	138	ff. 176ᵃ–178ᵇ	XIII²	Unasc.
Jesus	66	ff. 65ᶜ–88ᴮ	*ca.* 1300	Unasc.
Peterhouse	255, pt. iii	ff. 30ᴮ–33ᶜ	XIIIᵐ	Unasc.

85. *Correctorium Tocius Biblie*

I. Inc.: [a ten-line prologue] Publica collegi cupiens prodesse pusillis...
[text] Ut igitur de iam propositis evidencius agatur a prosodia...
Expl.: ...Versus et finis: Publica qui texit: hic correctorius exit: Si bene sit sic sit, si non, quis non maledixit?‖

II. Unpubl.

III. Unnoticed by the bibliographers until Cave (ed. 1720, p. 630) reported the Canterbury MS, this *Liber Correctorius* exists in several early unascribed copies and one later ascribed MS. The fact that the early copies

* Asc. to Robert of Winchelsea, Archbishop of Canterbury; has archdeacon's ending.

† This codex contains the same three works as Bodley MS 424; they may have come from the same scriptorium; has archdeacon's ending.

‡ *Mut. in init.* § With archdeacon's ending.

‖ In the Bodl. Auct. MS there is a short appendix (f. 410ᶜ): *Omnis diccio latina*..., part of which is also in the Canterbury copy, giving the pronunciation of about twenty-five words which *non accentuantur secundum modernam fratrum predicatorum consuetudinem*. It would appear to be a later addition.

are anonymous may justify some scepticism as to the truthfulness of the later ascription. There is much quotation from medieval grammarians throughout the text. The name we meet most frequently is *Magister Johannes de G.* The G. is at times expanded to *G'*, *Gerl'*, *Gall*, and refers, of course, to John of Garland. His *Compendium* is quoted (Fairfax MS, f. 8ᵃ). Paetow dated the composition of the *Compendium Grammatice ca.* 1234.* More frequently, however, it is *Magister Johannes in Speculo Ecclesie*. This is, in all probability, the *De Mysteriis Ecclesie*, which Paetow dated 1245.† Alexander de Villa Dei is commonly referred to as *Magister Alexander*, and there occur frequent quotations from his *Doctrinale*.‡ There are quotations from Alexander Neckham (†1217), Petrus de Riga (†1209), the *Lapidarius* (*Liber de Gemmis*) of Marbod§ (here called *libellus qui incipit Evax rex Arabum qui eciam dicitur lapidarius*), Walter of Châtillon, copious *versus* from Vergil's *Aeneid* and *Eclogues* and Ovid *in libro Eroydes*, and one reference to *liber quem Remigius scripsit de ebraycis nominibus* (Fairfax MS, f. 14ᵃ). Internal evidence compels us to date the *Correctorium* after 1245, but that late date leaves us almost a decade in which Grosseteste may have compiled the work. In view of his deep interest in grammar and etymology, there is no compelling reason, failing earlier contrary ascription, for rejecting the explicit attribution at the end of the Canterbury MS: *Explicit correctorium tocius biblie traditum a domino Roberto Grostede episcopo lincolniensi.*

The work was intended mostly to correct mispronunciation of words in which the quantity of the vowel, the derivation or the stress were currently misunderstood.‖ The author cites verses from recognized classics where the metre or the rhyme would show the proper stress or accent. In the MSS an accent-mark in red ink has been placed above the correct syllable. There is some divergence among the MSS, but nothing beyond the occasional omission of a *versus* which could be most simply explained as due to scribal independence.

IV. MSS:

Oxford				
Auct.	D. 3. I	ff. 407^{A}–410^{C}	XIII^{2}	Unasc.
Fairfax	27	ff. 7^{a}–24^{b}	XIV^{1}	Unasc.
London, B.M., Royal	I. A. VIII	ff. 411^{A}–421^{B}	XIII^{m}	Unasc.
Cambridge, C.C.C.	460	ff. 1^{a}–24^{b}	XIII^{2}	Unasc.
Canterbury, Ch. Ch.	D. 16 (58)	ff. 1^{a}–5^{a}	*ca.* 1400	Asc.

* L. J. Paetow, "Morale Scolarium of John of Garland" in *Memoirs of Univ. of California*, IV, pt. ii (Berkeley, 1927), 121. The Introduction lists the works of John, correcting the article by Hauréau in *Not. et Extr.* XXVII, pt. ii.

† *Op. cit.* p. 112 f.; ed. F. W. Otto, *Commentarii Critici in Codd. Bibl. Gissensis*... (Giessen, 1842), pp. 131–198.

‡ Ed. D. Reichling (Berlin, 1893). § *Patr. Lat.* CLXXIV, cols. 1737–1776.

‖ In a recent work, H. H. Glunz (*History of the Vulgate from Alcuin to Roger Bacon* (Cambridge, 1933), p. 285 f.) has mentioned this work and listed the four unascribed MSS, not noting the Grossetestian authorship; he did not note the copious quotations from grammarians of the early thirteenth century which help us to fix the *terminus a quo* of the composition. For the *Libri correccionum*, to be distinguished from the *Liber correctorius* or *Correctorium* with which we are concerned, see Denifle in *Archiv f. Litt.- und Kirchengeschichte d. Mittelalters*, IV (1888), 263 ff., 471 ff.

86. *De Cura Pastorali* (*Epistola* 127)

I. Inc.: Moyses qui tradente Domino susceperat...
Expl.: ...in ipsa superiori potestate obeditur.

II. Publ. by Luard, pp. 357–431, as Letter 127. See below, p. 212.

III. Although this work, addressed to the Dean and Chapter of Lincoln, *ca.* 1239, was one of the most important documents in the dispute between Grosseteste and his Chapter, there seems to be no thirteenth-century copy of it extant. It was used by Wyclyf and listed by Boston of Bury under the above title, by Bale and Pits as *Contra Prelatorum Ignaviam*, and by Tanner, who lists it once as a tractate *De Cura Pastorali* and once as a letter, citing the Cambridge and Cotton Otho MSS.

Both because of its great length and its impersonal tenor, it is not a letter in the ordinary sense, but rather a well-worked-out exposition of Grosseteste's conception of the episcopal function, based almost exclusively on Mosaic law. The spirit is neatly summed up in the beginning phrase of an early paragraph (p. 360): *Prelatus igitur, cuius typus est Moyses, non minutus potestate data aliis de spiritu suo in omnes suos subditos, plenam habet ordinariam et iudiciariam potestatem, ac per hoc plenam correccionem et reformacionem.* Although there are a few scattered quotations from the fathers, canon law is conspicuously absent.

IV. MSS (in addition to complete collections of Letters, q.v. below, p. 193 f.):

Oxford, Bodl.	312	ff. 172C–184D	XIV²	Asc.
London, B.M., Cotton	Nero D. II	ff. 267B–276B	*ca.* 1400	Unasc.
Cambridge, Trinity	B. 15. 23	ff. 74A–88C	*ca.* 1400	Asc.

87. *Dialogus de Contemptu Mundi*

I. Inc.: O munde immunde quare diligimus te? Hic est ergo fructus...
Expl.: ...mutabilitatis vicissitudine requiescat. Amen.

II. Unpubl.

III. This short work is ascribed to Grosseteste in the original hand in the early and unique copy. The rubric reads: *Incipit tractatus Roberti lincolniensis episcopi de contemptu mundi. Utitur enim quasi quodam dialogo inter corpus et animam.* Throughout the dialogue *R* for *Robertus* and *A* for *Anima* show the change in speaker. This tractate has not been noted in any Grosseteste bibliography. A later (*ca.* 1300) copy of the well-known *Visio Philiberti*,* also known as *Disputacio inter corpus et animam*, in MS 1583 (ff. 88B–89B) of the Vienna Nationalbibliothek bears the original rubric: *Incipit disputacio inter corpus et animam composita per magistrum Rudbertum grossi capitis linconiensem episcopum*, which testifies to the currency of a tradition that Grosseteste had written such a dialogue. As the Vienna copy is in a South German hand, and there is no evidence that the Cambridge MS has ever been outside England, we must suppose, if we accept the validity of the suggested

* See below, p. 247 f., *Spurium* 16.

tradition, that there was or is a copy of our authentic *Dialogus* somewhere on the Continent. It may yet be found.

IV. MS:

Cambridge, Trinity	B. 15. 38	ff. 77^a–79^b	XIII^m	Asc.

88. *De Dotibus*

I. Inc.: Primo tractandum est de dote...
Expl.: ...Isaie ii...vinee mee et non feci.

II. Unpubl.

III. The first mention of this treatise is by Bale. Pits and Tanner cite the Cambridge MS; Pegge copies Tanner's notice. Although there are but two MSS known, and the earlier of the two was written *ca.* 1350, there is no reason to reject the genuineness of the tract. The texts of the two copies are of independent traditions and must presuppose one or more recopyings, which might bring us well into the thirteenth century. It is safe to assume that it is a work of his later years, perhaps from his archidiaconal period, though it might be placed in the early years of the episcopate.

IV. MSS:

London, B.M., Cotton	Vesp. D. XXIII	ff. 15^b–19^b	XV^1	Asc.
Cambridge, Univ.	Ii. i. 19	ff. 209^D–211^B	XIV^m	Asc.

89. *De Eucharistia*

I. Inc.: Eucharistia dicitur ab eu quod est bonum et caris...
Expl.: ...potenciam per essenciam. Versus.... Panis mutatur specie remanente priore.

II. Unpubl.

III. This little work is distinctly Grossetestian in tone; it appears, furthermore, in a codex containing exclusively Grossetestiana. The lack of early copies, however, as well as its patently fragmentary nature would lead us to suspect that it is an extract, copied by a later scribe, from some unpublished larger work such as the *Dicta* or the *Moralia in Evangelia*, whose true context can be ascertained as soon as we have the longer works immediately available. Or again it might be one of the longer marginal notes which Grosseteste was in the habit of making in his own MSS.

IV. MS:

Cambridge, Trinity	B. 15. 20	cols. 519–520	*ca.* 1400	Asc.

90. *De Triplici Gracia*

See below, p. 231, *Dictum* 134.

91. *De X Mandatis*

I. Inc.: Sicut dicit Apostolus ad Cor. 12: Plenitudo legis est dileccio...
Expl.: ...genus lesionis exprimitur in istis sex mandatis.

II. Unpubl. save for a fragment by Brown, *Fasc. Rer. Expet.* II, 306–308.

III. This work, known to all the bibliographers beginning with Boston of Bury, is one of the best attested of Grosseteste's larger tractates. Most of the earliest MSS ascribe the work to him. Of its use in sermons in the century after the death of Grosseteste we can form only an imperfect picture. The preaching of that hundred years in England remains as yet insufficiently studied. But Wyclyf drew upon this treatise copiously in his homonymous work (ed. Loserth), e.g. pp. 9, 169 ff., 200, 233 ff., 306 f., as well as in his later *Opus Evangelicum*, I (ed. Loserth), 184.

Stevenson, p. 104 ff., following Pegge's suggestion (pp. 31, 269), connects the writing of this work with the agitation for the conversion of the Jews, 1230–1231, which called forth a similar treatise *De Cessacione Legalium* (see above, p. 121 f.). The suggestion is an attractive one, but, for the treatise on the Ten Commandments, needs further study. There is little in the text itself that would compel such an explanation, unless a restrained display of a knowledge of Hebrew history and law could be extended so far. There is no evidence in this work that Grosseteste had begun to use the Greek text of the LXX or any of the Greek fathers, a usage we have given reason for dating *ca.* 1230 (see above, p. 73). We should have expected him to make use of the LXX in a work concerned with the Mosaic code. On the other hand we notice an occasional specification of the number of a chapter in the New Testament, and several quotations from Aristotle's *De Animalibus*. These last two details would seem to fix the *terminus a quo* at 1225. We have then outside limits of *ca.* 1225 and 1230. A date nearer the former than the latter might be suggested by reason of the fact that Grosseteste habitually cites Scripture by the title of the book simply. He has not yet become used to quoting by chapter.

IV. MSS:

Oxford				
Digby	163	ff. 21^a–56^b	XV^{1}	Asc.
Laud Misc.	85	ff. 32^A–56^D	XIV^{2}	Asc.
	524	ff. 83^a–110^b	*ca.* 1400	Asc.
Balliol	35^B	ff. 114, 119★	1443	Unasc.
Exeter	21	pp. 170^a–212^b	XV^{1}	Asc. *mut. in fine*
Jesus	110	ff. 188^A–211	XV^{m}	Asc.
Lincoln	6	ff. 192^A–209^B+ *tabula*	XV^{1}	Asc.
	105	ff. 34^B–45^D	XIV^{2}	Asc.
London, B.M.				
Cotton	Otho D. x	ff. 213^a–227^b	XIV^{m}	Asc.
	Vitell. C. xiv	ff. 35^A–57^A	XIV^{2}	Asc.
Harley	1207	ff. 12^a–35^b	XIV^{2}	Unasc.
	1298	ff. 84^D–105^A	*ca.* 1400	Asc.
Royal	6. E. v	ff. 228^A–239^B	XIV^{m}	Asc.
	7. F. II	ff. 168^A–184^A	XIV^{m}	Asc.

★ Fragments of *Mandata* I and II.

London, B.M.				
Royal	11. B. III	ff. 319b–328b	*ca.* 1300	Unasc. Abr.
Cambridge				
Univ.	Ii. i. 26	ff. 39a–71a	XV1	Asc.
Trinity	B. 14. 36	ff. 128b–219b	XVm	Asc.
	B. 15. 20	cols. 674–742	XIV2	Asc.
Lincoln Cath.	125	ff. 50B–73D	XV1	Asc.
	180	ff. 120B–135D	XIV2	Unasc.
	202	ff. 1A–17D	XIVm	Asc.
Douai	451	ff. 1a–43a	XV1	Asc. Engl.
Vatican	lat. 4367	ff. 71a–104b	XIV2	Asc. Engl.

There are a few extracts from the discussion of *Mandatum* III in Trin. Coll., Cambridge, MS B. 15. 38, ff. 32a–33a, the earliest (XIIIm) MS of any part of the work. This MS contains much other Grosseteste matter.

92. *Glosule Varie*

Dr R. W. Hunt has come upon the following marginal glosses ascribed to Grosseteste in two MSS which he has kindly given me permission to print. It is probable that they will be found, on further investigation, to be extracts from some *dictum*, sermon or commentary. Thus far I have been unable to place them in their context.

MS York Cath. XVI. I. 5, XIII, Peter Lombard *In Psalmos*. On f. 11C, bottom margin, in a fifteenth-century hand:

Lincolniensis. Cor namque scrutari est investigare cogitaciones. Penes vero hominis scrutari est investigare appetitus et voluntates. Hoc enim sciendum est quod nulla cogitacio est peccatum nisi ipsam fecerit immundus affectus aut generet immundum effectum.

Idem. Nulla cogitacio, quamcunque fuerit immunda, cor humanum polluit, si voluntas non consentit. Set quia dissentis et non consentis pena est quam pateris cedit non ad culpam. Lincolniensis.

MS Hunter 58, Durham. Extracts from Jerome's *Breviarium Maius super Psalmos*, XV, 450, bottom margin:

R. Lyncolniensis. Cum duo convenerunt in unum et post divisi sunt, vis scire uter divisorum adhuc maneat in corporis unitate. Agnosce per simile membrorum sectorum. Si abscidatur membrum quod remanet dolet. Debet hoc nos ad unitatem invitare, quod pars separata a toto non movetur nisi pondere proprio in toto autem movetur pondere tocius. Sic si tu es in ecclesie unitate moveris sursum tocius ecclesie pondere, hoc est caritate.

93. *Nota de Graciis Deo Agendis*

I. Inc.: Nota quod quanto quis maiorem de deo habuit per scripturam noticiam...

Expl.: ...Ideo dicit Aristoteles in Ethicis: Scire aut parum aut nichil prodest ad virtutes.

II. Unpubl.

III. This short note of nineteen lines is ascribed in the original hand in the early and unique MS, which is probably the work of someone in the bishop's *familia* (see p. 74 f.). The quotation from Aristotle's *Ethics* might be of some help in dating the note *ca.* 1243 or later, but it is isolated and fragmentary.

IV. MS:

Cambridge, Gonv. & Caius	439	f. 52B	XIII¹	Asc.

94. *De Humilitate Contemplativorum*

I. Inc.: Discuciendum est diligenter a corde uniuscuiusque et maxime...
Expl.: ...nil scribatur nil legatur nisi solus ipse.

II. Unpubl.

III. Unnoticed by any of the early bibliographers, this short treatise was listed in M. R. James' *Catalogue of the MSS...of Gonville and Caius College, Cambridge*. The MS was, to all appearances, written by someone in the immediate *familia* of the bishop, though his handwriting occurs nowhere in the codex (see above, p. 74 f.). The ascription in the original hand, indented in the text, f. 56a, and repeated at the top of f. 56b, *dominus lincolniensis de humilitate contemplativorum*, dates the composition in the episcopal period. There are no other internal indications that would help in dating. We have called it a "treatise", but it was almost surely delivered as a sermon or collation. *Fratres karissimi* occurs once, and much of the argument is in the first and second persons plural. There is, however, the important lack of a sermon text, which allows us to classify it as other than a sermon.

IV. MS:

Cambridge, Gonv. & Caius	439	ff. 56a–57A	XIII¹	Asc.

95. *Meditaciones*

I. Inc.: Meditari debes quod mortaliter peccaveris...
Expl.: ...potest latere ubi intolerabile est apparere.

II. Unpubl.

III. Leland mentions a *Libellus meditationum*; Bale lists *Meditationum suarum Lib.* I. Tanner, citing Bishop Moore's MS, gives the incipit; Pegge takes his notice from Tanner. The MS tradition seems authentic.

IV. MSS:

Cambridge				
Univ.	Hh. iv. 3	ff. 98b–99a	XVm	Asc.*
Trinity	B. 2. 16	ff. 178a–179b	XIVm	Asc.

* This is the MS of Bishop Moore of Norwich, seen by Tanner. On f. 157b of this codex a contemporary scribe has written an abstract of the work, beginning: *Nota secundum Grosseteste quod octo sunt signa humilitatis....* (*Dictum* 142?)

The catalogue of the Douai MSS lists this work as *Perutilis meditacio Roberti Groceteste lincolniensis episcopi* in MS 269. The list was evidently compiled from the *contenta*, f. 140[a], where this title appears after *Secreta meditacio beati Ieronimi*. This work is not now in the codex, of English provenance, written XV[1].

96. *Moralitates super Evangelia*

I. Inc.: Intencioni quattuor ewangelistarum nichil eque vicio...
Expl.: ...ascendere possumus quod nobis patrare dignetur.

II. Unpubl.

III. For this very significant but relatively unknown work we have excellent internal and external authentication. The Trinity Coll., Oxford, MS is probably a copy of the archetype and bears an original ascription to Grosseteste. Thomas of Eccleston remarks in his *De Adventu Minorum* (ed. Little, Paris, 1909, p. 60 f.) that the Minorites under Grosseteste's tutelage *inestimabiliter infra breve tempus tam in questionibus quam predicacioni congruis subtilibus moralitatibus profecerunt*. This sort of exposition of Scripture with "moralities" is perfectly represented by our text. The four gospels are expounded *seriatim*, each text illustrated by one or more apt *exempla*, many of them, in this connection at least, apparently original with Grosseteste.*

The ascription on f. 1[a] of the Trinity MS reads: *Auctor huius libri est magister Robertus Grosseteste episcopus lincolniensis*. Just below in the same hand we read: *Thomas de londoniis precentor Theoulet* [i.e. Tewkesbury] *hunc librum perquisivit et de labore suo scribere fecit assignando eum claustro Theoulet ad necessitatem claustralium ibidem studentium*. We know from the statement of Eccleston that Grosseteste's lectures were given probably in 1229 and 1230—*infra breve tempus*—but the scribe's use of the title *episcopus* forces us to conclude that the actual writing of this MS was not done until 1235 or later. The *hunc librum* which he sought out so diligently—*perquisivit*—refers, in all likelihood, to Grosseteste's own copy, and as this copying may have taken place after Grosseteste's election to the bishopric we need not be disturbed by an apparent conflict in dates. This Thomas of London has thus far defied identification. There is, of course, no possibility of any confusion with the Thomas of London who was a benefactor of the Oxford Franciscans in 1341.†

The work is divided into four parts of seventy-eight, fifty-nine, ninety-eight and sixty-four chapters respectively. The title was known to Leland, Bale, Pits (who mentions the Trinity MS) and Tanner (who notes the Cambridge MS).

* Little suggested, *Arch. Franc. Hist.* XIX (1926), 808, that the Trinity MS was a copy of the work referred to by Thomas of Eccleston.

† See Little, *Grey Friars*, p. 92.

IV. MSS:

Oxford				
Balliol	35B	ff. 1^A–165^D	1443	Asc.*
Lincoln	79	ff. 11^a–248^b	XIII^m	Unasc.†
Trinity	50	ff. 2^A–6^A, *capitula*		
		ff. 7^A–409^B	XIII^1	Asc.
Cambridge, Univ.	Kk. ii. 1	ff. 183^A–304^C	XV^m	Asc.‡

97. *De Obsequiis Bene Dicendis*

I. Non versus de psalmo, non oracio de versu, non diccio de oracione, non sillaba de diccione, non litera de sillaba debet transiliri vel omitti, quia si omittatur litera erit vox non significativa ut *dominu* pro *dominus*. Unde quedam monialis cum devotissime gloriose virgini Marie deserviret quadam nocte in visione apparuit ei beata virgo Maria et inter cetera hec quoque dixit: "Noli timere, filia, matrem tuam que cotidie plurima mihi [f. 184^b] reddis obsequia. Sed si vis illa obsequia tibi magis prodesse et michi placere noli amodo ea tam velociter pronunciare. Nam placet michi peroptime angelica salutacio, et dum dicitur michi prolixius trahendo *Dominus tecum* ineffabiliter delector." Et illa devotissime gaudens duas particulas salutacionis beate virginis quas dicere consueverat ab illo die ut secundam partem diligencius et morosius dicere posset omisit.

II. Here published for the first time.

III. Previously unnoticed, this short *diccio* is first referred to by James and Jenkins in their catalogue of the Lambeth MSS (1932). It may be an extract, perhaps from the *Moralitates*, or a bit of table-talk taken down by one of his circle. The scribe of this valuable MS seems to have collected a number of intimate sayings of the bishop. See also pp. 125 f., 137, 155, and 157 f.

IV. MS:

London, Lambeth	499	f. 184^{a-b}	XIII^2	Asc. §

98. *Ordinacio de Pecunia Deposita in Cista S. Frideswyde*

I. Inc.: Omnibus Christi fidelibus.... Noverit universitas vestra quod cum burgenses Oxonie...

Expl.: ...presenti pagine sigillum nostrum duximus apponendum. Hiis testibus....

* The first leaf is now wanting, but it was seen entire by Langbaine who gives the correct incipit.

† Ascribed by Coxe, *Cat. Codd. MSS Coll. Oxon.* I (1852), Lincoln, p. 41, to Alexander Neckham on a basis of a late (*ca.* 1450) ascription pasted on the front flyleaf: *Moralia Magistri Alexandri Necham super evangelia cum tabula cum aliis contentis. Ex dono Magistri Roberti Flemmyng decani Lincolniensis.* The original scribe adds to our confusion by a note in red in the left margin of f. 1 which reads: *Moralia Magistri Alexandri de Ba super ewangelium.* This Alexander remains unidentified. It is not a known name for Alexander Neckham.

‡ This MS was noticed by Cave.

§ The text is immediately preceded by *Ro. Linc' epc.*

II. Publ. *Monumenta Academica* (R.S.) ed. H. Anstey (1868), p. 8; *Statuta Antiqua Univ. Oxon.* (ed. S. Gibson, Oxford, 1931), pp. 74–76.

III. For the foundation in 1240 of a chest at St Frideswyde's from which poor scholars might borrow without interest, see Rashdall, *Universities of Europe in the Middle Ages*, III (ed. Powicke and Emden, Oxford, 1936), 35 f., and also, Stevenson, p. 237 f., S. Gibson, *Statuta Antiqua*..., p. xl.

IV. MSS:

Oxford				
Univ. Archives	A. 1	f. 56^{a-b}	*ca.* 1325	Asc.
Bodl.	337 (Regist. D)	ff. 12^{b}–13^{a}	XIV^{2}	Asc.
Regist.	C	ff. 35^{b}–36^{a}	*ca.* 1400	Asc.

See also Gibson's description of the University Registers, *op. cit.* pp. x–xix.

99. *Parabola Domini Roberti Grosseteste*

For this parable and its moral, presented *in scripto* to Boniface, Archbishop of Canterbury, at Lyons in May, 1250, see below, p. 143 f.

100. *De Penis Purgatorii*

I. Inc.: In omnibus operibus tuis memorare novissima.... Intelligatis modo...

Expl.: ...in seculo permanebunt, de quo dolore ipse nos defendat qui sine fine vivit et imperat.

II. Unpubl. An edition of the Latin and Anglo-Norman versions together is in preparation by Miss Ruth J. Dean. See below, p. 158 f.

III. The number of ascribed copies of the Latin version is considerable, but none of the known copies can be dated earlier than the second half of the fourteenth century. It is interesting, though probably not significant, that, whereas there are several copies of the Anglo-Norman version of the thirteenth century, *none* bears any ascription, and that *all* the known copies of the Latin version, of the late fourteenth and fifteenth centuries, are ascribed.

The prologue, found with minor variants in all the Latin MSS, is as follows:

In omnibus operibus tuis memorare novissima tua et in eternum non peccabis. Dilectissimi fratres et sorores his omnibus qui istam compilacionem legerint vel ab aliis legi audierint, sanctus Robertus lincolniensis salutem et sanitatem corporis et anime in domino nostro Jesu Christo, qui verus est noster salvator, deinde indulgencie centum dies. Karissimi, per graciam domini nostri nos intendimus, secundum quod audivimus et in sacra scriptura didicimus, in ista compilacione loqui vobis de pena purgatorii ad salvacionem animarum vestrarum. Deus pro suo nomine benedicto...qui tota die venatus et nichil accipit. Intelligatis modo, karissimi....

The older MSS omit the *sanctus* before *Robertus*. Such pious emendations are not uncommon. The work was known to Wharton, Pits, Tanner and Pegge. In spite of the unanimity of MS attribution, the term *compilacio* should be emphasized.

IV. MSS:

Oxford, C.C.C.	155	ff. 3ª–10ᵇ	XV¹	Asc.
London, B.M.				
Add.	33957	ff. 44ᵇ–50ᵇ	XVᵐ	Asc.
Harley	3673	ff. 165ª–168ᵇ	XV¹	Asc.
London, Lambeth	500	ff. 72ª–89ª	XIV²	Asc.
Cambridge, Univ.	Kk. ii. 1	ff. 308ᶜ–309ᴰ	XVᵐ	Asc.
Dublin, Trinity	C. 4. 9	pp. 52–60	XV¹	Asc.
	C. 5. 17	ff. 111ᵇ–118ª	XVᵐ	Asc.

101. *De Penitencia David*

I. Inc.: Titulus Psalmi: Psalmus Davit. Cum venit ad eum Natan propheta...
Expl.: ...quando aliquis leticiam cordis sui pre gaudio exprimere non valet.

II. Unpubl.

III. Unknown to early bibliographers, this considerable item was first noticed in 1932 by James and Jenkins in their catalogue of the Lambeth MSS. It follows immediately after the *Oraciuncula post Prandium Gallice* (see below, p. 158), and is introduced by the rubric: *Idem super Psalmo: Miserere mei deus etc*. The *Idem*, like the *Idem* preceding the *Oraciuncula*, can refer only to Grosseteste, who was specifically mentioned as the author of the preceding item (see above, p. 135), and of the following *De Confessione et Modo Confitendi Peccata* (see above, p. 125). The work exhibits finely the characteristics of Grosseteste's exegetical method.

IV. MS:

London, Lambeth	499	ff. 184ᵇ–186ª	XIII²	Asc.

102. *De Sanguine Christi*

I. Inc.: Cum autem quod sacratissimus foret domini nostri...
Expl.: ...Et sic omnium cessare debent morsus detractorum.

II. Publ. in vol. VI (*Additamenta*) of Matthew Paris' *Chron. Maj.* (R.S.), pp. 138–144.

III. Matthew Paris tells the story* of this "determination" which took place at Westminster in October, 1247, on the occasion of the reception by the king of a crystal vase containing some of the drops of blood that fell from the body of Christ on the cross.

> Et cum inter loquendum aliqui de assidentibus obgrunnirent hesitantes, questionem hanc moverent, "Quomodo cum plene et integraliter tercia die post passionem resurrexerit Dominus, sanguinem in terra reliquerit?" Que questio ab episcopo Lincolniensi ad unguem tunc determinabatur, prout habetur in libro Additamentorum; prout huius pagine [scriptor] audivit, et verbo ad verbum satis dilucide scripsit, ad tale signum: [a chalice covered with a cloth].

* *Chron. Maj.* IV (R.S.), 640 ff. See also Stevenson, p. 263 ff.

The bibliographers have never listed this work as a separate treatise. There are not known to be any separate MS copies of the work. From the obvious care with which this "determination" has been prepared, it is hardly likely that it was delivered completely *ex tempore*.

IV. MS:

London, B.M., Cotton	Nero D. I	ff. 91^A–92^C	XIII^m	Asc.*

103. *Templum Domini* (*Distincciones* or *De Articulis Fidei*)

I. Inc.: Templum domini sanctum est quod estis vos. Sermo iste quamvis...

Expl.: ...ab eius servitute est esse in temperancia.

II. Unpubl.

III. The MS tradition of this work from the first half of the thirteenth century is abundantly clear. The great number of extant MSS bear witness to the wide diffusion and continued use of this outline of quasi-popular medieval theology. Much of the treatise is in diagrammatical form. It has been known to all the bibliographers. Matthew Paris (*Chron. Maj.* v (R.S.), 286)† ascribes a work under this title to John of Basingstoke. This may have been a sermon or even an independent tract, but it can hardly be that Matthew intended to contradict the evidence of MSS already written during Grosseteste's lifetime. If, on the other hand, he did refer to our treatise, he was clearly in error. Much of our MS evidence is older than the composition of Matthew's *Chronica Majora*. Thus far no copy of this work or any work with a similar title bearing an ascription to John of Basingstoke has been noted. In the earliest ascriptions Grosseteste is called *episcopus*. We must therefore place the composition of the work after 1235. There are no internal indications that would allow us to be more explicit.

Miss Roberta D. Cornelius has published‡ an English poem *Templum Domini* found in B.M. Add. 32578, ff. 105^a–116^a, which purports to be an "englishing" of Grosseteste's work. The author of the poem, however, has done no more than use Grosseteste's theological framework, and, as there is nothing original about that framework, even that dependence might be doubted.

IV. MSS:

Oxford				
Bodl.	36	ff. vi^a–x^a	XIII^m	Unasc.
	157	ff. 253^a–259^a	XIII^2	Unasc.
	631	ff. 183^b–196^b	XIII^1	Unasc.
Digby	149	ff. 46^a–55^b	XIII^m	Unasc.
Laud Misc.	112	ff. 317^a–324^C	XIII^2	Asc.
	368	ff. 74^a–83^b	XIII^m	Asc.

* It is generally accepted that this MS is the work of Matthew Paris himself.

† *Item aliud composuit* [magister Joannes Basingstoke] *in quo particule senten-ciarum per distincciones dilucidantur, quod sic incipit: "Templum Domini"; quod est perutile.*

‡ In *The Figurative Castle* (Bryn Mawr, 1930), pp. 90–112.

Laud Misc.	374	ff. 280^{A}–288^{D}	*ca.* 1400	R.G. MS
	497	ff. 304^{a}–311^{a}	XIII^{m}	Unasc.
Rawl.	A. 384	ff. 98^{a}–106^{b}	XIII^{2}	Asc.*
C.C.C.	32	ff. 77^{C}–85^{a}	XIII^{m}	Unasc.
Magdalen	202	ff. 163^{B}–170^{C}	*ca.* 1400	Asc.
Merton	257	ff. 140^{a}–147^{b}	XIII^{1}	Asc.†
Trinity	18	ff. 193^{a}–202	XIV^{1}	Unasc.
London, B.M.				
Arundel	52	ff. 100^{C}–107^{b}	*ca.* 1300	Unasc.
Burney	356	ff. 20^{b}–29^{b}	XIV^{2}	Unasc.
Harley	979	ff. 75^{a}–81^{a}	XIII^{m}	Asc.
	1897	ff. 1^{a}–8^{a}	XIII^{m}	Unasc.
	3244	ff. 138^{a}–145^{a}	XIII^{1}	Unasc.
Royal	5. F. xv	ff. 50^{a}–59^{b}	XIII^{m}	Asc.
	7. A. ix	ff. 91^{b}–102^{b}	XIII^{2}	Unasc.
	8. B. iv	ff. 92^{a}–99^{b}	XIV^{1}	Unasc.
	8. C. iv	ff. 2^{a}–7^{b}	XIII^{2}	Asc.
	8. D. iv	ff. 76^{a}–84^{a}	XIV^{1}	Asc.
	9. A. iii	ff. 47^{a}–57^{b}	XIV^{2}	Unasc.
	12. F. xv	ff. 165^{a}–175^{b}	XIII^{2}	Asc. XIV^{m}
Cambridge				
Univ.	Ii. i. 22	ff. 106^{a}–116^{a}	XIV^{1}	Unasc.
	Ii. i. 39	ff. 111^{a}–118^{b}	XV^{m}	Unasc.
	Kk. iv. 20	ff. 47^{b}–56^{a}	XIV^{1}	Unasc.
	Ll. i. 15	ff. 174^{a}–181^{a}	XIII^{m}	Asc.
C.C.C.	136	ff. 102^{a}–107^{a}	XIII^{2}	Asc. *mut.*
	150	ff. 118^{a}–122^{a}	XIII^{m}	Unasc. *mut.*
Emmanuel	27	ff. 69^{a}–75^{b}	XIII^{m}	Asc.
Jesus	66	ff. 50^{C}–59^{C}	*ca.* 1300	Asc.
Pembroke	245	ff. 210^{a}–216^{b}	*ca.* 1400	Asc.
St John's	15	ff. 71^{a}–77^{b}	XIII^{1}	Unasc.
	62	ff. 1^{a}–7^{a} + 128	*ca.* 1300	Unasc.
Trinity	B. 15. 20	cols. 487–508	XIV^{2}	Asc.
Leicester Corporation‡			XIII	Unasc.
Lincoln Cath.	202	ff. 221^{b}–224^{a}	*ca.* 1400	Asc.
	242	ff. 105^{a}–123^{b}	XV^{1}	Unasc. *mut.*
Manchester, John Rylands lat.	153§	ff. 3^{a}–14^{b}	XIII^{2}	Asc.‖
Bamberg	Q. iv. 6	ff. 305^{a}–320^{b}	XV^{m}	Asc. Ger.
	Q. iv. 39	ff. 87^{D}–97^{B}	1418	Asc. Ger.
Bern	260	ff. 43^{a}–47^{b}	*ca.* 1300	Unasc. Ger.¶
	271	ff. 13^{a}–21^{a}	XIV	Asc.

* The colophon reads: *Explicit summa quam Magister Robertus Grosseteste quondam episcopus lincolniensis nunc vero sanctus ad instruccionem sacerdotum et ad salutem animarum salubriter composuit.*

† The colophon reads: *Summa magistri Roberti lincolniensis episcopi de articulis ffidei et de ffide catholica et de omnibus rebus pertinentibus ad officium sacerdotale.*

‡ See *Hist. MSS Comm.* Report 8, Appendix 1, p. 420.

§ *Olim* Ashburnham 92.

‖ There was a copy in a Bible stolen from Reading Abbey in 1258, according to a detailed description left by *fr. Aluredus sacrista Radingie* in MS 371 of Lambeth Palace. See James and Jenkins, *Catalogue of MSS in Lambeth Palace* (Cambridge, 1930–1932), p. 504 f.

¶ Entitled *Speculum Sacerdotum Ecclesie.* I have not seen this MS and several others in this list for which insufficient data are given. See *Index Codicum.*

Graz, Univ.	655	ff. 107ᵃ–118ᵃ	XVᵐ	Asc. Ger.
	881	ff. 1ᵃ–11ᵇ of quire 18	1444	Unasc. Ger.*
Leipzig, Univ.	lat. 595	ff. 201ᵃ–216ᵇ	XV¹	Asc. Ger.
Lwów	824	ff. 35ᵃ–54ᵃ	1460	Asc. Pol.
Munich	Clm. 14658	ff. 1ᵃ–23ᵃ	XV¹	Asc. Ger.
	Clm. 14724	ff. 160ᴮ–163ᵃ	XIII²	Unasc. Ger.
Paris				
B.N.	lat. 3473	ff. 191ᵇ–209ᵃ	XVᵐ	Fr.†
	lat. 4936	ff. 49ᵃ–55ᵇ	XIII²	Asc. Fr.
	lat. 12312	ff. 211ᵃ–218ᵇ	XIV¹	Asc. Fr.
	lat. 15700	ff. 143ᵃ–152ᵃ	1449	Asc. Engl.
Mazarine	765	item 2	XIII	Asc.
Pavia, Univ.	69	ff. 25ᵃ–33ᵇ	XIII¹	Asc. Engl.
Rouen	533	ff. 118ᵃ–125ᵃ	XIIIᵐ	Unasc. Fr.
	558	ff. 184ᴬ–196ᴰ	XIIIᵐ	Unasc. Fr.
	591	ff. 86ᵃ–98ᵃ	XIIIᵐ	Unasc. Fr.
Salzburg, St Peter	b. x. 30	ff. 293ᴬ–295ᵇ	XVᵐ	Unasc. So. Ger. *mut.*
Toulouse	340			
Troyes	1077	ff. 1–6	XIII	Asc.
Vatican				
lat.	7688	ff. 43ᵃ–61ᵃ	XIII²	Asc. Engl.
Barb. lat.	488	ff. 78ᵇ–88ᵇ	XV²	
Venice, S. Marco	VI. 81	ff. 162ᵃ–193ᵇ	XIV¹	Unasc.

A brief extract from the *Templum* concerning the seven petitions of the *oracio dominica* appears in several late German MSS:

Berlin	lat. 826 (lat. theol. fol. 47)	ff. 346ᵇ–347ᵃ	1413	Asc. Ger.
	lat. 829 (lat. theol. fol. 311)	f. 116ᶜ⁻ᴰ	XVᵐ	Asc. Ger.

104. *De Triplici Rectitudine*

I. Inc.: Triplex est rectitudo in anima, scilicet voluntatis, verbi et operis...

Expl.: ...creatrix gradatim ascendere.

II. Unpubl.

III. This is a single paragraph in an early MS which contains other valuable items by Grosseteste (see Introd. p. 13). It would appear to be an extract from some longer work, or an *obiter dictum* orally delivered and copied by one of his household, or again it might be one of the longer *notule* with which he adorned his commentaries. It is to be dated in the episcopal period, if we may rely on the ascription *d. lincolniensis.*

IV. MSS:

Cambridge, Trinity	B. 15. 38	f. 33ᵇ	XIIIᵐ	Asc.

105. *De Tyrannide* (*De Principatu Regni*)

See below, p. 145 f.

* The librarian kindly informed me that there is a third MS of the *Templum* in the library, but he was unable to find it at that time (1933).

† Asc. *Raymundi episcopi Lingonensis*, doubtless scribal expansion of *R. epī lin'*.

106. *Versus de X Mandatis*

Appended to Sermon 83 (see below, p. 181) are the following verses, written in the same hand as the early (XIII^{m}) ascribed sermon. There is no reason to doubt Grosseteste's authorship.

London, B.M., Harley 979, f. 39^{b}:

Disce deum colere nomenque dei reverere;
Sabbata conserves, semper venerare parentes,
Noli mechari, metuas de cede notari,
Furta cave fieri, non sis testis nisi veri.
Hec cupiens queras nuptas non res alienas;
Sperne deos, fugite periuria, sabbata serva;
Sit tibi patris honor, sit tibi matris amor;
Non sis occisor, mechus, fur, testis iniqus,
Vicinique thorum relique, caveto suas.

107. Grosseteste at the Papal Curia in 1250

Though the bishop had won the long contest with his own chapter by 1246, his difficulties within his own diocese were not over. In the ensuing years his insistence on his right to visit monastic establishments in the diocese of Lincoln met with determined resistance. Grosseteste had appealed to Innocent IV and had received, in 1249, virtual confirmation of his rights from the pope.* But further complaints and appeals from the monastic bodies to the pope showed that he had not won his point so easily. It became clear that he would have to see the matter through in person at the curia, then at Lyons. This prospect was rendered more necessary by the harsh exactions of Boniface, Archbishop of Canterbury, who was claiming the right to visit throughout the whole province and, through his avaricious representatives, had coupled this not altogether unreasonable claim with unreasonable extortion. Indignation and fear for the state of the Church were not lessened by the knowledge that the archbishop was working hand in glove with the king. Grosseteste was, if we may trust the Dunstable chronicler,† chosen by common consent of the English bishops to present their case before the pope. Thus his own cause and that of the English episcopate combined to make his mission an important one. On the trip he was accompanied by the Bishops of London and Worcester, Robert Marsh (Archdeacon of Oxford), and John de Crackale (Archdeacon of Bedford). Adam Marsh, who had been with him on his visit to the Council of Lyons in 1245, was unable, to his great regret,‡ to go with him. The party left England early in March, 1250, and proceeded directly to Lyons. Hitherto we have been dependent upon Matthew Paris for an account of Grosseteste's dealings with the pope. But, as Stevenson has clearly shown,§ the account

* Matthew Paris, *Chron. Maj.* VI, 152. The *impetracio* is dated May 17, 1249.

† The meeting chronicled by the Dunstable annalist, *Ann. Mon.* III, 181, would seem, in the light of the speeches of Grosseteste at Lyons and the fact that he spoke as a representative of the English bishops, to have been a re-assembling of the group that met, according to Matthew Paris, *Chron. Maj.* V, 94, in London on Jan. 5, 1250.

‡ *Mon. Franc.* (R.S.), p. 156.

§ Cf. Stevenson, p. 281 ff.

of Matthew must rest, in some very important details, upon pure hearsay. Matthew is seldom elsewhere favourably disposed toward Grosseteste and in this case allows himself some unnecessary liberties. To have given any credence to an anecdote in which the pope includes Grosseteste under a general charge of cupidity, as he does,* materially weakens his whole account. We may safely treat his story of what happened at Lyons in 1250 with great reserve, and trust to a logical construction of the report given by Robert Marsh as reliable, largely because he collected Grosseteste's *dicta et scripta*, and was present at the hearings.

Until now the only work Grosseteste is known to have composed or delivered at the curia on this visit is the severe indictment of abuses prevailing in the Church, beginning: *Dominus noster Jesus Christus eternus eterni Dei patris filius*... and ending ...*dictis timore et desiderio cogentibus a me peccatore extremo est attemptatum.*† This memorandum was printed by Brown in the *Fasc. Rer. Expet.* II, 250–257, with the introductory paragraph of Robert Marsh, as found in a number of MSS. But the additional treatises or sermons composed and used by Grosseteste in defending his cause at Lyons have not been noticed. Eight MSS contain copies of what is evidently a collection made by Robert Marsh of Grosseteste's *dicta et scripta* with short explanatory rubrics which help us to connect the events in some logical order. It is singular that these MSS (save one, Royal 6. E. v) also contain the correspondence of Grosseteste, dated 1253, with the papal scriptor Innocent, concerning the pope's appointment of his nephew to a benefice in the diocese of Lincoln. Robert Marsh may have felt there was some topical coherence between the correspondence and the Lyons documents. There is no attempt to deceive, as the later letters are dated.

In the following summary of these writings and speeches of Grosseteste at Lyons the order in which they appear in B.M. Royal MS 6. E. v will be followed and parallels in the other MSS indicated. There is substantial uniformity among the MSS in this regard, as will be observed.

(1) Robert Marsh introduces the account of the proceedings with a detailed paragraph. The next paragraph begins the memorandum.

Anno domini millesimo cc^mo^ l, iii^o^ idus maii apud Lugdunum venerabilis pater Robertus lincolniensis episcopus constitutus in presencia domini pape et venerabilium patrum cardinalium solomodo astante sibi me magistro Ricardo‡ archidiacono suo Oxonie, captata prius brevibus benevolencia et suscitata attencione ad intendendum ab ipso manifestandis, tradidit quod subscribitur in uno rotulo scriptum domino pape, in altero rotulo domino Willelmo sabinensi episcopo cardinali, in tercio domino Hugoni tunc Sancte Sabine presbitero cardinali, in quarto domino Johanni Sancti Nicholai in carcere tulliano diacono cardinali, dicens in hiis singulis contineri quod eis manifestare voluit, quod scriptum a prenominato domino Johanne diacono cardinali in audiencia domini pape et cardinalium tantummodo incontinenti fuit perlectum in hiis verbis:

Dominus noster Jesus Christus eternus...extremo est attemptatum.

* *Chron. Maj.* v (R.S.), 95 ff.

† See below, p. 171, Sermon 14.

‡ All MSS read *Ricardo* erroneously for *Roberto*, doubtless expanded from an original *R.*

The introduction *and* memorandum are in the following MSS:

Oxford		
Bodl.	798	ff. 139^{A}–143^{C}
Exeter	21	pp. 132^{b}–133^{a}, 117^{a}–124^{b}
Merton	82	ff. 95^{C}–99^{D}
London, B.M.		
Lans.	458	ff. 145^{A}–147^{C}
Royal	6. E. v	ff. 126^{A}–128^{A}
	7. F. II	f. 115^{D}, Introd. sep.
Cambridge		
C.C.C.	257	f. 195^{a}, Introd. at end of collection
Gonv. & Caius	83	ff. 125^{D}–130^{B}
York Cath.	XVI. A. 6	ff. 182^{b}–183^{a}, 165^{a}–172^{a}
Paris, B.N.	lat. 10358	ff. 185^{b}–192^{b}

For additional MSS of the memorandum see below, p. 171. For dates of MSS listed here see below, p. 162 f. In several MSS it is asserted that Grosseteste preached the sermon before the pope, a tradition that may be explained by the relatively few copies made of Marsh's introduction.

(2) There follows here, in seven MSS, the correspondence concerning the pope's nephew.

Intelleximus vos litteram domini pape recepisse....

See Luard's ed. of Grosseteste's *Epistolae*, pp. 432–437, i.e. Letter 128, and below, pp. 192 f., 212 f.

Oxford		
Bodl.	42	f. 283^{a-b}
Merton	82	ff. 99^{D}–100^{D}
London, B.M.		
Lans.	458	ff. 147^{C}–148^{B}
	6. E. v	f. 128^{A-C}
Royal	7. E. II	ff. 385^{B}–386^{D}
	7. F. II	ff. 109^{A}–110^{B}
York Cath.	XVI. A. 6	ff. 172^{a}–173^{b}

It will be noticed that this 1253 correspondence is wanting in Exeter 21 and C.C.C., Cambridge, 257. The scribes may be credited with excluding it because of its lateness, inasmuch as they have included almost all the items having to do with the Lyons hearing.

(3) The next item in the MSS is the *Parabola domini Roberti Grosseteste lincolniensis episcopi* which begins:

Paterfamilias predives habet in una provincia decem exempli gracia pascuarum... *and ends* ...et defectum omnem reformare ut decet potens.

This *parabola* has a moral appended to it which is considerably longer than the *parabola* itself, applying the parable of the rich father to the Archbishop of Canterbury. The moral begins:

Hec parabola non indiget edisseri; plana est et de eius conspicue planicie nos episcopi Cantuarie provincie... *and ends* ...qui pro viribus parati sumus in hoc ducem deo preduce sequi.

This parable with its moral was directed, in writing, to the Archbishop of Canterbury, as we may infer from the direct form of address employed:

...*supplicamus*...*vobis reverende domine archiepiscope Cantuarie*... (Royal 6. E. v, f. 128[D]), and a reference in the next column to *huic scripto*. The presence of Boniface in Lyons in May, 1250* makes it almost certain that this parabola was addressed to him in person at approximately the same time as Grosseteste's *causa* was being heard.

Oxford, Merton	82	ff. 100[D]–101[D]
London, B.M.		
Lans.	458	f. 148[B–D]
Royal	6. E. v	ff. 128[C]–129[B]
	7. E. II	ff. 386[D]–387[D]
	7. F. II	ff. 110[B]–111[B]
York Cath.	XVI. A. 6	ff. 174[a]–175[a]

It will be noticed that Exeter 21 and C.C.C., Cambridge, 257 omit the *parabola*. In this as in several minor details their similarity is such as to suggest a common source.

(4) Immediately after the end of the moral begins Marsh's introduction to the complaint of the English clergy to the pope:

Itaque post primo proposita paucis elapsis diebus ad occurrendum si fieri posset imminentibus malis exacionibus et extorsionibus inconsuetarum procuracionum racione visitacionis a suis successoribus et archiepiscopis Cantuarie sic fuit in presencia domini pape et fratrum a dicto episcopo propositum:

Clerus Anglie dicit se precedentibus temporibus multipliciter fuisse gravatum tum per potestatem regiam cum iura ecclesiastica et libertates plurimum perturbavit... *ending* ...et non minus huius securum et huius sacre sedis clemencie condecens plurimum.

This is a sharp and detailed complaint of the English clergy against the archbishop's unusual exactions as well as against the support given the archbishop by the curia. We must assume that the terms of this complaint were agreed upon by Grosseteste's companions and probably discussed with other bishops before the party left England.

Oxford		
Exeter	21	pp. 124[b]–125[b]
Merton	82	ff. 101[D]–102[B]
London, B.M.		
Lans.	458	ff. 148[C]–149[A]
Royal	6. E. v	f. 129[B–C]
	7. E. II	f. 388[A–C]
	7. F. II	f. 111[B–D]
Cambridge, C.C.C.	257	ff. 189[b]–190[a]
York Cath.	XVI. A. 6	ff. 175[b]–176[a]

(5) The complaint was followed by Grosseteste's *propositum*, orally delivered, introduced by Robert Marsh's rubric:

Deinde sic proposuit idem episcopus coram eisdem tantum verbotenus:

Episcopi lincolnienses omnibus retro temporibus consueverunt visitare domos religiosas eiusdem diocesis sibi subiectas....

After a brief historical discussion of his own visitations in which he shows the great difference between his purposes and those of the archbishop who instituted visitations *ex cupiditate*, he ends:

...quod nullo modo debet archiepiscopus exigere inconsuetas procuraciones.

* Matthew Paris, *Chron. Maj.* v (R.S.), 138.

Oxford		
Exeter	21	pp. 125^{b}–126^{a}
Merton	82	f. 102^{B-D}
London, B.M.		
Lans.	458	f. 149^{B-C}
Royal	6. E. v	f. 129^{C-D}
	7. E. II	ff. 388^{C}–389^{B}
	7. F. II	ff. 111^{D}–112^{B}
Cambridge, C.C.C.	257	ff. 190^{a}–191^{a}
York Cath.	XVI. A. 6	ff. 176^{a}–177^{a}

(6) Grosseteste's arguments seem to have raised the question of *ius commune* as applied to the archbishop's rights to visit and provide. Robert Marsh now interjects a short explanation to Grosseteste's next *scriptum*, feeling, apparently, that its rather more abstract tenor demanded some justification.

Tercio si forte verba philosophica possent ex aliqua parte movere et ad amplius respondendum opinioni de iure communi quo dicebatur a quibusdam audientibus predicta: Ius commune est quod visitator procuretur, sic fuit ab eodem episcopo propositum in scripto:

The *tercio* is of some interest. *Primo* and *secundo* have not previously appeared, but *quarto* appears at the end of the coming *scriptum*, introducing a further memorandum. If we rightly divine Marsh's intention to enumerate the writings or speeches of Grosseteste delivered to the pope, there would be six. The *parabola* intended for the Archbishop of Canterbury is not counted. All six were, so far as we can judge, delivered or transmitted on the same day, May 13, 1250, to the pope and cardinals. The philosophical discussion of *ius commune*, *ius divinum* and *ius naturale* follows:

De regno et rege, tirannide et tiranno sic ait philosophus politicorum: Optime quidem... *and ends* ...iuvante domino sufficienter ostendetur.

This is without doubt the *abbreviacio de principatu regni et tirannidis* which Adam Marsh says he is returning to Grosseteste in a letter written probably early in 1252.* Grosseteste must have sent a copy of the work to Adam on his return from Lyons. This work has not hitherto been identified.

Oxford		
Exeter	21	pp. 126^{a}–127^{b}
Merton	82	ff. 102^{D}–103^{B}
London, B.M.		
Lans.	458	f. 149^{C-D}
Royal	6. E. v	ff. 129^{D}–130^{A}
	7. E. II	ff. 389^{B}–390^{A}
	7. F. II	f. 112^{B-D}
Cambridge, C.C.C.	257	f. 191^{a-b}
York Cath.	XVI. A. 6	f. 177^{a-b}

* *Mon. Franc.* p. 110; Stevenson, p. 31.

(7) Robert Marsh's rubric to the next memorandum follows immediately after the end of the work on kingship and tyranny. It is an appeal to *ius divinum*, i.e. scripture, against *ius commune sive positivum et eius apparatus.*

Quarto, quia adhuc quidam cardinalium adherebant iuri positivo et eius apparatibus plus quam iuri naturali et divino, fuit eis ab eodem episcopo traditum in scripto sic:
Ysaias ait 29° capitulo: eo quod appropinquat populus iste ore suo et labiis suis glorificat me, cor autem eius... *ending* ...et acerbissima mori dignatus est, ad cuius eciam imitacionem vos maxime pre omnibus tenemini.

Oxford		
Exeter	21	pp. 127^{b}–129^{a}
Merton	82	ff. 103^{B}–104^{A}
London, B.M.		
Lans.	458	ff. 149^{D}–150^{C}
Royal	6. E. V	f. 130^{A-D}
	7. E. II	ff. 390^{A}–391^{B}
	7. F. II	ff. 112^{D}–113^{D}
Cambridge, C.C.C.	257	ff. 191^{b}–192^{b}
York Cath.	XVI. A. 6	ff. 178^{a}–179^{b}

(8) The next item was not transmitted in written form, but was delivered orally, as we are informed by the rubric.

Tandem idem episcopus sic dixit pape domino et cardinalibus:
Secundum philosophiam omnis lex et omne iustum universaliter est verum, cum lex naturalis et iustum naturale sic universaliter est quod ipsum in se in sua universalitate consideratum.... *The speech ends* ...quod autem iniustum est in exterminium et ad infernalia deiciatis.

The argument is largely philosophical and not simple in its texture. Grosseteste may well have enjoyed it: it is doubtful if the cardinals could have.

Oxford		
Exeter	21	pp. 129^{a}–130^{a}
Merton	82	f. 104^{A-B}
London, B.M.		
Lans.	458	f. 150^{C-D}
Royal	6. E. V	ff. 130^{D}–131^{A}
	7. E. II	ff. 391^{B}–392^{A}
	7. F. II	ff. 113^{D}–114^{B}
Cambridge, C.C.C.	257	ff. 192^{a}–193^{a}
York Cath.	XVI. A. 6	ff. 179^{b}–180^{b}

(9) At this point, probably during an intermission in the proceedings, some member of the papal entourage sought to catch Grosseteste in a trap. Robert Marsh tells the story:

Interim dum predicta agerentur instante quodam nobili romano pluries apud eundem episcopum ut de beneplacito suo posset ingredi quandam prebendam ecclesie sue habentem curam animarum quam dixit sibi auctoritate domini pape fuisse collatam, et dicto episcopo more suo pluries ei manifestante qualem oportet esse pastorem animarum et quod si constitutus in officio pastorali illud rite non perageret, ipse est in seipso spiritualiter mortuus et animarum sibi commissarum occisor et antichristus et peior omni sodomita et huiusmodi plura, et superaddente episcopo quod non reputabat eum ad officium pastorale idoneum, sed si officium pastorale susciperet eo ipso incideret in mala pretacta et ideo de suo beneplacito nunquam optineret predictam prebendam. Ipse tandem et qui cum eo erant ex predictis indignati et offensi recesserunt clamantes: "factum domini pape, factum domini pape est et eius factis obloqueris". Et sic adeuntes dominum papam dixerunt: "episcopus talis publice vocat vos occisorem animarum et antichristum et omni sodomita peiorem et plura huiusmodi, quod incontinenti sumus parati probare". Unde dominus papa et plures de cardinalibus plurimum offendebantur. Quo audito idem episcopus coram papa et cardinalibus tantum in sue innocencie manifestacionem et offense predicte mitigacionem et eciam in audiencium edificacionem proposuit in hunc modum:

Ad vestram sanctitatem et sapienciam nolo ad presens uti prohemialibus sed statim me in medias res ponere. Conatum est ad avertendum cor vestrum a me et ad rapiendum mei in vestri odium et hoc occasione tali... *ending* ...ego conscienciam meam de mea affeccione vobis dixerim et per consequens non potest cor vestrum a me averti.

Oxford		
Exeter	21	pp. 130^{a}–132^{b}
Merton	82	ff. 104^{B}–105^{B}
London, B.M.		
Lans.	458	ff. 150^{D}–151^{C}
Royal	6. E. v	f. 131^{A-D}
	7. E. II	ff. 392^{A}–393^{D}
	7. F. II	ff. 114^{B}–115^{D}
Cambridge, C.C.C.	257	ff. 193^{a}–195^{a}
York Cath.	XVI. A. 6	ff. 180^{b}–183^{a}

This fervid defence of the probity of his intentions is apparently the last event of the public hearing. The results of his endeavours must be deduced from other sources. Marsh adds a postscript which appears in most of the MSS.

Postquam vero reversus in Angliam idem episcopus ne tantus sue peregrinacionis labor neclectus putaretur aut ab aliquibus in curia traderetur quibusdam familioribus suis cardinalibus scripsit in hunc modum.

Some of the MSS add a short recapitulation of the paragraph at the beginning of the whole collection as follows:

Anno domini M° ccl° feria vi^{ta} proxima post ascensionem domini que eo anno accidit iii° idus maii apud Lugdunum venerabilis pater Robertus lincolniensis episcopus constitutus in presencia pape Innocencii quarti et venerabilium patrum cardinalium solummodo astante me Ricardo archidiacono suo Oxonie etc. ut supra in principio istius quaterni.

Of the nine items listed above all but one (no. (2)) arose directly out of the mission of Grosseteste and his companions to Lyons in 1250, and were either transmitted to the pope and cardinals—or, in the case of no. (3), to Archbishop Boniface—in writing or delivered orally. Item (2) belongs to the year 1253, but must have seemed to Robert Marsh sufficiently germane to the earlier case in its fundamental thesis to warrant inclusion in the collection. This hitherto unnoticed collection is the most complete record of any of Grosseteste's public appearances, and furthermore unique in being a collection with explanatory rubrics made by a friend and member of his official family.

MISCELLANEOUS WORKS

108. *De Cane Ethimologia*

I. Inc.: Canis grecam ethimologiam habere dicitur. Grece enim cenos dicitur...

Expl.: ...Canes sunt domestica feritate atrociter mansueti subdole mordaces.

II. Unpubl.

III. This short etymology of sixteen lines appears only in the Durham MS in a section of the codex which contains exclusively Grossetestiana. It may have been a *notula* occasioned by some passage upon which Grosseteste was lecturing, taken down by a student in this form. There is one quotation, from Cassiodorus. Although it is possible that the reference to the Greek term in the incipit may indicate that at this time Grosseteste had begun his study of Greek, we have as yet no evidence for placing the beginning of his serious study of Greek earlier than the date at which this MS was written.* Cassiodorus, Isidore and Hugucius would have sufficed to build an entertaining etymology of almost any Latin word, particularly to a scholar of Grosseteste's resourcefulness.

IV. MS:

Durham Cath.	A. III. 12	f. 17^{C-D}	*ca.* 1230	Unasc.

109. *Liber Curialis*

I. Inc.: Curia regalis si te subnutreat alis,
Familie nectarius habearis, fabula nulla
Exeat ore tuo qua pro mendace proberis.
Sepius incurrit culpam viciosa loquela.
Sepius et levia confert mendacia fari
Et persepe vocat veris sermonibus uti...

Expl.: ...Mimus et invidia, tumor et fraus, ceca cupido,
Fictus amor, gula, predo, scelus, ipsa libido
Temporibus nostris regnant, cunctis dominando.

II. Unpubl.

III. The unique MS of this comprehensive guide to proper etiquette is early and ascribed. It seems to have escaped the bibliographers. One wonders if this composition has any connection with the incident recited in the *Lanercost Chronicle* (ed. J. Stevenson (Edinburgh, 1839), p. 44; see also Stevenson's *Grosseteste*, p. 7) when the Earl of Gloucester complimented Grosseteste on his courtly hospitality. There are precepts for *puer*, *dives*, *magni et potentes*, *mendicus* and *clericus* as to dress, conversation, eating,

* See above, p. 13 ff.

drinking and general demeanour. There are 669 lines in the poem. The rubric *Incipit liber curialis quem composuit Magister Robertus Grosteste* may fix the composition in the pre-episcopal period. It would, however, be strange if Grosseteste had conceived the idea of writing such a work before he had any social position which might have called it forth. He would have had to be at least archdeacon on this assumption, and the work would then be dated 1229–1235.

IV. MS:

Oxford, Trinity	18	ff. 168^{A}–172^{A}	XIII^{2}	Asc.

110. *Regule ad Custodiendum Terras*

I. Inc.: Quantum ad terras vestras forinsecas in primis faciatis...
Expl.: ...et nullus honor accressit domino vel domine.

II. Unpubl. See below, p. 158 f., for ed. of French *Reulles.*

III. This work is to be distinguished from the translation into English of Walter of Henley's French *Treatise on Husbandry.** The *Regule* were written for the Countess Margaret of Lincoln, widow of John de Lacy, Earl of Lincoln, during the period of her widowhood, 1240–1242.† The question of priority of the Latin or the French versions must remain open, but several suggestions may be made. Translation from French into Latin would *a priori* be less likely than the reverse. On the other hand it may be assumed to be almost self-evident that the Countess knew French, whereas her Latin might well have been elementary. But surely Grosseteste was equal to the approved diplomatic practice of publishing versions in two languages at the same time. The Latin text was known to Tanner, who cited this MS, and Pegge, who places the composition of the work in 1240 or 1241. The rubric in the MS reads: *Hic incipiunt regule quas bone memorie Robertus Grossetete fecit comitisse Lincolniensi ad custodiendum et regendum terras, ospicium, domum et familiam.*

IV. MS:

Oxford, Digby	204	ff. 3^{A}–5^{A}	XIII^{2}	Asc.

111. *Stans Puer ad Mensam (De Civilitate Morum)*

I. Recension 1 consists of the following seven lines only:

Stans puer ad mensam domini bona dogmata discat,
Sit vultu simplex, visum nec ubique revolvat;
Nec paries speculum, baculus vero sit tibi postis
Aut nares fodeat, propriam carnem neque scalpet,
Aut coram domino decet monstrare cachynnos.
Hec me qui docuit grossum capud est sibi nomen.
Presul et ille fuit, cui felix det deus omen.

* See below, p. 241, *Spurium* 1. See also Stevenson, pp. 230–234.
† See Stevenson, pp. 230–234.

Recension II is of forty to forty-seven lines, not including a twelve-line recapitulation.

Inc.: Stans puer ad mensam domini bona dogmata discas...
Expl.: (l. 38) Privetur mensa qui spreverit hec documenta.
(l. 39) Hec qui me docuit grossum caput est sibi nomen
(l. 40) Presul et ille fuit cui felix det deus.

III. In at least one of the recensions this poem has been known to most of the bibliographers. There can be little doubt as to the authenticity of Recension I. It follows immediately after the *Liber Curialis*, in the same hand, in the Trinity Coll., Oxford, MS, and l. 6 is, therefore, determinative. In Recension II, l. 1 of Recension I appears as l. 1, l. 2 as l. 3, l. 3 as l. 4, l. 4 as l. 5, l. 5, changed to *Nec coram dominis debes monstrare cacchinos* as l. 9, l. 6 as l. 41 and l. 7 as l. 42. The longer recension is obviously based on the shorter work with additional lines taken largely from the *Liber Curialis*, the whole in all probability the work of a fourteenth-century editor.

F. J. Furnivall published (E.E.T.S., Original Series 32 (London, 1868), pp. 26–33) an English work under this title, of fourteen stanzas of eight lines, ascribed to John Lydgate. He also published the Latin text as found in the Harley MS, in pt. ii of the same edition, pp. 30, 32. H. N. Macracken (*Minor Works of John Lydgate*, E.E.T.S., Extra Series 107 (London, 1911), p. xxviii) lists the known MSS of the English version and suggests that a French model was the basis for Lydgate's poem. It seems much more probable that Lydgate's English work was based on the longer recension of Grosseteste's seven lines.

IV. MSS:

Recension I:				
Oxford				
Bodl.	315*	f. 28A	XV1	Asc.†
Trinity	18	f. 172A	XIII2	Asc.
Recension II:				
Oxford				
Bodl.	837	f. 3C	XV1	Asc.
Rawl.	G. 60	f. 1a	XVm	Unasc.‡
London, B.M.				
Add.	37075	f. 22a–b	XVm	Asc.§
Harl.	3362	f. 6b	XVm	Unasc.‖

112. *Statuta Familie*

I. Inc.: Qui temporali serviret eterno intendat servire domino...
Expl.: ...oppressi vel affecti satagant ut competenter satisfiat.

* P. Leyser, *Historia Poetarum*... (Magdeburg, 1721), p. 998, lists this MS, under the number in Bernard's catalogue, 2712, remarking that these verses of Grosseteste are to be found at the end of a treatise of Richard Hampole.

† First six lines only.

‡ Forty-seven lines, ending: *Assumptoque cibo reddatur gracia Cristo.*

§ Forty-four lines. *Explicit liber urbanitatis.*

‖ Forty-two lines.

II. Unpubl.

III. There has been some confusion in the bibliographical tradition between this short ordinance and the *Regule* which Grosseteste sent to the Countess of Lincoln (see above, p. 149). Both are well authenticated, and, remarkably enough, each is extant in only a single MS, almost contemporary with Grosseteste. Both have been translated, the *Regule* from Latin into French (or *vice versa*) and the *Statuta* into English. The English translation of the *Statuta* is found in B.M. Sloane MS 1986, ff. 100^a–102^a, XV^m, and has the rubric:

Incipiunt statuta familie bone memorie dompni Roberti Grossetest lincolniensis episcopi. *The text begins:* Let alle men be warned þat seruen ȝou and warning be geue to alle men that be of howseholde to serue God and ȝou trewly... *and ends*...ffor of suche cometh grete descretion [!] and no worshippe therby growythe to the lorde.

This English version was printed by J. S. Brewer in *Mon. Franciscana* (London, 1858, R.S.), pp. 582–586, and again by F. J. Furnivall in E.E.T.S., Original Series 32 (London, 1868), pp. 328–333. A modernized text was also published by W. H. Hutton in his *Misrule of Henry III* (London, 1887), pp. 15–19. We have no indication that the actual work of translation can claim to be earlier than the unique Sloane MS.

The rubric of the Latin original reads: *Hec sunt statuta que Robertus Lincolniensis ordinavit et domis suis prepositis tradidit.*

IV. MS:

Cambridge, Univ.	Ee. i. 1	f. 259^{C-D}	XIII^m	Asc.

ANGLO-NORMAN WORKS

113. *Chasteau d'Amour*

I. Inc.: Ki ben pense ben peut dire...
Expl.: ...Ke a sa pes puissum venir.

II. Publ. by Matthew Cooke (London, Caxton Society, 1852), from the C.C.C., Oxford, and Harley MSS;* J. Murray (Paris, 1918), from all the MSS except the Hatton, Fitzwilliam, Digby and two Brussels copies. The section *Les iiii Filles de Dieu* (*Les iiii Sœurs* or *Les IIII Vertus*) was printed by Francisque Michel in the introduction of his *Libri Psalmorum versio antiqua*... (Oxford, 1860), pp. xxii–xxxi.

III. There has never been any valid doubt that this early allegory of the creation of the world and man, and man's fall and redemption, was the work of Grosseteste. J. Felten expressed the opinion† that some scribe affixed Grosseteste's name to a poem which may have had some Grossetestian theology as its basis. The reason for Felten's supposition is not made plain. There is certainly no basis for it in the literary or manuscript tradition. It will be noticed that of the sixteen known copies of the poem, complete or fragmentary, of which several date from the middle of the thirteenth century and the great majority were written within half a century after Grosseteste's death, only one, anonymous, fails to ascribe the poem to him. In the face of such evidence, approaching unanimity in a degree extremely rare in medieval manuscript tradition, serious doubts of authenticity are, at the very least, naïve. Recent studies‡ of the literary content and sources of the poem have made it clear that though there is much compilation and adaptation of earlier material in Grosseteste's *Chasteau*, the work was also, in its turn, a source of much allegorical and dramatic literature in his own time and in succeeding centuries.

The date of the composition is not easy to determine. If we accept the thesis that the *Vie de Tobie*, usually ascribed to Guillaume le clerc de Normandie, is dependent upon Grosseteste's *Chasteau* (see Traver, *op. cit.* p. 31 ff.), we must date the *Chasteau* at the beginning of the thirteenth century, inasmuch as Guillaume's known literary activity was limited to

* For corrections see F. Holthausen, "Die nordenglische Uebersetzung von Robert Grosseteste's *Chasteau d'Amour*", in *Anglia*, XIV (1892), 393–399.

† *Robert Grosseteste, Bischof von Lincoln* (Freiburg, 1889), p. 87 f. Miss Hope Traver, *The Four Daughters of God* (Philadelphia, 1907), p. 27, n. 1, does not accept Felten's position. A. Långfors in a recent study, "Notice des MSS... 535 et 10047" in *Not. et Extr. de la Bibl. Nat.* XLII (1933), 206, n. 1, treats Felten's suggestion seriously.

‡ Cf., e.g., R. Reinsch, "La vie de Tobie de Guillaume le clerc de Normandie..." in *Archiv* (Herrig), LXII (1879), 375–396; Traver; Murray; and Cornelius, *The Figurative Castle* (Bryn Mawr, 1930).

the last decades of the twelfth century and the first two of the thirteenth.* Such an early date, in view of the chronology of Grosseteste's life, quite apart from an analysis of style and content, seems quite unlikely. Långfors confirms this chronological improbability on a basis of a close examination of the content of the text (see Långfors' "Notice...", pp. 190–205), remarking that the *Chasteau* cannot be the source of the anonymous *Dialogus*, which is an integral part of the *Vie de Tobie*, or of the *Dit des quatre sereurs*, but rather that the *Chasteau* "est une imitation maladroite du poème anglo-normand anonyme" (p. 205). Accepting the implications of this conclusion which Långfors seems amply to have proved, the *terminus a quo* for the composition of Grosseteste's poem may safely be placed at some time in the second decade of the thirteenth century, and, more precisely, if we allow a Paris stay of 1209–1214, of which the probability is very strong, *ca.* 1215. Miss Murray (*op. cit.* pp. 62–64), from a study of certain rhymes—*eir, saveir*; *joie, voie*; *ferai, dei*, etc.—concluded that the poem was composed "vers 1230". Yet her own evidence favours an earlier date, as the forms she cites are found in authors who flourished in the second and third decades of the century.† This sort of evidence I am unable satisfactorily to evaluate, and must accept the conclusions of philologists. But in this case the evidence from philology is corroborated by the chronological probabilities of Grosseteste's life and movements. Everything considered, it appears safe to date the work between 1215 and 1230, with the probabilities favouring the early part of the period, while the impressions of his stay in France and acquaintance with Norman literary forms and traditions were still fresh in his mind. It is furthermore doubtful if his duties at Oxford, which were increasingly heavy during the 'twenties, would have allowed him much time for the composition of a long vernacular allegory.

The work is not mentioned by Boston of Bury; it is listed by Bale as *De Reparacione Lapsi*, beginning: *In principio creacionis mundi*, which is the incipit of the Latin prologue (Murray, p. 8), and by Pits, Tanner, Wharton and Pegge as *Chasteau d'Amour*.

IV. MSS:

Miss Murray (*op. cit.* pp. 22–23) described eleven MSS and listed the Fitzwilliam and Digby MSS without description. She had not used the Hatton or the two Brussels copies.‡ The dates given here will occasionally differ or be more specific. Långfors lists (*op. cit.* p. 207 f.) the MSS given by Miss Murray, accepting her dates save for the C.C.C., Oxford, copy which he puts "au début du XIVe siècle" and adds the Hatton MS (from Stengel)

* G. Paris, *La Littérature française du Moyen Âge* (5th ed. Paris, 1914), § 154.

† Miss Murray (*op. cit.* p. 63) dates Chardri 1210–1230. J. Vising, *Anglo-Norman Literature* (London, 1923), pp. 44, 48, gives "c. 1200" or "end of XII".

‡ She mentions one copy (2306) at Brussels, without giving the signature. Långfors corrects her description, but he was apparently unaware that the MS he was examining, 3357 (10747), was not the one mentioned by Miss Murray.

and Brussels 3357 (10747). He does not say that he has seen any of the English copies.

Oxford				
Bodl.	399	ff. 104^D–116^A	1300	Asc.*
	652	ff. 52^A–64^B	XIII^m	Asc.†, ‡
Digby	86	ff. 116^D–118^D	XIII^2	Unasc.§
Douce	132	ff. 23^A–36^C	XIII^2	Asc.†, ‖
Hatton	99	ff. 154^a–177^b	XIV^1	Asc.†, ¶
Laud Misc.	471	ff. 94^a–107^b	*ca.* 1300	Asc.†
C.C.C.	232	ff. 1^a–35^a	XIII^m	Asc.†
London, B.M.				
Egerton	846B	ff. 1^A–12^C	*ca.* 1325	Asc.†, **
Harley	1121	ff. 156^C–168^A	XIII^2	Asc.
	3860	ff. 48^A–61^C	XIII^2	Asc.
Royal	20. B. XIV	ff. 87^C–95^C	*ca.* 1300	Asc. 1505 lines
London, Lambeth	522	ff. 1^a–49^b	*ca.* 1300	Asc.††
Cambridge, Fitzw. Mus.	McClean 123	ff. 1^a–7^C	XIII^2	Asc. Fr.‡‡
Brussels, Bibl. Royale	2306 (9030–37)	ff. 255^A–269^A	XV^m	Asc. Fr.§§
	3357 (10747)	ff. 228^D–240^A	XIII^2	Asc. Lowl.†
Paris, B.N.	franç. 902	ff. 99^A–108^C	XIII^2	Asc. Engl.†

An English translation (XIV^m) is found in the Vernon MS in the Bodleian Library, ff. 292^a–296^b. It has been edited by C. Horstmann, E.E.T.S. 98 (1892).‖‖ A second, partial, English translation appears in B.M. Add. 22283 (XIV^m), ff. 84^b–87, which is closely related to the Vernon MS. Halliwell's edition of the *Castell of Loue* (1849) was based on a MS then in private hands, now Bodl. Add. B. 107. There is no reason to suppose that any of these three versions,¶¶ in their present form at least, are attributable

* To *Mestre Robert le Grosceteste.*

† With Latin prologue.

‡ Murray, p. 87.

§ Contains only the section *Des iiii files Deu*, ll. 204–468 of the poem. For this important MS see E. Stengel, *Codex...Digby* 86 (Halle, 1871), pp. 49–52.

‖ The Latin prologue is added *a.m. coeva* on f. 22^D in a hand that has made numerous marginal notations throughout the text.

¶ Ends l. 1540.

** Miss Murray prints, pp. 22–24, the prologue of this MS, observing that it is slightly different from the usual form.

†† Latin prologue *a.m. coeva.*

‡‡ With Latin prologue; ends l. 830, but only 811 lines.

§§ 1575 lines. The rubric reads: *Ci commence la Vye du doulz Jesu Crist et de son humanite faicte et ordonnee par saint robert grosseteste qui fuit evesque de nicole en la maniere qui sensieult.*

‖‖ See Murray, *op. cit.* pp. 81–85.

¶¶ These three versions were used by R. F. Weymouth in his *Castel of Loue* (London, 1864). See further F. K. Haase, "Die altenglischen Bearbeitungen von Grosseteste's 'Chasteau d'Amour' verglichen mit der Quelle" in *Anglia*, XII (1889), 311–374. Hupe published the text of the Egerton MS in *Anglia*, XIV (1892), 415–455, "Robert Grosseteste's Chasteau d'Amour (Castel of Love)". He treats Cooke's edition with scant respect.

to Grosseteste. There is a fourth, complete, translation in B.M. Egerton 927 (XIV²), ff. 1ª–28ª, which was done by a monk of Sawley.

This romance turned Munk of Salley out of a frenche romance that sir Robert Bishoppe a lyncolnne made and eked mekel therto as him thoght spedeful to edificacion and swetenes of devocioun and lering of lewed men... (MS *cit.* f. 1ª).

114. *Confessioun*

I. Inc.: Sire dieu omnipotent tut puissant donez moi dreite...
Expl.: ...a bone fin et me doint vie pardurable.

II. Publ. by Herman Urtel in *Zft f. rom. Philologie*, XXXIII (1909), 571–575.

III. Though extant in a single copy, nothing either in the language or the content would lead us to doubt the definite ascription. It does not appear to be a translation of any of his known Latin works on confession. The rubric reads: *Cest confessioun fist seint robert li evesque de nichole....*

IV. MS:

Hamburg, Stadtbibl.	Cod. Philol. 4° 296	pp. 59–66	XIV²	Asc. No. Fr.

115. *Iniunccio Penitenti Gallice*

The following injunction appears at the end of the *De Confessione et Modo Confitendi Peccata* (see above, p. 125 f.):

Ore ben frere le ordre e la perseverance e le amendement de vostre vie, e kan ke vus purrez fere de ben en la mesun deu deka vostre fin e le amendement ke vus a deu premettez. Totes cote choses vus serent en principale penance e en remission de ces pecchez ke ci avez comi e de tuz les autres trespas ke vus avez fet e vodriez comistre sil vus venisent a memorie. E dites avant ecclesia ke deu par sa merci vus doint veniam de preteritis et cautelam de futuris e a vostre fin vitam eternam, ou kil par la priere de sa duce mere e de tuz seins et totes seintes vus doint cele vie de mener en co secle et si espurger vostre vie par seinte confession, ke vus pussez apres le curs de ceste vie consequi vitam eternam, our ke deu vus doint ben vivre et ben morer e a la grant ioie parvenir. Amen.

There is a short section inserted in the text of the *De Modo*, f. 187ᵇ, which serves as the beginning of the penitent's confession, and consequently should be regarded as antecedent to the *Iniunccio.*

Io me faz confes a deu e a nostre dame seinte Marie e a tuz seins e a vus pere ke io par ma mauveite ai mut pecchee e offendu mon creatour e trespasse ses comaundemenz. Io ai mut pecche en penser, en parole e en fet.

As pointed out above (p. 125 f.), the work was composed after 1250.

IV. MS:

London, Lambeth	499	ff. 187ᵇ–188ª	XIII²	Asc.

116. *Le Mariage des Neuf Filles du Diable*

I. Inc.: Le diable se voleyt maryer...
Expl.: ...Que az toutz leals serra commune
Amen amen dye chekune.

II. Publ. by P. Meyer in *Romania*, XXIX (1900), 61–72, from the Rawl. Poet. MS. See also B. Hauréau, *Journal des Savants*, 1884, pp. 225–228, and Owst, *Literature and Pulpit*... (Cambridge, 1933), pp. 93–96.

III. This work is specifically ascribed to Grosseteste in the oldest extant MS, in the rubric, in the body of the prologue, and in the colophon. We read in ll. 13–15:

> Seynt Robert le translata
> En romaunz com orrecz ia
> Hors de latyn le fist atrere.

The "seynt" led Meyer to regard the work as probably not genuine. But there is no real incongruity in the appellation. In many early MSS of authentic works he is called *sanctus*, and we have Gascoigne's statement in his own hand in MS Bodl. 312, f. 184[D], that

> in littera testimoniali quam post mortem eius scripsit clerus Oxonie Clementi iiii[to] pape pro eius canonizacione fienda et in illa littera testatur universitas Oxonie quod propter magna et plura miracula et propter emanacionem olei ab eius tumba sanctus Robertus in tota Anglia dicebatur, et est copia huius littere in monasterio canonicorum de Osney.

We have also the title *Les Reulles Seint Robert* for another work (see below, p. 158 f.), and a thirteenth-century ascription referring to him as *beatus* (see above, p. 90). The use of the term in the thirteenth century simply reflects the high opinion held of him in all England at the time of his death, to which Gascoigne referred.*

This work is another attempt, similar in general tone to the *Peines de Purgatoire* (see below, p. 158), at popularizing, or perhaps we should say, visualizing, religion. Meyer, *op. cit.* discusses the Latin sources of the poem.

IV. MSS:

Oxford				
Fairfax	24	ff. 15[a]–18[b]	XIV[1]	Asc. in text†
Rawl. Poet.	241	pp. 196–207	XIII[2]	Asc.‡

Vising (*Anglo-Norman Literature*, p. 66) lists MS Rawl. C. 504 (XIII[2]) as a

* See further Stevenson, p. 327 ff., for early efforts for his canonization and the common use of *sanctus Robertus*. See also F. J. Tanquerey, *Recueil de lettres anglo-françaises* (1265–1399) (Paris, 1916), pp. 52 f., 55.

† This is an abridgment of the longer recension in the Rawl. MS and, furthermore, lacks several folia.

‡ The rubric reads: *Ici comence un tretitz coment le deable maria ces ix files a gent du secle et de sainte eglise solom Robert Groceteste*. The first twelve lines are from Ralph de Lenham's *Comput*.

copy of the poem, but there is to be found only the following anonymous diagram in the lower margin of f. 49[b].

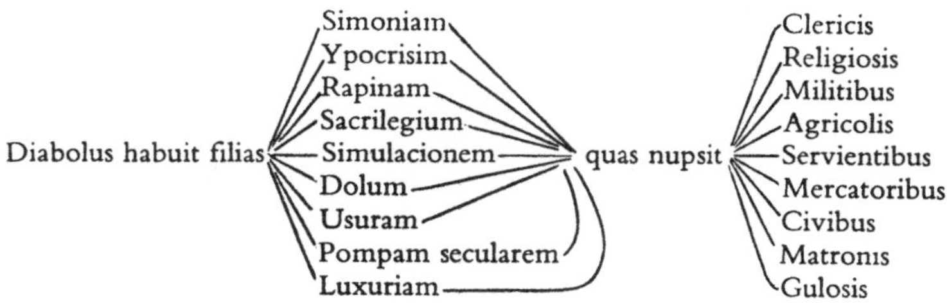

This miscellaneous codex contains *varia monastica* for Augustinian and Benedictine religious, but nothing else of Grosseteste. The names of the daughters and their spouses are the same as in the French version by Grosseteste. The same diagram is found on f. 91[A] of B.M. Royal 7. A. IX, also XIII[2] and anonymous. Our present information does not allow us to decide whether the Latin diagram is traceable to Grosseteste's treatise or his French work is based on an antecedent Latin work.

117. *Oracio ad Sanctam Margaretam Gallice*

I. The entire text, hitherto unpublished, follows:

Idem, scilicet Magister R. Grosseteste in oracione ad sanctam Margaretam: Gloriuse dame seinte Margarete. Io vus requor e encor merci ke vus eez merci de mei autresi uereiment cum io vus ai elu apres deu e sa duce mere nostre dame seinte Marie deuant totes autres. E a vus me tendrai auant tote les dames ke sunt ou estre purrunt; e vus auant totes amerai e honurai solum mon poer. E la grace ke deu par nostre requeste me durra, e ausi uereiment cum io nai iames en pense par la grace deu mon cor par ordure de la mauuaise char, ne de nuli autre soiller, e ausi uereiment cum io solum mon poure poer totes femmes, pur lamur de vus a ky io mai pris pur amer le plus honurai, e nomement celes ke par vostre nun sunt apelez, me seez eidant vers deu le tut pussant mon creatur. Kil eit merci de mei pur sa seinte pite e par vostre priere e pardoint mes pecches e me doint sa grace ke io puse sic transire per tempora ut non amittam eterna. E me seez ententiue eidere vers mon creatour ke io par sa mercy e par uostre priere puse si li plest sentir sa grace habundant en mei. E io vus premet leument ke si deus ad purveu ke io si prodome en tere deie estre ke io vus puse akun honur fere e enticerai autres al honur de vus, e io memes vus honurai si ke autres serrunt edefie par le bon esample ke nostre seignur par sa grace nostre aide en mei auera demostre. Quod mihi prestare dignetur et cetera.

III. This prayer was first noticed by James and Jenkins in their catalogue of the Lambeth MSS (1932), p. 696. For other short and ascribed works that appear in this MS, immediately preceding this prayer, see pp. 125 f., 135, 137, 158.

IV. MS:

London, Lambeth	499	f. 188[a]	XIII[2]	Asc.

118. *Oraciuncula post Prandium Gallice*

The complete text, as it appears in the unique MS, Lambeth 499, f. 184^b, is as follows:

Idem* post prandium hoc dicere consuevit: Deu seit od nus par sa pite e nus defende de mal e de pecche e nus doint fere sa volonte e nus meyne en saunte e consent a vifs e merci face a morz. Item Deu nus doint ben viure et ben morir e a la grant ioie paruenir. Item Deu seit od nus e nus doint sa grace e bone fin e vitam eternam. Item primo Benedicite. Responsio: Dominus nos custodiat et ab omni malo defendat et ad vitam eternam perducat.

For other items in this MS see preceding *Oracio*.

119. *Peines de Purgatoire*

I. Inc.: Ici comence romaunz estret hors de divinite solom l'ordeynement des philosophes.
In omnibus operibus tuis memorare...
A ses trechiers freres et soers en deu, as touz iceus ke ceste compilesoun lirunt...
Expl.: ...De celes peines deu nus defent par sa seinte pite.

II. See above, *De Penis Purgatorii*, II, p. 136.

III. See above, under the Latin *De Penis*. No MS of the French version is ascribed, and yet three and perhaps four of the French copies are earlier than the earliest Latin copy. The demand for works in French we know to have been on the decline in the second half of the fourteenth century, and we may thus account for the preponderance of French copies before that time.

IV. MSS:

Oxford, Bodl.	82	ff. 11^b–29^a	XIV^m	Unasc.†
	654	ff. 119^a–125^a	XIII^2	Unasc.
London, B.M.				
Arundel	288	ff. 84^A–91^D	XIII^2	Unasc.
Royal	16. E. II	ff. 3^a–24^b	*ca.* 1425	Unasc.
Cambridge, Trinity	R. 14. 7	ff. 111^D–115^A	XIV^1	Unasc.
Dublin, Trinity	E. 4. 30	ff. 109^a–119^b	1346	Unasc.

120. *Les Reulles Seint Robert*

I. Inc.: [prologue] Ci commencent les reulles que le bon evesque de Nichole sein Robert fist a la contesse de Nichole de garder e de governer terres...
[text] En dreit de vos foreyns teres a comencement...
Expl.: ...al Bristowe vez robes achatez a seynt Yve.

* The preceding item is specifically ascribed to Grosseteste. See p. 135.
† *Mut. e med. ad finem.*

II. Publ. by Miss E. Lamond in *Walter of Henley's Husbandry* (London, 1890), pp. 122–144 (from the Douce MS), with an English translation.

III. Owing to the confusion between Walter of Henley's *Husbandry* and Grosseteste's *Regule*, the French version, quite possibly the original of the *Regule*, escaped the notice of all the earlier bibliographers, in spite of the fact that there are more MSS of the French extant than of the Latin, and that one of these MSS is older than the Latin copy.

IV. MSS:

Oxford, Douce	98	ff. 182ᵃ–186ᵇ	*ca.* 1325	Asc.
London, B.M.				
Add.	33969	ff. 66ᵃ–78ᵃ	XIII²	Asc.
	38821	ff. 118ᵇ–121ᵃ	1289	Asc.
Harley	273	ff. 81ᴮ–85ᶜ	XIV¹	Asc.
	548	ff. 21ᵃ–27ᵇ	XV¹	Asc.
Sloane	1986	ff. 136ᵃ–139ᵇ	*ca.* 1400	Unasc.

Miss Lamond mentions (p. xliv) a fragment in the form of a roll, at Canterbury. She dates it "thirteenth century". I have not seen this roll.

SERMONS

I. The incipit and explicit of each sermon is given below.

II. E. Brown published, in *Fasc. Rer. Expet.* II, 250 ff., nineteen *Dicta* (see below, p. 214) which are listed in the MSS as Sermons and are given in the following list, as well as the *Sermo coram Papa et Cardinalibus* (Sermon 14). Little published excerpts from Sermon 8 from B.M. Royal 7. E. II in Appendix vii to his edition of the *De Adventu Minorum* of Thomas of Eccleston (Paris, 1909). Otherwise the sermons are both unpublished and unstudied. Occasional references to sermons of Grosseteste have been made by Loserth,* Owst,† Deanesly‡ and Welter§ in recent works, but almost exclusively to those published by Brown.

III. The bibliographers have listed indiscriminately and inclusively various MS collections of Grosseteste's sermons as well as single sermons, *Dicta* or sermons appearing as separate tractates. The confusion has not been entirely their fault. The MS tradition is appallingly irregular. Some sermons, more popular than others, may be preserved in almost a score of MSS; others, as well authenticated by age and specific ascription, may exist in only a single MS. Yet, in spite of the rather free selection the copyists have made, there may be traced some significant agreement among the important collections. From the appended table (p. 164 f.) it will be seen that there have been preserved two principal kinds of collection. The longer, of thirty-six to forty sermons, is preserved in five MSS, and a shorter, of fourteen to eighteen sermons, in nine MSS. The several shorter collections, of four to ten sermons, exhibit no marked independence of arrangement, though equally as old as the longer collections, i.e. XIV^m–XV.

The arrangement of the sermons may be taken as something of an indication of the tradition from which a given codex may have come. Three, B.M. Royal 6. E. v, 7. E. II and York Cath. XVI. A. 6, of the longer collections are obviously closely related. The York MS, *ca.* 1500, is almost certainly a copy of Royal 7. E. II, XIV². The Lansdowne MS, though containing all the sermons of the longer group, is completely independent as to arrangement. It is not sufficiently early, XIV², to compel recognition as representative of a good tradition. We may regard it as an arbitrary arrangement of these sermons. Royal 7. F. II has been accepted as representing the best arrangement of the longer tradition, and the sermons in the appended list numbered accordingly, but it is admitted that the margin of its superiority is very narrow. Its substantial agreement with Lincoln Cath. 202, XIV^m, for the first fourteen sermons; the important material agreement in the order of Sermons 6, 7, and 8 with the order in Royal 7. D. XV, the oldest, XIII², of all the collections; and the further fact that most of the MSS

* "Johann von Wiclif und Robert Grosseteste", *Sbte d. Kais. Akad.* 186 Bd., 2 Abh. (1918).

† *Preaching in Medieval England* (Cambridge, 1926) and *Literature and Pulpit*... (Cambridge, 1933), both *passim*.

‡ *Lollard Bible* (Cambridge, 1920).

§ *L'exemplum dans la littérature*... (Paris, 1927), see index.

containing fourteen to eighteen sermons agree, where there is any correspondence at all, with the order of Royal 7. F. II as to Sermons 1—13, have weighed heavily in its acceptance as the best tradition. But the confusion and divergence of arrangement remain considerable and suggest tentative explanations:

I. (*a*) There is an archetype behind Royal 7. F. II and Lincoln Cath. 202 from which the scribe of the latter copied Sermons 1–15, reversing 1 and 14, or

(*b*) There were two archetypes, one containing the first fifteen sermons and the other the remaining twenty-six. The latter theory appears likely in view of the fact that Royal 7. F. II contains Sermon 7 (*Exiit edictum...*) twice, once in the first lot of sermons and again as Sermon 31, i.e. in the second group. This duplication would be more simply explained if we suppose the scribe to have copied one collection which contained this sermon after having copied another collection which also contained it. If he were building a canon of Grosseteste's sermons on his own initiative, he would hardly have been guilty of that carelessness. We conclude, therefore, that Sermons 1–15 of Royal 7. F. II and the collection in Lincoln Cath. 202 probably come, with at least one intermediate step—note inversion of Sermons 1 and 14 in the Lincoln MS—from the same archetype. We designate these two MSS as Group I. Laud 374 is close to this group as is also, perhaps, Otho D. X.

II. Group II (Royal 6. E. V and 7. E. II, York Cath. XVI. A. 6) differ from Group I in that the first twenty-two sermons are in a variant order. Sermon 14 (*Dominus noster...*) everywhere shows a tendency to appear separately or out of order. From Sermon 24 to 37–39 the second archetype noticed in Group I has been drawn upon. The Prague Museum MS is related to this group, though independent in some ways, and, by reason of age (XIV^{m}) and provenance (Boh.), perhaps more valuable for the determination of the canon than an English copy. Laud 402, an arbitrary selection of eight sermons, may belong either to Group I or Group II. The presence of *Dictum* 135 (Sermon 62) indicates no more than the selectivity of the scribe.

III. Group III (Bodl. 830, Laud 374, Trinity Coll., Cambridge, B. 15. 20 and Pembroke Coll., Cambridge, 245) agree in the omission of Sermons 1, 2,* 7 and 14, and usually Sermons 16–20 out of the second part of the supposed composite of Group I. It is to be remarked that in nine MSS Sermons 16–20 appear *en bloc*; the three cases where they are not so arranged are not difficult to explain as arbitrary selections, evidenced by the arrangement of another *bloc* of sermons, 8–13.

IV. Group IV (Lincoln Coll. 56, Exeter Coll. 21, Lansdowne 458, Trinity Coll., Cambridge, B. 15. 20*) may be regarded as arbitrary selections of sermons by interested scribes. None of these MSS is early enough to demand special attention, though Exeter 21 is extremely valuable by reason of the quality of its text.

V. Group V. Royal 7. D. XV is the earliest collection extant (XIII^{2}), and contains numerous *Dicta* entitled *Sermones* as well as other sermons which appear in no other known MS. It is, excepting Durham MS A. III. 12, the oldest copy extant of any *Dicta*.

It hardly seems likely that we have all of the sermons Grosseteste preached. Some sermons at present anonymous or uncatalogued may eventually be identified as his. It is strange that we have so few MSS of his sermons dating from the thirteenth century. Counting the sermons and *Dicta*

* No. 5 in the Trinity MS.

originally intended or preached as sermons, ninety-two in all, and items 1, 2, 3, 16, 21, 22, 23, 25–27, 33, 35–42, 44, 46, 48, 53, 55, 56, 64–75, in the detailed description of Durham Cath. MS A. III. 12, which were certainly intended to be sermons, we have but 129 sermons. In view of his high conception of the preaching office and his eighteen years as bishop, the number of sermons is relatively small. We may hope for further discoveries.

IV. As the folia of MSS are given under the separate sermons, MSS which contain any sermons will only be listed and dated here. The date, in case a MS is the work of several scribes, refers only to that part in which the sermon occurs.

Oxford		
Bodl.	36	XIII^{1}
	52	XV^{1}
	57	XIII^{2}
	153	*ca.* 1400
	798	XIV^{2}
	801	XV^{1}
	830	XIV^{2}
Digby	191	XIII^{2}
Laud Misc.	374	*ca.* 1400
	402	XIV^{m}
	439	XIII^{m}
Rawl.	C. 531	XIII^{m}
Exeter	21	XV^{1}
Lincoln	56	XV^{1}
	105	XIV^{2}
Merton	47	*ca.* 1400
	82	*ca.* 1300
	127	*ca.* 1325
Univ. Coll.	109	XV^{1}
London, B.M.		
Cotton	Otho D. x	XIV^{m}
	Vitell. C. XIV	XIV^{2}
Harley	979	XIII^{m}
	1298	*ca.* 1400
Lans.	458	XIV^{2}
Royal	5. C. III	XV^{1}
	6. E. V	XIV^{m}
	7. A. IX	XIII^{m}
	7. D. XV	XIII^{2}
	7. E. II	XIV^{2}
	7. F. II	XIV^{m}
	8. E. XVII	*ca.* 1300
	9. A. XIV	XIII^{2}
	11. B. III	*ca.* 1300
London, Lambeth	171	*ca.* 1325
	523	XIV^{m}
Cambridge		
Univ.	Ll. i. 15	XIII^{m}
C.C.C.	156	XV^{2}
	257	XIV^{2}
	459	XIII^{m}

Gonv. & Caius	83	XV^{1}	
Jesus	66	*ca.* 1300	
Pembroke	245	*ca.* 1400	
St John's	15	*ca.* 1400	
Trinity	B. 15. 20	XIV^{2}	
	B. 15. 20*	XIV^{2}	
Cheltenham, Phillipps	3119	XIII^{2}	
Durham Cath.	A. III. 12	*ca.* 1230	
	B. III. 18	XV^{m}	
Lincoln Cath.	202	XIV^{m}	
York Cath.	XVI. A. 6	*ca.* 1500	
Berlin	lat. 361	XV^{1}	Ger.
Münster i. W.	165 (346)	XV^{m}	Ger.
Paris, B.N.	lat. 1727	*ca.* 1300	Engl.
	lat. 10358	XIII^{2}	Engl.
Prague			
Metrop. Chap.	272	*ca.* 1425	Boh.
Nat. Mus.	XII. E. 5	XIV^{m}	Boh.

In the following schema (pp. 164–165) the arabic numerals under a given MS press-mark indicate the order in which the sermons occur in that MS.

	Royal 7. F. II	Royal 7. E. II	York Cath. XVI. A. 6	Lincoln Cath. 202	Royal 6. E. V	Lans. 458	Bodley 830	Trinity, Cambr., B. 15. 20	Pembroke, Cambr., 245	Lincoln, Oxf., 56	Exeter, Oxf., 21	Laud 374	Cotton Otho D. X	Prague, N.M. XII. E. 5	Trinity, Cambr., B. 15. 20*	Laud 402	Bodley 153	Merton, Oxf., 47	Royal 7. D. XV	Durham Cath. B. III. 18
1. Pauper et inops	1	1	1	2	1	1	.	.	.	.	4	.	11	5	9	1	2	.	10	.
2. Erunt signa	2	2	2	3	2	3	.	5	.	.	3	.	10	6	6	2	.	.	1	.
3. Egredietur virga	3	3	3	4	3	14	2	1	1	11	.	1	2	7	2	3	.	.	.	.
4. Unguentum	4	4	4	5	4	15	3	2	2	8	.	2	3	8	3	4	5	.	.	.
5. Spiritus...per os	5	5	5	6	5	16	1	16	.	5	.	(sep.)	4	9	4	.	.	.	.	.
6. Convenitis ex	6	6	6	7	6	18	4	3	3	7	5	3	13	4	7	.	.	.	8	.
7. Exiit edictum	7	13	13	8	13	10	.	.	.	.	6	.	14	11	8	.	.	.	9	.
8. Beati pauperes	8	7	7	9	7	2	5	4	4	3	7	4	15	10	10	5	3	.	11	.
9. Manus in	9	20	20	10	20	34	6	5	5	4	.	5	5	16	.	.	4	.	.	.
10. Spiritus...descendit	10	21	21	11	21	24	7	6	6	.	.	6	6	17	.	.	.	.	.	.
11. Spiritus ubi vult	11	22	22	12	22	25	8	7	7	6	.	7	7	18	.	.	.	.	.	.
12. In libro Num.	12	18	18	13	18	6	9	8	8	.	1	8	8	.	.	7	.	.	.	.
13. Beatus Paulus	13	19	19	14	19	5	10	9	9	13	2	9	9	.	.	8	.	4	.	2
14. Dominus noster	14	40	40	1	39	13	.	.	.	.	8	.	12	.	5	.	1	2	12	3
15. Quoniam cog.	15	17	17	15	17	.	11	10	10	1	(sep.)	10	1	.	1	.	.	.	.	.
16. Canimus...Tota pulcra	16	8	8	.	8	17	.	11	11	9	9	11	.	12	.	.	.	.	.	.
17. Qui autem	17	9	9	.	9	9	12	12	12	2	13	12	.	13	.	.	.	.	.	.
18. Amice quomodo	18	10	10	.	10	8	13	13	13	10	.	13	.	14	.	.	.	.	.	.
19. Premonitus a	19	11	11	.	11	4	14	14	14	14	18	14	.	15	.	.	.	3	.	1
20. Cumque lavasset	20	12	12	.	12	7	15	15	.	12	.	15	.	.	.	.	.	.	.	.
21. Domum tuam	21	14	14	.	14	19	.	.	.	.	.	.	.	.	.	.	.	.	.	.
22. Legimus hodie	22	15	15	.	15	20	.	.	.	.	.	.	.	.	.	.	.	.	.	.
23. Et sedebit	23	16	16	.	16	.	.	.	.	.	.	.	.	.	.	.	.	.	.	.
24. Prelati et	24	23	23	.	23	27	.	.	.	15	10	.	.	.	.	.	.	.	.	.
25. Christus in	25	24	24	.	24	26	.	.	.	.	11	.	.	.	.	.	.	.	.	.

28.	Tribulatur homo	28	27	27	.	27	29	.	.	.	.	15	.	.	.	.	.	.	.	.	.
29.	Absintheum	29	28	28	.	28	28	.	.	.	.	16	.	.	.	.	.	.	.	.	.
30.	Ecclesia sancta	30	29	29	.	29	23	.	.	.	.	17	.	.	2	.	.	.	.	.	.
31.	Scriptum est*	32	30	30	.	30	22	.	.	.	.	.	.	.	.	.	.	.	.	.	.
32.	Deus est quo	33	31	31	.	31	21	.	.	.	.	.	.	.	.	.	.	.	.	.	.
33.	Ex rerum	34	32	32	.	32	11	.	.	.	.	.	.	.	1	.	.	.	.	.	.
34.	Natis et	35	33	33	.	33	12	.	.	.	.	.	.	.	3	.	.	.	1	.	.
35.	Egrede de	36	34	34	.	34	31	.	.	.	.	.	.	.	.	.	.	.	.	.	.
36.	Adulari est	37	35	35	.	35	.	.	.	.	.	.	.	.	.	.	.	.	.	.	.
37.	Contemplativorum	38	36	36	.	36	33	(*Spurium*, see below, p. 177)						.	.	.	.	.	.	.	.
38.	Post Moysen	39	37	37	.	37	.	.	.	.	.	.	.	.	.	.	.	.	.	.	.
39.	Ut iumentum	40	38	38	.	.	35	.	.	.	.	.	.	.	.	.	.	.	.	.	.
40.	Tenuisti	41	39	39	.	38	36	.	.	.	.	.	.	.	.	.	.	.	.	.	.
41.	Expoliantes	.	.	.	.	.	.	.	.	.	.	.	.	.	.	11	.	.	.	3	.
42.	Elevatus est	.	.	.	.	.	.	.	.	.	.	.	.	.	.	12	.	.	.	20	.
43.	Non est veritas	.	.	.	.	.	.	.	.	.	.	.	.	.	.	.	.	.	.	2	.
44.	Emptor est	.	.	.	.	.	.	.	.	.	.	.	.	.	.	.	.	.	.	4	.
45.	Qui seminat	(*Dictum* 11)			.	.	.	.	.	.	.	.	.	.	.	.	.	.	.	5	.
46.	In civitate	(*Dictum* 43)			.	.	.	.	.	.	.	.	.	.	.	.	.	.	.	6	.
47.	Vidimus	.	.	.	.	.	.	.	.	.	.	.	.	.	.	.	.	.	.	7	.
48.	Verbum et	(*Dictum* 131)			.	.	.	.	.	.	.	.	.	.	.	.	.	.	.	13	.
49.	Quemadmodum	.	.	.	.	.	.	.	.	.	.	.	.	.	.	.	.	.	.	14	.
50.	Omne capud	.	.	.	.	.	.	.	.	.	.	.	.	.	.	.	.	.	.	15	.
51.	Quasi cedens	.	.	.	.	.	.	.	.	.	.	.	.	.	.	.	.	.	.	16	.
52.	Hortamur vos	(*Dictum* 87)			.	.	.	.	.	.	.	.	.	.	.	.	.	.	.	17	.
53.	Nonne cor	(*Dictum* 72)			.	.	.	.	.	.	.	.	.	.	.	.	.	.	.	18	.
54.	Ascendit deus	(*Dictum* 50)			.	.	.	.	.	.	.	.	.	.	.	.	.	.	.	19	.
55.	Misericordia	(*Dictum* 2)			.	.	.	.	.	.	.	.	.	.	.	.	.	.	.	21	.
56.	Crux domini	(*Dictum* 119)			.	.	.	.	.	.	.	.	.	.	.	.	.	.	.	22	.
57.	Mali vellent	(*Dictum* 4)			.	.	.	.	.	.	.	.	.	.	.	.	.	.	.	23	.
58.	Secundum Aug.	(*Dictum* 6)		.	.	.	.	.	.	.	.	.	.	.	.	.	.	.	.	24	.
59.	Visitans	.	.	.	.	.	.	.	.	.	.	.	.	.	.	.	.	.	.	25	.
60.	Obtulerunt	.	.	.	.	.	.	.	.	.	.	.	.	.	.	.	.	.	.	26	.
61.	Elevata est	.	.	.	.	.	.	.	.	.	.	.	.	.	.	.	.	.	.	27	.
62.	Despondi vos	(*Dictum* 135)			.	.	.	.	.	.	.	.	.	.	.	.	6	.	.	.	.

Sermons 63–92 are *Dicta* or appear separately. See, however, the detailed description of Durham MS A. III. 12, pp. 76 ff. and 182 ff.

* Sermon 7 repeated = 31.

I

In the following tabulation of MSS the number in parenthesis indicates the order in which a given sermon appears in the collection.

1. Pauper et inops laudabunt nomen... × ...fulgebis gracia et misericordia.

Occasionally entitled *Sermo...ad fratres minores de laude paupertatis in festa sancti Martini*. See Little, *Eccleston*, p. 123.

Oxford		
Bodl.	153	ff. 207^{D}–211^{D} (2)
Laud Misc.	402	ff. 133^{a}–140^{a} (1)
Exeter	21	pp. 96^{a}–104^{a} (4)
London, B.M.		
Cotton	Otho D. x	ff. 246^{a}–250^{a} (11)
Lans.	458	ff. 117^{C}–119^{C} (1)
Royal	6. E. v	ff. 70^{A}–72^{D} (1)
	7. D. xv	ff. 16^{b}–21^{a} (10)
	7. E. II	ff. 251^{D}–258^{C} (1)
	7. F. II	ff. 10^{A}–13^{C} (1)
Cambridge, Trinity	B. 15. 20*	ff. 758^{A}–761^{A} (9)
Cheltenham, Phillipps	3119	ff. 62^{A}–66^{A}
Lincoln Cath.	202	ff. 185^{B}–189^{B} (2)
York Cath.	XVI. A. 6	ff. 1^{a}–9^{a} (1)
Berlin	lat. 361	ff. 230^{A}–235^{D}, with Sermon 8
Prague, Nat. Mus.	XII. E. 5	ff. 76^{A}–77^{D} (5)

2. Erunt signa in sole et luna et stellis.... Requirentibus discipulis... × ...regno patris sui sine fine.

Bale, *Index*, p. 375, lists *Sermones per adventum* with this incipit.

Oxford		
Laud Misc.	402	ff. 140^{a}–147^{a} (2)
Exeter	21	pp. 88^{a}–96^{a} (3)
London, B.M.		
Cotton	Otho D. x	ff. 243^{b}–246^{a} (10)
Lans.	458	ff. 122^{A}–124^{C} (3)
Royal	6. E. v	ff. 72^{D}–75^{C} (2)
	7. D. xv	ff. 1^{a}–2^{b} (1)
	7. E. II	ff. 258^{C}–264^{D} (2)
	7. F. II	ff. 13^{C}–17^{B} (2)
Cambridge, Trinity	B. 15. 20*	f. 756^{A-D} (6)
Lincoln Cath.	202	ff. 189^{B}–193^{D} (3)
York Cath.	XVI. A. 6	ff. 9^{a}–16^{a} (2)
Prague, Nat. Mus.	XII. E. 5	ff. 77^{D}–79^{C} (6)

3. Egredietur virga de radice Jesse etc. Novit caritas vestra... × ...usque ad summum eius.

Oxford		
Bodl.	830	ff. 140^{B}–144^{C} (2)
Laud Misc.	374	ff. 191^{D}–198^{B} (1)
	402	ff. 147^{b}–154^{a} (3)
Lincoln	56	ff. 148^{a}–152^{b} (11)

London, B.M.		
Cotton	Otho D. x	ff. 230^a–232^a (2)
Lans.	458	ff. 151^D–153^D (14)
Royal	6. E. v	ff. 75^C–77^D (3)
	7. E. ii	ff. 264^D–269^D (3)
	7. F. ii	ff. 17^B–20^B (3)
Cambridge		
Pembroke	245	ff. 159^a–164^a (1)
Trinity	B. 15. 20	cols. 357–368 (1)
	B. 15. 20*	ff. 745^C–748^C (2)
Lincoln Cath.	202	ff. 193^D–197^B (4)
York Cath.	xvi. A. 6	ff. 16^a–22^a (3)
Prague, Nat. Mus.	xii. E. 5	ff. 79^C–81^A (7)

4. Unguentum effusum nomen tuum... × ...huius mundi ad perpetue salutis portum.

Oxford		
Bodl.	153	ff. 217^C–219^A (5)
	830	ff. 144^C–149^A (3)
Laud Misc.	374	ff. 198^B–204^C (2)
	402	ff. 154^a–161^a (4)
Lincoln	56	ff. 141^b–146^a (8)
London, B.M.		
Cotton	Otho D. x	ff. 232^a–234^b (3)
Lans.	458	ff. 154^A–156^B (15)
Royal	6. E. v	ff. 77^D–79^D (4)
	7. E. ii	ff. 269^D–274^D (4)
	7. F. ii	ff. 20^B–23^B (4)
Cambridge		
Pembroke	245	ff. 164^a–168^b (2)
Trinity	B. 15. 20	cols. 369–380 (2)
	B. 15. 20*	ff. 748^C–751^B (3)
Lincoln Cath.	202	ff. 197^B–200^D (5)
York Cath.	xvi. A. 6	ff. 22^a–28^a (4)
Prague, Nat. Mus.	xii. E. 5	ff. 81^A–82^B (8)

5. Spiritus sanctus per os Salomonis in persona... × ...virginis Marie filiis hominum filio speciosissimo.

Oxford		
Bodl.	830	ff. 137^B–140^B (1)
Laud Misc.	374	ff. 1^A–4^B, as *Dictum* 1
London, B.M.		
Cotton	Otho D. x	ff. 234^b–236^a (4)
Lans.	458	ff. 156^B–157^D (16)
Royal	6. E. v	ff. 79^D–81^A (5)
	7. E. ii	ff. 274^D–278^A (5)
	7. F. ii	ff. 23^B–25^B (5)
Cambridge, Trinity	B. 15. 20	cols. 480–487 (16)
	B. 15. 20*	ff. 751^B–752^D (4)
Lincoln Cath.	202	ff. 200^D–202^D (6)
York Cath.	xvi. A. 6	ff. 28^a–31^b (5)
Prague, Nat. Mus.	xii. E. 5	ff. 82^B–83^A (9)

6. Conventis ex consuetudine ad collacionem quasi ad alicuius... × ... sit hic nobis huius collaciuncule finis.

Entitled in Royal 7. E. II *Sermo ad collacionem fratrum minorum.*

Oxford		
Bodl.	830	ff. 149^{A}–150^{B} (4)
Laud Misc.	374	ff. 204^{C}–206^{C} (3)
Exeter	21	ff. 104^{a}–105^{a} (5)
Lincoln	56	ff. 140^{a}–141^{b} (7)
London, B.M.		
Cotton	Otho D. x	ff. 252^{b}–253^{b} (13)
Lans.	458	ff. 158^{C}–159^{B} (18)
Royal	6. E. v	f. 81^{A-D} (6)
	7. D. xv	ff. 14^{a}–15^{a} (8)
	7. E. II	ff. 278^{A}–279^{B} (6)
	7. F. II	ff. 25^{B}–26^{A} (6)
Cambridge		
Pembroke	245	ff. 168^{b}–170^{a} (3)
Trinity	B. 15. 20	cols. 380–383 (3)
	B. 15. 20*	ff. 756^{D}–757^{B} (7)
Lincoln Cath.	202	ff. 202^{D}–203^{C} (7)
York Cath.	XVI. A. 6	ff. 31^{b}–33^{b} (6)
Prague, Nat. Mus.	XII. E. 5	f. 75^{C-D} (4)

7. Exiit edictum a Cesare Augusto.... Nato salvatore... × ...in libro vite ascribi cui cum patre...et gloria.

Oxford, Exeter	21	pp. 105^{a}–107^{b}, *frag.* (6)
London, B.M.		
Cotton	Otho D. x	ff. 253^{b}–254^{a} (14)
Lans.	458	ff. 136^{C}–139^{B} (10)
Royal	6. E. v	ff. 91^{D}–94^{C} (13)
	7. D. xv	ff. 15^{a}–16^{b} (9)
	7. E. II	ff. 301^{B}–307^{C} (13)
	7. F. II	ff. 26^{A}–27^{A} (7)
Cambridge, Trinity	B. 15. 20*	ff. 757^{B}–758^{A} (8)
Lincoln Cath.	202	ff. 203^{C}–204^{B} (8)
York Cath.	XVI. A. 6	ff. 61^{a}–69^{a} (13)
Prague, Nat. Mus.	XII. E. 5	ff. 84^{A}–85^{B} (11)

8. Beati pauperes quoniam.... Vos omnes et singuli huius sancte congregacionis... × ...in subiecta figura visibiliter descripsimus.

Often referred to (Bale, Pits, Tanner, etc.) as *Tractatus de Scala Paupertatis* and appears so in some MSS.

Oxford		
Bodl.	153	ff. 212^{A}–217^{B} (3)
	830	ff. 150^{B}–156^{C} (5)
Laud Misc.	374	ff. 206^{C}–215^{C} (4)
	402	ff. 161^{a}–170^{b} (5)
Exeter	21	ff. 107^{b}–117^{a} (7)
Lincoln	56	ff. 133^{a}–139^{a} (3)
London, B.M.		
Cotton	Otho D. x	ff. 254^{a} *et seqq.*, end indeterminate, burnt (15)
Lans.	458	ff. 119^{C}–121^{D}, first half only (2)
Royal	6. E. v	ff. 81^{D}–84^{C} (7)

Royal	7. D. XV	ff. 21^{a}–28^{b} (11)
	7. E. II	ff. 280^{C}–286^{A} (7)*
	7. F. II	ff. 27^{A}–31^{D} (8)
Cambridge		
Univ.	Ii. i. 19	ff. 201^{A}–208^{A}, separate as *Tractatus de Scala Paupertatis*
Pembroke	245	ff. 170^{a}–176^{a} (4)
Trinity	B. 15. 20	cols. 383–399 (4)
	B. 15. 20*	ff. 761^{A}–765^{A} (10)
Cheltenham, Phillipps	3119	ff. 66^{A}–70^{C}
Dublin, Trinity	B. 5. 4	ff. 62^{D}–69^{C}, separate
Lincoln Cath.	202	ff. 204^{C}–208^{D} (9)
York Cath.	XVI. A. 6	ff. 33^{b}–41^{b} (7)
Berlin	lat. 361	ff. 224^{A}–229^{D}, with Sermon I
Paris, B.N.	lat. 13573	ff. 2^{a}–10^{a}, separate as *Sermo ad Religiosos*
Prague, Nat. Mus.	XII. E. 5	ff. 83^{A}–84^{A} (10)

9. Manus in sacra scriptura frequenter.... Manus enim est... × ...sic semper cum domino permansuri.

Oxford		
Bodl.	153	f. 217^{B-C} (4)
	830	ff. 156^{C}–157^{A} (6)
Laud Misc.	374	ff. 215^{C}–216^{B} (5)
Lincoln	56	f. 139^{a-b} (4)
London, B.M.		
Cotton	Otho D. x	f. 236^{a-b} (5)
Lans.	458	ff. 179^{D}–180^{A} (34)
Royal	6. E. V	f. 104^{C-D} (20)
	7. E. II	ff. 330^{D}–331^{B} (20)
	7. F. II	ff. 31^{D}–32^{A} (9)
Cambridge		
Pembroke	245	f. 176^{a-b} (5)
Trinity	B. 15. 20	cols. 399–400 (5)
Lincoln Cath.	202	ff. 208^{D}–209^{B} (10)
York Cath.	XVI. A. 6	f. 99^{a-b} (20)
Prague, Nat. Mus.	XII. E. 5	f. 87^{C-D} (16)

10. Spiritus sanctus descendit super Christum in columbe specie... × ... que apte nata est ad formandum verbum.

Oxford		
Bodl.	830	f. 157^{A-B} (7)
Laud Misc.	374	f. 216^{B-D} (6)
Lincoln	56	ff. 139^{b}–140^{a} (5)
London, B.M.		
Cotton	Otho D. x	f. 236^{b} (6)
Lans.	458	f. 175^{A-B} (24)
Royal	6. E. V	f. 104^{D} (21)
	7. E. II	f. 331^{B-D} (21)
	7. F. II	f. 32^{A-B} (10)
Cambridge		
Pembroke	245	ff. 176^{b}–177^{a} (6)
Trinity	B. 15. 20	cols. 400–401 (6)
Lincoln Cath.	202	f. 209^{B-C} (11)
York Cath.	XVI. A. 6	ff. 99^{b}–100^{a} (21)
Prague, Nat. Mus.	XII. E. 5	f. 87^{C} (17)

* Entitled *Sermo de scala paupertatis in capitulo fratrum minorum.*

11. Spiritus ubi vult spirat et vocem.... Licet spiritus sanctus ubique sit per presenciam... × ...ad gracie magnitudinem reputatus in nichilum.

Oxford		
Bodl.	830	f. 157^{B-D} (9)
Laud Misc.	374	ff. $216^{D}-217^{B}$ (7)
Lincoln	56	f. 140^{a} (6)
London, B.M.		
Cotton	Otho D. x	ff. $236^{b}-237^{a}$ (7)
Lans.	458	f. 175^{B-C} (25)
Royal	6. E. v	ff. $104^{D}-105^{A}$ (22)
	7. E. II	ff. $331^{D}-332^{A}$ (22)
	7. F. II	f. 32^{B-C} (11)
Cambridge		
Pembroke	245	ff. $177^{a}-179^{a}$ (7)
Trinity	B. 15. 20	cols. 401–402 (7)
Lincoln Cath.	202	f. 209^{C-D} (12)
York Cath.	XVI. A. 6	f. 100^{a-b} (22)
Prague, Nat. Mus.	XII. E. 5	ff. $87^{D}-88^{A}$ (18)

12. In libro Numerorum scriptum est de levitis et scient singuli... × ... omnia innovanti et cum deo patre reconciliantis.

Oxford		
Bodl.	830	ff. $157^{D}-161^{B}$ (9)
Laud Misc.	374	ff. $217^{B}-222^{C}$ (8)
	402	ff. $174^{a}-179^{b}$ (7)
Exeter	21	pp. $73^{a}-77^{b}$, *mut. in init.* (1)
London, B.M.		
Cotton	Otho D. x	ff. $237^{a}-239^{a}$ (8)
Lans.	458	ff. $133^{B}-134^{D}$ (6)
Royal	6. E. v	ff. $99^{C}-101^{A}$ (18)
	7. E. II	ff. $318^{C}-322^{C}$ (18)
	7. F. II	ff. $32^{C}-35^{B}$ (12)
Cambridge		
Pembroke	245	ff. $177^{b}-181^{a}$ (8)
Trinity	B. 15. 20	cols. 402–412 (8)
Lincoln Cath.	202	ff. $209^{D}-212^{B}$ (13)
York Cath.	XVI. A. 6	ff. $83^{b}-88^{b}$ (18)

13. Beatus Paulus apostolus discipulum suum Titum in arte... × ... optimo usu et ordinatissimo fine composuerunt exterius.

Oxford		
Bodl.	830	ff. $161^{B}-168^{D}$ (10)
Laud Misc.	374	ff. $222^{C}-233^{D}$ (9)
	402	ff. $180^{a}-192^{a}$ (8)
Exeter	21	pp. $77^{a}-87^{b}$ (2)
Lincoln	56	ff. $154^{b}-161^{b}$ (13)
Merton	47	ff. $228^{b}-237^{b}$ (4)
London, B.M.		
Cotton	Otho D. x	ff. $239^{a}-243^{b}$ (9)
Lans.	458	ff. $129^{C}-133^{B}$ (5)
Royal	5. C. III	ff. $235^{C}-238^{A}$ (2)*
	6. E. v	ff. $101^{A}-104^{C}$ (19)
	7. E. II	ff. $322^{C}-330^{D}$ (19)

* In this MS Sermon 1 is *Dictum* 3.

Royal	7. F. II	ff. 35^{B}–41^{A} (13)
Cambridge		
Pembroke	245	ff. 181^{a}–189^{a} (9)
Trinity	B. 15. 20	cols. 412–432 (9)
Durham Cath.	B. III. 18	ff. 250^{C}–254^{D} (2)
Lincoln Cath.	202	ff. 212^{B}–217^{D} (14)
York Cath.	XVI. A. 6	ff. 88^{b}–99^{a} (19)

14. Dominus noster Jesus Christus eternus eterni Dei patris... × ...desiderio cogentibus a me peccatore extremo est attemptatum.

Published by Brown, *Fasc. Rer. Expet.* II, 250–257, presented to the Council of Lyons in 1250 and read aloud by Cardinal John of St Nicholas. See Stevenson, p. 285 ff.* Listed by Bale twice, once as beginning a *Homeliarum volumen*, and the second time as *Conciones ad romanum pontificem*, both notices are taken over by Tanner and Pegge, who cite Cambridge MSS. Many MSS have a rubric similar to that in Royal 7. E. II: *Hunc sermonem predicavit dominus R. Grostest lincolniensis episcopus coram domino papa et eius cardinalibus et toto clero in curia romana.* It is difficult to treat the rejection of the authenticity of this memorandum by Charles Jourdain in *Bull. de l'Acad. des Inscriptions et Belles Lettres* (1868), and reprinted in his *Excursions Historiques...* (Paris, 1888), pp. 149 ff., as seriously as the name of the learned author would ordinarily demand. Having seen none of the MSS, he remarks "les attributions qu'elles présentent sont équivoques, contradictoires et qu'elles méritent peu de créance". At least two of the MSS are of the thirteenth century and the majority are ascribed. See also below, p. 212 f.

Oxford		
Bodl.	52	ff. 127^{a}–136^{a}, separate
	153	ff. 204^{A}–207^{D} (1)
	798	ff. 139^{A}–143^{C}, separate
Exeter	21	pp. 117^{a}–124^{b} (8)
Merton	47	ff. 213^{a}–218^{a} (2)
	127	ff. 96^{A}–100^{B}, separate
London, B.M.		
Cotton	Otho D. x	ff. 250^{a}–252^{b} (12)
Lans.	458	ff. 145^{A}–147^{C} (13)
Royal	6. E. v	ff. 126^{A}–128^{A} (39)
	7. D. xv	ff. 28^{b}–34^{a} (12)
	7. E. II	ff. 380^{B}–385^{B} (40)
	7. F. II	ff. 41^{A}–44^{D} (14)
London, Lambeth	171	ff. 1^{a}–5^{b}, separate
Cambridge		
C.C.C.	257	ff. 185^{a}–189^{b}
Gonv. & Caius	83	ff. 126^{A}–130^{B}, separate, after *Dicta*
Trinity	B. 15. 20*	ff. 753^{A}–756^{A} (5)
Durham Cath.	B. III. 18	ff. 254^{B}–256^{D} (3)
Lincoln Cath.	202	ff. 181^{C}–185^{B} (1)
York Cath.	XVI. A. 6	ff. 165^{a}–172^{b} (40)
Paris, B.N.	lat. 10358	ff. 185^{b}–192^{b}, separate
Prague, Metrop. Chap.	272	ff. 82^{a}–90^{a}, separate, with letters

* See also above, p. 142 f.

15. Quoniam cogitacio hominis.... Confitendum est quod (quia)... × ...talis vicarii copiam confitendi potenciam.

This sermon occurs often separately as a *Tractatus de Confessione* or *Tractatus de Modo Confitendi*, and is so listed by Boston of Bury, Bale, Tanner and Pegge. Its appearance in all the principal sermon collections as well as its form show it to have been justly regarded as a sermon.

Oxford		
Bodl.	52	ff. 151^{a}–160^{b} (3)
	830	ff. 168^{D}–174^{B} (11)
Laud Misc.	374	ff. 233^{D}–241^{C} (10)
	439	ff. 79^{A}–81^{A}, separate
Lincoln	56	ff. 127^{b}–132^{a} (1)
	105	ff. 32^{A}–34^{B}, separate
Univ. Coll.	109	pp. 227^{a}–233^{a}
London, B.M.		
Cotton	Otho D. x	ff. 227^{b}–230^{a} (1)
	Vitell. C. XIV	ff. 31^{A}–34^{D}, separate
Harley	1298	ff. 105^{B}–108^{C}, separate
Royal	6. E. v	ff. 97^{B}–99^{C} (17)
	7. A. IX	ff. 115^{B}–118^{D}, *mut. in fine* (2)
	7. E. II	ff. 313^{D}–318^{C} (17)
	7. F. II	ff. 44^{D}–48^{D} (15)
	8. E. XVII	ff. 86^{A}–92^{C}, separate
Cambridge		
Univ.	Ll. i. 15	ff. 184^{A}–188^{A}, separate
C.C.C.	257	ff. 181^{a}–185^{a}, separate
	459	ff. 30^{b}–35^{b}, separate
Gonv. & Caius	138	ff. 172^{a}–175^{b}, with *Constituciones*
Jesus	66	ff. 59^{D}–65^{C}, separate
Pembroke	245	ff. 189^{a}–194^{a} (10)
Peterhouse	255, pt. iii	ff. 23^{A}–30^{B}, with *Constituciones*
Trinity	B. 15. 20	cols. 432–443 (10)
		cols. 508–519, separate
	B. 15. 20*	ff. 742^{D}–745^{C} (1)
Lincoln Cath.	202	ff. 217^{D}–220^{D} (15)
York Cath.	XVI. A. 6	ff. 77^{a}–83^{b} (17)

16. Canimus hodie: Tota pulcra es amica mea et macula non est in te. Non fuit... × ...creaturis omnibus restituit antiquam dignitatem.

Oxford		
Laud Misc.	374	ff. 241^{C}–242^{C} (11)
Exeter	21	p. 135^{a-b}, *bis* (9)
Lincoln	56	ff. 146^{a}–147^{b} (9)
London, B.M.		
Lans.	458	ff. 157^{D}–158^{C} (17)
Royal	6. E. v	ff. 84^{C}–85^{B} (8)
	7. E. II	ff. 286^{A}–287^{C} (8)
	7. F. II	ff. 48^{C}–49^{C} (16)
Cambridge		
Pembroke	245	ff. 194^{a}–195^{b} (11)
Trinity	B. 15. 20	cols. 443–447 (11)
York Cath.	XVI. A. 6	ff. 41^{b}–43^{b} (8)
Prague, Nat. Mus.	XII. E. 5	f. 85^{B-C} (12)

17. Qui autem sunt Christi.... Caro potest hic intelligi... × ...vero honoris suavitate fortiter attrahente.

Oxford		
Bodl.	830	ff. 174^{B}–175^{A} (12)
Laud Misc.	374	ff. 242^{C}–243^{D} (12)
Exeter	21	pp. 138^{a}–139^{b} (12)
Lincoln	56	ff. 132^{a}–133^{a} (2)
London, B.M.		
Lans.	458	f. 136^{A-C} (9)
Royal	6. E. v	f. 85^{B-C} (9)
	7. E. ii	ff. 287^{C}–288^{B} (9)
	7. F. ii	ff. 49^{C}–50^{A} (17)
Cambridge		
Pembroke	245	ff. 195^{b}–196^{b} (12)
Trinity	B. 15. 20	cols. 447–449 (12)
York Cath.	xvi. A. 6	ff. 43^{b}–44^{b} (9)
Prague, Nat. Mus.	xii. E. 5	f. 85^{C-D} (13)

18. Amice quomodo huc intrasti.... De hiis que in presenti sermone ... × ...potant sub specie vini de calice.

Oxford		
Bodl.	830	f. 175^{A-D} (13)
Laud Misc.	374	ff. 243^{D}–244^{C} (13)
Lincoln	56	ff. 147^{b}–148^{a} (10)
London, B.M.		
Lans.	458	ff. 135^{D}–136^{A} (8)
Royal	5. C. iii	f. 238^{A-C} (3)
	6. E. v	ff. 85^{D}–86^{A} (10)
	7. E. ii	f. 288^{B-D} (10)
	7. F. ii	f. 50^{A-C} (18)
Cambridge		
Pembroke	245	ff. 196^{b}–197^{a} (13)
Trinity	B. 15. 20	cols. 449–451 (13)
York Cath.	xvi. A. 6	ff. 44^{b}–45^{b} (10)
Prague, Nat. Mus.	xii. E. 5	f. 85^{D} (14)

19. Premonitus a venerabili patre.... Sacerdotes tui induantur.... Secundum hoc verbum... × ...prestante domino nostro Jesu Christo qui cum patre etc.

Not to be confused with Sermon 66 and *Dictum* 3.

Oxford		
Bodl.	830	ff. 175^{D}–185^{A} (14)
Laud Misc.	374	ff. 244^{C}–258^{C} (14)
Exeter	21	pp. 153^{a}–166^{b}, inc. (18)
Lincoln	56	ff. 161^{b}–171^{b} (14)
Merton	47	ff. 218^{a}–228^{b} (3)
London, B.M.		
Lans.	458	ff. 124^{C}–129^{C} (4)
Royal	5. C. iii	ff. 229^{C}–235^{C} (1)
	6. E. v	ff. 86^{A}–90^{D} (11)
	7. E. ii	ff. 288^{D}–299^{A} (11)
	7. F. ii	ff. 50^{C}–59^{A} (19)

Cambridge		
Pembroke	245	ff. 197^{a}–210^{a} (14)
Trinity	B. 15. 20	cols. 451–474 (14)
Durham Cath.	B. III. 18	ff. 245^{A}–250^{C} (1)
York Cath.	XVI. A. 6	ff. 45^{b}–58^{b} (11)
Prague, Nat. Mus.	XII. E. 5	ff. 86^{A}–87^{C}, inc. (15)

20. Cumque lavasset eos.... Sermo iste scriptus... × ...integri in nullo deficientes parante (prestante) domino Jesu Christo...in sec. sec.

Called in Lansdowne MS *Sermo in sinodo.*

Oxford		
Bodl.	830	ff. 185^{A}–186^{D} (15)
Laud Misc.	374	ff. 258^{C}–262^{D} (15)
Lincoln	56	ff. 152^{b}–154^{b} (12)
London, B.M.		
Lans.	458	ff. 134^{D}–135^{D} (7)
Royal	6. E. V	ff. 90^{D}–91^{C} (12)
	7. E. II	ff. 299^{A}–301^{B} (12)
	7. F. II	ff. 59^{A}–60^{C} (20)
Cambridge, Trinity	B. 15. 20	cols. 474–479 (15)
York Cath.	XVI. A. 6	ff. 58^{b}–61^{a} (12)

21. Domum tuam domine decet.... Domus dei est ecclesia... × ...ipse liber vite dominus noster Jesus Christus...et gloria.

London, B.M.		
Lans.	458	ff. 159^{B}–160^{A} (19)
Royal	6. E. V	ff. 94^{C}–95^{B} (14)
	7. E. II	ff. 307^{C}–309^{B} (14)
	7. F. II	ff. 60^{D}–62^{B} (21)
York Cath.	XVI. A. 6	ff. 69^{a}–71^{b} (14)

22. Legimus hodie. In ecclesia mundi... × ...ad simplicium instruccionem dictis.

London, B.M.		
Lans.	458	ff. 160^{A}–161^{B} (20)
Royal	6. E. V	ff. 95^{B}–96^{B} (15)
	7. E. II	ff. 309^{B}–311^{B} (15)
	7. F. II	ff. 62^{B}–63^{D} (22)
York Cath.	XVI. A. 6	ff. 71^{b}–74^{a} (15)

23. Et sedebit conflans et emundans.... In leccione epistole... × ... mundator omnium dominus noster Jesus Christus.

London, B.M., Royal	6. E. V	ff. 96^{B}–97^{B} (16)
	7. E. II	ff. 311^{B}–313^{D} (16)
	7. F. II	ff. 63^{D}–65^{D} (23)
York Cath.	XVI. A. 6	ff. 74^{a}–77^{a} (16)

24. Prelati et doctores ecclesie et apostoli oculi sunt... × ...dans cuncta moveri *or* ...axis processionem.

See *Dictum* 41.

Oxford		
Exeter	21	pp. 135^{b}–136^{b} (10)
Lincoln	56	ff. 171^{b}–172^{a} (15)

London, B.M.		
Lans.	458	f. 176^{A-C} (27)
Royal	6. E. v	ff. 105^{A-B} (23)
	7. E. II	ff. $332^{A}-333^{A}$ (23)
	7. F. II	ff. $65^{D}-66^{B}$ (24)
York Cath.	XVI. A. 6	ff. $100^{b}-102^{a}$ (23)

25. Christus in scriptura frequenter sol... × ...sed ego elegi vos.

Oxford, Exeter	21	pp. $136^{b}-137^{b}$ (11)
London, B.M.		
Lans.	458	ff. $175^{D}-176^{A}$ (26)
Royal	6. E. v	f. 105^{B-C} (24)
	7. E. II	f. 333^{A-C} (24)
	7. F. II	f. 66^{B-D} (25)
London, Lambeth	523	f. 121^{a-b} (2)
York Cath.	XVI. A. 6	f. 102^{a-b} (24)

26. Jeronimus in libro de membris domini... × ...exclamabant dicentes hec dicit dominus deus.

Oxford, Exeter	21	p. 137^{b} (12)
London, B.M.		
Lans.	458	ff. $178^{D}-179^{A}$ (32)
Royal	6. E. v	f. 105^{C} (25)
	7. E. I	f. 333^{C} (25)
	7. F. II	f. 66^{D} (26)
York Cath.	XVI. A. 6	f. 102^{b} (25)

27. Ad verificacionem sequencium proprietatum dei... × ...proficere et perfectus esse.

Oxford, Exeter	21	pp. $139^{b}-141^{a}$ (14)
London, B.M.		
Lans.	458	ff. $177^{C}-178^{B}$ (30)
Royal	6. E. v	ff. $105^{C}-106^{A}$ (26)
	7. E. II	ff. $333^{D}-334^{D}$ (26)
	7. F. II	ff. $66^{D}-67^{D}$ (27)
York Cath.	XVI. A. 6	ff. $103^{a}-104^{a}$ (26)

28. Tribulatur homo cum amittit... × ...salvacio et tandem beatitudo.

Oxford, Exeter	21	pp. $141^{a}-142^{b}$ (15)
London, B.M.		
Lans.	458	f. 177^{A-C} (29)
Royal	6. E. v	f. 106^{A-C} (27)
	7. E. II	ff. $334^{D}-335^{D}$ (27)
	7. F. II	ff. $67^{D}-68^{C}$ (28)
York Cath.	XVI. A. 6	ff. $104^{b}-105^{b}$ (27)

29. Absintheum calidum est et siccum... × ...penam diluas et culpam.

Oxford, Exeter	21	pp. $142^{b}-144^{a}$ (16)
London, B.M.		
Lans.	458	ff. $176^{C}-177^{A}$ (28)
Royal	6. E. v	ff. $106^{C}-107^{A}$ (28)
	7. E. II	ff. $335^{D}-336^{C}$ (28)
	7. F. II	ff. $68^{C}-69^{B}$ (29)
York Cath.	XVI. A. 6	ff. $105^{b}-107^{a}$ (28)

30. Ecclesia sancta celebrat hodie solempnitatem... × ...pro nobis resurrexit gloriosus.

Oxford, Exeter	21	pp. 147^{a}–153^{a} (17)
London, B.M.		
Lans.	458	ff. 172^{D}–175^{A} (23)
Royal	6. E. V	ff. 107^{A}–109^{A} (29)
	7. E. II	ff. 336^{C}–341^{A} (29)
	7. F. II	ff. 69^{B}–72^{D} (30)
York Cath.	XVI. A. 6	ff. 107^{a}–112^{b} (29)
Prague, Nat. Mus.	XII. E. 5	ff. 74^{B}–75^{A} (2)

31. Scriptum est de levitis scilicet de ministris tabernaculi... × ... miserabilimi erimus.

In some later MSS this sermon has an appendage, appearing without break or separate rubric. This appendage is indicated below with an *.

Oxford		
Bodl.	36	ff. 46^{A}–50^{D}, separate
	801	ff. 193^{a}–203^{b}, with Sermon 32
Digby	191	ff. 168^{A}–172^{B}, separate, *mut. in fine*
London, B.M.		
Lans.	458	ff. 169^{A}–172^{D} (22)*
Royal	6. E. V	ff. 109^{A}–112^{C} (30)*
	7. A. IX	ff. 66^{a}–68^{a} (1)
	7. E. II	ff. 341^{B}–348^{D} (30)*
	7. F. II★	ff. 78^{A}–83^{C} (32)*
London, Lambeth	523	ff. 131^{b}–138^{a} (4)
Cambridge, St John's	15	ff. v^{a}–xi^{b}, separate*
York Cath.	XVI. A. 6	ff. 113^{a}–123^{a} (30)*
Paris, B.N.	lat. 1727	ff. 134^{D}–138^{C} (2)*

32. Deus est quo nichil melius excogitari potest... × ...quo nichil melius cogitari potest.

See above, p. 125, *De Confessione II*.

Oxford, Bodl.	801	ff. 173^{a}–193^{a}, with Sermon 31
London, B.M.		
Lans.	458	ff. 161^{B}–169^{A} (21)
Royal	6. E. V	ff. 112^{C}–119^{C} (31)
	7. E. II	ff. 348^{D}–364^{D} (31)
	7. F. II	ff. 83^{C}–96^{B} (33)
York Cath.	XVI. A. 6	ff. 123^{a}–144^{a} (31)
Paris, B.N.	lat. 1727	ff. 125^{B}–134^{D} (1)

33. Ex rerum iniciatarum et mutabilium et... × ...et glorie inmensitas in sec. sec.

London, B.M.		
Lans.	458	ff. 139^{B}–143^{B} (11)
Royal	6. E. V	ff. 119^{C}–122^{D} (32)
	7. E. II	ff. 364^{D}–372^{B} (32)
	7. F. II	ff. 96^{B}–102^{C} (34)
York Cath.	XVI. A. 6	ff. 144^{a}–154^{a} (32)
Prague, Nat. Mus.	XII. E. 5	ff. 73^{A}–74^{B} (1)

★ Sermon 31 in this codex is Sermon 7, *Exiit edictum*, repeated. See above, p. 168.

34. Natis et educatis et assuefactis que... × ...scrutatorem et testem absolutus et iustificatus.

Bale (*Index*, p. 374), followed by Pits, calls this *De Cura Pastorali*.

Oxford, Merton	47	ff. 209^{b}–212^{b} (1)
London, B.M.		
Lans.	458	ff. 143^{B}–145^{A} (12)
Royal	6. E. v	ff. 122^{D}–124^{A} (33)
	7. E. II	ff. 372^{B}–375^{D} (33)
	7. F. II	ff. 102^{C}–105^{B} (35)
York Cath.	XVI. A. 6	ff. 154^{a}–158^{a} (33)
Münster i. W.	165 (346)	ff. 68^{a}–75^{a}, separate
Prague, Nat. Mus.	XII. E. 5	f. 75^{A-C}, as *Cur Deus Homo* (3)

35. Egrede de terra tua et de cognacione tua... × ...ubi Christus manet cum patre sine tempore...qui vivit...per omnia sec. sec.

London, B.M.		
Lans.	458	f. 178^{B-D} (31)
Royal	6. E. v	f. 124^{A-C} (34)
	7. E. II	ff. 375^{D}–376^{D} (34)
	7. F. II	ff. 105^{B}–106^{A} (36)
London, Lambeth	523	ff. 124^{b}–126^{a} (3)
York Cath.	XVI. A. 6	ff. 158^{a}–160^{a} (34)

36. Adulari est libidine placendi alii... × ...ex necessitate adulari voluerit.

London, B.M., Royal	6. E. v	f. 124^{C-D} (35)
	7. E. II	ff. 376^{D}–377^{B} (35)
	7. F. II	f. 106^{A-C} (37)
London, Lambeth	523	ff. 120^{a}–121^{a} (1)
York Cath.	XVI. A. 6	ff. 160^{a}–161^{a} (35)

37. Contemplativorum oculi aquilinos... × ...contrectavit sicut dominus noster Jesus Christus.

See below, p. 250 f., *Spurium* 24, *De Septem Gradibus Contemplativorum*. The work appears among the sermons in the following MSS:

London, B.M.	
Lans.	458 (33)
Royal	6. E. v (36)
	7. E. II (36)
	7. F. II (38)
York Cath.	XVI. A. 6 (36)

It also appears in Royal 11. B. III, f. 277^{a-b} (*ca.* 1300, a MS which contains Sermon 8, the *De Doctrina Cordis* (see *Spurium* 18, p. 248 f.) and the genuine *De X Mandatis*. All these works in this codex are unascribed.

38. Post Moysen et eius successorem... × ...replasmacionem similiter et octavum psalmum in Christum dixit.

London, B.M., Royal	6. E. v	f. 125^{C-D} (37)
	7. E. II	ff. 378^{D}–379^{C} (37)
	7. F. II	ff. 107^{D}–108^{B} (39)
York Cath.	XVI. A. 6	ff. 163^{a}–164^{a} (37)

39. Ut iumentum factus sum aput te.... Iumenta nomen... × ...et gracia et neutrum sum altero.

London, B.M.		
Lans.	458	f. 180^{A-B} (35)
Royal	7. E. II	f. 379^{D} (38)
	7. F. II	f. 108^{B-C} (40)
York Cath.	XVI. A. 6	f. 164^{a} (38)

40. Tenuisti manum dexteram meam.... Manus dextera hominis... × ...deberet turbinem metere.

According to a colophon in Royal 7. F. II, this sermon was preached before the pope and cardinals *in curia romana*, but I am sure this is a copyist's error.

London, B.M.		
Lans.	458	f. 180^{B-C} (36)
Royal	6. E. V	f. 125^{D}, variant beginning *Iocunditas mentis* (38)
	7. E. II	ff. 379^{D}–380^{B} (39)
	7. F. II	ff. 108^{C}–109^{A} (41)
York Cath.	XVI. A. 6	ff. 164^{a}–165^{a} (39)

41. Expoliantes veterem hominem induite.... Vetus homo peccatum, novus... × ...peccata in vera contricione.

London, B.M., Royal	7. D. XV	ff. 5^{b}–8^{a} (3)
Cambridge, Trinity	B. 15. 20*	ff. 765^{A}–766^{A} (11)

42. Elevatus est sol et luna stetit. Ubi habemus "sol et luna stetit" ... × ...fontibus acquam vivam emanantibus humectat.

London, B.M., Royal	7. D. XV	ff. 42^{b}–44^{a}, entitled *Sermo de Ascensione* (20)
Cambridge, Trinity	B. 15. 20*	f. 766^{A-D} (12)

43. Non est veritas, non est misericordia.... Hec terra quam... × ... operabimur in patria.

London, B.M., Royal	7. D. XV	ff. 2^{b}–5^{b} (2)

44. Emptor est qui rem in hunc usum secundum causam... × ...et ad quid restituit.

London, B.M., Royal	7. D. XV	f. 8^{a-b} (4)

In this MS there follow as separate sermons *Dicta* 11 and 43 (Sermons 45 and 46). See under *Dicta*.

47. Vidimus stellam eius in oriente.... Karissimi facimus hodie festum ... × ...in illo celesti gaudio ad quod etc.

London, B.M., Royal	7. D. XV	ff. 11^{b}–13^{b} (7)

In this MS Sermons 6, 7, 1, 8 and 14 follow directly, then *Dictum* 131 (q.v.), i.e. Sermon 48.

49. Quemadmodum luna a sole lucem receptam... × ...ecclesia per predicatores eundem rorem largitur.

London, B.M., Royal	7. D. XV	ff. 34^{b}–35^{b} (14)

50. Omne capud languidum et omne cor... × ...negacionisque motibus admolitos consuetudinis sue.

London, B.M., Royal 7. D. xv ff. 35^b–36^b (15)

51. Quasi cedens exaltata sum in.... Accedet homo ad cor... × ...sic exaltata et quare tantum.

London, B.M., Royal 7. D. xv ff. 37^a–38^b (16)

In this MS there follow, as the next three sermons, *Dicta* 87, 72, and 50, i.e. Sermons 52, 53, 54; then Sermon 42, and four more *Dicta*, 2, 119, 4, 6, i.e. Sermons 55, 56, 57, 58.

59. Visitans visitavi vos et vidi omnia.... Vos audite parabolam... × ... nec in cor hominis ascendit quam preparavit...ad quam nos perducat etc.

London, B.M., Royal 7. D. xv ff. 51^a–54^b (25)

This sermon appears only in this MS, written in a different hand, though similar to and contemporary with the hand of the preceding authentic sermons. It is not specifically ascribed, but the spirit and technique are clearly Grossetestian, and considerable weight may be attached to the quotation, f. 54^a, from Aristotle's *Ethics*: *quia non ramunculus viriditatem boni operis habet, nisi manserit in radice dileccionis. Ethicorum* 8: *Amicicia est virtus maxime necessaria ad vitam*, and to another from Bk. II of the *Physics*. The sermon must be dated *post* 1243.

60. Obtulerunt.... Hodie celebrat ecclesia purificacionem... × ...qui pro nichilo ducunt in minimis transgredi.

London, B.M., Royal 7. D. xv ff. 55^a–57^a (26)

61. Elevata est nubes de tabernaculo.... In quinta visione apocalypsis legitur... × ...in eternum tecum est mihi negare; non poteris quod potuero.

London, B.M., Royal 7. D. xv ff. 57^a–60^b (27)

62. Despondi vos uni viro virginem.... Virgo hec casta sancta est... × ...in vinculo pacis permaneamus per infinita secula.

Oxford, Laud Misc. 402 ff. 171^a–174^a (6)

Dictum 135, q.v.

63. Posuit stellas in firmamento celi. Vos minores... × ...curiam regis celorum cui est honor et gloria.
Dictum 137. *Sermo ad sacerdotes in Synodo de hoc verbo....* Listed by Wharton.

64. Rex sapiens stabilimentum.... Verba... × ...firmam petram domini nostri Jesu Christi.
Dictum 51. *Sermo synodalis.*

65. Sint lumbi vestri precincti.... Officium nostrum qui... × ...operum execucione ad laudem et gloriam...in sec. sec.
Dictum 138. *Sermo in celebracione ordinum de hoc verbo....* Listed by Wharton.

66. Sacerdotes tui induantur.... Versus iste generaliter... × ...epulemur et conregnemus cum eo per infinita sec. sec.
Dictum 3, not to be confused with Sermon 19. Wharton calls *Sermo ad clerum in Ps. cxxxii.* 9.

67. Fugit Matathias et filii.... Mons frequenter in scriptura... × ...appropinquacionem non considerare.
Dictum 14.

68. Osee ait.... Non est veritas... × ...intuentes pretendens.
Dictum 21. Appears in Cambridge, Trin. Coll. B. 15. 38, ff. 38^{a}–39^{a} (XIII^{m}) as *Sermo ad religiosos.*

69. Exemplum esto fidelium... × ...et fide et castitate.
Dictum 35, q.v. In Cambridge, Trin. Coll. B. 15. 38, ff. 41^{a}–42^{a}, as *Sermo ad Prelatos.*

70. Ieiunium a cibis corporalibus... × ...ieiuno bis in sabbato.
Dictum 36, q.v.

71. Comedite amici et bibite... × ...de laude caritatis.
Dictum 37, q.v. In Cambridge, Trin. Coll. B. 15. 38, f. 39^{a-b}.

72. Pax vobis.... Luc. 24. Consuetudo... × ...exultabunt in deum vivum.
Dictum 38. In Cambridge, Trin. Coll. B. 15. 38, ff. 39^{b}–40^{a}, as *Sermo de multiplici pace.*

73. Prelati et doctores ecclesie... × ...tanto apparet minus.
Dictum 41. In Cambridge, Trin. Coll. B. 15. 38, ff. 40^{a}–41^{a}, as *Sermo ad Prelatos.* In Durham Cath. A. III. 12, ff. 12^{A}–13^{B}, and Eton MS 8, ff. 19^{B}–20^{C}.

74. De hostio tabernaculi non exibitis... × ...sine fine ferventes.
Dictum 52, q.v.

75. Apparuerunt apostolis dispartite... × ...sine fine nostra conversacio.
Dictum 89, q.v.

76. Ezechielis xxxiv: Ve pastoribus... × ...querunt plus hiis.
Dictum 90, q.v.

77. Simon, diligis me... × ...et vita dominus noster.
Dictum 91, q.v.

78. Preibis enim ante faciem domini... × ...de exilio reduccio.
Dictum 108, q.v.

79. Filius dei volens ostendere... × ...minimum mutatum aureum.
Dictum 101, q.v.

80. Recte iudicate filii... × ...cum interfectis cadatis.
Dictum 103, q.v.

81. Restat agere de luxuria ordine precassato. Luxuria est incontinencia corporis... × ...censentur ut ex supradictis diligens lector colligere poterit manifeste.

Pavia, Univ.	69	ff. 85ª–88ᵇ, separate, XIIIᵐ, Asc. Engl.

Bale lists as from Gascoigne (*Index*, p. 376) a title *Contra luxuriam* li. i. Gascoigne's reference to it is explicit: *Illud scriptum ex manu sua propria ego T. Gascoigne vidi Oxonie anno Cristi* 1455 *et est inter minores in libro registratum episcopus lincolniensis*, Oxford, Lincoln Coll. 117, f. 138ª.

82. Beati pauperes spiritu. Matt. v. Videndum quot modis sit paupertas ... × ...suam reservant. Exemplum de divite et Lazaro Luc. 16.

London, B.M., Royal	11. B. III	ff. 316ᵇ–319ᵇ, separate, *ca.* 1300, Unasc. with Grosseteste's *De X Mandatis*, also Unasc.

83. Decalogus est sermo brevis decem dei mandata continens... × ... assumpta comprehendunt.

London, B.M., Harley	979	ff. 37ᶜ–39ᴮ, separate, XIIIᵐ, Asc.

For the *Versus de X Mandatis*, appended to this sermon, see above, p. 141.

84. Maria optimam partem elegit.... Bene novit caritas... × ...servus vero peccati minus quam nichil.

Oxford, Bodl.	57	ff. 180ᵇ–182ᵇ, separate, XIII², Asc. Noticed by Paul Meyer in *Romania*, XXXV (1906), 581

85. Nostra conversacio est in celis.... Verba sunt Apostoli... × ...est in celis quod ipse prestare dignetur.

Oxford, Rawl.	C. 531	ff. 213ᶜ–216ᴰ, separate, XIIIᵐ, Asc. as *Sermo ad religiosos*

86. Primum quidem omnium mandatorum est: non habes deos alienos coram... × ... *There may be two endings:* (*a*) ...nec sic actuosus ut contemplacionem non requirat dei, *or, after a diagrammatical* scala humilitatis et scala superbie, (*b*) ...in duobus restant contemptus dei.

Paris, B.N.	lat. 1727	ff. 138ᶜ–139ᴮ or 140ᴬ, Asc. Engl.

87. Cum in *Ierarchia Celesti* IX distinguantur ordines scilicet 3... × ... vehemens ad suplicium peccatorum.

Oxford, Bodl.	867	ff. 104ª–110ª, XIV², Asc., rubricked *Sermo Roberti lincolniensis de triplici ierarchia humana*

This is the *Sermo in Hierarchiam Triplicem* listed by Tanner as found in Bodley MS Sup. M. 4 art. 4. Pegge suggested that there was some confusion with Grosseteste's commentaries on the Pseudo-Dionysian works, but he was in error and Tanner's data are correct. The MS bears still the earlier press-mark Sup. M. 4.

88. Erat Ihesus eiciens demonium.... Legitur in fine ewangelii quod ... × ... deo coniungamur per graciam et in futuro per gloriam.

Durham Cath. A. III. 12 ff. 15^D^–16^B^, Imbedded in earliest (*ca.* 1230) collection of *Dicta*. See Introd. p. 16, and pp. 76 and 214 f.

89. Venite cogitemus contra Jeremiam cogitaciones.... Et est vox iudeorum... × ... ut sic simus socii passionum Ihesu Christi per quod et erimus participes eius resurreccionis et consolacionis.

Durham Cath. A. III. 12 f. 16^B–D^

90. Orietur vobis timentibus nomen meum [Mal. iv. 2].... Excecatis non est sol... × ... ipse deus veniet et salvabit nos.

Durham Cath. A. III. 12 ff. 16^D^–17^B^

91. Accepit Simeon puerum.... Sciendum est quod sicut ille accepit ... × ... timor domini expellat peccatum. Beatus igitur vir qui semper est pavidus.

Durham Cath. A. III. 12 f. 17^B^

92. Erat exspectans consolacionem.... Ita et nos. Delicata enim est ... × ... propositum ad effectum perducere propter artam dietam.

Durham Cath. A. III. 12 f. 17^B–C^

This sermon is followed by the *De Cane Ethimologia* (see above, p. 148) and that in turn by the *Convertimini ad me in toto corde*, here incomplete, but complete on f. 78^A–B^ in another, contemporary, hand (see below, p. 183).

II

The following sermons and *dicciones* exist, unless otherwise specified, at least so far as is known at the present time, in a single MS, Durham Cath. A. III. 12. The MS is rich in Grosseteste material (see Introd. p. 13 ff.), but contains no ascription of any of the works to him. The section ff. 78^A^–87^D^ contains many sermons that appear among the *Dicta* or in the definitive *Comm. in Psalmos* (see above, p. 75 f.). The remaining sermons are unmistakably by the same person. As Grosseteste remarks in the *Recapitulacio* appended to the *Dicta* (see below, p. 214) that he had made a selection from his sermons for the purposes of the collection of 147 *Dicta*, we must assume that there were many of his minor writings which he thought unsuitable for the purposes for which the *Dicta* were chosen. The authenticity of these unascribed sermons seems to me beyond doubt: their presence among other authenticated works of his which are also unascribed, thus putting them all on the same level;

their tone; the fact that sermons by other writers are definitely ascribed to them so that the reader knows that he has another series of sermons, would all indicate the intent of the scribe.

1. Convertimini ad me in toto corde vestro.... Omne enim peccatum reducitur... × ...nobis ita geiunare ut possimus ad patriam pervenire, quod nobis etc.

f. 78^{A-B}. Two-thirds of this sermon appears on f. 17^{D}. A new gathering begins f. 18^{A}, in another hand in the middle of a running commentary on selected psalms. There is no indication of authorship. The bibliographers have mentioned a series of sermons beginning *Convertimini*. The better-known collection with this incipit is by Robert Holcot. This present series may be the one intended by the early tradition.

2. Milicia est vita hominis super terram. Miles dura sustinet et tamen de... × ...lacrimantes. Unde dominus per Ysaiam...et vos esurietis. Donet igitur dominus.

f. 78^{B-D}.

3. Exemplum esto fidelium.... Apostolus doctor sollicitudinem omnium pastorum... × ...ut predictum est ut nomen eternum habeatis, quod nobis....

ff. 78^{D}–79^{A}. Dictum 35 treats the same subject, but is considerably reworked and expanded.

4. Nolite fieri sicut equus.... Equus superbus et cervicosus est et mulus et... × ...precipitatur in ruinam et cum impetu cadit in infernum.

ff. 79^{A-B}. See below, p. 190, ff. 124^{C}–125^{C} of this MS.

5. Quoniam tanquam fenum velociter arescet. Fenum significat hominem ... × ...quem feci tecum fenum quasi bos comedet.

f. 79^{B-C}. In *Comm. in Psal.*, Eton MS 8, ff. 21^{C}–22^{B}. *Dictum* 53. The section in the *Comm.* is twenty lines longer than in the Durham MS.

6. Qui manet in caritate in deo manet et deus in eo. Verbum domini in sacra... × ...ego in vobis et in epistola. Qui manet in deo manet etc.

ff. 79^{C}–80^{A}.

7. Conceperunt laborem et peperunt. Verbum est enim non solum quod sonat... × ...ad decipiendas animas. Ps. v. Sepulchrum patens est guttur.

ff. 80^{A}. In *Comm. in Psal.*, Eton MS 8, ff. 5^{D}–6^{A}, ending ...*et ego suscipiam te*, i.e. ten lines less than in the Durham MS, where the preceding paragraph ends as in the *Comm.*

8. Lavabo per singulas noctes lectum meum...et hoc merito quod defeci sensu....

f. 80^{A-B}. This is the first of eight short paragraphs, from two to nine lines in length, which are either short quotations from Augustine, Cassiodorus, *et al.*, or definitions or similitudes such as are found in the shorter *Dicta*.

9. Quinque sensus porte sunt per quas intrat mors... × ...canticum laudis et exultacionis.

f. 80^B^. In *Comm. in Psal.*, Eton MS 8, ff. 6^D^–7^A^. *Dictum* 7. Followed by a column of glossed quotations, then

10. Celum significat summa invisibilia... × ...ibat per loca arida non inveniens requiem.

f. 80^C–D^.

11. Pisces significant malos homines qui in loco... × ...ut sic intremus in gaudium.

f. 80^D^.

12. Paradisus voluptatis significat ecclesiam... × ...penitencie et desiderium celestis patrie.

ff. 80^D^–81^A^. Includes paragraph: *Adam significat*....

13. Hoc viso igitur considerandum qualiter hec upradicta virtutis descripcio... × ... in anima que non informatur a deo vera virtus non sit?

f. 81^A–B^. Part of *Dictum* 56; also in this MS, ff. 13^D^–14^B^.

14. Quoniam non in finem.... Paupertas generaliter dicta est defectio vel carencia... × ...populum suum et pauperum suorum miserebitur.

f. 81^B–C^. *Dictum* 94. In *Comm. in Psal.*, Eton MS 8, f. 6^B–D^.

15. Ecclus. x. Timor domini non despicere hominem iustum pauperem ... *nine lines of scriptural quotations.*

f. 81^C^.

16. Hec sunt que paupertatem secuntur et animum inflammare debent ... × ...prodest ei inopia sua, excercet corpus, non opprimit.

f. 81^C–D^.

17. Divites qui congregant superflua unde pauperes sustineri deberent ... × ...tales precidit bonis loco eorum plantatis.

f. 81^D^. *Dictum* 46 complete, nine lines.

18. Ysidorus quod homines habeto ad misericordiam. Nullus a te tristis habeat... × ...fructum remuneracionis amittit.

f. 81^D^. Seven lines.

19. De tuis iustis laboribus ministra pauperibus. Non auferas uni... × ... et reddit audacis in rebus ignaris.

f. 81^D^.

20. Serve nequam omne dimisi tibi quoniam rogasti me. Due sunt regule... × ...per artam viam ad gaudia eterna pertingamus.

ff. 81^D^–82^A^.

21. Serve nequam etc. Rex iste qui posuit racionem servis suis... × ...ut ad vitam et requiem perveniamus ad quam nos perducat.

f. 82^{A-B}. There follow three paragraphs of quotation and paraphrase from Bernard, Gregory and Isidore, then

22. Ecce nunc dies salutis ad literam iam instant dies in quibus... × ... igitur dicitur penitencia dies salutis quia ad veram salutem perducit ad quam nos....

ff. 82^{C}–83^{C}.

23. Cum appropinquasset Ihesus Iherico etc. Si linguis hominum loquar. ...Notandum quod sicut es... × ...et alibi regni eius non erit finis. Explicit ars predicandi.

ff. 83^{C}–84^{D}. See above, p. 121.

24. Clama ne cesses quasi tuba ex alta vocem tuam... × ...includitur. Clamare habet optimum.

ff. 84^{D}–85^{A}.

25. Ecclesiasticus. Humilia valde caput tuum quoniam vindicta carnis ... × ...quia hic agitur de humilitate unde vide humilitatem etc.

f. 85^{A-B}. There follows a combined quotation of three lines: *Ecce odor filii mei... × ...abundanciam aggratulatur.*

26. Ego flos campi.... Verba sunt Salomonis sub persona Christi loquentis... × ...precibus beate virginis cuius festa celebramus, ut ipsa pro nobis intercedat apud dominum.

f. 85^{B-C}.

27. Pulcra ut luna. Luna gerit typum causa cuiuslibet ecclesie quam ... × ...prelati quos premunt diviciarum honera.

ff. 85^{D}–86^{B}. In *Comm. in Psal.*, Eton MS 8, f. 8^{A}. *Dictum* 71.

28. De superbia que est amor proprie excellencie nascitur invidia ... × ...a vicio detraccionis non sunt immunes.

f. 86^{B-D}. In *Comm. in Psal.*, Eton MS 8, ff. 9^{D}–10^{C}; again in Durham MS, f. 6^{A-B}, but five lines shorter than here. *Dictum* 128.

29. Yas grece venenum dicunt et inde iaspis quod morsu venenato ... × ...erga homines deus exercuit imitari neglexit.

ff. 86^{D}–87^{B}. Also in Durham MS, f. 6^{B-D}. *Dictum* 88.

30. Pupilla est pura cordis intencio in deum sine illa intelligencia... × ... delectat frigus quod est privacio ardoris concupiscencie.

f. 87^{B}. In *Comm. in Psal.*, Eton MS 8, f. 10^{C-D}; also Durham MS, f. 6^{D}. *Dictum* 77.

31. Cupiditas est amor immoderatus adipiscende et retinende pecunie ... × ...Refugit enim avaricie plurimorum consorcia.

f. 87^{B-C}. In *Comm. in Psal.*, Eton MS 8, f. 9^{B-D}; also Durham MS, ff. 6^{D}–7^{A}. *Dictum* 140, though here four lines longer than *Dictum*.

32. Tenebrosa aqua in nubibus haeris. Calore solis elevatur vapor ... × ... potestatem claudendi celum nubibus ne pluat. Apostolus v [*sic*].

f. 87^{C-D}. In *Comm. in Psal.*, Eton MS 8, ff. 10^{D}–11^{A}. Also in this MS, f. 7^{A}. *Dictum* 78.

33. Ignis aliquando zelum dei exprimit, aliquando spiritum sanctum ... × ... et ibi consumpti sunt.

f. 87^{D}. Incomplete in nineteen lines. In *Comm. in Psal.*, Eton MS 8, f. 11^{A-D}; also in this MS, f. 7^{B-C}. *Dictum* 79.

This is the end of this gathering of ten folia. As none of the other gatherings in this hand appears to fit after this one, nor indeed to be out of place, we are compelled to assume that a gathering—of what size we cannot say—has disappeared. The next two gatherings, ff. 88–103, contain several sermons ascribed to *Frater Jordanus Ord. Pred.* and one, f. 89^{D}, ascribed to *Magister Rogerus Sarisberiensis.* From the fact that the sermons proceed according to the calendar of saints' days, we may infer that the whole—twenty-three sermons—of this group comes from a collection quite different from that containing the work of Grosseteste.* The following gathering, ff. 104–111, is, excepting only the last leaf, f. 111, the work of the scribe who wrote the *Dicta* and sermons of Grosseteste on ff. 78 ff. Again we have a number of Grosseteste's *Dicta* to authenticate the rest of the gathering.

34. Plorabitis et flebitis vos. Mundus autem exaudebit. Mundus autem sedet... × ... seipsum querit et respondet: durus quid amas caro.

ff. 104^{A}–105^{A}. On f. 104^{B} we read ...*nisi forte obiciatis michi quod clerici habent eas cum requie et sine labore quia in labore hominum non sunt clerici quia oxonie* [*parisius* is written above *oxon̄*] *defertur eis habundanter argentum.* Grosseteste often speaks with feeling about the clergy's cynical greed for money.

35. Ite in castellum quod circa vos est.... Tollens Iacob virgas populeas et... × ... audivit nec in cor hominis ascendit.

ff. 105^{A}–106^{A}. The following *Dictum* may have been suggested by the last quotation of this exposition.

36. Qui finxit sigillatim corda etc. Cor hominis est quod primum in eo... × ... in execucionibus negociorum sunt animosi.

f. 106^{A-B}. In *Comm. in Psal.*, Eton MS 8, f. 21^{A-C}; also in this Durham MS, f. 13^{B}–, broken up in several parts. *Dictum* 42.

37. Et lingua vera meditabitur iusticiam etc. Lingue sunt predicatores quod... × ... tota vita prelati que volvitur per septem dies.

f. 106^{B}. The next column is blank.

* See A. G. Little and Miss D. Douie, "Three Sermons of Friar Jordan of Saxony, the Successor of St Dominic in England, A.D. 1229" in *EHR*, LIV (1939), 1–19.

38. Ambrosius enim fuit opprobrio Petro crux domini que tantum ei gloriam dedit... × ... presumere debes quod ei bonum consulat.

ff. 106^{D}–107^{B}. Made up mostly of quotations from Anselm, Gregory and Isidore.

39. Dixi custodiam vias meas etc. Est verbum mentis unde dicit: dixi... × ... os tuum loquebatur sed mens tua usuras cogitabat.

f. 107^{B-C}.

40. Benedictum lignum per quod fit iusticia. Salomon dicit quod verbum dei... × ... Istud lignum benedictum est a deo in effectu et opere.

ff. 107^{C}–108^{A}.

41. Qui vicerit non ledetur a morte secunda. Verba sunt spiritus sancti loquentis... × ... in eternam gloriam de qua omnes dicunt: Quid est hoc quod nec oculus vidit nec aures audiunt?

f. 108^{A-D}.

42. Ascendam in palmam et apprehendam fructus eius. Christus caput ecclesie... × ... resurreccionis et ascensionis, que quidem gloria est vita eterna ad quam nos....

ff. 108^{D}–109^{C}.

43. Ascendit deus in iubilacione. Dominus noster Jesus Christus... de sinu patris descendit... × ... ut egipticis fuit qui advolavit nebulo.

ff. 109^{C}–110^{C}. All eight steps of the ascent are described. This seems to be the first draft of *Dictum* 50. It appears also in the longer form in the *Comm. in Psal.*, Eton MS 8, ff. 23^{D}–26^{B}. There is an intermediate form in the Durham MS in this same hand, f. 118^{A-C}, covering only four of the eight steps of ascent, but in a form nearer that of the *Dictum* and the *Comm. in Psal.* Much of the verso of f. 110 and f. 111 is covered with the fine writing we have supposed to be that of Bertram of Middleton (see Introd. p. 16). On f. 112^{A} our neat calligraphic hand begins again.

44. Judith una mulier hebrea fecit confusionem magnam. Judith interpretatur... × ... Ecce quod fatuus est malos exaltando eciam ecclesiastice.

f. 112^{A-C}.

45. Vidi cervos [*sic*] in equis et principes quasi ambulantes super terram ... × ... in terris quid facturi sumus in celis.

f. 112^{C}.

46. Erubescant et conturbentur etc. Si enim penitet aliquod peccati ... × ... sacrificio dei glorificacio ad penitenciam de exilio reduccio.

ff. 112^{C}–113^{A}.

47. Ne quando rapiat ut leo animam meam. Leo a leon grece quod est rex... × ... album predicatorem scilicet castum maxime veretur.

f. 113^{A-B}. In *Comm. in Psal.*, Eton MS 8, f. 5^{C-D}; also Durham MS, ff. 5^{A-B} and 113^{A-B}. *Dictum* 122. There follow sixteen lines of quotations from scripture on returning good for evil.

48. Posui tibi aquam et ignem ad quod volueris porrige... × ...est qui iactat a se scutum sapiencie eodem modo.

ff. 113^{B}–114^{D}.

49. Dixi custodiam vias meas etc. Lingua hominis sapientis est calamus ... × ...quo ad facilitatem et sensum recepcionis.

f. 115^{A-B}. In *Comm. in Psal.*, Eton MS 8, f. 26^{B-D}. About one-third of *Dictum* 54.

50. Idem est lapis in terra quod os in carne, stabilitas scilicet et firmitas ... × ...inventa dat omnia sua et operat eam.

f. 115^{B-C}. In *Comm. in Psal.*, Eton MS 8, f. 32^{B-D}. *Dictum* 117.

51. Apocalipsis xxiº. Fundamentum primum iaspis. Iaspidis multa sunt genera... × ...posita quasi castri anime propugnaculum est.

f. 115^{C-D}. This is the first of the twelve stones of the Apocalypse. In *Comm. in Psal.*, Eton MS 8, ff. 32^{D}–33^{A}. First part of *Dictum* 100, slightly abridged.

52. Deus est protector etc. Dans scutum paciencie quod scutum est impressum... × ...se senciunt frustratos conatu nocendi.

f. 115^{D}. About two-thirds of *Dictum* 112.

53. Lapis Christus ut in psalmo lapidem quem reprobaverunt etc.... × ... turbine umbraculum ab escu.

f. 116^{A}. Here in diagrammatical form. As prose in *Comm. in Psal.*, Eton MS 8, f. 32^{D}. May be a part of *Dictum* 100 or 112.

54. Saphirus lapis fulgens est simillimus celo purpureo... × ...vespas qui exterminabitur cananeum.

f. 116^{A-B}. In *Comm. in Psal.*, Eton MS 8, f. 33^{A-D}. The second stone of the Apocalypse. Part of *Dictum* 100.

55. Diligam te domine virtus mea. Diligendus est deus ab omnibus. Si enim... × ...in claustro moriantur ut eternaliter vivant qui sic deum diligant.

f. 116^{B-D}.

56. Calcedonus quasi ignis luberne pollentis speciem retinet et habet ... × ...luce veritatis fulgida summe pulcritudini configurata.

ff. 116^{D}–117^{A}. In *Comm. in Psal.*, Eton MS 8, ff. 33^{D}–34^{A}. Part of *Dictum* 100. The third stone of the Apocalypse.

57. Hodie cum omni devocione ad memoriam redemptoris nostri revocamus... × ...salutis nostre precium quod tam copiose effundisti.

f. 117^{A-B}.

58. Smaragdus nimie viriditatis est a deo ut herbas virentes frondes...
Sardonicem faciunt duo nomina sardus et onix...
Sardus sed sardius dicta eo quod reperta sit... × ...sine contencione aliqua videbantur occidi.

ff. 117^{B}–118^{A}. In *Comm. in Psal.*, Eton MS 8, ff. 34^{A}–35^{A}. Parts 4 and 5 of the stones of the Apocalypse. Part of *Dictum* 100.

59. In ascensu autem spirituali gradus ascensionis nobis sunt necessarii ... × ...precincta herenti et horrenti gressum quod retrahenti.

f. 118^{A-C}. In *Comm. in Psal.*, Eton MS 8, ff. 23^{D}–25^{A}. The first four steps of the ascent. See above, p. 187, Durham MS, f. 109^{C}. Part of *Dictum* 50.

60. Qui considerant in virtute sua et in multitudine diviciarum.... Quod sunt... × ...thesaurizatis nobis in novissimis diebus.

f. 118^{C}. On Psal. xlviii. 7.

61. Et precium redempcionis etc. Dant precium redempcionis qui dant elemosinam... × ...primus habere quod necesse est secundus quod satis est.

ff. 118^{C}–119^{B}. On Psal. xlviii. 9. In *Comm. in Psal.*, Eton MS 8, ff. 27^{A}–28^{A}. There follows a quotation of eight lines from Chrysostom.

62. Immola deo sacrificium laudis. Laudare aliquem est opera bone et recte... × ...sicut expresse docet Augustinus in libro de civitate dei.

f. 119^{B-D}. On Psal. xlix. 14. In *Comm. in Psal.*, Eton MS 8, ff. 31^{C}–32^{B}. *Dictum* 104.

63. Malum coram te feci. Boecius. Magna nobis indicta est necessitas ... × ...vereri potest; cito erit mundus.

f. 119^{D}. Quotations from Seneca and Boecius applied to Psal. l. 6.

64. Asperges me ysopo et mundabor.... Ysopus calidus est in tercio gradu... × ...gloriam que a solo deo est non vultis.

ff. 119^{D}–120^{A}. On Psal. l. 9. In *Comm. in Psal.*, Eton MS 8, f. 30^{B-D}. *Dictum* 105.

65. Cor contritum non conteritur nisi quod durum est et frangibile ... × ...durissimam et scio quoniam non confundar.

f. 120^{A-C}. On Psal. l. 19. In *Comm. in Psal.*, Eton MS 8, ff. 30^{D}–31^{C}. *Dictum* 106.

66. Quis dabit mihi pennas columbe? Rabanus. Columbe eo quod ad earum... × ...dyaboli astucias prevideat, agnoscat et declinet.

ff. 120^{C}–121^{A}. On Psal. liv. 7. In *Comm. in Psal.*, Eton MS 8, ff. 28^{A}–29^{A}. *Dictum* 107.

67. Ab altitudine diei. Dies est sol lucens super terram. Est autem sol alcior... × ...amoris posita quasi castri propugnaculum.

f. 121^{A-B}. The last twelve lines are identical with the ending of the section on f. 115^{D}, i.e. about half *Dictum* 112. In *Comm. in Psal.*, Eton MS 8, ff. 29^{A}–30^{B}, omitting last third of *Dictum*.

68. Sequitur in abstinencia autem pacienciam quia ut aid Beda abstinencia... × ...Quam gloriosa dicta sunt de te civitas dei.

ff. 121^{C}–122^{A}. The last four steps in the ascent. See above, f. 118^{A-C}. *Dictum* 50, last half.

On f. 122^{C} the script changes, assuming a chartish appearance. From occasional lapses, however, it seems to be the work of the same scribe. This section, continuing to f. 127^{D}, contains exclusively sermons. For their authenticity I have no better proof than their appearance in this place in this codex and their strongly Grossetestian tone and method.

69. Renovamini spiritu mentis vestre.... Virtutem verbi domini dei ostendit... × ...ad iuventutem glorie. Dominus igitur det nos renovari in iuventute gracie, ut tandem renovemur iuventute glorie.

ff. 122^{C}–123^{B}. On Ephes. iv. 23.

70. Non est nobis colluctacio adversus carnem.... Apostolus in hodierna epistola... × ...super rotam mutabilitatis constitutum recipiamus in premium quod nobis....

ff. 123^{B}–124^{C}. On Ephes. vi. 12.

71. Diliges dominum deum tuum.... Sapiens corde precepta suscipit, stultus... × ...hiis tribus de causis est diligendus. Rogate igitur deum etc.

ff. 124^{C}–125^{C}. On Matt. xxii. 37. The figure of the *equus superbus diaboli* appears. See f. 79^{A-B} of this MS: *Nolite fieri sicut equus*..., above, p. 183.

72. Ecce ego mittam in fundamentis Sion.... Dicit Salomon in Prov. ... × ...mel de petra oleumque de saxo durissimo.

ff. 125^{C}–126^{A}. On Is. xxviii. 16.

73. Tempus belli...qui lapidem preciosum invenit. Stultus est nisi bene ... × ...pertineant, nude huiusmodi idonei sunt ad bellum Christi.

f. 126^{A-D}. Entitled: *in prima dominica adventus*. The margins of ff. 126^{b} and 127^{b} have about a dozen Anglo-Norman prayers, written in plummet and now only partially legible, in the same hand that has made pencil notations throughout the codex. They seem to be prayers to St Joseph. I have not been able to identify them.

74. Sponsabo te in sempiternum. Sponsabo te in iusticia et in iudicio ... × ...precessit. Unde psalmista: potasti vos vino compunccionis.

ff. 126^{D}–127^{B}. On Hosea ii. 19.

75. Sancti per fidem vicerunt regna. Hoc nomen sancti sonat firmitatem ... × ...quod possumus venire ad gaudia eorum in celis quod nobis....

f. 127^{B-D}. Entitled: *Sermo de omnibus sanctis.*

There follows, in the same hand, ff. 128A–136C, in seventy-one *capitula*, the *Allegorie in Novum Testamentum*, beginning: *Primi parentes humani generis...*, usually ascribed to Hugo de Sancto Victore (ed. *Patr. Lat.* CLXXV, cols. 751 ff.), followed in turn, ff. 136C–138D, by an *Admonicio pia*, beginning: *Audi fili admonicionem patris tui; inclina aurem tuam...*, divided into twenty-one *capitula*. The last leaves, ff. 138D–144D, of this gathering contain miscellaneous sermons, in a different but contemporary hand, mostly on texts from the Pauline epistles. The next unit is of forty folia, ff. 145a–184b, slightly wider than the preceding, in two quite different hands. It is an exhaustive topical concordance of the Bible in five books. There are three columns to the page, the separate topics are written in red, and the book of the Bible, the chapter and the section, *a–e*, followed by a portion of the text, averaging about three words, complete the reference. The early date of this concordance is attested by the presence of several notes in plummet by the same hand that has dated the sum of his penances *iiii kal. marc. anno ab incarnacione domini* M° CC° XXXI on f. 130B. A paleographical judgment of the date of the two hands of this concordance would put them both *ca.* 1225, confirming 1231 as a *terminus ad quem*. It is certainly one of the earliest concordances to use the chapter-division of Stephen Langton.* This compilation would yield interesting data on the text of Langton's Bible. Its importance is not lessened by the fact that it is immediately followed by Langton's *Postilla* on Ecclesiastes, beginning *Hoc nomen Ecclesiastes interpretatur concionator et refertur...* (ff. 185A–189D),† and a fragment of his commentary on Exodus (ff. 190A–193C). Though these two commentaries may be by one of the hands that worked on the concordance, they are written on folia formerly two inches wider than the concordance, $9\frac{3}{4} \times 12\frac{5}{8}$ in., and now folded over at the edge. They must also be dated *ca.* 1225. There are more folia of this same material, ff. 220A–223A, in the same hand. From f. 194A to 219B is an early (*ca.* 1225) work on the sacraments of the Church which is *mutilus in initio*.

* See in general H. Denifle, "Die Handschriften der Bibel-Correctorien des 13. Jhdts." in *Archiv f. Litt.- und Kirchengeschichte d. Mittelalters*, IV (1888), 263 ff., 471 ff.

† Cf. G. Lacombe, "Studies on the Commentaries of Cardinal Stephen Langton" in *Archives d'Histoire doctrinale et littéraire du Moyen Âge*, V (1930), 145, where it is listed as beginning on f. 1 of this MS.

LETTERS

The collection of 128 letters* of Grosseteste has been recognized as a source of historical, religious, philosophical and political information since early in the fourteenth century. The letters were abundantly used by Burley, Wyclyf, Hus and Gascoigne. The authenticity of the collection as we have it has never seriously been questioned. But the actual time at which the letters were gathered into a canon or by whom has never been learned. We have no MS of the whole collection that we can date earlier than *ca.* 1400. Separate letters, for various reasons, have appeared as integral tractates or, again, may have survived apart from the collection as such. We do, however, have good evidence that the collection was made by *ca.* 1300, even if we are unable to say that Grosseteste himself was responsible for the selection of some and the rejection of other letters. MS 8336 of the Phillipps collection at Cheltenham is a miscellaneous codex of great value for early Franciscan history†, written by William Herbert not later than 1314. On f. 181[a] are short extracts from eight of Grosseteste's letters, numbered in the MS by the same numbers that appear in later collections: 33, 34, 75, 78, 79, 103, 104, 112. For several pages, to f. 183[b], short extracts from sermons are occasionally ascribed to Grosseteste. We can therefore place the establishment of the canon of his letters as completed at the very beginning of the fourteenth century, without being able to be more precise.

It is hardly possible that Grosseteste can have had any hand in the collection or arrangement of the letters, for, though a general chronological sequence is faintly discernible, it is too uncertain and unreliable to have come from anyone reliably conversant with the persons or events involved; there is no topical arrangement, nor any grouping by correspondents. The relatively small number of letters, in view of an obviously great correspondence, is astonishing. There are numerous references in extant letters to letters which appear now to be lost beyond hope of recovery,‡ though some as yet unsuspected treasure of manuscripts may fill in the gaps and disappoint our pessimism.

In the following list of the letters, a tentative effort has been made to revise the dates assigned to the letters by Luard. The results do not satisfy me, for I am quite sure, *a priori*, that some source of information which would have improved the conjecture has often been overlooked. Yet it seemed expedient to make the effort. Luard's dates are given in square brackets. If there has appeared to be no reason to revise his date, or if it has been impossible, for a variety of reasons, the date remains as his.

* So numbered usually. Two numbers, 52 and 72, serve for two letters each. We have, *in toto*, 134 letters.

† See A. G. Little in *EHR*. XLIX (1934), 302.

‡ Kington, in his *History of Frederick II*, I (London, 1862), 448, speaks of a correspondence between Grosseteste and the Emperor. He adduced no evidence, nor does any seem to have been discovered since he wrote.

Editions: E. Brown published, in the *Fasc. Rer. Expet.*, Letters 4, 8, 10–12, 17, 22–30, 32, 35–38, 40–52, 53–56, 61, 66, 68, 71, 72, 73–104, 106–126; H. R. Luard, in *Roberti Grosseteste Episcopi Quondam Lincolniensis Epistolae* (R.S.), London, 1861, published 133 Epistolae.

MSS (for MSS of Ep. 1 see above, p. 98 f.; of Ep. 52*, p. 126 f.; of Ep. 127, p. 129; of Ep. 128, p. 143):

Library	MS	Folios	Date	Contents
Oxford				
Bodl.	42	f. 283^{a-b}	XIII^{2}	Ep. 128
	52	ff. 136^{b}–137^{b}	XV^{1}	Ep. 128
	312	ff. 126^{A}–184^{D}	XIV^{2}	113 Epp.
	750	ff. 124^{b}–125^{b}	XIII^{m}	Ep. 130
	798	ff. 122^{C}–127^{D}	XIV^{2}	Excerpts, Epp. 2–89
Digby	218	ff. 92^{a}–94^{a}	XIV^{2}	Excerpts, Epp. 2–89
	220	ff. 81^{A}–83^{D}	XV^{1}	Epp. 1 & 5. See p. 98
Laud Misc.	439	f. 253^{A-B}	XIII^{m}	Ep. 130
C.C.C.	280	ff. 163^{a}–168^{b}	XVII	*Tabula epistularum* 128
Merton	47	f. 208^{a-b}	*ca.* 1400	Ep. 85
London, B.M.				
Cotton	Otho C. xiv	ff. 1^{a}–89^{b}	*ca.* 1400	Excerpts*
	Vesp. A. xviii	ff. 91^{a}–92^{a}	XIII^{2}	Ep. 128†
	Vesp. E. iii	ff. 41^{a}–42^{a}	XIII^{2}	Ep. 128 (*Burton Annals*)
	Vitell. C. xiv	ff. 3^{D}–6^{C}	XIV^{2}	Excerpts, Epp. 2–89†
Lans.	964	ff. 114^{b}–118^{b}	XVII	Excerpts‡
Royal	5. A. xii	ff. 247^{C}–248^{C}	XV^{1}	Ep. 128†
	5. C. iii	ff. 259^{B}–263^{B}	XV^{1}	Excerpts, Epp. 2–89
	6. E. v	ff. 132^{A}–135^{A}	XIV^{m}	Excerpts, Epp. 2–89
	7. E. ii	ff. 386^{A-D}, 393^{D}–396^{B}	XIV^{2}	Epp. 128, 131†
Sloane	683	ff. 2^{a}–22^{a}	XIV^{2}	Excerpts, Epp. 1–123†
Stowe	930	ff. 54^{b}–55^{b}	*ca.* 1270	Ep. 128†
London, Lambeth	203	ff. 193^{b}–194^{b}	XIV^{1}	Ep. 128†
Cambridge				
Univ.	Ii. i. 19	ff. 208^{A}–209^{D}	XIV^{1}	Ep. 128
C.C.C.	107	f. 94^{b}	XV^{1}	Ep. 131
	123, pt. ii	ff. 1^{A}–61^{b}, 64^{a}–67^{a}	1456	Epp. 1–128, out of order
	156	f. 109^{a-b}	1465	Ep. 128†
	385	pp. 84–87	XIII^{2}	Ep. 128†
	453	pp. 1–395	*ca.* 1400	Epp. 1–127
Sid. Suss.	92, pt. ii	ff. 1^{a}–50^{b}	XVII	Epp. 1–58§
Trinity	B. 15. 20	ff. 883^{B}–890^{D}	XIV^{2}	Excerpts, Epp. 2–89†

* Badly damaged by fire of 1731. Apparently a selection, but it is difficult now to know how many or what letters it contained.

† Not noticed by Luard.

‡ Letters wanting in Brown's *Fasc. Rer. Expet.*

§ Copied from *libro imperfecto manuscripto in bibliotheca dunelmensi.* See Luard, *op. cit.* Introd. p. xcvii. The Durham codex seems to have disappeared.

Cheltenham, Phillipps	8336	f.	181a	ca. 1310	Excerpts. See p. 192
Hereford Cath.	Reg. Ric. de Swinfield	f.	12a	XIV¹	Ep. 48
Lincoln Cath.	Reg. Joh. d'Alderby	f.	275	XIV	Ep. 129*
Paris, B.N., Moreau	1260			XVIII	Excerpts
Prague					
Univ.	lat. 763	ff.	1a–77a	ca. 1410	Shorter coll. Boh.†
	Czech 232	ff.	108b–111a	XV¹	Ep. 128 Boh.‡
Metrop. Chap.	272	ff.	2a–79b	ca. 1425	Shorter coll. Boh.§
	509	ff.	175A–227C	XV¹	Shorter coll. Boh.‖
	693	ff.	153b–159b	ca. 1410	Epp. 10, 9, 25, 75, Boh.
	1572	ff.	1a–71a	XV¹	Shorter coll. Boh.¶
Wolfenbüttel	Theol. 2207 12°	ff.	193b–196b	XVm	Ep. 128 Engl.

In spite of a striking similarity in the selection of the letters copied by Czech scribes, it would seem unnecessary to assume a previous tradition of a shorter collection. There is no MS of the letters now in Bohemia of English provenance. It is more probable that a selection was made by some Czech scribe who was in England in the early years of the fifteenth century at the time when works of Wyclyf were being so hurriedly copied. This probability would doubtless hold for other works of Grosseteste that appear in Bohemian MSS after 1405–1410—*Dicta*, sermons, and even minor philosophical works. The reason for this interest in Grosseteste was of course that Wyclyf regarded him so highly and the Czechs were thus led to seek his original works.

1. Rogavit me dulciflua dileccio tua, quatenus scriberem... × ...rescribendo errorem meum corrigas.

To Adam Rufus. The first half appears separately as *De Forma Prima Omnium*. See above, p. 98. The second half is known as *De Intelligenciis*. See above, p. 104. Luard dates before 1210, but see under the separate tractates. Pp. 1–17. Quoted by Wyclyf, *De Ente Predicamentali*, p. 147. On p. 261 in this same volume the letter is quoted, but the work is not by Wyclyf. See above, p. 99.

* Printed from this MS by Wood, *Hist. et Antiquitates Univ. Oxon.* I, 94. I have not examined the register.

† Contains fifty-nine letters, omitting 7, 17, 78 and 126 of those listed below in n. §, but adding 8, 10, 75, 88, 89 and 102. Ep. 88 is repeated.

‡ Followed, ff. 111b–115a, by a literal Czech translation of the letter, both the Latin and the Czech versions being entitled *Epistola Luciperi*.

§ Contains, in the following order, fifty-seven letters, viz. 1, 7, 9, 58, 59, 25, 112, 51, 52, 74, 17, 122, 6, 85, 86, 87, 88, 77, 71, 73, 101, 111, 90, 96, 98, 100, 107, 84, 108, 109, 7, 20, 35, 23, 36, 44, 19, 46, 48, 47, 49, 76, 79, 78, 101, 126, 29, 30, 33, 31, 34, 57, 37, 38, 39, 40, 41, 13, 72 (of which the second half comes first). Repetition of Epp. 7 and 101 may be noted.

‖ Contains fifty-seven letters with 101 repeated, omitting 7, 29, 100, 111 of those found in MS 272, but containing 8, 10, 75 and 89.

¶ Contains fifty-three of the above fifty-seven letters, repeating 10 and 38, omitting 6, 17, 29, 46, 74 and 126, but containing instead 89 and 102.

2. Novit sinceritas caritatis vestre scriptum esse, quoniam... × ...accepcius compleri posse credidit.

To Fr. Agnellus Pisanus, Provincial of the Franciscans in England, and the convent in Oxford. [1225.] To be dated between 1229 and 1232, during Grosseteste's occupancy of the archdiaconate of Leicester. Pp. 17–21.

3. Unitati vestre reverende, quantas valeo, licet non quantas debeo ... × ...opportunius differendum. Valeat semper in domino vestra veneracio.

To the Dean, William of Tournay, and Canons of Lincoln. [1231.] Pp. 22–25.

4. Scripsi vobis literam humiliter supplicantem ut diem pacis... × ...sed nomini tuo da gloriam. Valeat in domino veneracio vestra.

To the Abbot, Adam of Latebury, and Convent of Reading. [1231.] Pp. 25–33. Brown, II, 307–309.

5. Munificencie liberalitatis vestre gracias ago affectuosas que plurimis ... × ...nec irritatur, caritas. Valeat in domino domina mea carissima.

To Margaret de Quincy, Countess of Winchester. [1231.] See above under *De X Mandatis* (p. 131) and *De Cessacione Legalium* (p. 121). Pp. 33–38. English translation by Friedman, *Robert Grosseteste and the Jews* (Cambridge, Mass. 1934), pp. 12–18.

6. Magnorum animorum est, alios beneficiis prevenire... × ...quod est verbum Dei. Valeat in domino...sublimitas.

To Richard Marshall, Earl of Pembroke. [Probably 1230–1231.] Pp. 38–41.

7. Fama magnis laudibus vestram extollit sapienciam... × ...variis occupacionibus detentis onerosus esse.

To Richard Marshall, Earl of Pembroke. [Probably 1230–1231.] Inscribed simply *suus Robertus Grosseteste*, without further title, this letter could perhaps better be assigned to the period between 1232, when he resigned his preferments, and 1234, the date of Marshall's death. Pp. 41–43.

8. Desideranti tibi valetudinis mee statum agnoscere... × ...esset graviter oppressurum. Vale in Christo.

To his sister Juetta (Yvette). Written probably immediately after he resigned his preferments; he refers also to his recent severe illness and subsequent recovery. To be dated then late in 1232 or early in 1233. [1232.] Pp. 43–45. Brown, II, 310. Quoted by Wyclyf, *De Officio Regis*, pp. 85 and 132.

9. Recepta epistola tua dulciflue consolacionis necnon et pie aggratulacionis... × ...misericorditer abluat et abstergat.

To Master Adam Marsh. [1232.] Allowing time for the *mordaces detracciones* and *graves contemptus* which he mentions as consequent upon his resigning his preferments, we must still date in 1232, as Adam Marsh is not yet addressed as *Frater*, which we know him to have become in that year. Pp. 45–47.

10. Te, quem in Christo consuevi diligere, non possum non diligere ... × ... novum commutacionis. Vale in Christum, ut audeam aliquando subscribere, vale in Christo.

To an unnamed cleric, *Magister N.* We have no means of knowing when or to whom this letter was written. From its place in the collection and from the simple *Robertus Grosseteste*, we should place it in the period 1232–1235 or before 1229. [1232–1234.] Pp. 48–50. Brown, II, 310 f.

11. Benevolencie dileccionis vestre qua soliciti estis de processu et ... × ... quoniam merces vestra copiosa est in celis.

To Master Michael Beleth. From *Robertus divina permissione lincolniensis electus*. Written, therefore, between March 27 and June 3, 1235. [1235.] Pp. 50–54. Brown, II, 311 f.

12. Cum Apostolus ad Romanos dicat: Hoc iudicate magis, ne ponatis ... × ... preces monachis effuderunt.

To Edmund, Archbishop of Canterbury. *Robertus...electus*, i.e. March to June, 1235. [1235.] Pp. 54–56. Brown, II, 313.

13. Dileccionis vestre literas recipimus, continentes quod cum simul nolitis ... × ... predicatores interim curabo supplere.

To William de Cerda. From *Robertus...electus*. Date as preceding letter. [1235.] Pp. 57–59.

14. Compertum est apud me vestre sanctitatis votum salutem ... × ... in hac parte non repellatis neque inexauditas dimittatis.

To Alardus, Provincial of Dominicans in England. Written just before Michaelmas, 1235. [1235.] P. 59 f.

15. Quia ex debito officii mihi licet indigno impositi ... × ... nutante et incerta varietate. Valete in domino.

To Alardus, Provincial of Dominicans in England, and *diffinitores* in a chapter soon to be held at York. Written probably immediately after and supplementary to Ep. 14, which is mentioned in this letter. [1235.] P. 61.

16. Novimus quod zelus domus Dei vos comedit et desiderium illius ... × ... poteritis festinacione. Valete in Christo Jesu Domino nostro.

To John of St Giles. Written probably in the summer of 1235, before John had left Mainz. When Grosseteste wrote to Alardus (Ep. 14), he knew of the approximate date of John's arrival in England. We are therefore justified in assuming that Grosseteste had received a reply to this letter (Ep. 16) before writing to Alardus. Ep. 16 would then have been written at least some three or four weeks before Ep. 14. [1235.] P. 62 f.

17. Recepimus literas dileccionis vestre, novit Dominus dolorem et anxietatem ... × ... vita separabit me a diligendo vos in Domino.

To William Raleigh, Treasurer of Exeter. Raleigh was Treasurer of Exeter in 1237,* and from this office elected Bishop of Winchester late in 1238, though his election was rejected by the king, and Bishop of Lichfield, Feb. 24,

* Le Neve, *Fasti*, I, 414, who misquotes *Pat. Rolls*. It should be 21 Henry III. m. 9.

1238/9. From the statement ...*iampridem paratus fui testibus*... we must presuppose a prolonged controversy. I suggest the end of 1236, i.e. before the London Council of 1237. [1235.] Pp. 63–65. Brown, II, 314.

18. Recepimus literas venerabilis viri domini Boecii domini pape nuncii... × ...sed Illum tantum qui potest corpus et animam mittere in gehennam.

To John Romanus, Subdean of York. John was Subdean from 1228 until perhaps 1241.* Luard dates the letter "1235?" Stevenson dates "probably 1236",† with which I would agree. The vicariate of Chalgrave was not filled by Grosseteste before June 27, 1238.‡ Pp. 65–67.

19. Licet lex amicicie res eciam que videntur impossibiles ad possibilem ... × ...malos potest esse amicicie copulacio.

To John Blund, Chancellor of York. Our knowledge of Blund is as yet unsatisfactory. He was Chancellor in 1231 and 1244,§ and probably all the intervening time. If the letters are in chronological order Luard's suggestion of "1236?" is acceptable. P. 68 f.

20. Diligencie et laboris tui mercedem retribuat tibi bonorum... × ... Hanc paginam tecum ad me reportes et vale.

To Adam Marsh. After Adam has spoken with John of St Giles, Grosseteste asks him to meet him at Liddington. The itinerary of Grosseteste|| contains only one reference to Liddington in 1236, Sept. 22, and several in 1237. He was in Liddington on March 19, 1237, on April 6, and from May 17 to June 26 of the same year. As the wording of the letter gives the impression that Grosseteste was using Liddington as a temporary headquarters, the early summer of 1237 seems the most probable period for the letter to have been written. This later date is corroborated by a reference to *peticionibus...ad curiam transmittendis,* which would ill accord with an earlier period. [1236?] Pp. 69–71.

21. Noveritis quod dominus rex nuper apud Northamptoniam ad brevem... × ...per censuram ecclesiasticam compescendo. Valeatis etc.

To the archdeacons of the diocese of Lincoln. [1236.] I have been unable to identify the regulations made for the Northampton fair by the king. P. 71 f.

22. Quia ad pastoris spectat officium his qui ignorant et errant... × ... presumpserint canonica punientes districcione.

To the archdeacons of the diocese of Lincoln. [1236.] Pp. 72–76. Brown, II, 314 f.

23. Cum ad imitacionem beati apostoli Pauli exhortantes nos imitatores ... × ...de incendio sempiterni ignis eripere. Vale.

To William Raleigh, Treasurer of Exeter. Obviously a continuation of the correspondence noted in Ep. 17. 1237 is a likely date. [1236.] Pp. 76–94. Brown, II, 316–322. Quoted by Wyclyf, *De Officio Regis*, p. 123; *De Potestate Pape*, p. 233; *De Civ. Dominio*, IV, 397.

* Le Neve, *Fasti*, III, 127 f. Simon of St Giles was Subdean in 1241, but if or how long before is not yet known.

† *Op. cit.* p. 139.

‡ *Rotuli Grosseteste*, p. 313.

§ Le Neve, *Fasti*, III, 163.

|| *Rotuli Grosseteste*, p. x.

24. Recepi rescriptum tuum in quo mihi gracias refers de eo... × ...a caritate tua que est in Christo Jesu Domino nostro.

To William Raleigh, Treasurer of Exeter, in answer to a reply to the preceding letter. 1237. [1236.] Pp. 95–97. Brown, II, 323 f.

25. Quanto fervencius te diligo et ex affeccione paterna brachiis... × ... indicaturus es in triumphante ecclesia.

To Hugh de Patteshull. Hugh was Treasurer of the Exchequer, 1234–1236;* he resigned the living of Elkington in 1240,† and seems to have died as Bishop of Coventry by 1241.‡ Grosseteste had instituted him to Old Warden in Feb. 1237.§ In this letter Grosseteste urges Hugh not to assume more duties than he can discharge. [Not after 1236?] Pp. 97–100. Brown, II, 324.

26. Literas paternitatis vestre ea qua decuit reverencia recepi pro abbate ... × ...in manus Dei, de quibus non est qui possit eruere.

To Edmund, Archbishop of Canterbury. A long story of litigation and complicated disputes lies behind this letter. A number of persons are named, but we are not able to infer anything definite from their offices, which, when mentioned, are found to have been held over a considerable period. The letter is obviously from the early part of the episcopate; the reference to the summons to the king's court would place it about 1238. [1236.] Bale lists this letter as beginning the *Epistolae Familiares* which he had seen in a Cambridge Univ. MS. (*Index*, p. 374). I do not recognize the MS as any thus far known. Pp. 101–105. Brown, II, 325 f.

27. Noverit paternitas vestra quod abbas de Ramesey, ordinis beati Benedicti... × ...de facili posset pravorum molimine subverti.

To Edmund, Archbishop of Canterbury, containing a royal letter dated May 4, 1236. [1236.] Pp. 105–108. Brown, II, 326 f. *Raynaldi Continuatio*, II (XXI), 153.

28. Cum paterna et pastorali solicitudine anime mee proximam... × ... ne unquam offendatis ad lapidem pedem vestrum.

To Edmund, Archbishop of Canterbury. Written some time after the previous letter, probably within the year. Pp. 108–113. Brown, II, 327–329. *Raynaldi Continuatio*, II (XXI), 174.

29. Cum summus pontifex personas crucesignatorum et ipsorum bona ... × ...consonum eciam inimicis benefacere.

To King Henry III, asking for the release from prison of Richard Syward. [1236.] An entry in the *Cal. of Pat. Rolls*, 1236, p. 158, notes the imprisonment of Richard Syward under date of Sept. 24, 1236. P. 114 f. Brown, II, 330.

30. Scriptum est, Caritas paciens et benigna est, ideoque tolerat... × ... poterimus inoffensa rectitudine iusticie.

To Philip de Kyme. [1236?] De Kyme († 1242) had resented Grosseteste's rejection of his presentee and had appointed another as prior of Kyme. This other would seem to have been Roger de Toft, appointed between June 27, 1236 and June 27, 1237.|| P. 116 f. Brown, II, 330 f.

* Tout, *Chapters in Administrative History*, VI (Manchester, 1933), p. 18.

† *Rotuli Grosseteste*, p. 193.

‡ Le Neve, *Fasti*, II, 352, and *Rotuli Grosseteste*, p. 204.

§ *Rotuli Grosseteste*, p. 307 f.

|| *Rotuli Grosseteste*, p. 11.

31. Gracie quam nobiscum fecistis in concessione fratrum nobiscum ... × ... salva ordinis integritate et honestate.

To Frater Helias, Minister-General of the Franciscans. After Ep. 41. [1236?] P. 117 f.

32. Cum domus Dei, testante propheta Filioque Dei, domus sit oracionis ... × ... Circumcisionis Domini nullatenus permittatis fieri.

To the Dean and Chapter of Lincoln. Luard places the letter "probably in 1236" perhaps on the assumption that Grosseteste would take the first opportunity to forbid the "feast of fools", scheduled for the feast of the Circumcision. In this case the letter would have been written shortly before Jan. 1, 1236, unless, having seen, the first time in his episcopate that the feast was held, its licentious character, he forbade its return, and then we should have to date the letter *ca.* Christmas, 1236. The first suggestion seems more probable. P. 118 f. Brown, II, 331.

33. Gracias Deo referimus quod cum graciarum accione molestias ... × ... per Dei graciam, ad nutum vestre voluntatis.

To John de Foxtone. [1236?] According to Matthew Paris, *Chron. Maj.* IV, 378, miracles had been worked at the tomb of a certain Magister Johannes de Foxtuna in 1244. The *dilectus noster in Christo dominus J. de Bannberry*, who had brought one book back to Grosseteste (p. 120), appears often as a witness to episcopal documents between Feb. 1237 and the middle of 1239.* The earlier of these two *termini* would seem to be the earliest date we could assign to this letter. P. 119 f.

34. Religionis sanctitas, religioseque persone, quam sint venerande ... × ... quod eorum multitudo sit aliis egestatis occasio.

To Alexander Staneby (Stavensby), Bishop of Coventry and Lichfield. [1236?] A date early in 1237 would best accord with the probabilities of the case.† Pp. 120–122.

35. Etsi ex generali debito subieccionis, quo non solum populus ... × ... et ecclesie sue sancte per tempora longa.

To Pope Gregory IX. [1236?] Certainly very early in episcopate. Pp. 123–125. Brown, II, 331 f. Quoted by Wyclyf, *De Civ. Dominio*, IV, 395.

36. Sicut super mundi cardines mundus innititur ... × ... suscipiat benigne caritatis amplexacio.

To Cardinal Egidius, about the same time as Ep. 35, as Grosseteste has but recently become a bishop, *gradum adeptus...altiorem* (p. 127). [1236?] Pp. 125–128. Brown, II, 332 f. Quoted by Wyclyf, *De Potestate Pape*, p. 256.

37. Etsi faciem vestram corporalem non viderimus, credimus tamen ... × ... sed solam eternam salutem querimus animarum.

To Frater Raymond de Pennaforte. [1237?] This letter, with Epp. 38, 39, 40, 42, and 43, is concerned with the appointment and maintenance of Simon of Arden as Grosseteste's proctor at Rome for the duration of the litigation with the Chapter. Matthew Paris tells us the litigation began in 1239 (*Chron.*

* *Rotuli Grosseteste*, pp. 253, 185, etc.

† See Eccleston's *De Adventu Minorum* (ed. Little, Paris, 1909), p. 100 and n. *c*.

Maj. III, 528). As Simon of Arden appears as a witness in a Lincoln document as late as August 4, 1238 (*Rotuli Grosseteste*, p. 186), and he was rector of Ab-Kettleby in 1238, it is likely that all letters indicating his impending or actual presence in Rome should be dated late 1238 and 1239. Pp. 128 f. Brown, II, 333. Quoted by Wyclyf, *De Potestate Pape*, p. 262.

38. Caritati vestre, que, sicut nos prevenit cognicione, sic eciam... × ... cum nomen episcopale resonet in supra intendere.

To Frater Ernulph, Papal Penitentiary. [1237.] From the phrase *ex bone memorie fratris Ade Rufi* we know that Adam Rufus is already dead, but the exact date of his death is not yet known, though there are good reasons for placing it before 1235.* This letter is to be dated at the same time as Ep. 37. P. 129 f. Brown, II, 333 f.

39. Si de nominis vestri titulo aliqua omisimus aut non recte... × ...ex ipsius mole sed ex donantis affeccione.

To Ranfred, Papal Notary. [1237?] Concerned with the same business, though less directly than other letters, it mentions John de Ferentino as Archdeacon of Norwich, which we know him to have been in 1236.† His archidiaconate should then be extended to 1239. Pp. 130–131.

40. Credimus vestram caritatem memoriter tenere quanta familiaritate ... × ...super his per latorem presencium significare velitis.

To Frater Jordan, Prior-General of the Dominicans, written about the same time as the preceding three letters. [1237.] Pp. 131–133. Brown, II, 334.

41. Quia filii vestri, fratres minores in Anglia sui gracia... × ...hesitantis propulsio, tribulati consolacio.

To Frater Helias, Minister-General of the Franciscans. [1237.] There is no mention of any specific persons nor of Grosseteste's case at Rome, but the recurrence of several complete sentences appearing in the letter to Frater Jordan (Ep. 40) would lead us to accept the contemporaneity of the two letters. P. 133 f. Brown, II, 334 f.

42. Pro salubri consilio, affabili colloquio et dulci solacio... × ...floreat suavius, et fructificet fertilius.

To Frater Ernulph, Papal Penitentiary. [1239.] As Simon of Arden has arrived in Rome and enough time has elapsed for Ernulph to have entertained him, and for word to have got back to Grosseteste, we must place this letter at least some months after the letters asking for the support of friends in Rome, i.e. about the middle of 1239. P. 134 f. Brown, II, 335.

43. Quia caritatis latitudo neque stat neque coarctatur... × ...debent dileccioni, semper esse paratos.

To John de Ferentino, Papal Chamberlain. [1237.] This letter belongs with the Rome correspondence, i.e. 1239. See above, Ep. 39. P. 135. Brown, II, 335. Quoted by Wyclyf, *De Potestate Pape*, p. 258.

* Cf. Eccleston, *De Adventu Minorum* (ed. Little, Paris, 1909), p. 21, n. *b*; Little in *Arch. Franc. Hist.* XIX (1926), 832, n. 7.

† Le Neve, *Fasti*, II, 478.

44. Ex fido relatu didici quod bone memorie Hugonem... × ...quam vestri gracia fecistis cum eodem vivo.

To Cardinal Thomas de Episcopo, Cardinal priest of S. Sabina (†1243). [1237?] This is the sort of letter a newly consecrated bishop would write to a dear friend of his predecessor. Its general tone would have no point after a few years had elapsed. No mention is made, as in the preceding letters, of Grosseteste's pending business at the papal court. Failing contrary evidence, 1236 would seem the latest reasonably understandable date. Pp. 135–137. Brown, II, 335 f.

45. Epistolam reverende paternitatis vestre per dominum Cestrensem ... × ...amantem redamare potero. Valeat paternitas vestra in Domino.

To Cardinal Egidius. [1237?] It is difficult to date this letter satisfactorily. Receipt of a letter from Cardinal Egidius *per dominum Cestrensem...transmissam nuper* may mean that the Bishop of Lichfield had brought a letter to Grosseteste from Rome, or that it was a circular letter or that Egidius had addressed a letter to Grosseteste "in care of" the Bishop of Lichfield. The first of the three is the most natural suggestion. But then the question arises which Bishop of Lichfield would be meant. Alexander Staneby died Dec. 26, 1238. He had spent many years in Italy and, before election as bishop, had been *clericus de camera domini Pape*, and consequently better known to the papal court than Grosseteste. The letter to the latter might conceivably have been sent first to Staneby. We do not have any information that he was in Rome in the years immediately preceding his death. Matthew Paris tells us (*Chron. Maj.* III, 385) that he was in England and Wales early in 1237. There is no mention of Grosseteste's pending suit at the papal court. P. 137 f. Brown, II, 336.

46. Magistrum Ricardum de Cornubia vestri testimonii titulus... × ...et foveat recollectum. Valeat in Deo paternitas vestra.

To Cardinal Egidius. [1237?] Le Neve (*Fasti*, II, 184) says that Richard de Cornubia was collated to St Martin's about 1250. In Grosseteste's *Rotuli* (p. 43), Magister Ricardus Cornubiensis is admitted as rector of the church at Skremby in Grosseteste's fifth year, i.e. 1239–1240. In this letter Grosseteste specifies that Richard is to come into residence in Lincoln and has assigned him *fructus prebende Sancti Martini in Dernesthall in qua institutus est*. The weight of evidence seems to favour the later date (1250), though the silence of the *Rotuli* is disturbing. This Richard must not be confused with the Frater Ricardus Rufus Cornubiensis† who joined the Franciscan order between 1235 and 1238. Grosseteste would have used the "Frater" scrupulously. Pp. 138–140. Brown, II, 337.

47. Considerantes quod de vestra eminenti sciencia... × ...racione deficiatis, cum dicetur: Redde racionem villicacionis tue.

To Master Richard of Cornwall. [1237?] Written at the same time as Ep. 46. P. 140. Brown, II, 337.

* *Annales Monastici* (R.S.), II, 299.

† See Eccleston, *De Adventu Minorum* (ed. Little, Paris, 1909), pp. 24, 37, and Little in *Arch. Franc. Hist.* XIX (1926), 841 ff.

48. Sicut senciunt sancti et iusti, equa iniquitas est non punire... × ... mansuetudinis et non magister crudelitatis. Valete.

To Simon de Montfort. [1238.] The reference to Simon de Montfort's extortion from Simon Curlevache (Matthew Paris, *Chron. Maj.* III, 479 f.) is quite explicit. This dates the letter early in 1238.* Pp. 141–143. *Reg. Ricardi de Swinfield* (Cant. and York Soc., ed. W. W. Capes, London, 1899), *s.a.* 1238; Brown, II, 338 f.

49. Literas sanctitatis vestre ea qua decet reverencia suscepi... × ...non possim pre confusione. Valeat paternitas vestra in Domino.

To Cardinal Otho, Papal Legate. [1238.] The Acto here mentioned as Otho's clerk by Grosseteste is spoken of, in the same capacity, by Matthew Paris (*Chron. Maj.* III, 419) under the year 1237. See below, Ep. 74. Grosseteste refers to *nepos domini pape promotus in unam de optimis prebendis lincolniensis ecclesie* since his consecration. This promotion does not appear to have been traced. See Stevenson, p. 207. Pp. 144–146. Brown, II, 339.

50. Quoniam debitores sumus evangelizandi verbum Dei... × ...instrumentorum transcripta, nobis faciatis habere. Valete.

To Robert de Hayles, Archdeacon of Lincoln. [1238.] Written after the Council of London in November, 1237, and before the death of Robert of Hayles which must have occurred early in 1238, as Thomas Wallensis appears as his successor before June 17, 1238.† P. 146 f. Brown, II, 340.

51. Roberto archidiacono lincolniensi viam universe carnis ingresso ... × ...quemadmodum Paulus ait ad Timotheum, Nemo adolescenciam tuam contemnat. Valete.

To Thomas Wallensis. [1238.] Pp. 147–151. Brown, II, 340 f.

52. Sanctitatis vestre literas recepimus in forma deprecatoria ut Thomam ... × ...beneficii, conferatur. Valeat sancta paternitas vestra per tempora longiora.

To Cardinal Otho, Papal Legate. [1238?] Grosseteste objects to the appointment of Thomas Ferrers, younger son of the Earl of Derby, to a benefice, on grounds of extreme youth. Grosseteste institutes William de Horton to the suggested benefice, Rand, Lincolnshire, before June 27, 1241.‡ The letter falls somewhere between 1238 and 1241. We cannot yet be more definite. Pp. 151–154. Brown, II, 342 f.

52*. Debentes de vobis racionem bonam reddere, que racio, secundum Augustinum... × ...pro posse nostro adiuvante Domino Jesu Christo canonice punituros.

The *Constituciones Roberti Episcopi* sent to clergy of the diocese of Lincoln; often appears separately under that title in MSS, and so listed by bibliographers. [1238?] Pp. 154–164. See above, pp. 126 f. for other MSS and printings.

* C. Bémont, *Simon de Montfort* (transl. E. F. Jacob, Oxford, 1930), p. 26, places the incident of the extortion in 1239. Matthew Paris is quite clear in placing it early in 1238.

† *Rotuli Grosseteste*, p. 22 ff.

‡ *Rotuli Grosseteste*, p. 53.

53. Licet gloria bonorum sit ab intus, nesciatque sinistra eorum... × ...et contagiosa scabies lacius serpat. Valete.

To the Abbot and Convent of Fleury. [1238?] Pp. 166–168. Brown, II, 343.

54. Secundum vocem Domini, Si cecus ceco ducatum prebeat... × ...et eciam turpissime morti tradere. Valete.

To the Abbot and Convent of Fleury [1238?] requesting that a prior be named for Minting Abbey. As Brother John was instituted soon after June 27, 1238 (see *Rotuli Grosseteste*, p. 27), the letter is probably to be dated in the spring of the same year. P. 168 f. Brown, II, 344.

55. Adiuvante Domino veniemus ad partes vestras et cognoscemus evidencius... × ...semper dum vivimus capiat incrementum. Valete.

To Alan of Cestreham, Abbot of Leicester. [1238?] Grosseteste refers to previous letters from Alan complaining of the bishop's severity. The correspondence is doubtless to be connected with Grosseteste's reforming activities of 1237–1238. Pp. 169–171. Brown, II, 344.

56. Scripsistis nobis vos multum admirari super eo quod vos... × ... caritate noveritis nos affectare. Valeat dileccio vestra in Domino.

To William, Earl of Warren. [1238.] The Earl died May 27, 1240. Pp. 171–173.

57. Quiescens hac septimana proxima paululum ab exteriorum tumultu ... × ...reputabit eam in tanti boni comparacione. Valete.

To the Abbot and Convent of Bury St Edmunds. For a discussion of the contents of the letter see above, p. 70 f. Luard suggests (without date) that the letter was written to Walter of St Edmund, Abbot of Peterborough, a suggestion accepted by Stevenson (p. 165), but Pauli's contention (p. 52), that the letter was addressed to St Edmundsbury, seems perhaps more acceptable. Grosseteste's relations with the latter house were close and scholarly. We have a record of his exchange of MSS with the monastery in Pembroke, Cambridge, MS 7. See Introd. p. 25 ff. The phraseology in the salutation *Abbati et conventui de Burgo* is a usual term for St Edmundsbury, whereas in the *Rotuli Grosseteste* Peterborough is usually *Burgum Sancti* (*Beati*) *Petri*. Pp. 173–178.

58. Non solum ex relacione fame cuius odor bonus mundum replet ... × ...Incolumitatem vestram conservet Altissimus per tempora longa mihi et Ecclesie sue.

To Pope Gregory IX. [1238?] As it mentions *dissensiones* in the Franciscan order, which we may properly connect with the antecedents of the deposition of Frater Helias in 1238, we suggest late 1237, a date which would apply to the following letter as well. Pp. 179–181.

59. Cum fratres minores per regnum Anglie constituti sua salubri predicacione... × ...plurimum exterminate. Valeat in Domino sancta paternitas vestra.

To Cardinal Raynald, Bishop of Ostia, bespeaking his protection for the Franciscans. [1238?] See Ep. 58. P. 181 f.

60. Quia fides per dileccionem operans vos indissolubiliter unit Christo ... × ... viribus omnibus non impediet. Valeat sancta paternitas vestra per tempora longiora.

To Cardinal Otho, papal legate. [1238.] Pp. 182–185.

61. Quod inter tot et tantas occupaciones tam dulcifluo ... × ... gemitibus ab eo postulari. Valeat sancta paternitas vestra per tempora longiora.

To Cardinal Otho, papal legate. [1238.] Pp. 185–188. Brown, II, 345 f.

62. Rogavit nos dileccionis vestre sinceritas quatenus scriberemus ... × ... sciamus, universa consummabit. Valeat fraternitas vestra in Domino.

To Ralph de Neville, Bishop of Chichester. [1238.] Pp. 188–190. Brown, II, 346 f.

63. Quia omnia in nobis honeste et secundum ordinem fieri decet ... × ... eorundem sanctorum impetrare satagatis consolacionem.

To the Abbot and Convent of Ramsey. [September, 1238.] Pp. 190–192. Brown, II, 347 f.

64. Non solum abundans, sed et superabundans multiplicium ... × ... honeste petitum concedere. Incolumitatem vestram ... et Ecclesie sue.

To Pope Gregory IX, commending to him his proctor, Simon of Arden· [1238.] It must have been, at the earliest, late in 1238, as, early in August of that year, Simon was a witness of a Leicester institution. See *Rotuli Grosseteste*, p. 186. P. 192 f. Brown, II, 348.

65. De vestra promocione, sicut literatorie rogastis, gracias ... × ... adornatus et reparacio. Valeat in Domino sancta paternitas vestra.

To Cardinal Raymond, Deacon of St Eustace. [1239?] The vicar of Maxey referred to must be Henry of Bledelawe. See *Rotuli Grosseteste*, p. 169. Raimundus Nonnatus, O. Merc., was promoted cardinal early in 1239 and died Aug. 26, 1240.* The letter is to be dated then about the middle of 1239. Grosseteste's case at the curia is still in process. P. 193 f. Brown, II, 348 f.

66. Sufficienti nobis constat certitudine, quod vestra dileccio sincera ... × ... propagentur latitudinem. Valeat dileccio vestra in Domino.

To John de Ferentino, Papal Chamberlain. [1239.] P. 195. Brown, II, 349.

67. Dileccionis vestre lumen quod super omnes generaliter effunditis ... × ... consolidet fervore. Valeat sancta paternitas vestra in Domino.

To Cardinal Egidius. [1239?] Expressing gratitude for kindness, the letter is rather vague as to detail. If it refers to help rendered to Grosseteste's proctor, Simon of Arden, while in Rome, the middle of the year 1239 would best satisfy known conditions. P. 196.

68. Longo cremento solidata robora apta sunt ad supportandum ... × ... intuitu caritatis excludere. Valeat sancta paternitas vestra in Domino.

To Cardinal Thomas. [1239?] Simon of Arden is mentioned as still in Rome. The letter could, therefore, have been written as late as the beginning of 1241. P. 196 f. Brown, II, 350.

* See Eubel, *Hierarchia Catholica Medii Aevi*, I (Münster, 1898), 6.

69. Aque multe non poterunt extinguere caritatem et flumina non obruent eam... × ...radiis transitus preparetur. Valeat sancta paternitas vestra in Domino.

To Frater Ernulph, Papal Penitentiary. [1239?] Another letter to gain support for his *negocia* at the Roman curia. P. 197 f.

70. Paternitatis vestre dulciflua benignitas, studens beneficiis precurrere ... × ...sacrificium pinguius. Valeat in Domino sancta paternitas vestra.

To Cardinal Raynald, Bishop of Ostia. [1239?] A letter of thanks for help given to Simon of Arden, *lator presencium*. P. 198 f.

71. Secundum legem divinam et naturalem, filii carnales parentibus ... × ...unum in Christo qui est pax nostra, qui fecit utraque unum. Valete.

To the Dean and Chapter of Lincoln. [1239.] See Matthew Paris, *Chron. Maj.* III, 528. Pp. 199–203. Brown, II, 350 f.

72. Dei filius de sinu patris venit in uterum virginis, de qua natus est homo... × ...gratos ei qui seipsum pro nobis tradidit. Valete.

To John Romanus, Subdean of York. [1239?] Grosseteste does not specify which church in Stamford was contemplated, and it is not possible, therefore, to date the letter. There were numerous institutions in Stamford in the years 1237–1240. See *Rotuli Grosseteste*, pp. 22, 30, 32, 41, etc. P. 203 f. Brown, II, 351 f.

72*. Dominus rex Anglie constituit abbates iusticiarios itinerantes ... × ...et habeatis ibi hoc breve. Teste me ipso, etc.

To Edmund, Archbishop of Canterbury. [1236?] See Stevenson, p. 172 ff. Pp. 205–234.

73. Exposita prudentibus Deumque timentibus intencione vestra... × ... paratus ero iusticie cederę et veritati. Valete.

To the Dean and Chapter of Lincoln. [1239.] Pp. 235–240. Brown, II, 352–354.

74. Rogavit nos paternitatis vestre sanctitas per magistrum P.... × ... magistrum Attonem satagat ordinare. Valeat sancta paternitas vestra per tempora longiora.

To Cardinal Otho, Papal Legate. [1239?] Written evidently soon after the arrival of Otho in England, June, 1237, this letter gives full reasons for refusing a prebend to Acto (Atto), Otho's clerk. See above, Ep. 49, which was probably an earlier letter which Otho had not seen fit to accept as final. An intermediary, *magister P. clericus vester*, would seem to have acted for Otho after the first refusal. Pp. 241–243. Brown, II, 354 f.

75. Recepimus literas dileccionis vestre insinuantes pondus vestre tribulacionis... × ...utilitatem speramus posse proficere. Valete.

To Simon de Montfort. [Probably August, 1239.] P. 243 f. Brown, II, 355.

76. Redeuntes ad nos a vestre paternitatis sanctitate clerici... × ...ex cordis procedit simplicitate. Valeat paternitas vestra per tempora longiora.

To Cardinal Otho, Papal Legate. [1239.] Pp. 245–247. Brown, II, 356.

77. Cum ad pastoris pertineat officium oves suas cognoscere... × ...ut habeat vestra sanctitas recommendatum. Incolumitatem...Ecclesie sue. [As in Ep. 58.]

To Pope Gregory IX. [1239.] Grosseteste refers to his *nuncius specialis* who is soon to arrive in Rome. This *nuncius* we may assume to be Simon of Arden, who can hardly have arrived in Rome before January, 1239. The letter is then to be placed toward the end of 1238.* P. 248 f. Brown, II, 357.

78. Humor subtilis eciam partes minimas infundit... × ...irroracione non sit exclusa. Valeat paternitas vestra in Domino.

To William of Auvergne, Bishop of Paris (1227–† 1248). [1239.] There is nothing in the letter by which it can be satisfactorily dated. A certain *R. clericus* of Grosseteste is not identifiable. P. 250. Brown, II, 357.

79. De rescripti vestri melliflua dulcedine et de vestra benignissima ... × ...pro nobis scripsimus respondere. Valeat paternitas vestra per tempora longiora.

To Cardinal Otho, Papal Legate. [1239.] Grosseteste mentions the proctor of the Dean and Chapter of Lincoln at Rome since Whitsuntide, but he does not mention his answer to that move, which we should expect him to have done, had he already sent Simon of Arden to Rome as his proctor. The late summer or autumn of 1238 best suits the known conditions. Pp. 250–253. Brown, II, 358.

80. Sicut tibi mandavi per W. de Hemmyngburge clericum meum ... × ...prodesse poterunt, secundum quod Dominus tibi inspiraverit.

To Simon of Arden, Grosseteste's proctor at Rome. [November, 1239.] Pp. 253–260. Brown, II, 359–361.

81. Significavi nuper vestre sanctitati quod cum ad visitacionis... × ... semper proficiat in augmentum. Incolumitatem...longa. [As in Ep. 58.]

To Pope Gregory IX. [November, 1239.] P. 260 f. Brown, II, 361.

82. Cum obsistentibus impedimentis gravibus nequit inferiorum... × ... nostre modicitatis suscipere. Valeat paternitas vestra per tempora longiora.

To Cardinal Otho, Papal Legate. [In or soon after November, 1239.] Pp. 262–264. Brown, II, 362.

83. Malorum principiis obsistendum est, quia "Sero medicina paratur ... × ...ad bravii comprehensionem. Valeat paternitas vestra semper in Domino.

To Edmund, Archbishop of Canterbury. [1240.] Pp. 264–266. Brown, II, 363.

* Simon of Arden witnesses a Lincoln document *ii non. Augusti pontificatus nostri anno iiij*, i.e. 1238. *Rotuli Grosseteste*, p. 186.

84. Insinuatum est nobis quod vos H. decanum Christianitatis Lincolnie ... × ... ecclesiasticam libertatem taliter deperire. Valete.

To Robert of Lexington and his co-Justices-Itinerant in Lincoln. [1240.] The story of extortion from a rural dean at Lincoln would suggest a period after the appointment of Robert of Lexington as head of the itinerant justices in the northern counties in the spring of 1240. See Matthew Paris, *Chron. Maj.* IV, 34. Pp. 266–268. Brown, II, 364.

85. Qui ad ministerium aliquod, utile multis et necessarium ... × ... nostro idoneum vobis demus pastorem. Valete.

To the Convent of Messenden. [1240.] Pp. 268–270. Brown, II, 364 f.

86. Gracias agimus Domino Jesu Christo, pastori summo, qui ecclesie sue ... × ... in vestri adventus recentia. Valeat paternitas vestra semper in Domino.

To Boniface, Archbishop-elect of Canterbury. [Written soon after Sept. 17, 1243] the date of the election of Boniface. The references to the disputed election of William Raleigh would indicate that this letter was written after receipt of the papal letter of confirmation by Henry III, and considerably before the king's change of heart. P. 271 f. Brown, II, 365 f.

87. Secundus ramus a radice caritatis procedens est dileccio proximi ... × ... commodo quantolibet temporali. Valeat vestra paternitas semper in Domino.

To Boniface, Archbishop-elect of Canterbury. [1243?] More probably written after arrival of Boniface in England, early in 1244. Pp. 273–275. Brown, II, 366 f.

88. Cum diocesis nostra multum sit diffusa multumque inhabitata ... × ... de dulci prodit caritatis radice. Valeat paternitas vestra in Domino.

To Boniface, Archbishop-elect of Canterbury. [1243?] As Ep. 87. P. 275 f. Brown, II, 367.

89. Accedentes nuper ad nos clerici vestri ex parte vestre paternitatis ... × ... debeant voluntati complacere. Valeat paternitas in Domino.

To Boniface, Archbishop of Canterbury. [1245.] Written from [Lyons, i.e. between Jan. 15 and Mar. 5, 1245]. P. 276 f. Brown, II, 367 f.

90. Naturaliter indicta est, non solum hominibus et mansuetis ... × ... pure et irreverberate contemplemini.

To the Dean and Chapter of Lincoln. [1240?] Probably after Epp. 96 and 97. Pp. 277–284. Brown, II, 370 f.

91. Rescripsistis nobis quasi pro competenti responso ... × ... unde non exibit donec ultimum quadrantem persolverit. Valete.

To the Dean and Chapter of Lincoln. [1240?] The mention of participation of the king and his *prohibicio* would seem to correspond best with the story of the state of the quarrel reported by Matthew Paris (*Chron. Maj.* IV, 156) as of the year 1241. See Stevenson, p. 198, n. 4. Pp. 285–287. Brown, II, 370 f.

92. Non scimus ex integro cur tocies ad curiam domini regis ... × ... illud revocari similiter satagant. Valete.

To the Dean and Chapter of Lincoln. [1240?] This letter is later than Ep. 91. Some considerable time must be accounted for. I suggest 1241–1242. Pp. 287–290. Brown, II, 371 f.

93. Rogastis nos et obsecrastis ad pacem inter nos et capitulum... × ...et conturbacionis simul commixta confusio. Valeatis etc.

To the Dean and Chapter of Salisbury. [1240?] Probably about the same time as Ep. 92. P. 290 f. Brown, II, 372.

94. In principio litere vestre promittitis verba pacis in spiritu... × ...vos publice excommunicatos denunciari faciemus. Valete.

To the Dean and Chapter of Lincoln. [1241?] Odo of Kilkenny is mentioned as having prosecuted the cause of the chapter at the curia, and the references to the monks of Canterbury make it fairly clear that the see is still vacant. Late in 1241 or 1242. Pp. 291–295. Brown, II, 373 f.

95. Muri fortitudo et civium ad muri propugnacula prudens... × ... sicut alias per literas nostras vos rogasse meminimus. Valete.

To the Dean and Chapter of Lincoln. [1242?] The attacks on Lincoln may be supposed to be Henry III's demands for money for his Poitou campaign. See Matthew Paris, *Chron. Maj.* IV, 189, *s.a.* 1242. P. 296 f. Brown, II, 374 f.

96. Scribit Salamon in Parabolis quod omni tempore diligit qui amicus est... × ...tam anxio necessitatis articulo.

To Hugh of Norwold, Bishop of Ely. [1242?] See Ep. 90. This and the following, Ep. 97, should antedate Ep. 90. Pp. 297–299. Brown, II, 375.

97. Rogatis quod ex parte vestra absencia non offendar... × ...si viriliter egeritis, adepturi. Valete.

To Master Richard of Kirkham. [1242.] See above, Epp. 90 and 96. P. 299 f. Brown, II, 376.

98. Legimus de Moyse, quod ipse erat mitissimus hominum... × ... decet, non violenciam. Valeat paternitas vestra semper in Domino.

To Walter Cantilupe, Bishop of Worcester. [1242?] This letter can only refer to the first attempt at settlement of Grosseteste's dispute with his chapter, 1239–1240, as related in Ep. 80, and must therefore have been written early in 1240. A previous correspondence on the same subject is mentioned. Pp. 300–302. Brown, II, 376 f.

99. Intimavit nobis ex parte dileccionis vestre dilectus clericus... × ... sed quid nobis videatur, respondere. Valeat paternitas vestra in Domino.

To Walter Cantilupe, Bishop of Worcester. [1242?] Bishop Walter has been asked to accompany Henry III to France. This is doubtless the Poitou campaign of 1242. As Henry embarked on May 15 of that year, the letter would have been written some time previously. The *Magister Leonardus* mentioned in the letter (p. 302) appears as a witness to Lincoln documents *ii kal. Decembris anno sexto* (i.e. 1240). See *Rotuli Grosseteste*, pp. 55, 207. Pp. 302–304. Brown, II, 377.

100. Scriptum est, Ne dicas amico tuo, vade et revertere, et cras dabo tibi... × ...memores esse dignemini. Valeat paternitas vestra in Domino.

To Matthew, Provincial Prior of the Dominicans. [1242?] Fr. Bede Jarrett dates Matthew on a basis of Luard's conjectural date of 1242.* There is, however, no exact internal or external evidence for a specific date for this letter. Matthew died 1254. P. 304 f. Brown, II, 378.

* *The English Dominicans* (London, 1921), p. 219.

101. Super eo quod statum vestre dominacionis et domine... × ... vobiscum vestris adversis. Valeat dominacio vestra per tempora longiora.

To King Henry III. [1242?] Written certainly before May 15 of this year. As a reply to the king, after he had left for France, it would have no point. It is probable, even, that the king's letter to Grosseteste, and this, Grosseteste's reply, were both written before the January, 1242 meeting of parliament at which Henry's request for a subsidy was refused. From Grosseteste's answer, we would infer that Henry was trying subtly to influence the powerful bishop in anticipation of his request for financial aid from parliament. Pp. 306–308. Brown, II, 378 f.

102. Audivimus excellenciam vestram Willelmo de Compton, custodi ... × ... regalis excellencia revocare. Valeat dominacio vestra per tempora longiora.

To King Henry III. [1243.] P. 308 f. Brown, II, 379.

103. Scriptum est in libro Sapiencie: Sicut sol oriens mundo... × ... instanciam liberare curetis. Valeat serenitas vestra semper in Domino.

To Queen Eleanor. [1243?] Undoubtedly written at the same time as Ep. 102, asking that the queen use her influence with the king to restrain him from encouraging disturbances in the English Church. She was with Henry in Bordeaux from the summer of 1242 until late in 1243. P. 310 f. Brown, II, 380.

104. Rediens ad nos a vestre paternitatis presencia magister S. de Ardene ... × ... et ipse sit vite et immortalitatis medicamentum. Valeat sancta paternitas vestra per tempora longiora.

To Cardinal Otho, Papal Legate. [1240?] This letter cannot have been written later than the autumn of 1238, as Simon of Arden, *clericus noster* (who leaves for Rome late in 1238; see Ep. 64), is mentioned as having brought back from Cardinal Otho the report that the latter, influenced by *susurri malignorum*, by whom we are doubtless to understand the emissaries of the chapter, was displeased with Grosseteste. Pp. 311–313. Brown, II, 380 f.

105. Ex relacione dilecti in Christo filii magistri R, intelleximus... × ... sed plurimum augmentum suscipere. Valeat sancta paternitas vestra per tempora longiora.

To Cardinal Otho, Papal Legate. [December, 1240.] P. 313 f.

106. Literas vestras super facto vicarie de Pincebec recepimus... × ... per alium ad vestram presenciam evocetis. Valete.

To Master Martin, Papal Chamberlain. [1244?] Martin arrived in England early in 1244. This letter is an answer to a request from Martin for information concerning the vicariate of Pinchbeck; it does not, however, reflect the bitter opposition to Martin that arose later in the year. See Matthew Paris, *Chron. Maj.* IV, 368, 374, etc. Summer 1244 is the most probable date. Bk. VI of the *Nicomachean Ethics* is quoted. See above, p. 65 f. Pp. 315–317. Brown, II, 381.

107. Ex relatu fide digno audivimus quod plurimi sacerdotes... × ... impedire curetis. Valeat sancta paternitas, etc.

A letter to the archdeacons of the diocese of Lincoln. [1244?] The letter could as well have been written in 1238 or 1239 as in 1244. P. 317 f. Brown, II, 382. A translation of most of this letter appears in W. H. Hutton's *Misrule of Henry III* (London, 1887), pp. 10–12.

108. Regulam beati Benedicti, que supereminentis est sanctitatis... × ... in districto iudicio condemnacionem. Valete semper in Domino.

To the Abbot and Convent of Fleury. [No date.] This letter cannot be precisely dated on internal evidence, yet it may be remarked that considerable time and some correspondence have transpired since Ep. 54, which, compared to this letter, is quite mild. Grosseteste names four monks that he has removed for vice or laxity, Philip, Theobald, Walrand and Girard. Pp. 318–321. Brown, II, 382 f.

109. Receptis literis apostolicis continentibus quod edificia fratrum minorum... × ...patentes susceperimus responsum. Valeat caritas vestra semper in Domino.

To the Abbot and Convent of Cîteaux. [1244?] Thomas of Eccleston does not mention the house at Scarborough, founded probably before 1240 (see ed. Little, p. 153), but Matthew Paris refers (*Chron. Maj.* IV, 280) to the dispute with the Cistercians *s.a.* 1243, and Adam Marsh speaks of it with some feeling. *Mon. Franciscana*, I, 406. Pp. 321–323. Brown, II, 383 f. Translation in *Mon. Franciscana*, I, 642 f.

110. Nacta plenissime fiducia scribendi vestre paternitati... × ...confidenter committimus dileccioni. Valeat sancta paternitas vestra semper in Domino.

To Cardinal Otho, Papal Legate. [Soon after August 23, 1243.] Pp. 324–328. Brown, II, 384 f.

111. Benedictus Deus, qui post tempestatem tranquillum faciens... × ... habere velit recommendata. Incolumitatem vestram conservet Altissimus ecclesie sue sancte per tempora longiora.

To Pope Innocent IV. [Soon after June 24, 1243.] P. 328 f. Brown, II, 386.

112. Homo quidam peregre proficiscens, servis suis bona sua tradidit ... × ... Vermis enim eorum non morietur et ignis non extinguetur. Valete.

To the archdeacons of the diocese of Lincoln. [November, 1244.] Pp. 329–333. Brown, II, 386 f.

113. Vestre dileccionis ad nos fervorem, quem frequenter prius in vestris ... × ...domini Pape prosequentes. Valeat paternitas vestra semper in Domino.

To William Raleigh, Bishop of Winchester, and Walter Cantilupe, Bishop of Worcester. [1245.] Written from Lyons, soon after his arrival, Jan. 7, 1245. The council did not open until June 26.* P. 333. Brown, II, 388.

* So Matthew Paris. See Hefele-Leclercq, *Histoire des Conciles*, V (Paris, 1913), 1633.

114. Veros non molestat amicos, sed magis consolatur, quicquid sapienter ... × ... pro omnibus episcopis est pronunciatum. Valeat paternitas vestra semper in Domino.

To William of Nottingham, Provincial Minister of the Franciscans in England. [Probably October, 1245.] Written on the way home from the Council of Lyons in 1245. He mentions the death of Alexander of Hales (Aug. 15, 1245) and hopes to land on the Isle of Wight by Oct. 14. P. 334 f. Brown, II, 388. *Mon. Franciscana*, I, 627 f. *partim*.

115. Vestre caritatis erga parvitatem meam concepte sinceritas ... × ... memoria efficaciter innovetur. Valeat paternitas vestra semper in Domino.

To Cardinal Hugh of St Cher. [Late in 1245], on return from Council of Lyons. P. 335 f. Brown, II, 388 f.

116. Ex obediencia plerumque facere cogimur quod et cum tristicia facimus ... × ... gracia eosdem invenietis. Valeat semper in Domino sancta paternitas vestra.

To Walter Gray, Archbishop of York. As Ep. 115. P. 337. Brown, II, 389.

117. Me reverso in Angliam, occurrente domino regi revertenti ... × ... vobis cercius innotescat. Incolumitatem vestram conservet Altissimus ecclesie sue per tempora longiora.

To Pope Innocent IV. [After his return in 1245.] Henry III returned from Wales at the end of October (Matthew Paris, *Chron. Maj.* IV, 487). The paths of Grosseteste and the king must have crossed. The interview that took place can be dated almost to the day, i.e. Oct. 28 or 29. The letter to the pope must have been written immediately thereafter. P. 338 f. Brown, II, 389 f.

118. Credentes vos zelo fervere salutis animarum, ex desiderio salutis ... × ... humiliter exaudire compellant. Valeat paternitas vestra in Domino.

To T. [1245.] See *Rotuli Grosseteste*, p. 290. "W" was succeeded by "R" as Archdeacon of Huntingdon *anno* XII, i.e. 1246–1247. "T" seems, therefore, to have refused, probably 1246, the archdeaconry offered. P. 339 f. Brown, II, 390.

119. Scripsit nobis reverenda dominacio vestra vos mirari non modicum ... × ... honori regio non prospiciunt. Valeat dominacio vestra semper in Domino.

To King Henry III. [1246.] The letter to which this is obviously a reply is dated April 1, 1246, and is given by Matthew Paris, *Chron. Maj.* IV, 554. Pp. 340–342. Brown, II, 390 f.

120. Ego et frater Ada de Marisco, qui vos specialiter diligit in Domino ... × ... in hac vita degentis in habitu seculari. Valete.

To John of Offinton. [1246?] The earliest reference to John of Offinton in Grosseteste's *Rotuli* is as a witness to an institution in Saddington, where John appears as a canon of Lincoln, Mar. 25, 1247 (p. 428). This letter is to be dated some time previously, as it is a simple request that John come to England. P. 342 f. Brown, II, 391.

121. Accedens ad nos dilectus filius magister Robertus precentor ... × ... salutem operemini, preparacio. Valete semper in Domino.

To the Dean (Henry of Lexington) and Chapter of Lincoln. [1246.] P. 343 f. Brown, II, 391 f.

122. Scriptum est, Iustum non contristabit quicquid ei acciderit, quod ... × ... eadem iuvante gracia vobis deesse poterimus. Valete.

To the Dean (Henry of Lexington) and Chapter of Lincoln. [1246.] It is difficult to assign any specific date between the years 1245 and 1253 to this short letter, which merely asks for the co-operation of the Dean and Chapter. P. 345 f. Brown, II, 392.

123. Periti edificiorum constructores omni prospiciunt diligencia ... × ... est tempus aliud conveniencius accommodandum. Valete.

To the Masters Regent in Theology of Oxford. [1246?] Wood printed this letter in *Hist. et Antiqq. Univ. Oxon.* I, 91 f., and dated it 1240. Luard's suggestion of 1246 seems more probable. P. 346 f. Brown, II, 392 f. Wood, *ubi supra.*

124. Ex dominacionis vestre precepcione vobis hanc scribimus pagellam ... × ... avariciam, attencius audiatis. Valeat et vigeat dominacio vestra per tempora longiora.

To Henry III. [1245?] Grosseteste had examined Robert Passelew as to his theological preparation in 1244. See Matthew Paris, *Chron. Maj.* IV, 401. From a letter (Ep. 126) to Archbishop Boniface, telling of his refusal to institute Passelew to St Peter's, Northampton, we conclude approximate contemporaneity of Epp. 124 and 126, probably early in 1246. It will be recalled that Grosseteste had an interview with the king at the end of October. This letter presupposes some correspondence. Pp. 348–351. Brown, II, 393 f.

125. Audivimus excellenciam regiam adversus nostram parvitatem ... × ... ipsum concorditer consencient. Valeat et vigeat dominacio vestra per tempora longiora.

To King Henry III. [1245?] Shortly after the previous letter, i.e. early in 1246. Pp. 351–353. Brown, II, 394.

126. Novit vestra paternitas vos ideo in capite constitutos episcoporum ... × ... vos eorum devocio et in gloria vestra macula ponatur. Valeat paternitas vestra semper in Domino.

To Boniface, Archbishop of Canterbury. [1245?] Some negotiations between Passelew, Grosseteste and Boniface's *officialis* is presupposed. It must be dated in 1246, probably early in the year. Pp. 353–356. Brown, II, 395 f.

127. Moyses, qui tradente Domino, susceperat gubernaculum tocius populi ... × ... omnium supremo in ipsa superiori potestati obeditur.

To the Dean and Chapter of Lincoln. [1239?] Appears separately in numerous MSS as *De Cura Pastorali*, and is so listed by the bibliographers. See above, p. 129. Bale (*Index*, p. 374) lists separately as *Contra prelatorum ignaviam.* Pp. 357–431.

128. Noverit discrecio vestra, quod mandatis apostolicis affeccione ... × ... et non Pater Domini nostri Jesu Christi qui in celis est.

To Master Innocent, Notary of Pope Innocent IV. [1253.] The letter is usually preceded by a copy of the pope's letter to Master Innocent, prefixed by Grosseteste's words: *Intelleximus vos literam Domini Pape recepisse in hec verba.* (Luard, p. 432 f.) Pp. 432–437. Matthew Paris, *Chron. Maj.* V, 186, whence it was reproduced, i.e. from the older edition of Matthew Paris's work, in the

1658 ed. of Grosseteste's *De Cessacione Legalium*, pp. 26–29. Publ. also as Ep. CCXVI of Adam Marsh's letters (*Mon. Franciscana*, I, 382–385), and in *Burton Annals* (R.S.), ed. Luard, pp. 311–313. Quoted by Wyclyf, *De Officio Regis*, p. 82.

For the discussion arising out of faulty MS tradition which confused the notary with the pope of the same name, see Charles Jourdain, *Bulletin de l'Académie des Inscriptions et Belles-Lettres*, 1868, pp. 13–29, reprinted in his *Excursions Historiques à travers le Moyen Âge* (Paris, 1888), pp. 147–171. See above, under Sermon 14, p. 171. Jourdain's objection to the authenticity of this and other cognate works is based on an examination of none of the MSS. One sentence will sufficiently illustrate his argument. "Ainsi, n'est-il pas remarquable que la prétendue lettre de Robert de Lincoln à Innocent IV contre les empiétements de la cour de Rome ne se retrouve pas dans les plus anciens [MSS] qui contiennent les lettres de ce prélat?" This letter appears, contrary to the statement of Jourdain, in at least four MSS of the thirteenth century (see above, p. 193), and in several others which antedate any known MS of the whole collection. Though the letter is not addressed to the pope directly, there can be small doubt that Grosseteste intended the letter to reach Pope Innocent IV, expressly appending it, as his reply, to the pope's letter to Archbishop Boniface. A. L. Smith followed Jourdain's arguments, in his *Church and State in the Middle Ages* (Oxford, 1913; Ford Lectures for 1905), p. 101 ff. Mgr Mann, though noting Smith's doubts, takes a more favourable view of the authenticity of the letter. See his *Lives of the Popes*, XIV (London, 1928), 258 ff.

129. Scripserunt nobis dilecti in Christo filii Cancellarius et Universitas ... × ... ut debeatis propensius in Domino commendari. Datum apud parcum Stowe viii Id. Maii, pontificii nostri an. xiii.

To Master Robert Marsh. [May 8, 1248.] Pp. 437–439. A. Wood, *Hist. et Antiqq. Univ. Oxon.* I, 94 f.

130. Cum nos, licet immeriti, simus ex officii debito verbi Dei... × ... et nos ex taciturnitate accusacionem, faciatis apercius pervenire.

To the clergy of the diocese of Lincoln. [1250.] Pp. 439–442.

131. Utinam fideles et grati venerande matris anglorum ecclesie filii ... × ... ad immensum cedet meritorum cumulum apud Deum.

To the Lords and Commons of the kingdom, and the citizens of London. [1252.] Pp. 442–444.

132. Literas domini J. Sarraceni subdiaconi et capellani domino pape ... × ... per literas vestras patentes constare faciatis....

To the archdeacons of the diocese of Lincoln. August, 1247. Encloses letters from Pope Innocent IV and papal commissioners, urging collection of papal tax for the crusade decreed by the 1245 council at Lyons. *Apud* Matthew Paris, *Chron. Maj.* VI, 134.

A letter to Friar Ralph of Colebruge, second Regent Master of the Oxford Franciscans, and Adam Marsh, was probably written in 1249. See A. G. Little, "Franciscan School at Oxford" in *Arch. Franc. Hist.* XIX (1926), 837 f.

DICTA

Dicta 147 (*Dictamina*)

I. Inc.: Amor multipliciter videtur dici...
Expl.: ...cognicionis iusticie et misericordie.

II. E. Brown published in the Appendix to the *Fasc. Rer. Expet.* (1690), pp. 258–305, *Dicta* 3, 18, 23, 35, 51, 90, 101, 103, 112, 113, 127–130, 134–138, 140, 142, 144, from some not too good MS, perhaps Trin. Coll., Cambridge, MS B. 15. 20, in which there are some notes in Brown's hand.

III. These 147 *Dicta* were collected and arranged by Grosseteste himself from sermons and lectures of his earlier years in Oxford (and perhaps Paris) as he tells in the *recapitulacio* appended to many of the MSS:

In hoc libello sunt 147 capitula quorum quedam sunt brevia verba que dum in scolis morabar scripsi breviter et in composito sermone ad memoriam; nec sunt de una materia nec adinvicem continuata, quorum titulos posui ut facilius quod vellet lector posset invenire. Spondent itaque plerumque plus aliqui tituli quam solvant capitula lectori. Quedam vero sunt sermones quas eodem tempore ad clerum vel ad populum feci.

A corroboration of this statement is found in Durham Cath. MS A. III. 12 (see Introd. p. 16, and above, p. 182 f.) which contains at least thirty-three of these *Dicta* in such an order, interspersed with other sermons, etymologies and brief comments, as to lead to the conclusion that he made a selection from this and other similar *corpora* of his accumulated writings on theological subjects. As this MS was written in or near 1231, we can assign many of the *Dicta*, particularly those *ad clerum*, to the archidiaconal period, 1229–1232. Those written while he was still *in scolis* can best be ascribed to the period of his lectureship to the Franciscans, though there is no compelling reason why much of this material may not have been composed earlier. It would be difficult, on the other hand, without very good proof, to place any considerable amount of it before 1220. His interests in mathematics and science must have remained predominant until about that date.

Another fact of no small interest comes to light from a comparative examination of the *Dicta* and Grosseteste's *Commentarius in Psalmos*, which exists in its entirety, so far as is known, in only two MSS: Eton Coll. MS 8 and Bologna, Archiginnasio MS A. 893 (see above, p. 75 f.). Into this haphazard commentary have been incorporated thirty-seven of these articles which Grosseteste has collected as *Dicta*. As suggested above (p. 76), the lack of organization would best be explained if we suppose a pupil or friend to have been responsible for the assembling of the *commentarius* out of sayings of Grosseteste, or perhaps from random notes in the bishop's own hand.

Twenty-seven of the *Dicta* are either rubricked as sermons in the MSS of the 147 *Dicta*; are clearly sermons from their text; or appear in MSS separately as sermons.

We have a great number of MSS of the whole collection, but none earlier than 1300. The work was evidently more congenial to the preacher of the fourteenth and fifteenth centuries; it was indeed in such demand that a standardized *tabula* of subjects with references to the text, divided into 333 sections, was assembled, and appears in many of the later MSS, prefixed, usually, to the text.*

IV. MSS:

Oxford				
Bodl.	798	ff. 1A–121B + *tabula*	XIV²	Asc.
	830	ff. 1A–137A + *tabula*†	XIV²	Asc.
Digby	218	ff. 94C–97C (*tabula* only)	XIV²	Unasc.
Laud Misc.	374	ff. 4C–191C	*ca.* 1400	Asc.
Balliol	35B	f. 114A	1443	Asc.‡
Exeter	21	pp. 1a–70a + *capitula*	XV¹	*Mut. in init.*
Lincoln	56	ff. 2a–127b + *tabula*	XV¹	Asc.
Magdalen	202	ff. 4C–120D + *tabula*	*ca.* 1400	Asc.
London, B.M.				
Cotton	Otho D. x	ff. 65a–147a + *tabula*	XIVm	Asc.
Royal	5. C. III	ff. 184A–229C	XV¹	Asc.§
	7. D. xv	ff. 1a–60b	XIII²	Asc.
Cambridge				
Univ.	Ff. iii. 15	ff. 1a–193a	*ca.* 1500	Asc.‖
	Ii. ii. 27	ff. 112A–199B + *tabula*	XIV²	Asc.
C.C.C.	257	ff. 9a–179b + *tabula*	XIV²	Asc.
Gonv. & Caius	83	ff. 1A–119C + *tabula*	XV¹	Asc.
	380	ff. 1A–139B + *tabula*	XIV²	Asc.
Pembroke	245	ff. 5A–159A + *tabula*	*ca.* 1400	Asc.
Peterhouse	204, pt. ii	ff. 1A–79D + *tabula*	XV¹	Asc.
Trinity	B. 15. 20	cols. 1–357	XIV²	Asc.
	B. 15. 20*	ff. 766D–883B	XIV²	Asc.
	B. 15. 38	ff. 35a–42a	XIIIm	Asc.
	O. 4. 40	ff. 9A–167B + *tabula*	XV¹	Asc.
Eton Coll.	117, vol. 1	pp. 1a–205a + *tabula*	XV¹	Asc.
Lincoln Cath.	68	ff. 181b–190a	XIV²	Asc.¶
	180	ff. 1A–5A, *tabula* only	XIV²	Asc.
	188	ff. 14A–144A + *tabula*	XIV²	Asc.
	202	ff. 18A–141C + *tabula*	XIVm	Asc.**
Cracow, Jagellon.	1601	pp. 22–299	1416	Asc. Boh.

* J. Loserth used Prague Univ. MS 409 of the *Dicta* in his "Johann von Wiclif und Robert Grosseteste", *Sbte d. kais. Akad.*, Phil.-hist. Kl., Bd. 86, 2. Abh. (Vienna, 1918), but restricted himself to the *Dicta* published by Brown.

† The *tabula*, almost as often as not, precedes the text. In a few cases it is in another part of the codex. I have not thought it necessary to specify in each case.

‡ Has only the last five lines of the *Dicta*. See above, p. 134 f., under *Moralitates*.

§ Selected *dicta* only. See under Sermons, above, pp. 170, 173.

‖ Purports to contain *additamenta* of Thomas Rotherham († 1500), Bishop of Lincoln, 1471–1480. The additions are not considerable.

¶ *Tabula* and *prohemium* only.

** No. 464 of the MSS of the Earl of Kingston, destroyed by fire at Thoresby, April 4, 1745, bore the title *Robt. Grosthead seu Grouthead Episc. Lincoln. Dicta et Sermones CC. 5.*

Prague				
Univ.	409	ff. 71^{A}–224^{D}+ *tabula*	1414	Asc. Boh.
	470	ff. 1^{A}–160^{B}	1414	Asc. Boh.
	1444	ff. 4^{C}–124^{C}+ *tabula*	1414	Asc. Boh.
	1450	ff. 12^{A}–153^{B}	1407	Asc. Boh.
	1456	ff. 1^{A}–193^{D}	*ca.* 1410	Asc. Boh.
	1740	ff. 1^{A}–164^{A}	*ca.* 1410	Asc. Boh.
	1963	ff. 1^{a}–205^{b}	1414	Asc. Boh.
	2302	ff. 1^{A}–141^{B}	1419	Asc. Boh.
Metrop. Chap.	509	ff. 1^{A}–172^{C}	XV^{i}	Asc. Boh.
Nat. Mus.	XII. E. 5	ff. 44^{A}–71^{A}	XIV^{m}	Asc. Boh.*

In the following list a reference like "Sermon 66" means that the *Dictum* has also been listed among the Sermons, above, p. 180.

1. Amor multipliciter videtur dici. Consuevimus enim dicere amorem ... × ... cum dicuntur amare pecunias et cibos et homines.

On the true nature of Christian love.

2. Misericordia est amor sive voluntas relevandi miserum a sua miseria ... × ... sicut dicit scriptura: Date elimosinam et ecce omnia munda... Luc. ii.

Sermon 55. On the fruits of mercy. A sermon, appearing in the early collection, Royal 7. D. xv. See above, p. 179.

3. Sacerdotes tui induantur iusticiam. Versus iste generaliter competit ... × ... induti epulemur et conregnemus cum eo per infinita secula seculorum.

Sermon 66. On the perfect righteousness of the priesthood: the need for a perfect morality as an example to the laity. Brown, II, 301–305.

4. Mali vellent queque agant prava recta et iusta esse... × ... perpetuam penam propter perpetuitatem sue prave voluntatis.

Sermon 57, appearing in the early collection, Royal 7. D. xv. How the evil desire their works to appear righteous; on the gravity of venial as well as mortal sin. See above, p. 179. Quoted by Wyclyf, *De Civ. Dom.* IV, 517 ff.

5. Iudicia de hiis que possunt bene et male fieri secundum diversas intenciones... × ... ob eius iusticiam ad penam non iudicabimur.

How Satan would have us espouse Pride, appealing to us falsely through our reason.

6. Secundum Augustinum: Mendacium est cum quis aliud habet in animo... × ... in cinerem fumumque exalant quasi adhuc ardeant.

Sermon 58, appearing in the early collection, Royal 7. D. xv. How great a sin is falsehood in word or deed. See above, p. 179. Quoted by Wyclyf, *De Civ. Dom.* I, 342.

* The scribe of this MS was evidently cognizant of the relation between Grosseteste's *Comm. in Psal.* and the *Dicta*. On f. 64^{B}, after giving the titles of *Dicta* 102–107, he has written *require in psalterio*. The same *renvoi* occurs for *Dicta* 112, 117, 119, 121, 122 and 140. So far as I know, so close a familiarity with the works of the bishop is shown by no other medieval scribe.

7. Quinque sensus porte sunt per quas intrat mors ut dicit Ieremias 9: Mors... × ...introducit celebratque canticum laudis et exultacionis.

A similitude: how the senses, like gates, allow mortal sins to enter. See above, p. 184, no. 9.

8. Respectus dei est eius cognicio et voluntas tollendi tenebras culpe ... × ...reminisci facit et arefacta aromatica fragrare facit.

"Like a ray of the sun which dissipates the shadows of sin and evil desire."

9. Velociter currit sermo eius. Sermo interior in sermone exteriori ... × ...velud quibusdam pedibus motivum ipsum deportatur.

The word of God, *quasi pedibus*, carries the mind of the hearer from worldly to celestial things.

10. Emptor est qui rem in hunc usum factam ut detur pro re alia donat ... × ...precio a quibus de quo emendo liberavit et ad quid restituit.

Sermon 44. How God redeemed mankind. "The son of God bought and redeemed mankind from God the Father as from a just king, and from the devil a cruel tormentor, giving himself as a man as the price." Quoted by Wyclyf, *De Civ. Dom.* III, 284. See above, p. 178.

11. Qui seminat in benediccionibus.... Cor. 9. Semina autem... × ... et habebit penam debitam illicito appetitui voluptatis. I Cor. 7.

On the fruitfulness of charity.

12. Fraus palliata est in superficie omnibus formis consequentibus ... × ...omnique talium instrumenta manu gestat.

On the subversive power which deceit gives the deceiver.

13. Manus vestre pollute sunt sanguine.... Ysa. 59. Alieni sanguinis ... × ...sunt iniquitate quando particiones operum sunt pollute.

A similitude: as he who sheds another's blood is said to have another's blood on his hands, and as a man's life-blood is in his possessions, so he who takes another's property has his hands soiled with another's blood.

14. Fugit Matathias et filii eius in montes.... Mons frequenter in scriptura... × ...ascendentis et descendentis non prosequimur.

Sermon 67. A similitude: the ascent to the mount of celestial contemplation is strewn with ten stepping stones over which the religious, guided by his rule, will know how to climb. See above, p. 180.

15. Sompnus plerumque in scriptura peccatum signat ut in 1° Apostoli ... × ...nisi finis appropinquacionem non considerare.

How the Apostle Paul uses sleep as a figure for sin; how evil desires come upon us in our dreams; how, when we sleep, the fleeting things of this world take on the likeness of beatitude, but do not have it.

16. In Johanne scriptum est: Heri hora septima reliquit eum febris ... × ...oransque ibi pro filio suo infirmo sepe exauditur.

How the seventh hour signifies the beginning of the decline of the physical, outer man and of the passing of the vain and the transitory, and the beginning of the ascendance of the inner man, of hope, of our journey to the City of Consolation.

17. Contempnenda sunt hec mundana propter eorum velocem transitum ... × ... ne caritate in te extincta inimicus dei efficiaris.

How quickly the things in which men glory pass; how easily, like a river, they take us on *in mari penarum*; how the believer should beware of vain things. In the *Comm. in Psal.*, Eton MS 8, ff. 22[B]–23[A].

18. Paciencia est animi a molestiis inflexibilitas. Paciens enim est... × ... non solum in nobis paciencia sed eciam virtus quecumque alia.

How patience, more than an immobile bulwark, is an active force which sustains and guides the believer's soul. Brown, II, 293–295.

19. Vidi et ecce manus missa ad me.... Liber iste sacra scriptura est ... × ... completa sustinet ne vergant in detrimentum.

On the excellence of Holy Scripture. How the four senses of Scripture satisfy every need of the human mind, and Scripture itself is written on the human heart as the image of God and the figure of His substance.

20. Lucas dicit: Surrexit dominus vere.... Fuerunt heretici qui dixerunt ... × ... interpretatur obediens facta est Christi Dei et hominis manifestacio.

On the three principal errors concerning the resurrection: Docetism, of those who *dicebant illum fuisse verum hominem sed non vere mortuum*, of those who *dixerunt illum fuisse verum hominem ante passionem et vere mortuum in passione, sed in resurrexione non revixit homo sed totus fuit deificatus et in deitatis essenciam totaliter transivit.*

21. Osee ait 4: Non est veritas.... Hec terra que vacua est... × ... ad sanguinem attactu pretereundum est ad presens.

Sermon 68. Of the manifold nature of truth, and of the general unwillingness of mankind to seek it; how the absence of truth implies the presence of the vices flowing from *mendacium*, theft, murder and adultery. See above, p. 180.

22. Membrum corporis utpote oculus vel os vel manus dicitur... × ... geometria circulum aliter compotista et aliter poeta.

How the names of the diverse members of the body are used in various disciplines: in theology a member is so denominated when it performs fully the functions for which God made it. Each science construes differently an identical term.

23. Cum humilitas sit amor persistendi in ordine sibi congruo... × ... humilitatis nostre flumine ipsum aspergendo.

On the pervasive influence of humility: the example of Christ. Brown, II, 292 f.

24. Quedam sunt que possunt et bene et male fieri secundum... × ... visus penetrat, intima apparent manifeste sordibus plena.

On the danger of judgments based on insufficient knowledge.

25. Habitantibus in regione umbre.... Ysa. 9. Ad intelligenciam huius ... × ... oculi mentales humani poterant sustinere.

How spiritual death has its rise in the will of the reasonable creature: a distorted will keeps the light of righteousness from the soul as shadows before the sun.

26. Optimus modus dandi est cum res data sub hac condicione... × ... non plene perfruemur nisi in patria.

How the virtue of giving is conditioned by the intention of the giver and the use made of it by the recipient. Quoted by Wyclyf, *De Dom. Div.* p. 213.

27. Debet unusquisque diligere proximum suum quantum se diligit ... × ... amor hominis spiritualis est odium hominis carnalis.

On the proper love of our fellows: "but the carnal man loves himself since he loves the pleasures of sense, of knowledge and of power".

28. Satisfaccio est ad honorem eius apud quem delictum est, solucio ... × ... sunt penalitates in satisfaccionem culpe portande.

On satisfaction: man could never satisfy God by works of mercy as penance for his sins, if he had not sinned and thus caused misery for which *opera misericordie* are necessary.

29. Corpus viri melius est et nobilius est quavis arbore... × ... non sunt naturales, sed nature bone corrupciones.

A man is more noble than the rest of creation, so the knowledge of his procreation is more noble and fine than a knowledge of the like processes of lower beings, but its abuse correspondingly ignoble.

30. Natus ad regnum nisi de genere esset... × ... nisi causa honesta et necessitatibus compellentibus.

A short paragraph. Unlike worldly kingdoms, any believer is heir to the heavenly kingdom.

31. Quies opponitur motui, sed requies proprie opponitur labori... × ... contrarium dignat nox et requies sabbati.

Exegesis of *quiescere* and *laborare*: how sin makes our labour more fatiguing.

32. Unumquodque operum nostrorum voluntariorum faciunt tria ... × ... operatur voluntas totum sapiencia totum potencia.

How *sapiencia, voluntas* and *amor* combine, in varying measure, in every voluntary act. A single paragraph. Quoted by Wyclyf, *De Mandatis Divinis*, p. 98.

33. Philippe, qui videt me.... Quia quantum quis agnoscit filium ... × ... hominis proprium licet non eius diffinicionem.

Of the confusion into which non-Christians must fall on the subject of the godhead: how only the doctrine of the Trinity clarifies this confusion.

34. Cum audienda est laus domini, debet auditor ab aula... × ... debet suscitare attencionem in audiente.

When God's praise may be heard, all vain and worldly sounds should be driven from our ears. A paragraph.

35. Exemplum esto fidelium.... Paulus doctor gencium solicitudinem ... × ... et conversacione et caritate et fide et castitate.

Sermon 69. Of the manifold responsibilities of priests and prelates toward their parishioners. Cf. Durham Cath. MS A. III. 12, ff. 78[D]–79[A], for a re-working or perhaps the original of this *Dictum*. Often entitled *Sermo ad clerum* (Wharton, etc. and MSS). Publ. Brown, II, 297–300. Quoted by Wyclyf in *De Mandatis Divinis*, p. 402 ff.

36. Ieiunium a cibis corporalibus parum aut nichil prodest... × ... numeraret ieiunium dicens: Ieiuno bis in sabbato.

Sermon 70. Abstinence from bodily foods is imperfect fasting: perfect fasting is a cheerful and pious abstinence from illicit desires and sins of the heart.

37. Comedite amici et bibite.... Consuetudo curialis est in conviviis ... × ... adversitatibus tollerat dicit Augustinus de laude caritatis.

Sermon 71. A similitude. On feasts: the true bread is the body of Christ, the true drink His blood; the true meat is Holy Scripture, the true milk the doctrine of our faith. See above, p. 180.

38. Pax vobis. Luc. 24. Consuetudo regum potentum est... × ... caro nostra simul exultabunt in deum vivum.

Sermon 72. How the peace of Christ is superior to the peace brought by the armies of the kings of this world: His is a peace brought by love, theirs by destruction. See above, p. 180.

39. Si quis iaceret super terram supinus impotens... × ... trahitur quid alium retrorsum cadens labitur.

A similitude: the sinner sunk in sin, as a weak man lying on the ground, lifting his hand for help, should accept help from God's proffered hand.

40. Anima quattuor virtutibus quasi camisia, pellicia, tunica et passio ... × ... et delicata est hillaritas bene operandi.

A similitude showing how the four virtues clothe the soul.

41. Prelati et doctores ecclesie in corpore Christi comparantur oculis ... × ... quanto minori affeccione tanto apparet munus.

Sermon 73. A similitude: as the eye guides the other members of the body, so should the clergy guide those members of the body of Christ who must depend on them. See above, p. 180.

42. Cor hominis est quod primum in eo fungitur... × ... in execucionibus negociorum sunt animosi.

On the diversity of meaning of "heart" in Scripture, literal and derived. A sermon. See p. 186, no. 36.

43. In civitate Jerusalem, anima scilicet, preest rex superior... × ... ut punirentur aliqui sed ut punicio vitaretur.

A similitude: the soul is a city, the king the reason of Scripture, the citizens the spiritual virtues, the walls the thought of the pains of Hell, the enemies the evil spirits that storm the walls by prompting the soul to vain pleasures. In the *Comm. in Psal.*, Eton MS 8, f. 38[A–C].

44. Johannes erat lucerna; similiter lucerne erant omnes sancti... × ... in vocem sponsi et non reflecteretur in se.

A similitude: a lamp must be lit and may be extinguished. God lights the believer's soul, but that light may be put out by vain curiosity, pride or evil desire.

45. Qui erant sub lege erant spiritualiter in nocte, quia inter oculos ... × ... sed ambulant in tenebris et nesciunt quo vadunt.

A similitude: the soul, like the starry heavens, has light and darkness; grace and faith, like the rays of the sun, dissipate the shadows of sin and doubt. In *Comm. in Psal.*, Eton MS 8, f. 4^{A-B}; also Durham Cath. A. III. 12, f. 4^{B}, five lines longer than in Eton MS.

46. Divites qui congregant superflua unde pauperes sustineri deberent ... × ... tales precidit bonis in loco eorum plantatis.

A short similitude: the rich who divert to their own use the property of the poor are like a parasite in the body which must be cut out and cast away. In Durham Cath. A. III. 12, f. 81^{D}. See p. 184.

47. Superbia est amor excellencie proprie. Humilitas est amor persistendi ... × ... inferioribus elementis et corruptibilibus perturbato.

How pusillanimity arises out of pride. Cf. *Dictum* 127.

48. Sicut vox exterior assumpta a verbo interiori eius signum ... × ... illius artis et invisibilis verbi visibile verbum.

A similitude: as the spoken word is but the sign of the inner word, so the sensible works of creation are signs of the invisible and eternal Word.

49. Caput anime est potencia memorandi, intelligendi, diligendi deum ... × ... dicitur acuet duram iram in lanceam.

Of the image of the Trinity in the sensible soul; of righteousness, love and prudence.

50. Ascendit deus in iubilacione.... Filius dei qui a sinu patris manens ... × ... superiori gradu omnes regule agendorum ad proximum.

Sermon 54. On the eight steps in the ascent of the soul: *fides, operacio misericordie, sciencia, abstinencia, paciencia, pietas, amor eternus* and *caritas*. Appears as *Sermo in ascensione domini* in Cambridge, Trin. Coll. MS B. 15. 38, ff. 35^{a}–38^{a}, and as Sermon 19 in Royal 7. D. XV, f. 42^{a-b}. See above, p. 179. It appears also partially in Bodl. 867, ff. 94^{b}–96^{a}. In the *Comm. in Psal.*, Eton MS 8, ff. 23^{D}–26^{B}, and in the Durham Cath. MS A. III. 12, ff. 109^{C}–110^{B}. See above, p. 187, no. 43; p. 189, no. 59; p. 190, no. 68.

51. Rex sapiens stabilimentum est.... Verba sunt sapientis, Sapiencie cap. 6 ... × ... firmam petram Dominum nostrum Jesum Christum.

Sermon 64. How the priesthood is in a sense a royal office, enjoying its prerogatives and obligations in things spiritual. *Secundum regis officium est subditos moribus informare: hoc expresse nobis convenit....* Quoted by Wyclyf, *De Mandatis Divinis*, p. 402 ff. Mentioned by Wharton, II, 345, as *Sermo ad clerum.* Publ. Brown, II, 258–260.

52. De hostio tabernaculi non exibitis septem diebus usque ad diem ... × ... caritate que nunquam excidit sine fine ferventes.

Sermon 74, to ordinands on the symbolism of the "door of the tabernacle" which may become, through pride, the door by which one leaves the militant Church, or, through humility and charity, the door into the Church triumphant. On the possibilities of the ministry. *Harum beatitudinum spiritualissimam mutacionem nunc michi videntur habere fratres minores qui in vite sancte excellencia admiranda de seipsis faciunt mirabilia. Simus igitur et nos eorum imitatores.... Commutemus in nobismetipsis regnum cupiditatis in regnum caritatis* (MS Bodl. 830, f. 45[B]). This is a stirring sermon.

53. Fenum signat hominem carnalem sicut dicit Ysay... × ...vero virtutum non sine verbi boni semine.

On contempt of the world. Cf. p. 183, no. 5. In the *Comm. in Psal.*, Eton MS 8, ff. 21[C]–22[B], and in Durham Cath. A. III. 12, f. 79[B–C] (twenty lines shorter than the *Dictum*).

54. Lingua hominis sapientis...sicut ait propheta.... Hic colamus ... × ...vero cum imperat quietem a tali mocione.

As a man speaketh so is he; how clean speech marks the believer. In the *Comm. in Psal.*, Eton MS 8, f. 26[B–D]; also in Durham Cath. A. III. 12, f. 115[A–B] (a third of the *Dictum*). See p. 188, no. 49.

55. Dedite in lucem gencium.... Verba sunt prophete que nunc recitat ... × ...quia quot membrorum est capiti attribuitur.

On John the Baptist: the four kinds of light that illumine the world; how John was the bearer of the light of a life of repentance.

56. Bonitas que opponitur malicie vel viciositati est amor ordinatus ... × ...iniustus est qui a regno iusticie ipsum repellit.

A morality: of the fruits of ordinate love; how it is the source of the cardinal virtues. In Durham Cath. MS A. III. 12, f. 13[B]–14[B], in variant form, and f. 81[A–B] *partim*. See also above, p. 184, no. 13.

57. Quid appetibilium non confert timor domini vis sapienciam... × ... ne pereas si amas, time ne displiceas.

A morality: how fear worketh wisdom and wisdom salvation, even if the fear be only fear of punishment.

58. Si oculus corporalis eget et non plene sanus posset... × ...eger non est potens ad eandem perfecte videndam.

A short similitude on the health and sickness in the eye of the body and the eye of the mind. In *Comm. in Psal.*, Eton MS 8, ff. 13[C]–14[A]; also in Durham Cath. A. III. 12, ff. 7[D]–8[B], in lower margin.

59. Egritudinem oculi dicimus quandoque aut humorem... × ...sint alie morborum divisiones et cetera.

On the essential nature of sickness: a departure from the perfect natural state. A single paragraph.

60. Omnis creatura speculum est, de quo resultat similitudo... × ...hic incepit edificare et non potuit consummare.

On the similarity of the mind of man to the Trinity: memory, intelligence and love. A characteristically Augustinian exposition.

61. Conclude elemosinam.... Elemosina in sinu pauperis... × ...sed eciam ipsius erogacionem approbancium.

How almsgiving is salutary for the recipient.

62. Sicut boni predestinati scribuntur in libro vite et in celo ... × ... veri sunt in sermone prophetico intelliguntur.

What it means for the righteous to be written in the book of life and the evil in the book of this world.

63. Cum quis a deo recedit abiit cum filio prodigo in regionem ... × ... non sibi dissimilis asperima oculis egris.

How, like the Prodigal Son, the sinner departs from God, yet is drawn back by his own need and the Father's love.

64. Conceperunt laborem et pepererunt iniquitatem. Verbum est non solum ... × ... dicit: reverte ad me et ego suscipiam te. Jer. 3.

A similitude: how thoughts, like seeds, grow into something much bigger. Satan plants evil thoughts in the mind and they grow into evil deeds. In the *Comm. in Psal.*, Eton MS 8, ff. 5ᴰ–6ᴬ, and see p. 183.

65. Qui honorat servum alicuius in quantum servus eius est ... × ... dant sua bona nequicie peccato et diabolo.

How honour given to charlatans and quacks is honour given to Satan. A short paragraph.

66. Diabolus et vicia fortissima sunt ad tenendum prostratum ne surgat ... × ... unus spiritus cum deo sunt longe debiliora.

A morality: on the power of vices and the Devil to keep even a strong man from rising out of his bondage to sin; how they are unable to pull down a man who is standing upright, strong in his righteousness.

67. Omnia opera nostra in amore magnitudinis nostre radicantur ... × ... vestit, esurientes pascit ceteraque opera misericordie facit.

A morality: the two sources of all our deeds are either charity or pride.

68. Opera bona extra caritatem facta, licet non mereantur celum tamen ... × ... misericordie exhibentes promereri non possunt sibi.

How every good work, even if not arising out of charity, has a certain inherent goodness, even if the doer is evilly actuated.

69. Caritas est amor rectus et amor rectus est amor recti ... × ... ab omni insultu insuperabile omniaque possidentem.

Of the different ways in which those actuated by charity and those actuated by pride or evil desires love and fear God.

70. Iusticia reddit unicuique quod suum est sed nunquid in potestate ... × ... graciosam sive pro male meritis penam iustam.

How justice demands that each shall have what is his, and receive the just deserts for his deeds. In *Comm. in Psal.*, Eton MS 8, f. 8ᴮ⁻ᶜ.

71. Pulcra ut luna. Luna gerit tipum tam ecclesie et cuiuslibet ... × ... sunt prelati quos premunt diviciarum onera.

On the figurative use in Scripture of the moon for the Church, the soul and the Blessed Virgin. In the *Comm. in Psal.*, Eton MS 8, f. 8ᴬ; also in Durham Cath. A. III. 12, ff. 5ᴮ–6ᴬ and ff. 85ᴰ–86ᴮ. See p. 185, no. 27.

72. Nonne cor nostrum ardens.... Verba sunt duorum discipulorum ... × ... sermone exteriori et exponit scripturas duplici sermone interiori.

Sermon 53. How those illumined by the divine fire regard temporal things as foolishness; how the believer should know this divine fire when it comes to him.

73. Vinum bonum dat nutrimentum corpori, sanitatem reddit... × ... deducet me in lucem videbo iusticiam eius.

On the salutary properties of good wine: how it clarifies sluggish blood and makes us forget our needless melancholy. In the *Comm. in Psal.*, Eton MS 8, f. 39^{B-D}. This is of a piece with Grosseteste's recommendation to a too often penitent friar that a glass of good wine occasionally would help to order his conscience better. *Mon. Franciscana*, I, 64; see also Stevenson, p. 333.

74. Est autem iusticia triplex, prima est que consistit in doctrina... × ... coram ipso sed ex fide per dileccionem operante.

On the threefold nature of righteousness: observance of laws of human reason; external observance of the commandments of God; righteousness dictated by obedience to Scripture and guided by charity.

75. Est ira duplex quia simpliciter ira est appetitus pene... × ... de priori dicitur irascimini et nolite peccare.

On the twofold nature of wrath: a desire for pain to oneself as a purge; a desire for pain to another. A short paragraph.

76. Domine deus meus exaltasti.... Terra est caro hominis... × ... mundum in celo conversantur cum angelis.

A contrast between those whose lives are of the earth earthy and those whose thoughts are raised to heavenly things.

77. Pupilla est pura cordis intencio in deum sive ipsa intelligencia... × ... delectat frigus quod est privacio ardoris concupiscencie.

A comparison between the eye of the spirit and the eye of the flesh. In the *Comm. in Psal.*, Eton MS 8, f. 10^{C-D}; also in Durham Cath. A. III. 12, f. 6^{D} and f. 87^{B}. See above, p. 185, no. 30.

78. Calore solis elevatur vapor de terra et aquis marinis qui... × ... potestatem claudendi celum nubibus ne pluat.

A similitude: how Christ is signified by a cloud. The warmth of the sun is the grace of the Holy Spirit which raises and purifies our desire. Yet there is the great difference that earthly clouds lose by giving off rain. In the *Comm. in Psal.*, Eton MS 8, ff. 10^{D}–11^{A}; also Durham Cath. A. III. 12, ff. 7^{A} and 87^{C-D}. See p. 186, no. 32.

79. Ignis aliquando zelum dei exprimit, aliquando spiritum sanctum ... × ... est species elementorum et caritas forma virtutum.

Of the various properties of fire and how these properties correspond to the Holy Spirit, charity, cupidity, malice, understanding, wrath, trial and carnal passion. In *Comm. in Psal.*, Eton MS 8, f. 11^{A-D}; also Durham Cath. A. III. 12, ff. 7^{B-C} and 87^{D}. See above, p. 185, no. 33.

80. Molendus est animus inter spem et timorem quasi inter duas molas ... × ... qui de uno pane et de uno calice participamus.

A similitude: how the soul of man must be ground between hope of eternal salvation and fear of punishment as between two millstones.

81. Cervus signat viros sanctos deum desiderantes, unde Psalmus: Sicut cervus... × ... induerit immortalitatem et corruptibilis homo incorrupcionem.

A morality: On the habits and qualities of the deer and the serpent. In the *Comm. in Psal.*, Eton MS 8, ff. 11[D]–12[C]; also Durham Cath. A. III. 12, ff. 7[C]–8[A].

82. Miserere mei domine quoniam.... Psal. 6. Stimulus ad orandum ... × ... et testimonium quia superbis deus resistit.

On the extrinsic need for prayer: the shortness of life, the infirmities of the flesh and our limited knowledge. In the *Comm. in Psal.*, Eton MS 8, ff. 4[D]–5[C]; also Durham Cath. A. III. 12, f. 4[C–D].

83. Passer a parvitate vocatus passer est nimia velocitate celerimus ... × ... dic ut lapides isti panes fiant.

A similitude: how by its sagacity in evading capture, its willingness to take refuge and its love for the heights, the sparrow may be said to resemble the nobler believer.

84. Ex usuris adquisicionem iniustam esse et non quam patefacit auctoritas... × ... inter scopulos ac latencia saxa demergens.

A short treatise on usury. The selling price of an article should not be determined by expectation of its future value, but by its present value.

85. Vas eleccionis est mihi ille.... Vas consuevit fieri de massa solida ... × ... amatorum mundi vilia sunt et abiecta.

In praise of the apostle Paul; on the meaning of "a chosen vessel".

86. Nolite esse prudentes apud vosmetipsos... quia hec est bonitas se et... × ... ad curandum et sanandum adhibita est medicina.

On the obligation incumbent on every man, as a member of a body, to help and not to harm his fellow members.

87. Hortamur vos ne in vacuum.... Gracia dei est bona voluntas ... × ... hic inflictas dum est locus penitencie murmurant.

Sermon 52. How the gifts of God should not be abused; how the righteous man owns all things, the unrighteous nothing. See above, p. 179.

88. Ioth (Yas) grece, ut dicit Ysodorus, venenum dicitur et inde aspis... × ... erga homines deus exercuit mutari neglexit.

A disquisition on the habits of the asp: how it hides in caverns and stops its ears against the voice of the enchanter. In *Comm. in Psal.*, Eton MS 8, ff. 8[C]–9[B]; also in Durham Cath. A. III. 12, ff. 6[B–D] and 86[D]–87[B]. See above, p. 185, no. 29.

89. Apparuerunt apostolis dispartite lingue.... Quia spiritus sancti adventum... × ... desiderio ut sit in gloria sine fine nostra conversacio.

Sermon 75. On the descent of the Holy Spirit in tongues of fire upon the apostles; on the principal properties of fire: heat and light, and the significance of these properties to the secular and regular clergy.

90. Ezech. xxxiv. Ve pastoribus Israel.... In sermone quem postremo loquebar... × ...non que Christi sed que sua sunt querunt plus hiis.

Sermon 76. The opening sentences of this sermon indicate that an immediately preceding sermon has treated the matter of what constitutes a good pastor. But as that is not the distinctive subject-matter of *Dictum* 89, it is difficult to place this sermon with regard to the antecedent. This sermon elaborates on what constitutes a bad pastor. It is rather long. Publ. Brown, II, 263–267.

91. Simon, diligis me.... In penultimo sermone quem feci vestre caritati... × ...qui est via, veritas et vita, Dominus noster Jesus Christus....

Sermon 77. A sequel to the preceding sermon (*Dictum* 90). On the nature of spiritual love: why and how the believer should love God and Christ.

92. Cum dolor sit sensus absencie appetiti lacrima que ex dolore... × ... viciorum tollunt et fluxum luxurie arefaciunt.

On the virtue of suffering the pains and misery of life gladly: tears are or should be commensurate with the guilt. In Durham Cath. A. III. 12, f. 3^{B-C}.

93. In semine est virtus inclinativa ad formam et ad speciem... × ...de parte non seminabili singulariter fiat.

How Christ, free from the taint of concupiscent generation, could not have been in Adam or Abraham by *racio seminalis*. Cf. Wyclyf, *De Statu Innocencie*, p. 502.

94. Paupertas generaliter dicta est defectus vel carencia rei... × ...sunt omnes thesauri sapiencie et sciencie absconditi.

On the three kinds of poor: those who lack worldly possessions yet without desiring them; those who have such possessions but love them with a moderate love—these are poor in spirit; those who lack, but desire, these things. On the real poverty of Christ. In *Comm. in Psal.*, Eton MS 8, f. 6^{B-D}; also Durham Cath. A. III. 12, ff. 3^{A} and 81^{B-C}, where the subject is continued for two more columns, to f. 82^{A}; see above, p. 184 f.

95. Ambo huius scuti fulget luce inaccessibili angelus... × ...dabis eis scutum cordis laborem tuum.

On the shield of faith, accompanied by a diagram. In Durham Cath. A. III. 12, f. 14^{A-B}.

96. Bona voluntas generalis qua vult homo esse talis... × ...scuti proprii est dexterum cornu scuti amici.

On the significance of the shield of good will; of the excellence of loving protection of one's friend. In Durham Cath. A. III. 12, f. 15^{A-B}.

97. Frumentum granum tritici hanc habet proprietatem ab omnibus ... × ...verbum quasi saniem per os digestum valet.

A comparison between the growth and functions of grain and man. In the *Comm. in Psal.*, Eton MS 8, f. 40^{B-C}.

98. Folium verbum signat iuxta illud: Et folium eius non defluet... × ... De fructu oris homo saciabitur bonis.

A similitude: how the word of God is like a leaf adorning and protecting a tree, likened unto the believer. In the *Comm. in Psal.*, Eton MS 8, f. 2^{B-D}; also in Durham Cath. A. III. 12, ff. 2^{D}–3^{A}.

99. Mons signat dominum salvatorem, unde Isa. 2: Erit in novissimis ... × ... que in fine credet quando reliquie salve fient.

On the many figurative senses of mountain in Scripture: the Saviour, the Church, holy men, heretical teaching, the Jewish people, etc. In the *Comm. in Psal.*, Eton MS 8, ff. 2^{D}–3^{D}; also Durham Cath. A. III. 12, ff. 3^{D}–4^{A}.

100. Johannes in Apocal. 21 ait: Fundamentum primum iaspis. Iaspidum ... × ... in humilium animo memoria designatur.

On the twelve stones of the Apocalypse, their figurative uses in Scripture and the Fathers. In the *Comm. in Psal.*, Eton MS 8, ff. 32^{D}–37^{D}; also Durham Cath. A. III. 12, ff. $115^{C–D}$ and 116^{A}–118^{A} (parts). See above, p. 188 f., nos. 51, 54, 56, 58.

101. Filius dei volens ostendere ad quid nos prelatos plebi sui prefecit ... × ... in corruptibilem velut obolum minimum mutatum aureum.

Sermon 79. On the pastoral office; how Christ exemplified the true pastor. Quoted by Wyclyf, *De Mandatis Divinis*, p. 43. Publ. Brown, II, 260–263.

102. Ab altitudine diei timebo ego.... Ps. 99. Dies est sol lucens super terram... × ... sapiencie parvitas et oblivionis multitudo.

A similitude: how the distance of the sun from us, his changing orbit, his varying warmth, signify Christ and His light. In the *Comm. in Psal.*, Eton MS 8, ff. 29^{A}–30^{B}; also Durham Cath. A. III. 12, f. $121^{A–B}$. See above, p. 189, no. 67.

103. Recte iudicate filii.... Ps. 58. Si vis recte iudicare primo considera ... × ... ne incurvemini sub vinculo et cum interfectis cadatis.

Sermon 80. On the qualities demanded of a judge: love of truth, impartiality, courage, patience and the fear of God the Supreme Judge. In *Comm. in Psal.*, Eton MS 8, ff. 38^{C}–39^{B}. Publ. Brown, II, 274–276. Wharton, II, 345, mentions a *Dictum de bono judice in Psal. LVII.* I (a slip for "LVIII"?).

104. Laudare aliquem est bona opera bone et recte voluntatis eius ... × ... scit infinita sicut expresse dicit Augustinus in libro de Civ. Dei.

Why, in general, a person should be praised; more specifically how we praise any reflection of God in His creatures, and therefore, with *laus stans perpetua*, God Himself. In *Comm. in Psal.*, Eton MS 8, ff. 31^{C}–32^{B}; also Durham Cath. A. III. 12, f. $119^{B–D}$. See above, p. 189, no. 62.

105. Ysopus calidus est in tercio gradu. Valet contra catarrum et vocis raucidinem... × ... et gloriam que a solo deo est non vultis.

A similitude: humility, like hyssop with its many curative qualities, is the remedy for the ills brought on by pride. In the *Comm. in Psal.*, Eton MS 8, f. $30^{B–D}$; also in Durham Cath. A. III. 12, ff. 119^{D}–120^{A}. See above, p. 189, no. 64.

106. Cor contritum non conteritur nisi quod durum est et frangibile ... × ... ut petram durissimam et scio quoniam non confundar.

How the hardness of the sinner's heart may be softened, as it were, in a mortar, by the threefold pestle of shame, the ugliness of the sin and remorse. In the *Comm. in Psal.*, Eton MS 8, ff. 30^{D}–31^{C}; also Durham Cath. A. III. 12, f. $120^{A–C}$. See above, p. 189, no. 65.

107. Psalmo 54 legitur: Quis mihi dabit pennas sicut columbe? Rabanus ait... × ...quodammodo astucias prevideat, agnoscat et declinet.

On the figurative meanings of "dove" in Scripture: God, the Holy Spirit, the Apostles, the Jews and charity. In Durham Cath. A. III. 12, ff. 120[C]–121[A]. See above, p. 189, no. 66.

108. Preibis enim ante faciem domini.... Luc. 2°. Vita vestra quibus sermo... × ...dei glorificacio ad patriam de exilio reduccio.

Sermon 78. On the life of penance: how the religious shows his hatred of sin; how satisfaction is the release of a debt to one against whom we have sinned.

109. Theos grece deus latine et mutatur aspiratum in *d* et *o* in *u*... × ... quia beati pacifici quoniam filii dei vocabuntur.

On the derivation of *deus* from the Greek θεός which in turn may come from *theo*=*curro*, or *themotis*=*caliditas*, or *letor*, or *pono*; a brief moral interpretation of each meaning.

110. Castrimargia nomen grecum est unde derivatur hoc nomen... × ... a lemos quod est guttur quasi gutturis insania.

On the derivation of *castrimargia*. Aristotle's reference to *margos* in the *De Animalibus*. On the difference between *castrimargia* and *lemargia*, the two Greek words for gluttony.

111. In Iob legitur quod fuerunt ei tres filie et quod vocavit Iob... × ... quod ei splendeo et inde dicitur margarita.

A short comparative study of the names of the three daughters of Job as given in the Vulgate and the LXX. This has every indication of having been composed at about the same time as the *Comm. in Galathas*. See above, p. 73.

112. Dominus est protector meus dans scutum paciencie, quod scutum ... × ... vicia singula cum virtutibus conveniunt.

A description of the three shields: patience, i.e. the internal shield; the external shield of fear, weakness and ignorance; a third but false shield of pride, bearing the vices simulating their corresponding virtues. In the *Comm. in Psal.*, Eton MS 8, ff. 37[D]–38[A]; also Durham Cath. A. III. 12, f. 115[D] (part). See above, p. 188, no. 52. Publ. Brown, II, 276–280.

113. Prophecia maxime proprie dicta videtur esse futurorum... × ... lateret eum veritas quam determinate pronunciavit.

On the nature of prophecy; on Paul's vision on the road to Damascus; on true and false prophets. Publ. Brown, II, 281–284.

114. Qui a veritate recedit ad fallaciam arcium magicarum... × ...in primis tollat et sic ab errore fallacie revocet.

How easily we are misled by an occasional realized hope into thinking that the arts of magic have power over events.

115. Quelibet bona congregacio conventualis arbori bone assimilari potest... × ...arbor mala que excidetur et in ignem mittetur.

A similitude: how a good convent may be likened to a sound tree: the knowledge and will of the abbot is the heart of the tree, the knowledge and love of a single rule is a root, the love of being governed by these rules is the force drawing the food from the earth through the roots, etc.

116. Exequie et sepulcrorum construccio non prosunt defunctis ut scribitur... × ...defunctis facta nunquid pro eisdem fieri possunt?

A question: funerals and tombs are supposed to be of no benefit to the dead, yet they are called "good works" if done *ex caritate*, but other *opera meritoria* are supposed to benefit the dead. There seems to be some confusion in our current doctrine.

117. Idem est lapis in terra quod os in carne, stabilimentum scilicet et firmitas... × ...margarita inventa dat omnia sua et comparat eam.

A similitude: how Christ is the solid adamantine rock around which the earth (the human race) is made; the earth is not pure rock as Christ is not pure man; of the many qualities of this rock. In the *Comm. in Psal.*, Eton MS 8, f. 32^{B-D}; also Durham Cath. A. III. 12, f. 115^{B-C}. See above, p. 188 no. 50.

118. Omnis sciencia sillogistica est sicut rethe contextum secundum ... × ...ad que de vagitate et tenebris fluminis attrahentur.

On the nature and functions of a net: how the syllogism is like a triangular net (from Aristotle, *Prior Analytics*, I): how theology turns the syllogism to spiritual uses and catches in its net *pisces spiritales* who are willingly caught.

119. Crux domini nostri Ihesu Christi signum appellatur frequenter in scriptura... × ...polluta est; convenienter in sanguine dicitur esse polluta.

Sermon 56. On the significance of the Cross: the meaning of the four arms of the Cross; how the believer should take to himself this figure of the Cross and crucify the flesh. In *Comm. in Psal.*, Eton MS 8, ff. 16^{D}–19^{B}; also Durham Cath. A. III. 12, ff. 10^{C}–12^{A}, both lacking the last paragraph.

120. Mare mundum turbulentum signat, unde Jonas 9: Proicite me ... × ...quibusdam quasi pinnulis in anteriora se extendit.

On the diverse meanings of "sea" in Scripture and the Fathers: baptism, the human race, the Church; the latter sense a significant figure, where the good and bad features are aptly typified.

121. Ursus dictus quod ore suo formet fetus quasi orsus, nam informes ... × ...similitudinem tu filios tuos instituere tibi similes non potes.

On the figurative significance of the bear, his qualities and habits. In the *Comm. in Psal.*, Eton MS 8, f. 6^{B}.

122. Leo dicitur a leon grece quod est rex latine, quia ipse est rex bestiarum... × ...album predicatorem scilicet castum maxime veretur.

On the noble qualities of the lion: how the lion typifies Christ the King of kings; how Satan is the king of the children of pride. In the *Comm. in Psal.*, Eton MS 8, f. 5^{C-D}; also Durham Cath. A. III. 12, ff. 5^{A-B} and 113^{A-B}. See above, p. 187, no. 47.

123. Vitis plantacionem Noe primus adinvenit. Dicta est: vitis quia vini... × ...sciencie sicut vinum sibi fructiferum fructificat.

A similitude: how the vine typifies the *plebs ecclesie*, with its roots, leaves and fruit.

124. Secundum Aristotelem sapor videtur fieri exaccione suci terrei ... × ... sine sapore et dulcedine mediocre.

A morality: on the essence of flavour: of the relation of flavour to nutritive value; how sweetness is wisdom incarnate and how the soul is nourished by this sweetness.

125. Sanctorum congregacio terra vivencium est que bene terre comparatur... × ... operibus exterioribus fructificantes supportant.

A similitude: how the congregation of the saints, like the elements of the terrestrial universe, are all drawn toward a centre, which is Christ. In the *Comm. in Psal.*, Eton MS 8, f. 8[A–B]; also Durham Cath. A. III. 12, f. 6[A].

126. Interrogatus unusquisque vestrum an desideraret et deligeret societatem... × ... insensibiliores brutis magis irracionabiles et posteriores.

How in our ignorance we so often rejoice the evil spirits by our sins, and actually join forces with them against the *celestes cives*.

127. Superbia est amor excellencie proprie cum scilicet aliquis vel superiorem... × ... filii dei qui semetipsum formam servi accipiens exinanivit.

A longer essay on pride (see *Dictum* 47), its degrees and terrible effects; how the roots of pride may be removed by considering our infirmities and knowing that what is good in us is ours by grace. Publ. Brown, II, 285 f.

128. De superbia que est amor excellencie proprie nascitur invidia ... × ... qui omnes a vicio detraccionis non sint immunes.

How pride is the source of jealousy, the evil of invidious criticism of others. In *Comm. in Psal.*, Eton MS 8, ff. 9[D]–10[C]; also Durham Cath. A. III. 12, ff. 6[A–B] and 86[B–D]. See above, p. 185, no. 28. Publ. Brown, II, 287 f.

129. Colleccio creditorum ad iusticiam que unum fidei corpus consistit ... × ... non est alia fides sed eadem antiquorum et nostra.

What is meant by an "article of faith": the details of our faith cannot be believed without being known: they are based on Scripture which it is the believer's duty to know *in parvo et in magno*. Publ. Brown, II, 281.

130. In omni operacione dei est prestacio alicuius boni non debiti ei cui ... × ... tanto ei qui vindicatur maioris boni prestacio.

How God's punishment, however well deserved, is often actuated by mercy; how God's rewards are given more out of mercy than from the just merits of the receiver. Publ. Brown, II, 295 f.

131. Verbum et sapiencia patris, Ihesus Christus, assimulat se plantacioni ... × ... roborabitur ad videndum lumen divinitatis eius.

Sermon 48. A similitude: How Christ in His passion was like a rose. The five leaves covering it may be likened to the five books of the Mosaic law under which Christ lived until the time of His *expansio in cruce*. See above, p. 178.

132. Homo integratur ex anima et corpore constante ex omnibus membris... × ... idem pectus et integrum post coste ablacionem.

Wherein consists the wholeness of a man: not in size or weight or number of bones, but in completeness of function and in fulfilment of the purposes of a given member.

133. Sentire pollucionem in sompnis et sentire fluxum seminis per morbum... × ...castitatem in mentis habitu sed non in corporis actu.

On the grades of chastity: on conjugal chastity and the divine purpose of marriage. How the Fathers of the early Church were as chaste as modern virgins *in habitu mentis*, but, because of the need to propagate the people of God, *non in corporis actu*. This is without doubt the *De Pollucione Nocturna* listed by Bale and Tanner.

134. Gracia est bona voluntas dei qua vult nobis dare quod non meruimus ... × ...per motum tum per solis radios tum per confricacionem.

On the gifts of God's grace: how man is justified by God's choice *ab eterno*: what is *gracia gratificans* and the grades of grace. The last paragraph seems extraneous and is essentially the argument found in *De Motu Corporali et Luce*, Baur, pp. 90–92. Quoted by Wyclyf, *De Dom. Divino*, pp. 236 ff., 247 ff. This *dictum* appears separately as *De Triplici Gracia* in Cambridge, Gonv. and Caius MS 131, pp. 79–80, *ca.* 1425, in the hand of Walter Crome (this MS cited by Tanner); also in Eton MS 117, ff. 206[a]–207[b], XV[1], Asc. Publ. Brown, II, 282.

135. Despondi vos uni viro virginem castam exhibere Christo. Virgo hec... × ...in vinculo pacis permaneamus per infinita secula seculorum.

Sermon 62 (q.v., p. 179). *Sermo ad conventum monachorum.*

136. Orare est exprimere alicui mentis desiderium quo desideratur ab eo... × ...sacco et cinere quos abiecimus saccum alium, et cinerem adiungamus.

On prayer. How the inner desire and the expression should be one. The laity, not knowing the meaning of the Lord's prayer that they repeat, should fervently desire truly good things for themselves and others; how we should express repentance for our sins in our prayers. Publ. Brown, II, 283 f.

137. Posuit stellas in firmamento celi. Vos minores prelati stelle firmamenti... × ...introducatis in curiam regis celorum...gloria in secula seculorum.

Sermon 63 (q.v., p. 179). Publ. Brown, II, 268–270.

138. Sint lumbi vestri precincti et lucerne ardentes in manibus... × ...in bonorum operum execucione ad gloriam domini nostri Jesu Christi.

Sermon 65 (q.v., p. 179). Publ. Brown, II, 271–274.

139. Possibile imo forte necesse est cum aliquis post caritatem... × ... redicionis in transitoriam purgantem fuit commitata.

On the gravity of lapsing from a state of *caritas* by committing a mortal sin: how the lapse identifies the will actuating the present sin with the will before the state of *caritas*, nullifying all the benefits of previous repentance and forgiveness.

140. Cupiditas est amor immoderatus adipiscende et retinende pecunie ... × ...facta est in spem illius perdicio eorum.

On the insatiability of the desire for money, and the hypocrisies it leads us into. In the *Comm. in Psal.*, Eton MS 8, f. 9[B–D]; also Durham Cath. A. III. 12, ff. 6[D]–7[A], 87[B–C], here slightly longer than the *dictum*. See p. 185, no. 31.

141. Humilitas est amor persistendi in ordine sibi congruo... × ... obprobria qui verbo virtutis sue supportat omnia.

How the Christian's proper *ordo* is that of repentance, to which humility is well suited, yet the humility of the *miser* should not be forced upon him by his worldly superiors. See *Dictum* 47. Publ. Brown, II, 288–290.

142. Humilitas est qua homo sui verissima cognicione ipse sibi... × ...ex virginitate tamen ex humilitate concepit.

How the truly humble man desires to glorify God by his own humility: the three grades of humility and the signs of humility. Publ. Brown, II, 290–292. This is probably Bale's *De Humilitate Domini* (*Index*, p. 374). Bale may have taken the title from Cambridge Univ. MS Hh. iv. 3, f. 157[b] (XV[m]), where this *Dictum* occurs separately.

143. Cum dives dicatur quia multa possidet propria ille merito... × ... promittitur paupertati premium regni celorum.

Poverty is a glorious state because like the celestial, where there will be no property. A very short paragraph.

144. Virtuti et potestati oracionis nulla poterit potestas creata... × ... omnia quecunque petieritis in oracione credentes accipietis.

No earthly power can compare with the power of prayer. A short paragraph. Publ. Brown, II, 285.

145. Quis edificans domum non diligenter considerat et quantum ... × ...in corpus suum admittit consimiles operaciones.

How we build our eternal life here in our earthly pilgrimage: we should build of the best material so that our eternal home will be perfect.

146. Plerique homines huius temporis dicunt se ieiunare et tamen... × ... hostilem irrisionem non ad dileccionis intencionem.

How fasting, intended as a memorial of Christ's passion and death, is travestied by many who do not even hunger.

147. Ut (Et) ait Ysidorus aqua dicta est quod superficies eius equalis sit ... × ...reddit haustus cognicionis iusticie et misericordie.

On the diverse qualities of water: of certain wells whose waters have different effects: forgetfulness and memory (in Bohemia), fertility, properties curative of various human ills; of the properties of the waters of various lakes in Italy, Idumea, Ethiopia and Africa. In the *Comm. in Psal.*, Eton MS 8, ff. 14[B]–16[D], and Durham Cath. A. III. 12, ff. 8[D]–10[C], slightly shorter than the *dictum*.

DOUBTFUL WORKS

1. *Pseudo-Andronici de Passionibus*

I. Inc.: Quid est passio? Passio est irracionalis anime mocio et preter...
Expl.: ...Fortitudo autem sciencia durorum et non durorum et neutrorum.

II. Unpubl. Greek text ed. F. G. A. Mullach, *Fragmenta Philos. Graeca*, III (1881), 570–574.

III. Pelzer* was the first to suggest (1921) that Grosseteste was in all probability the translator of this first half of the Περὶ παθῶν of the Pseudo-Andronicus. The Latin text occurs in Peterhouse, Cambridge, MS 116, immediately following the *De Virtute*, which in turn follows the composite text of the *Ethics* and the Greek commentators. The other works are well authenticated, and Pelzer argues that the presence of this short work in an early Grosseteste MS gives us reason to posit him as the translator of it as well. Franceschini accepts the probability,† noting, furthermore, the presence of the work in the valuable Ambrosian MS E. 71 sup. which contains the *De Virtute* and the *De Lineis Indivisibilibus*, both ascribed to Grosseteste. See above, p. 67 f. But the *De Passionibus* is not even there ascribed. Its presence in the codex might, therefore, be construed in the opposite sense to that accepted by Franceschini. A scribe so well informed as the writer of this codex, who has given us the authorship of two works furnished by no other known scribe, cannot have omitted to tell us, if he knew, that Grosseteste translated this work. His silence on this point warns us to make no undocumented assumption.‡ The nature of the work is slightly different from that which usually attracted Grosseteste. It is purely a catalogue of the passions, with the Greek name of the passion defined, e.g.:

> Achthos autem tristicia gravans. Achos autem tristicia discordiam faciens. Penthos autem tristicia intemporanee mortis. Sphakelismos autem tristicia vehemens.... Epicherecakia autem delectacio in proximorum infortunis. Goeceia autem delectacio secundum decepcionem vel incantacionem. Eupatheie species tres: bulisis, gaudium, eulaneia....

It is more probable that this work, used by Albertus Magnus and Thomas Aquinas, was translated by someone in the Grosseteste circle than that Grosseteste himself was responsible for the actual translation. The presence of the work in the Ambrosian MS suggests the period of the Council of

* "Les Ouvrages de Morale...", *Rev. Néo-Scolastique de Philosophie*, XXIII (1921), 322.

† *Roberto Grossatesta...*, p. 61.

‡ Pelzer accepts (*ubi supra*) this argument from conscious silence in arguing that Bartholomew of Messina did not translate the second chapter of the *De Bona Fortuna*, *art. cit.* p. 320 f. Conclusions from the argument are always liable to reversal from new data, but have much inherent strength if the documentation already available is typical and thorough.

Lyons, *ca.* 1245. See above, p. 67. Someone of his *familia* then with him may have been the translator.

IV. MSS:

Cambridge, Peterhouse	116	ff. 242^{B}–243^{A}	XIII^{2}	Unasc.
Milan, Ambros.	E. 71 sup.	f. $158^{B–D}$	XIII^{m}	Unasc. So. Fr.

2. *Ars Algorismi in Communi*

I. Inc.: Dicente Boecio in principio Arismetrice omnia que a primeva rerum...

Expl.: ...extraccione tam in numeris cubicis quam quadratis.

II. Unpubl.

III. This work is apparently ascribed on the front leaf of the Dublin MS (*ca.* 1325) in this form:

Computus dn̄i Roberti Lincoln'
De Arte Algorismi in communi — lincoln'
Item alius tractatus eiusdem magis in speciali.

At first glance it would seem to be the clear intention of the scribe to indicate that all three works are by *lincoln'*. But an examination of the text itself soon causes doubts to arise as to whether Grosseteste would have written what we find here. A pseudo-Greek etymology like this:

> Algorismus dictus autem ab *algos* quod est ars et *rithmus* numerus, quasi ars numerandi, vel ab *en* quod est in et *gogos* duccio et *rithmus* numerus, quasi induccio in numerum vel ab *algo* inventor et *rithmus*...

can hardly be by Grosseteste. He was familiar early in his career with the important mathematical works of the Arabians current in Western Europe,* and must have known enough of their terminology to know that *Algorismus* was not of Greek derivation. The probability then arises that the scribe meant to connect the first and third of these three items, after noticing that he had written *eiusdem*. The bracket which he has made would seem to point to two, the first and third, and to omit the second. It must furthermore be remarked that this work is but a reworking of the current *Algorismus* and not an original treatise at all. It might even be safer to regard the work as a *spurium*.†

IV. MSS:

Oxford				
Digby	97	ff. 156^{b}–164^{a}	1395	Unasc.
Laud Misc.	644	ff. 127^{b}–130^{b}	XIII^{2}	Unasc.
London, B.M., Royal	12. F. xix	ff. 183^{a}–184	XIV^{1}	Unasc.
Dublin, Trinity	D. 4. 27	ff. 99^{b}–104^{a}	*ca.* 1325	See above

* See above, Introd. p. 30 ff.

† A note (XIII^{2}) in the margin of f. 127^{a} of Digby MS 168, reading...*quere plus in fine compoti mei Lincolniensis, scilicet cum algorismo suo*... might indicate that the owner of this codex considered a part of Grosseteste's *Compotus* an *Algorismus*, but at best the phraseology is inconclusive. See W. D. Macray, *Cat.... MSS... Digby* (Oxford, 1883), col. 175.

3. *De Astronomia*

I. Inc.: Investigantibus astronomie raciones ponendum est primo punctos esse...

Expl.: ...unius hore bisse momentum est dimidium momentum.

II. Unpubl.

III. Boston of Bury, followed by Bale, Tanner and Pegge, lists a *De Astrologia*. We have no means of saying positively that such a title is not possible, for, from a knowledge of the rest of Grosseteste's works, and from evidence in his own hand in Bodl. Savile MS 21 (see above, Introd. p. 30ff.), we know him to have been interested in astrology early in his career. His interest in mathematical astronomy was paramount throughout his life. But the present tractate is not ascribed to Grosseteste until *ca.* 1400, and then in the colophon: *Explicit Lincolniensis in theorica spere*. The earliest MS, Rawl. D. 893, XIII[m], is slightly incomplete *in fine* and bears no ascription. The subject-matter is quite similar to that in the Cambrai *Theorica Planetarum* (see above, p. 118), but the work is not so long. It is not impossible that we have Grosseteste's own abridgment of the *Theorica*. The Digby colophon might be construed as supporting such a supposition. Baur's suggestion (p. 143*) that Paris B.N. 7413 contains a copy of this treatise is unfounded. In the Vatican MS the work follows immediately after Grosseteste's *De Sphera* and *Compotus*. But as both these genuine works are ascribed and our present treatise bears no ascription, its position might well argue against its authenticity.

IV. MSS:

Oxford				
Digby	97	ff. 138[a]–142[a]	1395	Asc.
Rawl.	D. 893	ff. 129[b]–134[b]	XIII[m]	Unasc.
Vatican, Pal. lat.	1414	ff. 62[C]–66[D]	XIII[2]	Unasc. Lowl.

4. *De Aversione a Summo Bono*

I. Inc.: Primum in via mali est actualis aversio a summo bono quod patet...

Expl.: ...est Antichristi unde Zach. hanc excecacionem tangit Iob dicens [incomplete in middle of column].

II. Unpubl.

III. This treatise follows immediately the diagram appended to the *De Effectibus Virtutum* (see below, p. 236).* Written by the same scribe, it is quite obviously the work of the author of the preceding treatise. It is longer and a larger number of authorities are quoted. Noticeable is a stanza apparently taken from Isidore's *Etymologiae* (f. 45[C]) beginning: *Apothou ceraton hoc est a cornibus apte*. There are other occasional Greek or pseudo-

* For contents of this MS see above, Introd. p. 13 ff., and above, pp. 182 ff., and *Index codicum*, s.n.

Greek etymologies, but the author is relying on Isidore, Jerome or Augustine. This bent would accord with the temper of Grosseteste at the time of the composition of this codex, *ca.* 1225–1230. As he began serious study of Greek *ca.* 1230, we should expect to find his own etymologies after that time. Some of the chapter-headings are: *De contemptu generali, De omissione, De libidine, De voluptate, De voluptate vituperabili, De delectacione, De viciis nature, De fragilitate, De mollicie, De lassitudine, De pronitate, De nequicia, De rebellione.*

Publication of the *Dicta* or the Sermons might furnish adequate grounds for rejection or acceptance, but what slight evidence is now available makes Grosseteste's authorship probable.

IV. MS:

Durham Cath.	A. III. 12	ff. 41B–48D	*ca.* 1230	Unasc. *mut. in fine*

5. *De Effectibus Virtutum*

I. Inc.: Nichil fit in terra sine causa, dicit Iob v, et ita omne quod fit...

Expl.: ...gracia principium omnium subiectorum fides.

II. Unpubl.

III. There is no conclusive evidence to show that this is a work of Grosseteste. It appears in a single MS, Durham Cath. A. III. 12, in a hand that has written numerous Grosseteste items, all unascribed, e.g. f. 78 ff., in such order as to show exceptional closeness to the source. See above, pp. 16 and 182. The internal evidence may not be conclusive in favour of Grosseteste as the author, but several separate facts are worth noting. The treatise must have been written before 1231, the *terminus ad quem* of the writing of the codex (see above, p. 14 f.), and not much before 1225, as all biblical references are by chapters. The preaching office is treated in Grosseteste's typical style. The distinction between the Old and New Testaments, worked out at greater length in the treatise *De Cessacione Legalium*, written *ca.* 1231, is clear and explicit. The work is followed by a diagrammatical summary of the effects of the virtues and vices after the fashion of the *Templum Domini*. Though no single fact is conclusive as to the authorship, the cumulative effect of all the details of evidential value is very strongly in favour of Grosseteste as the writer.

IV. MS:

Durham Cath.	A. III. 12	ff. 38A–39C + diagram, ff. 39B–41A	*ca.* 1230	Unasc.

6. *De Gloria in Infirmitatibus*

I. Inc.: Gloriandum est in infirmitatibus quia sanant a peccatis preteritis...

Expl.: ...voluntarius usus naturam utramque coniungeret.

II. Unpubl.

III. This short work would seem to be almost an abstract of a projected longer work. Many sentences are not completed; biblical references are barely indicated and *exempla* mentioned in such a way as to indicate that the hearer or the scribe might be expected to fill in the necessary details. There is one unspecified quotation from Aristotle. The work appears in Gonv. and Caius MS 439 immediately after the *Comm. in Epist. Pauli ad Rom. V–XVI* (see above, p. 74 f.), with no sensible break, in the same hand that has written several ascribed Grosseteste items. There is no specific reference to *lincolniensis* in this *opusculum*, nor have we any external evidence for Grosseteste's authorship. It must therefore be placed among the *dubia*. Yet it gives the impression of having been taken down by this scribe from Grosseteste's *leccio*. It is strongly Grossetestian in the vigour of style and thought, the wealth of knowledge of Scripture shown, and in vocabulary. It may well have been delivered as a sermon to the clergy of his chapter. The XIV^{m} hand conjectured (see above, p. 75) to be that of the Bury librarian has written in the margin: *notate clerici.*

IV. MS:

Cambridge, Gonv. & Caius	439	ff. 70^{b}–71^{a}	XIII^{1}	Unasc.

7. *De Homine Creato*

I. Inc.: Quoniam dictum est mihi ut meipsum cognoscam sustinere...
Expl.: ...est ut quicquid supra illud est non aliud quam racio est.

II. Unpubl.

III. A work *De homine* is ascribed to Grosseteste by Bale, Pits and Tanner, beginning: *Adam, ubi es?* I suggest below (p. 251, *Spurium* 25) that confusion may have arisen with a work of Langton. In Gray's Inn, London, MS 13, the first item, ff. 1^{A}–16^{B} (XIII^{m}), is an anonymous work which an eighteenth-century owner of the codex has ascribed in the *contenta*: *Grostest de homine creato, corrupto, restaurato.* In the course of the tractate almost no authorities are quoted; there are arguments strikingly similar to certain passages in Grosseteste's *De Anima* and *De Intelligenciis.*

[f. 9^{C-D}] Invisibilis et incorporea est anima. Si enim visibilis esset, corporea esset et partes haberet, neque tota simul in uno loco esset. Nullum enim corpus aut simul tangi potest. Anima vero in quibuscunque suis motibus vel actibus tota simul adest tota, videt tota....Habet anima vires quibus corpori commiscitur quarum prima est naturalis, secunda vitalis, tercia animalis, et sicut deus trinus et unus, verus et perfectus, omnia tenet, omnia implet, omnia sustinet, omnia supersedet et circumplectitur, sic anima hiis viribus per totum corpus diffunditur, non locali distensione, sed vitali intensione.

Cf. Baur, pp. 114–117, 250–255. The least that can be said is that the fundamental point of view adopted in this treatise is essentially that of Grosseteste, and the details of expression strikingly like his in several authentic works. The late ascription is more than likely traceable to Bale and Pits and is of little weight of itself, and the internal evidence is not strong enough, unsupported, to justify more than a suspicion of Grosseteste's authorship. So far as I am aware, the work is extant in this single copy.

8. Sermons in Gonville and Caius MS 439

(i) *De Arbore Bona*

I. Inc.: Non potest arbor bona....Mt. 7. Ut in ovili dominico lupus dinoscatur...

Expl.: ...et erunt fructus eius in cibum.

II. Unpubl.

III. This short sermon, rubricked *Sermo dominica septima post pentecosten*, follows immediately the *De gloria in infirmitatibus* (see above, p. 236 f.). It bears no ascription of any sort. Nevertheless it has some definite connection with the *Comm. in Epist. Pauli ad Rom. V–XVI* (see above, p. 74 f.) by reason of the rubric and its distinctively Grossetestian style. Plato is quoted: *homo est arbor eversa*. The sermon is found on f. 71ª of the MS.

(ii) *De Duabus Tunicis*

I. Inc.: Cum prohibentur indui due tunice expresse monetur non dupliciter...

Expl.: ...

II. Unpubl.

III. It is difficult to know where this sermon was intended to end. Toward the bottom of the first page, f. 71ᵇ, there is in the left margin: *Dominica 20ª post pentecosten*, preceded by a ¶, which usually indicates, in this MS, a new subject. That is not, however, the case here. On the next page, f. 72ª, there are four such signs. The first is followed by: *Dominica 23ª post pentecosten*. If the hypothesis that these sermons were taken from Grosseteste's *lecciones* to his *familia* is possible, this time-discrepancy could be explained by one of his frequent absences from Lincoln and subsequent return and resumption of his exegesis.

9. *Theorica Planetarum Correcta*

I. Inc.: Circulus ecentricus dicitur vel egresse cuspidis vel egredientis...

Expl.: ...splendor erit lune planete et non corporaliter.

II. This "correction" has not been published. The original has often been printed, under the name of Gerard of Cremona: 1472, 1477, 1478 (twice), 1480, 1518 (as by John of Cremona), 1531, etc.*

III. This is not an original work, but a correction of the very common *Theorica Planetarum*. According to Bjornbö† there are two recensions, a

* See Boncampagni, *Gherardo Cremonese* (Rome, 1851), p. 97.

† *Acta Mathematica*, v (1905), 112 ff. He lists fifty-eight MSS. The list could easily be doubled.

Continental, by Gerard of Sabionetta (*fl.* 1250), and an English, ascribed in several MSS to Walter Brito († 1372) and again to Simon of Bredon,* fellow of Merton. Collation of the text of our MS with the usual Continental text shows that we have an expansion by a trained mathematician, approximately one-fifth longer than the original. The difficulty in the way of accepting this early fourteenth-century ascription is the fact that Gerard of Sabionetta is generally supposed to have composed the work between 1250 and 1260. This late date would render a "correction" by Grosseteste improbable, unless we were to suppose that he procured a copy at Lyons in 1250 and set to work immediately to correct the text. But this supposition puts some strain on chronological probabilities. The eventual solution of our doubt as to the authenticity† of Grosseteste's "correction" will depend largely on the correct determination of the date of composition of the original, whether by Gerard or perhaps by John of Sacro Bosco. The complete MS tradition remains to be examined. Bale (*Index*, p. 373) lists this incipit. The colophon reads: *corepta secundum Lincolniensem.*

IV. MS:

Cambridge, Univ.	Ii. i. 13	ff. 59ᵃ–61ᵇ	*ca.* 1325

Bodley MS 300 contains, ff. 40ᶜ–44ᴮ, a *Theorica Planetarum*, ascribed in the colophon to Grosseteste. It is, however, the ordinary version of Gerard, with inconsiderable scribal variants, and has none of the additions of the Cambridge MS. The same is true of Oxford, Univ. Coll. 41, f. 28ᵃ (35ᵃ), listed by Baur, p. 122*. Cambridge Univ. MS Ii. i. 27, ff. 171ᵃ–178ᵃ, written by Frater Thomas de Wyndele in 1424, is entitled *Theorica Planetarum lyncolniensis*. Like the Bodley MS 300 it is the usual *Theorica* of Gerard. Baur's notice (p. 122*) of *De Cursu Planetarum Quedam* ascribed to Grosseteste in Vat. Urb. lat. 1428, f. 174ᵇ, is misleading. The *Compotus* of Grosseteste ends on this page, and the scribe has added some notes of his own, but there is no separate work of Grosseteste in this codex until his *De Sphera*, ff. 180ᴬ–186ᴬ. See above, pp. 95 f. and 115 f.

10.

Concerning the following doggerel quatrain we should hesitate to pronounce, and reproduce it simply as it appears. Of Grosseteste's versatility there has never been any doubt. He might even have been capable of this, but it seems more likely to have been the work of the fourteenth-century scribe whose initials happened to be R.G.

Salisbury Cath. MS 55, f. 186ᵇ, XIV

Hoc opus est factum
Scriptor tenuit bene pactum
Non petit incaustum
Set vini nobilis haustum
Per R. G.

* See Powicke, *Merton Books*, p. 138.

† Baur's summary rejection of the work (p. 122* f.) was due to a failure to notice the real nature of the work, and a confusion with other badly catalogued items in other MSS.

SPURIOUS WORKS

A personality so commanding as Grosseteste becomes, in the course of time, a magnet for attributions of many works which are found, on closer examination, to be falsely so ascribed. Some of these writings appear, aside from one or more MS ascriptions to Grosseteste, completely anonymously. Others, whose real authors are discoverable beyond any reasonable doubt, may appear in a few MSS ascribed to Grosseteste, or again anonymously. Some works whose real authors remain to-day hidden to us, graced with the dubious honour of a catholic appeal, have been ascribed to Grosseteste among half a dozen possible candidates for the title. Occasionally it is possible to trace with a large degree of confidence the source of the false attribution to Grosseteste. More often we must take refuge in pleasant speculation. Many of the items in the following list of works designated as spurious have been discussed by Baur. When our conclusions agree substantially with his, the reader is referred to his edition. Additional evidence is sometimes available. Bale is the source of most of the false attributions in modern catalogues of MSS, and his errors have been perpetuated and even augmented by succeeding bibliographers. The total of errors is greatest in the latest of the compilers, Pegge, who, however, quite honestly indicates the source of his information, and, as he does not pretend to any familiarity with the MSS, we may disregard his evidence as derived. He will seldom be quoted in the following list.

Though Tanner, in addition to compiling from his predecessors, had seen a great number of MSS, he was often quite uncritical in assigning a single work to two or even three authors. He was, furthermore, apparently unmindful of the fact that the validity of MS attributions varies with their age. In the case of the older bibliographers, we may assume that they have seen no inconsiderable number of MSS which have since been lost or destroyed, or have filtered into private or otherwise inaccessible collections. Such MSS, it is to be hoped, may yet be rediscovered and identified.

In the following list works erroneously ascribed to Grosseteste in MSS by any of the bibliographers or by more recent serious writers are cited, and an effort is made to show why it is necessary to reject them as spurious. Here, as throughout this catalogue, the incipits and explicits are usually fuller than in the bibliographers without specific notice being taken of the expansion.

1. *De Agricultura, Translacio Anglice.*

Bale, Pits and Tanner list a work under this title beginning: *Pater etate decrepita filio dicebat.** This undoubtedly refers to the English translation of Walter of Henley's *Treatise on Husbandry*, found in a late fifteenth-century MS, B.M. Sloane 686, f. 1 ff. which begins:

> The tretyce off husbandry þ[t] maystur Groshe...made þe whiche was bishope off lycōll. he transelated þis booke out off ffrenshe in to englysshe. þe begyninge off þis booke....†

Miss Lamond suggested (p. xxx f.) that the reason for this attribution was that "some knowledge survived of the fact that Grosseteste had written Rules [see above, pp. 149, 158 f.] for the management of an estate and household, and that the transcriber supposed this treatise to be identical with that of the Bishop of Lincoln". The absence of any evidence contemporary with Grosseteste that he made any translation at all from French into English, the lateness of the language in which this translation is written, and the probability that it was written too late for Grosseteste to have known it, all combine to make the ascription false. Miss Murray (*Château d'Amour*, p. 19) accepts as certain a translation by Grosseteste of Walter's *Treatise on Husbandry*. This erroneous ascription is accepted as late as 1934 by L. M. Friedman in his *Robert Grosseteste and the Jews* (Cambridge, Mass. p. 10). Grosseteste's *Reulles* are doubtless the source of all these misunderstandings, as they appear in both Latin and French, and treat the same general subject as Walter of Henley's *Treatise on Husbandry*.

2. *De Anima.* See below, p. 259, *De Potenciis Anime. Spurium* 45.

3. *In Apocalypsin Joannis.*

Bale, Pits and Tanner list a commentary beginning: *Vidi in dextra sedentis super....* This would appear to be a false attribution to Grosseteste of Nicholas of Lyra's commentary on the Apocalypse (ed. Rome, 1471, and often since), extant in many MSS in England and on the Continent. No MS of any work ascribed to Grosseteste bearing this incipit or even this title has come to light. We have no evidence that he was particularly interested in apocalyptic literature.

4. *Arismetrica de Arte Mensurandi Altitudines et Profunditates.*

Baur (p. 143*) mentions this work as found in Munich Clm. 11067, f. 201,

* Bale, *Index* (ed. Poole), p. 379: *Robertus Grossetest transtulit de gallico in latinum.* See Lamond, *ed. cit.* p. xxxviii.

† Printed first *ca.* 1510 by Wynkyn de Woorde and reproduced in facsimile by F. H. Cripps-Day in *The Manor Farm* (London, 1931), pt. vii. For other editions, *op. cit.* pp. 6–8. A second MS, Trin. Coll., Cambridge, O. 1. 13 (1037), ff. 177, 188–194, XV, has substantially the same ascription as the Sloane MS.

written in 1449/50, and ascribed to Grosseteste. This MS does not now, however, contain any work ascribed to Grosseteste. Formerly Grosseteste's *De Prognosticacione* (see above, p. 103 f.) was to be found between present ff. 84 and 85. An incomplete *De Composicione Chilindri* beginning: *Ad chilindri composicionem quod dicitur horalogium viatorum* occupies ff. 200^{A}–201^{A}. On f. 201^{B} is a *Tabula collecta Oxonie de ascensione solis ad omnes horas diei*. The MS is dated in various places 1445–1448. It is barely possible that we have here some reference to Grosseteste's expansion of sections of Gerbert's *De Geometria* which we have in his own hand. See above, Introd. p. 32.

5. *De Aseneth Filia Pharaonis, Translacio ex Greco.*

Because of the fact that this work,* beginning: *Et factum est in primo anno septem annorum ubertatis*... and ending ...*et Ioseph nuncupatus est pater eius in terra Egipti*, occasionally appears in the same codex as Grosseteste's translation of the *Testamenta XII Patriarcharum*, it has long been thought that Grosseteste was the author of this translation as well.† M. R. James was the first to express doubt of Grosseteste's authorship,‡ because of the age of a copy in Corpus Christi College, Cambridge (MS 424), which he dated "XII?" If this had been the only copy on the borderline between the twelfth and thirteenth centuries, it would have been possible to explain the apparently early script as that of an aged scribe writing in an isolated centre. Such cases are not uncommon. But an Oxford copy (Rawl. G. 38) must be dated before 1200, much too early for Grosseteste to have been the translator.§ The list of MSS given below is not offered as complete. No MS thus far noticed bears any indication of the identity of the translator. The story is of course found in the *Speculum Historiale* of Vincent of Beauvais (I, chaps. 118–122).

MSS:

Oxford, Rawl.	G. 38‖	ff. 90^{a}–97^{b}	XII^{2}
London, B.M.			
Add.	18210‖	ff. 49^{D}–54^{D}	XIII^{m}
Egerton	2676¶	ff. 53^{a}–65^{a}	XIII^{m}
Cambridge			
C.C.C.	424	ff. 42^{a}–59^{b}	*ca.* 1200
Trinity	1440	ff. 47^{a}–54^{a}	XIV^{2}

* Ed. Batiffol in *Studia Patristica*, I (1889), 89–115, from the two C.C.C., Cambridge, MSS, with the Greek text, pp. 39–86.

† See Sandys, *Hist. of Classical Scholarship*, I (Cambridge, 1921), 576.

‡ See his *Cat. of MSS*...*C.C.C., Cambridge, s.n.*

§ Franceschini, *op. cit.* p. 47, doubts the authorship of Grosseteste on grounds of style and because Vincent of Beauvais, though mentioning Grosseteste as author of the *Testamenta*, does not mention him as author of the *Historia Aseneth*, and also because Fabricius finds the work to have appeared before the thirteenth century. No specific MS is mentioned or dated.

‖ With the *Testamenta* and Ἰησοῦς of Suidas, both asc.

¶ With the *Testamenta*.

(Graz, Univ.	978	ff. 173^a–180^b	1464	So. Ger.)*
Liége	184†			
Vienna, Nat. Bibl.	13707	ff. 201^A–202^D	1472‡	So. Ger.

6. *De Astrolabio.*

A work with this title beginning: *Astrolabii circulos et membra nominatim...* and ending ...*diametri putei ad totam eius profunditatem* is listed by Bale and Tanner. The latter lists three MSS which contain the work: Digby 98 (ff. 145^b–148^a, *ca.* 1400); Bodley NE F. 10, 11 (=Bodley 300, ff. 81^C–84^B, XV^1) and Laud E. 105, f. 158. The last indication is incorrect. The old signature Laud E. 105 is now Laud lat. 116, which contains *Roberti Valturii... de re militari* (XV^m). Of Grosseteste's interest in and expert knowledge of the use of the astrolabe and the quadrant we have excellent evidence in his own hand in Savile MS 21. See above, Introd. p. 30 ff. Baur remarked (p. 145*) that the work is ascribed to Grosseteste in the Digby MS. There is no ascription of this work in the rubric, colophon or in the *contenta*, though later in the codex there are genuine ascribed works of Grosseteste. See above, pp. 10, 93, and 103 ff. The work *De Astrolabio* is written by the same hand that wrote these genuine works. But the scribe is explicit with regard to the authorship of these works, and his silence as to the author of the *De Astrolabio* would almost of itself rule out Grosseteste. Failing specific positive evidence, we must simply remark that we have no evidence for Grosseteste's authorship. See also Baur p. 68*. Also in Digby 167, ff. 64^a–67^a (XIV), Unasc.

7. *Commentarius in Boecii De Consolacione Philosophie.*

A commentary with this title, beginning: *Boecius iste nobilissimus civis romanus*, is ascribed to Grosseteste by Leland, Bale and Tanner, and literary tradition has generally accepted the attribution.§ But actual ascription goes back to the end of the fourteenth century in England.|| The commentary is the work of William of Conches, to whom it is ascribed in the earliest MSS dating from the twelfth century. There are the following copies of the work:

London, B.M.				
Harley	2559	f. 34^a, beg. only	XIII^1	Unasc.
Royal	15. B. XIII	f. 1^A ff.	XIV^m	Unasc.
Cambridge, Jesus	70	ff. 1^a–89^a	*ca.* 1400	Asc. R.G.
	74	ff. 1^a–129	XV^1	Unasc.
Klosterneuburg	138	ff. 61^b–62^b	1372¶	

* The rubric reads here correctly: *Historia Asseneth sumpta ex prima parte speculi hystorialis....* It is not the earlier translation, but follows immediately after the *Testamenta.* This section from Vincent's *Speculum* appears separately also in Weimar, Q. 117, ff. 33^b–36^a, XIV^m.

† See above, p. 44, under *Testamenta.* The *Cat. Général* dates the MS "XII", in this case probably too early. ‡ With the *Testamenta.*

§ See, e.g., M. Manitius, *Gesch. d. lat. Lit. d. Mittelalters*, II (Munich, 1923), 651.

|| Baur remarks (p. 46* f.) that Gascoigne was the first to ascribe this commentary to Grosseteste. There is some mistake in Baur's construction of the text of Gascoigne's *Liber Veritatum*, which neither in the edition of Thorold Rogers nor, I am kindly informed by Miss Winifred Pronger who has read the whole MS carefully, in the autograph of Gascoigne ascribes the commentary to Grosseteste.

¶ Asc. XVI to Bartolomeus de Sancto Concordio, O.P.

Leipzig—mentioned by Obbarius, *Boethii De Consolatione Philosophiae* (Iena, 1843), pp. xxvii, l and lxi.

Orleans	230 (274)	ff. 1^a–44^b	XII^2	Asc. Conches
Paris				
B.N.	lat. 1326			
	lat. 13334	ff. 45^a–51^b	XII^2	Unasc.
	lat. 14380*	ff. 66^A–99^D	*ca.* 1300	Asc. R.G.
St Germain	1381			Unasc.
Tours	699	ff. 1^C–128^D	XV	Unasc. *mut. in fine*
Troyes	1101	ff. 1–19	XII^2	Asc. Conches
	1381	f. 34 ff.	XII	Unasc.

Charles Jourdain, in his article "Des Commentaires Inédits de Guillaume de Conches et de Nicolas Triveth sur la Consolation de la Philosophie de Boèce" in *Not. et Extraits des MSS de la Bibl. Nat.* xx (1862), 40–80 (reprinted in *Excursions Historiques...à travers le Moyen Âge* (Paris, 1888), pp. 29–68), noticed the early French MSS of this commentary without remarking on the later ascription to Grosseteste. Baur correctly rejected the work as not by Grosseteste, but without mentioning Jourdain's work or MSS other than the Jesus Coll. 70 and the Paris B.N. lat. 14380, both ascribed to Grosseteste. His reasons for rejecting the work were based on internal evidence. We are happily not dependent on that kind of evidence, as the twelfth-century ascriptions to William of Conches are determinative. My data on many of the MSS are incomplete, as Jourdain's article seemed to make further examination unnecessary.

8. *Canon Misse.*

This work,† beginning: *In virtute sancte crucis et sacramento altaris...* and ending *...est conveniencia, in tercio differencia*, is ascribed to Grosseteste in the *contenta*, *ca.* 1300, of Pavia MS 69. The *contenta* is the work of an Italian owner of this codex of English provenance, and, as it is evident that the edges were cut and the book rebound toward the end of the thirteenth century, we may posit some misreading of a partially obliterated ascription, or an arbitrary expansion of the letter "R" erroneously to *Robertus*, instead of *Richardus*. The work is by Richard of Wedinghausen, a Premonstratensian,‡ and is found in the following MSS known to me:

Oxford, Rawl.	A. 384	ff. 93^A–97^B	XIII^2	Asc.§
London, B.M., Royal	4. B. VIII	f. 244^b ff.	XIII^m	Unasc.
	8. A. XI	f. 2^b ff.	XIII^1	Unasc.
	8. A. XV	f. 163^b ff.	XIII^m	Unasc.
	8. A. XXI	f. 157^b ff.	XIII^1, *frag.*	Unasc.
Cambridge, Univ.	Ll. i. 15	ff. 188^B–192^D	XIII^2	Unasc.
Pavia, Univ.	69	ff. 92^a–95^b	XIII^1	Asc. R.G. in *contenta*, *ca.* 1300, *manu italiana*

* This is the MS St Victor 200 mentioned by Jourdain. Asc. to Grosseteste on backflyleaf, XV^1.

† Ed. *Patr. Lat.* CLXXVII, col. 455 ff. in appendix to the works of Hugh of St Victor, as by John of Cornwall, and so in Tanner, p. 432.

‡ See B. Hauréau in *Not. et Extraits*, XXIV ,pt. ii, who called him "Richard de Prémontré". Hauréau dealt particularly with Troyes MS 302.

§ The rubric reads: *Incipit tractatus a Ricardo premonstratensis ordinis editus de canone misse.*

9. *In Catonis Disticha* (*Parvus Cato*).

Beginning: *Cum animadverterem quamplurimos homines*... and ending ...*Hec brevitas fecit sensus coniungere vivos*, this work is listed as a work of Grosseteste by all the bibliographers from Bale. No MS evidence for such an ascription has appeared, save as Baur remarks (p. 48* f.) upon an eighteenth-century note in Peterhouse, Cambridge, MS 215, f. 59[a], at the beginning of a copy of this work, *per Robertum Grosseteste*, but as the note refers to the page in Bale's *Scriptores* where the ascription first occurs, we need not attach too much weight to it. The work itself appears in a great number of MSS of the first years of the thirteenth century if not earlier, and therefore may be assumed to be pre-Grossetestian. I am not aware that the author of this quasi-commentary is known. The numerous marginal and interlinear glosses in the Peterhouse MS were written *ca.* 1275. There has not appeared thus far any cogent reason to connect them with Grosseteste or his circle. See James' *Catalogue of MSS*...*Peterhouse*, p. 260. I suspect this MS of being the one noted by Leyser, *Historia Poetarum et Poematum Medii Aevi* (Magdeburg, 1721, 1741), p. 998, as containing *Cato et alia* by Grosseteste, among the MSS of Thomas Gale, Professor of Greek at Cambridge and Dean of York († 1702).

10. *Compendium Philosophie*.

Under this title, or *Compendium Scienciarum*, the work beginning: *Felix prior etati que tot sapientes*... and ending ...*prudencie lectoris relinqui nos*, ascribed to Grosseteste by Leland, Bale, Pits, Tanner, Luard, Hauréau, Felten, Felder, Stevenson and, as late as 1932, by Harvey,* is the *De Divisione Scienciarum* of Gundissalinus (ed. by Baur in *Beiträge*, IV, Hefte 2–3 (Münster, 1903)). Baur (pp. 124*–126*) gives a history of the perpetuation of the erroneous ascription.

11. *Compendium Sancti Augustini De Civitate Dei*.

Listed without incipit by Boston of Bury, Bale, Tanner and Wood (*Hist. et Antiqq.* p. 78), this work has generally been disregarded by later bibliographers. Powicke, however, has recently suggested (*Merton Books*, p. 163) that MS 140 of Merton College, Oxford, may contain this work. The text, ff. 175[A]–197[C], *ca.* 1300, begins: *Gloriosa dicta sunt de te, civitas dei. Ps.* 86. *Cum Romam sochorum irrupcione*... and ends ...*cum verba fide resurreccionis future ad eternam beatitudinem ad quam nos perducat. Expliciunt abreviaciones de civitate dei per ignotum.* In the prologue, however, we read, f. 175[B]:

> Itaque frater Robertus de Kilwardby qui postea cantuariensis erat archiepiscopus tandem portuensis cardinalis ut libri huius leccionem faciliorem redderet dum in ordine nostro sacre doctrine intendebat premissa singulorum librorum intencione in omni capitulorum ab olim brevibus titulis distinctorum singillatim et compendiose conscienciam annotavit.

We have therefore an item which we should in all likelihood add to the list of the works of Kilwardby. Boston of Bury may have seen a copy ascribed simply to *Robertus* and assumed that Grosseteste was intended. Aside from this attribution, no evidence has appeared that Grosseteste compiled any

* *Oxford Companion to English Literature* (Oxford, 1932), p. 339.

such *Compendium*, though his own copy of the *De Civitate* was copiously annotated. See above, p. 27 ff.

12. *De Composicione Chilindri.*

A work with this title, beginning: *Investigantibus (nature) chilindri composicionem qui dicitur horologium*... and ending ...*Et sic per umbram scies altitudinem cuiuslibet rei erecte* has been ascribed to Grosseteste in an occasional catalogue of MSS, e.g. Coxe, *Cat. Codd. Bodl.* I, 458. No MS thus far noticed can with safety be dated earlier than *ca.* 1275. Furthermore, in MSS where this work appears along with genuine works of Grosseteste that are specifically ascribed, this work remains unascribed. Scribes may have felt that there was sufficient similarity of subject-matter to warrant grouping the works together, but their silence as to the author is perhaps more eloquent than the grouping. It is often called *Chilinder Oxoniensis* in MSS, but considerable liberty has been taken with the text and the accompanying computations.

The following MSS are known. There are probably many more extant.

Oxford				
Bodl.	464	ff. 204^{a}–205^{b}	*ca.* 1300	Unasc.*
Digby	98	ff. 166^{A}–167^{D}	XIII^{2}	Unasc.†
Laud Misc.	644	ff. 219^{A}–220^{D}	XIII^{2}	Unasc.‡
Univ. Coll.	41	ff. 35^{a}–36^{a}	1301	Unasc.
London, B.M., Royal	12. C. XVII	ff. 91^{D}–94^{C}	*ca.* 1350	Unasc.
	12. E. XXV	ff. 145^{b}–147^{a}	XIII^{2}	Unasc.
Erfurt, Amplon.	Q. 349	ff. 150^{C}–153^{B}	XIV^{2}	Unasc. No. Ger.
	Q. 385	ff. 143^{a}–145^{a}	XIV^{m}	Unasc. No. Ger.
Münster i.W.	741 (530)	ff. 74^{b}–75^{b}	*ca.* 1400	Unasc. Ger.
Vienna, Nat. Bibl.	5239–5239*	ff. 8^{*a}–10^{*a}	*ca.* 1400	Unasc. Ger.
	5303	ff. 247^{b}–250^{a}	*ca.* 1500	Unasc. Ger.
	5418	ff. 168^{a}–171^{b}	XV^{m}	Unasc. Ger.

13. *De Computo Ecclesiastico* (*Summa de Symbolo*).

This work, often denominated by its incipit *Qui bene presunt presbyteri*... ending ...*in cibum, sanguinem in potum*, has been ascribed to many authors, among them to Grosseteste by Bale, Pits and Tanner. So far as I am aware, no MS ascribing the work to Grosseteste has been noted. It is occasionally ascribed to William de Monte (Montibus), Chancellor of Lincoln († 1213), but in its present form it can hardly be his work, as he is quoted in the text. It is more likely to be the work of Richard of Wetherstede (Wetheringsett), *al.* Grant, *al.* of Leicester, Chancellor of Lincoln, 1221–1229, and Archbishop of Canterbury, 1229–1231. See Warner and Gilson, *Cat. of Royal MSS* (London, 1912), under MS 4. B. VIII; P. Glorieux, *Répertoire des Maîtres en Théologie de Paris au XIIIe Siècle*, I (Paris, 1933), 280. See also J. C. Russell, *Dict. of Writers of Thirteenth-Century England* (London, 1936), p. 196, who does not seem to have noted Glorieux's list of MSS. See further R. W. Hunt, "English Learning in the Late Twelfth Century" in *Transactions of the Royal Hist. Soc.* fourth series, XIX (1936), 22.

* With Grosseteste's *De Prognosticacione*.

† With the *Calendarium* and *De Sphera*.

‡ With the *Computus* and *De Lineis*. See Baur, p. 151* f.

14. *De Coniugio.*

Pits, Wharton, Cave and Tanner ascribe to Grosseteste a work with this title, beginning: *Coniugium quod eciam matrimonium*... and ending ...*homines ad nupcias frequenter iterandas.* Bale (*Index*, ed. Poole, p. 368) ascribes this work to Robert Criklade and Pits (p. 234) has a second ascription to Robert Criklade. Pits mentions a *MS in Cantabrigia in pub.* There are two copies of the work in Cambridge University Library, to either of which he may have had reference, viz.

Ii. i. 22	ff. 120ª–127ᵇ	XIV¹	Unasc.
Mm. v. 32	ff. 95ᵇ–113ᵇ	*ca.* 1200	*a magistro Gualterio compositus*

MS Ii. i. 22 contains the *Templum Domini* (see above, p. 138 f.), which may have led Pits to assume Grosseteste's authorship of the *De Coniugio.* But the work is certainly not his. It forms part vii of Hugh of St Victor's *Summa Sententiarum* (ed. *Patr. Lat.* CLXXVI, cols. 156–174). The ascription in the earlier (*ca.* 1200) Cambridge MS to *Magister Gualterius* (probably Walter of St Victor, † after 1180) suggests a need for a re-examination of the composition of the *Summa.**

15. *Difficilia Naturalis Sciencie.*

Bale, Pits and Tanner list among Grosseteste's works a treatise under this title, beginning: *Studiosissime sepiusque rogatus*... and ending ...*et alia corpora sunt equivoce in loco.* Baur has pointed out that this is the *Summule in libros Physicorum* of William of Ockham (ed. Bologna, 1494; Venice, 1506; Rome, 1637, etc.). Perhaps the earliest known copy of this treatise is in Lincoln Cathedral Library, MS 180, ff. 71ª–88ᴰ, XIVᵐ, written by Johannes de Argentina and ascribed to Ockham. See also Little, *Grey Friars*, p. 227.

16. *Disputacio inter Corpus et Animam.*

Inc.: Vir quidam extiterat dudum heremita Philibertus...
Ecce mundus moritur viciis sepultus...
Noctis sub silencio tempore brumali...
Expl.: ...Et me in manibus Christi totum commendavi.

This poem, with and without prologues, known also as the *Visio Philiberti*, is ascribed, in one fairly early Vienna MS and in several later South German copies, to Grosseteste. But G. von Karajan placed the rise of the poem in the twelfth century.† B.M. Royal MS 7. A. III contains a form of the poem and certainly dates from the twelfth century.‡ It has been published several times: Hamburg, 1669, by Chr. von Stökker; by Karajan in 1839, and by Th. Wright among *Poems Attributed to Walter Mapes* (London, 1841), and

* See Grabmann, *Gesch. d. scholastischen Methode*, II, 124–127, and J. de Ghellinck, *Le Mouvement théologique du XIIᵉ Siècle* (Paris, 1914), pp. 158–160, etc. and literature there cited.

† In *Frühlingsgabe für Freunde älterer Literatur* (Vienna, 1839). See also P. Leyser, *Hist. Poetarum et Poematum Medii Aevi* (Magdeburg, 1721, 1741), p. 996.

‡ Daunou, in *Hist. litt. de la France*, XVIII (Paris, 1835), 442, suggested that it was a translation of an older French poem, appearing to regard it as not by Grosseteste.

by Éd. Du Méril in *Poésies populaires* (Paris, 1843). C. S. Northup has recently given a translation of the whole poem.* For the early history of this type of poetry and the literature, see R. Batiouchkof in *Romania*, xx (1891), 1–55, 513–578. Some MSS ascribing the work to Grosseteste are

Graz, Univ.	1294	ff. 88^{B}–95^{a}	1360	So. Ger.
Leipzig, Univ.	lat. 803	ff. 1^{A}–3^{D}	XV^{1}	So. Ger.
Paris, B.N.	lat. 10636	ff. 8^{a}–14^{a}	XV^{2}	Köln
Prague, Univ.	2385	ff. 119^{a-b}, 275^{C}–277^{A}	XV^{m}	Boh.
Salzburg, St Peter	b. VI. 3	ff. 240^{b}–245^{a}	XV^{m}	So. Ger.
Vienna, Nat. Bibl.	1583	ff. 88^{B}–89^{D}	*ca.* 1300	Ger.

Northup listed fifteen MSS. There are probably about forty copies of the work extant. Its authorship has not, so far as I know, been incontestably established.† It has been variously ascribed to Hildebert of Le Mans, Peter of Blois and Walter Mapes. The oldest MS of the poem I have seen, Klosterneuburg 270, verso of flyleaf, XIII^{2}, has the ascription: *Incipit carmen cancelarii parisiensis.* No ascription so old has hitherto been noticed. Walther notices a Basel MS, A. v. 14 f. (XV) which ascribes the poem to *Philippus cancellarius parisiensis* († *ca.* 1236).

17. *Distincciones.*

Tanner lists a *Liber Distinctionum ordine alphabetico*, and mentions MS Westm. 8. G. ii. The Westminster MS may be the present Gray's Inn MS 23, which contains such a work, ff. 1^{A}–143^{B} (XIV^{1}), beginning: *Abeuncium per hunc mundum alii*... and ending ...*intremus ad nupcias cum domino nostro Jesu Christo.* There is no ascription in the text, but on the second front flyleaf is written, in an early fifteenth-century hand, *distincciones lincolniensis.* The text is the work of Nicholas of Gorham († *ca.* 1295), ascribed to him in numerous MSS, e.g. Bodl. Laud Misc. 555, ff. 1^{A}–167^{B}, *ca.* 1325. The fact that Grosseteste's *Templum Domini* is often called *Distincciones* (see above, p. 138 f.) in early MSS may have misled Tanner into making this erroneous ascription.

18. *De Doctrina Cordis.*

Inc.: Preparate corda vestra domino...

Expl.: ...qui in eo et per eum habebunt.

Publ. Naples, 1607, as by Fr. Gerard Leodiensis. See *Hist. litt. de la France*, XIX, 130 f.

* *PMLA.* VI (1901), 503–525.

† See also Manitius, *Gesch. d. lat. Lit. d. Mittelalters*, III (Munich, 1931), 951 ff. More recently F. J. E. Raby, in his *Hist. of Secular Latin Poetry in the Middle Ages*, II (Oxford, 1934), 302 f., regards the ascription to Grosseteste as well founded. See also H. Walther, *Das Streitgedicht i. d. lat. Lit. d. Mittelalters* (Munich, 1920), p. 69 ff., for other MSS and a discussion of authorship. He favours Grosseteste as the author without, I feel, giving sufficient attention to the lateness of the ascriptions to Grosseteste and the absence of any ascription in English MSS of the poem which are quite numerous: he lists twenty-two. On his own copious evidence the confusion in tradition is so great as to make us despair of being able to trace the author of this reworked poem at all; yet on a basis of priority of ascription, Philip the Chancellor is the most likely author.

Bale was the first to ascribe this work to Grosseteste, and has been followed by subsequent bibliographers, though Pegge noted the Naples print and the ascription. The work has also been ascribed to another British author, John of Wales, and often appears with the *De Lingua*, sometimes ascribed to Grosseteste. See below, p. 252 f. The author to whom the *De Doctrina* is most commonly ascribed is Gérard de Liége, but Hugo of St Cher, Albertus Magnus and Albert of Brescia have also been credited with its authorship. In a recent study Dom A. Wilmart has listed fifty MSS now extant and twenty apparently lost, and contends at some length for the authorship of Gérard de Liége.* Dom Wilmart's arguments are inherently strong, yet the simple priority of a MS not noticed by him bearing an ascription to another author would seem sufficient evidence to lead us to doubt strongly the probability of Gérard's authorship. Breslau MS I. Q. 108, written early in the second half of the thirteenth century, has this colophon: *Explicit liber de doctrina cordis editus a domino Guidone monacho ordinis cysterciensis et cardinale urbis Rome.*† This early ascription, the earliest found in the thirty MSS of this work examined by me, is corroborated by another ascription, also earlier than the majority of attributions, though not older than some ascriptions to Gérard, in B.M. Arundel MS 320, of the first years of the fourteenth century. This MS gives every indication of having been written in the Lowlands. At the end of the prologue we read: *Incipit liber de doctrina cordis editus a Gwidone.* It must be remarked that the great majority of the earliest copies are unascribed. Whether by Guido or Gérard, it is only important for our present purposes that Grosseteste was not the author. A few MSS not noticed by Dom Wilmart are listed here.

Oxford				
Lat. theol.	f. 6	ff. 1^{a}–208	XIII^{2}	Unasc.
Univ. Coll.	62	ff. 1^{A}–63^{A}	*ca.* 1425	*Extracta lincolniensis de lingua*
Cambridge, St John's	199	ff. 1^{A}–109^{C}	XIII^{2}	Asc. XVII to R.G.
Durham Cath.	B. III. 18	ff. 257^{A}–291^{C}	XV^{m}	Asc. XVII to R.G.
	B. III. 19	ff. 148^{A}–202^{D}	*ca.* 1400	Asc. to R.G.
Edinburgh, Univ.	85	ff. 1^{a}–135^{a}	XV^{1}	Unasc.
Breslau	I. Q. 108	ff. 1^{C}–58^{B}	XIII^{2}	Asc. to Guido. Ger.
Prague, Univ.	1516	ff. 66^{C}–83^{C}	*ca.* 1400	Asc. to Hugo. Boh.
Würzburg	M. ch. f. 229	ff. 2^{A}–74^{C}	XV^{2}	Asc. to Hugo. Ger.

There is a German fifteenth-century translation in Klosterneuburg MS 363, ff. 132–159. An English fifteenth-century "Doctrine of the Herte" in Fitzwilliam, McClean MS 132, ff. 1^{a}–117^{a}, seems to have no relation to our Latin treatise.

19. *Enchiridion.*

This title, without incipit, was first listed by Boston of Bury and repeated by Bale. Tanner suggests that the work is the *Manuel de Peches quod gallice scripsit Rob. Grost. et in angl. rythmos transtulit Rob. Brunensis.* There is no MS

* "Gérard de Liège: Un Traité inédit de l'Amour de Dieu" in *Rev. d'Ascétique et de Mystique*, XII (1931), 349–430.

† Made cardinal Dec. 1262, † 1272. See C. Eubel, *Hierarchia Catholica Medii Aevi*, I (Münster, 1898), 8.

evidence connecting Grosseteste with the Anglo-Norman original, whereas William of Waddington's authorship is clearly established. See summary of literature in J. Vising, *Anglo-Norman Language and Literature* (Oxford, 1923), p. 57.

There is another work, however, which may have been responsible for the false attribution to Grosseteste of a work bearing this title. Pavia Univ. MS 69, of English provenance, contains, ff. 1A–19A, XIII[1], a work with the rubric: *Incipit Encheridion penitentis ex summa Reymundi et ex distinccionibus W. Autissiod. et R. lincolniensis et R. de Leycestria.* The work begins: *Fidei est credere quod omnes nascimur....* There appear to be no specific quotations from Grosseteste in the body of the text. The *Distincciones* referred to would be his tractate *Templum Domini*, often appearing in MSS as *Distincciones Roberti lincolniensis.* See above, p. 138.

20. *Commentarius in Ethica Nicomachea.*

See above, p. 85 f., under *Notule in Ethica Nicomachea et in Commentatores Grecos.*

21. *Super Evangelia.*

Bale and Tanner list under this title a treatise beginning: *Missionem filii legimus duplicem...* but judge it to be the same as the *Moralitates super Evangelia.* See above, p. 134. This incipit does not appear in the *Moralitates*, nor have I found it in any MS.

22. *Exposicio in Verba Cantici.*

Wharton lists this work with the incipit: *Nigra sum sed formosa.* We might regard it as "genuine but lost" were it not for the fact that it is nowhere mentioned before Wharton. It might conceivably be one of the "lost" sermons, or one of the *dicta* that Grosseteste discarded in his final selection. See above, p. 214.

23. *De Fide Resurreccionis.*

Tanner lists a work under this title beginning: *Dominus ac redemptor noster...* which he had found in B.M. Cotton MS Otho D. x. There was once such a treatise in this codex (see Introd. p. 11) which still contains a great number of works of Grosseteste. But we have no means of knowing whether this treatise was ascribed to Grosseteste, as the part containing it was destroyed in the fire of 1731. Inasmuch as this work has appeared nowhere else ascribed to Grosseteste, we may suggest that it is the *Postilla in Mattheum* of Peter of Babylon, known to Boston of Bury, Bale and Tanner, which has this incipit. If Tanner found it in the Cotton MS unascribed, he might easily have been led to think that its presence in a predominantly Grossetestian MS justified an ascription to Grosseteste.

24. *De Septem Gradibus Contemplativorum.*

Inc.: Contemplativorum oculos aquilinos obtutus...
Expl.: ...concretum scilicet dominum nostrum Jesum Christum qui est benedictus in secula seculorum.

This short work, published among the works of Bonaventura in the Vatican

(1696) edition and by Peltier (1868), is found in four important and generally reliable collections of Grosseteste's sermons: B.M. Royal MSS 6. E. v, 7. E. II, 7. F. II and Lansdowne MS 458. It is found, according to the editors of the Quaracchi edition of the works of Bonaventura (1882 ff. vol. VIII, p. cxiv) in seventy MSS, of which twenty-six (only three of the fourteenth century) ascribe it to Bonaventura,* five to St Bernard, three to Thomas of Vercelli and one to St Thomas Aquinas.† The editors pointed out that there were three principal recensions, one noticeably the oldest. It is this oldest recension that has been published. The other recensions appear to be no more than reworkings of a tract that, because of confusion or doubt as to its authorship, had not become sacrosanct and consequently could undergo editing. Furthermore hardly any two MSS can be found to agree in detail. Bodley MS 36 is the oldest of the more than two score MSS of the treatise I have seen, and should not be dated later than XIII^{m}, written by an English scribe.‡ This early copy in England would confirm the rejection by the Quaracchi editors of Bonaventura's authorship. P. Glorieux in his compendious *Répertoire des Maîtres en Théologie de Paris au XIIIe Siècle* (Paris, 1933, I, 278) has ascribed the work to Thomas Gallus, Abbot of Vercelli († 1226 or 1246). The summary nature of the *Répertoire* did not permit of a discussion of the authorship, which would have involved an examination and redating of the oldest MSS, but the authorship of Thomas Gallus seems more likely than that of Grosseteste. Were the work by Grosseteste, in view of the number of English MSS of the thirteenth century, we should have expected earlier copies than the B.M. (XIV^{m-2}) MSS to be ascribed. The Continental tradition is, in general, earlier and more considerable as to copies extant than the English.

25. *De Homine.*

Bale, Pits and Tanner list a work under this title beginning: *Adam, ubi es? qui legis intelligat....* We may suspect confusion of the bibliographers with the work of Stephen Langton, *De Viciis et Virtutibus*, with this incipit.§ No other work beginning thus has been noted. The title suggests further confusion, as it does not agree with that given to Langton's work. Cf. the *dubium*, *De Homine Creato*, above, p. 237.

26. *Sancti Ignacii Epistole*, middle recension, often ascribed to Grosseteste. See above, p. 58 ff.

27. *Lexicon Greco-Latinum.*

Franceschini has lately raised the question of the possible Grossetestian authorship of the Greco-Latin lexicon,|| first noticed by M. R. James in

* Paris, B.N. lat. 2042, *ca.* 1310–1320, Fr., ff. 86^{C}–89^{A}, ascribes the work to Bonaventura. *It is the earliest ascription I have seen.*

† There was no list of these seventy MSS, but the number could doubtless be increased to well over one hundred.

‡ The presence of this item, ff. 75^{C}–76^{B}, is not mentioned in the *Summary Catalogue.*

§ See G. Lacombe and B. Smalley, "Studies on the Commentaries of Stephen Langton" in *Archives d'Histoire doctrinale et littéraire du Moyen Âge*, v (1930), 183, where reference to Bale's *Index* (i.e. ed. Poole) should be corrected from p. 427 to 417.

|| *Roberto Grossatesta...*, p. 68 ff.

1910, in MS 9 of the College of Arms in London.* James had argued that the lexicon came from Grosseteste's circle, but was not to be attributed to him. A *magister Nicholaus* he identified as *Nicholaus grecus*, Grosseteste's collaborator in the translation of the *Testamenta XII Patriarcharum*. Dialectic peculiarities indicate that the compiler was a Greek from Sicily or southern Italy with some familiarity with Byzantine Greek.† Franceschini sees in these facts reasons for believing that the lexicon was brought to England by one of the *coadiutores* that Grosseteste imported into England from Magna Graecia. But this is almost impossible. The lexicon is the work of an English scribe, writing a characteristic neat developed chancery hand. On paleographical evidence we must say the lexicon can hardly have been written before *ca.* 1275. See plate accompanying James' article, p. 408. Such lexicons were not, as a general rule, recopied, and we may safely assume that this copy is the original. The presence of dialectical Greek, localizable in Magna Graecia or Byzantium, raises no difficulties. An English scholar, working under the guidance of south Italian or Byzantine Greeks, would naturally reproduce their peculiarities. We conclude, therefore, that James' theory of authorship is the more satisfactory. It may furthermore be remarked that Grosseteste knew the difference between Ionian and Attic Greek, but makes no reference to Byzantine Greek as such in any of his known etymological glosses.

28. *De Lingua.*

This work, beginning: *Lingua congruit in duo opera, scilicet in gustum et in locucionem*... and ending ...*misericors est et mater misericordie*, is quoted by the author of the longer recension of the *Summa Iusticie* (see below, p. 263 ff.) as his own work ...*ut in nostro tractatu De Lingua*. The *De Lingua* contains, furthermore, a reference to a *tractatus de laude salvatorum*, evidently by the same author. See Lincoln Coll., Oxford, MS 56, f. 317^{a}. The *De Lingua* often appears in MSS with the *Summa Iusticie*. I have noticed no copy older than the earliest copy of the *Summa*, but it is manifestly an earlier work of the same author, who may be Johannes Guallensis. This work must be distinguished from a work with the identical incipit, found partially in Merton MS 272, f. 295^{A-D}, XIII^{m}, unascribed; Vatican Chigi MS A. v. 159, ff. 1^{A}–91^{B}, XIII^{m}, asc. *magistri Roberti*; and Melk 965, ff. 2^{A}–160^{A}, XIII^{2}, asc. *magistri Roberti Hylewardi*, that is, Robert Kilwardby. The Vatican MS is of English provenance, the Melk copy is more likely by a Lowlands scribe. Many of the MSS of the *De Lingua* have a *tabula* of the work. See also below, p. 263 f.

MSS:

Oxford				
Bodl.	81	ff. 2^{b}–189^{b}	part *ca.* 1300, rest XIV^{m}	Unasc.
Jesus	110	ff. 5^{A}–180^{D}	XV^{m}	Asc. R.G.
Lincoln	56	ff. 178^{b}–308^{a}	XV^{1}	Asc.‡
	105	ff. 47^{A}–104^{C}	XIV^{2}	Unasc.§

* In *Mélanges offerts à M. Émile Chatelain* (Paris, 1910), pp. 396–411.
† See James, *op. cit.* p. 406 ff., Franceschini, *op. cit.* p. 69 f.
‡ With *Dicta* and *De Venenis*. § With other asc. works.

Merton	187	ff. 2^A–135^C	1437	Asc.
Oriel	20	ff. 140^a–270^b	XV¹	Unasc.
Univ. Coll.	62	ff. 1^A–63^A	*ca.* 1425	Asc.*
London, B.M.				
Arundel	47	ff. 14^b–87	XIVᵐ	
	200	ff. 49^a–149^b	XV¹	Unasc.
Harley	5275	ff. 1^a–58^b	*ca.* 1400	Asc.†
	5369	Item 3	XV¹	
Cambridge				
Univ.	Ff. iii. 24	ff. 117^a–234^b	XVᵐ	Unasc.
Clare	22	ff. 1^a–106^b	XV	Asc.‡
Pembroke	246	ff. 5^a–246^b	XV¹	Asc.
Trinity	B. 15. 35	ff. 158^b–232^b	XIV²	Unasc.
Durham Cath.	B. III. 18	ff. 128^A–227^D	XVᵐ	Asc.
	B. III. 19	ff. 1^A–141^D	*ca.* 1400	Asc.
Lincoln Cath.	123	ff. 1^a–141^b	*ca.* 1400	Unasc. *mut.*
	125	ff. 74^A–226^B	XV¹	Asc.§
	126	ff. 1^a–110^A	XV¹	Asc.‖
Worcester Cath.	Q. 72	ff. 43^A–124^D	XV¹	Unasc.¶
Vatican	lat. 4348	ff. 1^A–112^C	XIVᵐ	Unasc. Engl.**

29. *De Lingua Abreviatus.*

Trinity Coll., Dublin, MS 207 (B. 4. 25) contains, ff. 23^A–50^A, XIV², an unascribed *De Lingua Abreviatus*, beginning: *Peccatum est vitandum sextuplici ab causa*, identical with Bodl. Laud Misc. MS 206, ff. 1^b–55^b, XV¹, where it is called *De Septem Viciis* and ascribed to Grosseteste. The work is an obviously late compilation from such common sources as the *Summa de Viciis* of Guillelmus Peraldus, the *De Venenis* and the *De Lingua*. The ascription to Grosseteste would seem purely gratuitous.

30. *Commentarii in Logicam.*

Bale, followed by later bibliographers, lists this inclusive title. We may, failing some early trustworthy ascriptions, regard it as respectful optimism on the part of Bale, unless, as is remotely possible, chap. 7 of the *Compendium Scienciarum*, the *De Divisione Scienciarum* of Gundissalinus, is meant.

31. *Manuel des Pechiez.*

Miss Hope Emily Allen has revived (*Romanic Review*, VIII (1917), 446–449) the theory that Grosseteste may have been the author of the *Manuel des Pechiez*, usually ascribed to William of Waddington. She reprints an account by Samuel Pegge given in his *Life of Robert Grosseteste* of a MS of Thomas Tyrwhitt, bought at Thomas Martin's sale (Pegge, p. 275). Miss Allen remarks that "the manuscript here described cannot be identified with any copy of the *Manuel des Pechiez* among those already listed; nor can it

* Only excerpts from *De Lingua* and *De Corde*.

† *Mut. in initio.*

‡ This codex was lost or misplaced when I visited the library in December, 1931.

§ With *De X Mandatis, De Venenis* and *Oculus Moralis.*

‖ *Mut. in fine.*

¶ With *Oculus Moralis.*

** First half of work only.

be otherwise traced". The MS is in all probability the B.M. Royal 20. B. XIV which Miss Allen had previously described, inasmuch as the contents seem to be the same. If that is so, no reliability can be placed on Pegge's statement, because Grosseteste's name does not occur, in this MS, in connection with the *Manuel des Pechiez*, though it does appear in the *Chasteau d'Amour*. But Pegge's statement is otherwise suspect. He says that the *Templum Domini* (*De Articulis Fidei*), q.v. above, p. 138, was translated into French verse. There is no known evidence for this. The *Manuel* could hardly be confused with the *Templum*, save by a very careless and casual person who neglected to read either work. More weight might be attached to the statement of Robert Mannyng of Brunne at the beginning of his *Handlyng Synne*: "Here begynneþ þe boke þat men clepyn yn frenshe Manuele Pecche þe whych boke made yn frenshe Roberd Gros-test, Bysshop of Lyncolne." But, in view of the fact that no one of the twenty MSS of the French text of the *Manuel* so much as mentions Grosseteste, we can safely regard the ascription of Mannyng, written some considerable time after the death of Grosseteste, as a gratuitous addition intended to give authority to the work he was rendering into English.

32. *Postilla super Evangelium Marci.*

H. H. Glunz, in a recent book,* ascribes to Grosseteste a commentary on Mark beginning: *Vidi et ecce quatuor quadrige egrediebantur*... found in the same Pembroke Coll., Cambridge, MS 7 which contains the *Postilla in Psalmos* of Stephen Langton ascribed to Grosseteste as *Memoriale* by early bibliographers. See next item. This commentary on Mark, ff. 228^{A}–267^{D}, is written by the same scribe as the *Postilla*, i.e. *ca.* 1200. There are some marginal notes in Grosseteste's hand at the beginning of the work, and, at the foot of the first page, Grosseteste began the name of the author in plummet: *venerabilis magistri*, but did not finish. There are at least four other copies of this commentary, viz. Bodley, Laud Misc. MS 291, ff. 93^{A}–153^{B}, written at the end of the twelfth century. In this codex the gospel is divided into thirteen chapters. A third copy is in Bodley MS 494, ff. 55^{D}–111^{C}, written about the same time. This codex was given by Hugh de Wilton, Archdeacon of Taunton, to the church of St Peter in Exeter. The date of Hugh's death is uncertain, between 1219 and 1244. A. Landgraf has noted† a MS in the B.N. in Paris, lat. 15269, of the thirteenth century, which contains, ff. 117^{a}–152^{a}, this *Glosa in Marcum* and *glose* on the other gospels, ascribed to Petrus Comestor. Another copy is in MS 11 of my own collection, ff. 1^{A}–34^{D}, unascribed. This codex gives every indication of having been written at Paris *ca.* 1200. All five copies, to judge from misreadings or *lacunae* in the text, are either copies of divergent archetypes or were care-

* *History of the Vulgate in England from Alcuin to Roger Bacon* (Cambridge, 1933), p. 280, and extracts from Pembroke MS in Appendix F, pp. 355–359.

† "Recherches sur les Écrits de Pierre le Mangeur" in *Rech. de Théol. anc. et méd.* III (1931), 341–372, particularly pp. 366–372. He treats at length the earlier suggestion of Lacombe in *Archives d'Histoire doctrinale et littéraire du Moyen Âge*, V (1930), that these glosses may have been the work of Langton, and points out the lack of any early ascription to Langton. Landgraf's arguments from internal evidence point conclusively to Petrus Comestor as author.

lessly written for commercial purposes. The Pembroke MS, which Grosseteste soon tired of correcting and was probably glad to trade for something more useful to him (see above, Introd. p. 26), is the worst from the point of view of text.

33. *Memoriale.*

Under this title Pits and Tanner listed a work beginning: *Est introitus interior*. Pits specifies a MS in Pembroke College, Cambridge. This is, of course, the present MS 7 which has on the front flyleaf in Grosseteste's hand: *Memoriale magistri Roberti Grosseteste pro Exameron Basilii*, which, as M. R. James pointed out,* constitutes, when connected with the fact that the book was at Bury St Edmunds in the early fourteenth century, evidence of a transaction whereby Grosseteste acquired from the Bury monks a copy of the *Paraphrasis Eustachii Exameron Basilii*, a rather rare work at that time in England, in return for this codex containing miscellaneous *postille* and commentaries. The incipit given by Pits and Tanner is that of the first item in the MS, ff. 1^{A}–132^{B}, the *Postilla in Psalmos* of Stephen Langton.† This MS must be dated *ca.* 1200, one of the earliest copies of the work. See also above, Introd. p. 25 ff.

34. *De Mendicantibus.*

There is in B.M. Harley MS 1002, ff. 94^{b}–95^{b}, *ca.* 1400, a short *questio* ascribed to Grosseteste. It begins: *Questio utrum viri ad corporales labores validi...* and ends *...populo christiano scandalo et gravamen*. But in spite of this specific ascription, the *questio* must be rejected as a later composition. It is surely a product of the fourteenth century, reflecting throughout the bitter struggle between the conventuals and the spirituals. Certainly in Grosseteste's lifetime no occasion had arisen for him, a good friend of both the Franciscan and the Dominican orders, to say (f. 96^{a}): *Callidissimus hostis multos ypocritas sub habitu monachorum, hoc est religiosorum, usquequam dispersit Sathanas*. In Bodley MS 52, ff. 140^{b}–145^{b}, XV^{1}, a tractate with this incipit, with substantial variants throughout the text, is ascribed to Thomas Wylton. In two other MSS, Bodley 158, ff. 147^{a}–152^{b}, XIV^{2}, and Lambeth 357, ff. 63^{b}–66^{b}, XV^{1}, it is unascribed. There is a tradition connecting the work with Richard Fitz-Ralph, Archbishop of Armagh († 1360).

35. *Commentarius in Metaphysica Aristotelis.*

Stevenson (p. 43 f.), through a misunderstanding of the meaning of *procuracio* in the Durham College Rolls (ed. Blakiston, Oxford Hist. Soc. III, 37) attributed a commentary on the *Metaphysics* to Grosseteste, and remarked that it was lost. Baur (p. 40*) showed that the *procuracio eiusdem* referred to a Robert of Graystones who had presented to Durham College *inter alia* a copy of Grosseteste's *In Posteriora* and an anonymous *Exposicio super Meta-*

* *Catalogue of MSS...of Pembroke College, Cambridge* (Cambridge, 1905), p. 7.

† See G. Lacombe, "Studies in the Commentaries of Stephen Langton" in *Archives d'Histoire doctrinale et littéraire du Moyen Âge*, V (1930), 37, and P. Glorieux, *Répertoire des Maîtres...*, I (Paris, 1933), 240. This MS seems not to have been noticed by either of these scholars.

physica. Miss Sharp, accepting Stevenson's attribution,* overlooked Baur's correction. It may be added that we should hardly expect a commentary on the *Metaphysics* from Grosseteste. His interests lay elsewhere.

36. *De Natura Luminis et Diaphoni.*

Boston of Bury, followed by Bale, Pits and Tanner, listed a work under this title, beginning: *Considerandum quippe est.* The work is, however, an excerpt from Bk. II, lect. 19, of the commentary on the *De Anima* of Aristotle by Thomas Aquinas.†

37. *De Oculo Morali.*

Inc.: Si diligenter voluerimus in lege domini meditari...

Expl.: ...illic eriguntur. Ad illud regnum nos perducat qui sine fine vivit et regnat.

Publ. 1475 (asc. to John Pecham), 1496 (asc. to Pierre de la Sépière), 1496 (in Italian translation), 1641, 1655, 1656.

This popular work has been variously ascribed in the MSS: to John Pitsanus (Pecham), to John of Wales, to Duns Scotus, to Raymond Jordan († 1381), to Pierre de Limoges (de la Sépière) and to Grosseteste. The evidence of the oldest MSS, however, is virtually unanimous in ascribing it to Pierre de Limoges († 1306). This was pointed out as long ago as 1869 in the *Hist. litt. de la France* (xxv, 194 ff.).‡ All the English bibliographers, beginning with Bale, have ascribed the work to Grosseteste. Recently J. T. Welter has discussed the work at some length in his masterly study of the *Exemplum*, § and added a partial list of about seventy MSS in European libraries. He lists but nineteen MSS in English libraries. I give below a more complete list of MSS in the British Isles. In many of these MSS a *tabula* precedes or follows the text.

MSS:

Oxford				
Bodl.	122	ff. 6^a–54^b	*ca.* 1400	Unasc.‖
	315	ff. 28^B–59^D	XV^1	Asc. R.G.?¶
	742	ff. 302^A–340^C	1444	Asc. XVII R.G.?**
Digby	77	ff. 109^a–148^a	XIII^2	Unasc.
Laud Misc.	519	ff. 127^a–246^a	XV^m	Unasc. Ger.
	527	ff. 220^a–256^a	XIV^1	Asc. R.G. *a.m.* XIV^2
	677	ff. 148^C–231^C	XIV^2	Unasc. Ger.

* *Franciscan Philosophy at Oxford in the Thirteenth Century* (Oxford, 1930), p. 14.

† See M. Grabmann, *Die Werke d. Heiligen Thomas von Aquin* in the Münster *Beiträge* (1931, Bd. xxii, Hefte 1–2), p. 346, and P. Mandonnet, *Des Écrits authentiques de S. Thomas d'Aquin* (2nd ed. Freiburg, 1910), p. 151.

‡ B. Hauréau, author of this article on Jean de Galles, reviews the divergent ascriptions of Wadding, Oudin, Sbaralea and the incunable editions, and favours Pierre de Limoges. See also H. Spettmann, "Das Schriftchen 'De Oculo Morali' und sein Verfasser", in *Arch. Franc. Hist.* xvi (1923), 309–322.

§ *L'Exemplum dans la Littérature religieuse et didactique du Moyen Âge* (Paris, 1927), p. 177 ff.

‖ *Mut. in initio.*

¶ *Secundum magistrum de Lunochia.*

** *Magister de Lunochia.*

Balliol	274	ff. 166ᵃ–204ᵃ	1409	Unasc.
Magdalen	6	ff. 3ᵃ–59ᵇ	XIV¹	Asc. R.G.*
	202	ff. 183ᴮ–216ᶜ	XV¹	Asc. R.G.
Merton	43	f. 54ᵃ, five lines	XIV¹	Asc. R.G. XIV²
	82	ff. 64ᴬ–95ᴮ	*ca.* 1300	Unasc.
	216	ff. 203ᵃ–229	XIV²	Asc. R.G. *a.m.*
Oriel	20	ff. 271ᵃ–309	XV¹	Asc. R.G.
Univ. Coll.	62	pp. 1ᵃ–63ᵃ	*ca.* 1425	Asc. R.G.†
London, B.M.				
Arundel	200	ff. 15ᵃ–43ᵇ	XV¹	Asc. R.G.‡
Cotton	Otho D. x	ff. 2ᵃ–21ᵇ	XIVᵐ	Unasc.
	Vitell. C. xiv	ff. 7ᴬ–30ᴮ	XIV²	Asc. R.G.
Royal	6. E. v	ff. 211ᴮ–227ᴮ	XIVᵐ	Asc. R.G.
	7. C. i	ff. 3ᴬ–32ᴬ	XIV²	Unasc.
	12. D. vii	ff. 103ᴬ–135ᴰ	*ca.* 1300	Unasc. Ital.
	12. E. xxi	ff. 105ᵃ–145ᵃ	XV¹	Asc. R.G.
London, Lambeth	137	ff. 280ᴰ–309ᴰ	XIV¹	Unasc.
	483	ff. 4ᵃ–70ᵇ	XIV²	Asc. R.G.
	523	ff. 1ᵃ–85ᵃ	XIV²	Unasc.
Cambridge				
Univ.	Ii. ii. 27	f. 111ᴬ⁻ᴮ	XIV²	*Capitula* only
	Ll. i. 15	ff. 53ᵃ–80ᵃ	XIII²	Unasc. Lowlands
Gonv. & Caius	200	pp. 3–140	XIV²	Unasc.‡
Jesus	67	ff. 170ᵃ–275ᵇ	XIV²	Asc. R.G.
Pembroke	229	ff. 119ᴬ–154ᴰ	XIV²	Unasc.
Peterhouse	279, pt. ii§	ff. 1ᵃ–24ᵇ	XIV²	Asc. R.G. XV²
Sid. Suss.	85	ff. 147ᵃ–190ᵃ	XIII²	Unasc.
Trinity	B. 15. 35	ff. 232ᵇ–251ᵃ	XIV²	Unasc.
Dublin, Trinity	115 (A. 5. 3)	ff. 301ᵃ–361ᵃ	1377	Asc. R.G.
Durham Cath.	A. iv. 18	ff. 1ᵃ–62ᵇ	XV¹	Asc. R.G.‖
	B. iii. 18	ff. 292ᴬ–319ᴬ	XVᵐ	Asc. R.G.
	B. iii. 19	ff. 203ᶜ–239ᶜ	*ca.* 1400	Unasc.¶
Lincoln Cath.	125	ff. 1ᴬ–34ᴰ	XV¹	Unasc.
Manchester, John Rylands	181	ff. 1ᵇ–51ᵇ	XVᵐ	Asc. Pecham
Worcester Cath.	F. 115	ff. 211ᴬ–227ᴬ	XIV²	Unasc.
	Q. 14	ff. 115ᵃ–183ᵃ	XV¹	Unasc.**
	Q. 72	ff. 125ᴬ–160ᶜ	XV¹	Unasc.
	Q. 97	Unfoliated	XVᵐ	Unasc.

38. *De Penitencia.*

A tractate beginning either *Ne tardeas converti ad dominum* or *Peniteas cito peccator* is ascribed to Grosseteste in several late MSS, e.g. Cambridge Univ. Kk. iv. 20, XIV¹, ff. 44ᵃ–47ᴬ, and by Bale and Tanner. It is the metrical work, often glossed, but originally by either John of Garland—though it does not seem likely to me (cf. Hauréau, *Notices et Extraits*, xxvii, pt. ii, p. 10)—or William de Montibus (so ascribed in Cambridge Univ. Ii. i. 26, XIII¹, ff. 1ᴬ–3ᴬ) and printed in *Patr. Lat.* ccvii, col. 1153 ff., among the works of Peter of Blois.

* And John of Wales, XIV².

† With extracts from *De Lingua.*

‡ *Mut. in initio.*

§ Now St John's MS 91, pt. ii.

‖ The ascription to Grosseteste of the eighteenth century; the MS is *mut. in initio et in fine.*

¶ With asc. *De Corde* and *De Venenis.*

** With *De Lingua.*

At all events it antedates Grosseteste, and he may quite well have used it in his own *De Modo Confitendi* (see above, p. 126) as a source. The rubric of this latter work, in the oldest MS, reads: *Diversi tractatus penitencie in unum redacti secundum magistrum Robertum Grosseteste.*

39. *Commentarius in Physica Aristotelis.*

Tanner mentioned a commentary on the *Physics* in Bodley e Museo MS 130 (ff. 1ᵃ–19ᵇ). Baur (p. 20*) gave the modern signature, e Museo 230, and judged the work to be an abbreviation of the *Summa in Physica* (see above, p. 83) intended for students. It is not, however, an abridgment of the *Summa*, but an independent work, of about the same length. The work begins: *Quoniam autem ut dicit Aristoteles hinc opinamur unumquodque scire cum causas cognoscimus*... and ends ...*quod indivisibile, immobile, incorruptibile est nullam magnitudinem habens.* In spite of the ascription by the scribe of the text, *ca.* 1425, the probabilities are all against Grosseteste's authorship. We have already a genuine commentary on the *Physics*, attested by two good and fairly early MSS (see above, p. 82), and the *Summa*, for which the tradition is unimpeachable. It seems *prima facie* unlikely that Grosseteste would have written a third. The work may have been written by someone who was familiar with Grosseteste's *Summa*, though it does not show any sign of being influenced by the full commentary. There are no distinctively Grossetestian ideas in the treatise. The sections on eternity and motion, on which subjects Grosseteste had very definitely un-Aristotelian ideas, are noticeably lacking in any Grossetestian characteristics and read like the exaggeratedly logical treatises of the middle and late fourteenth century. Grosseteste avoided formal logic wherever he could. This is certainly a case where Baur's criterion of a great discrepancy in "Sprache und Terminologie" (p. 23*) would apply. The colophon might be read so as to give rise to a suspicion of fraud. *Explicit optimum opus super octo libros physicorum secundum Lincolniensem.* The *optimum*, in view of the absence of other copies, sounds hopeful on the part of the scribe. It is even more suspicious that the same scribe has written other commentaries which are unmistakably identical in tone and manner of argument. They follow in order of their appearance in the MS.

40. *Commentarius in De Anima*, ff. 20ᵃ–65ᵃ, beginning: *Iste est primus liber de anima qui prima sua divisione*....

41. *Commentarius in De Celo et Mundo*, ff. 65ᵇ–88ᵃ, beginning: *Iste est liber Aristotelis intitulatus de celo et mundo in quo determinat de toto universo*....*

42. *Commentarius in De Generacione et Corrupcione*, ff. 90ᵃ–123ᵃ, beginning: *Iste est liber de generacione et corrupcione in quo determinat philosophus de corpore mobili ad formam*....

43. *Commentarius in Meteora*, ff. 126ᵃ–140ᵃ, beginning: *In isto libro qui liber metheororum intitulatur*.... This last is the unpublished commentary of Walter Burley on the *Meteora*, extant and ascribed in many English MSS. Bale and Leland must have assumed the authenticity of all the works in this MS, as they

* For his *Questiones in De Celo et Mundo*, see above, p. 86.

have listed all the titles, though without incipits. Tanner mentions the MS and gives the incipits of all the works, but notices that the last four bore no ascription, but were only *cum Lincoln. in Libr. Physic. e Mus.* 130 *in Bibl. Bodl.* There is no good reason to ascribe any of them to Grosseteste.

44. *Poetria Aristotelis, Translacio ex Greco.*

Grabmann noted* the ascription in Erfurt Amplon. Q. 16 (not 66, as Grabmann gives), ff. 1^a–16^a, XV[1], to Grosseteste of a translation of the *Poetria Aristotelis.* The rubric reads: *Incipit primus liber poetrie Aristotelis. Prologus linconiensis translatoris.* This is the translation by Hermannus Alemannus of the commentary of Averroës on the *Poetics* of Aristotle.

45. *De Potenciis Anime.*

Walter Burley's unpublished treatise *De Potenciis Anime,* beginning: *Ut dicit philosophus* 2° *de Anima*... and ending ...*in duo membra, sicut affectivus et sensitivus,* was ascribed to Grosseteste by Leland, Bale, Pits and Tanner. The source of this error is, happily, easily traced. An early copy of the work, Digby MS 172, ff. 1^A–6^B, *ca.* 1300, bears no inscription in the original hand. The *contenta,* however, in a later hand, *ca.* 1350, list *linc' de potenciis anime,* which has been copied at the top of f. 1^a. Yet Burley's authorship is well established by a number of contemporary ascriptions. The work contains a quotation from the *De Sensu et Sensato* of Albertus Magnus, not composed before 1256,† several years after Grosseteste's death. A Hebrew translation of this work, probably from this MS, as it ascribes it to Grosseteste, was noted by Steinschneider, *Hebräische Uebersetzungen* (Berlin, 1893), p. 476. See above, under *De Anima,* p. 89 f.

46. *De Preceptis.*

In a recent article I accepted,‡ somewhat uncritically, the MS ascription of a tractate beginning: *Primum preceptum est non adorabis deos alienos*...*scultile scilicet rei non existentis*... and ending ...*nullus est finis. Erit hic ergo consummatus,* found as a separate work in Pavia MS 69, ff. 67^A–85^C, XIII[1], Engl. See above, Introd. p. 19 f. I am informed by Dr R. W. Hunt that this tractate forms the last part of the *Qui bene presunt* of Richard of Wetherstede, sometimes ascribed to William de Montibus. See above, p. 19. The Italian scribe may easily have misread or misgrouped the *contenta* or misconstrued the change of hand between the separate parts of the *Qui bene presunt.* It is not insignificant that in the ascription the Italian scribe writes *lincolniensis.* The second *l* would indicate that he had before him the writing of an English scribe. The normal Italian way of writing the name was almost anything but this.

* *Aristoteles-Uebersetzungen d. XIII. Jhdts.* (*Beiträge,* Münster, 1916), p. 257.
† See Fr. Pelster, *Kritische Studien zum Leben und zu den Schriften Alberts des Grossen* (Freiburg i.B. 1920), p. 161, n. 2. See also my note "The *De Anima* of Robert Grosseteste" in *New Scholasticism,* VII (1933), 202.
‡ "A XIIIth Century *Oure Fader* in a Pavia MS" in *Modern Language Notes,* April, 1934, pp. 235–237.

47. *In Predicamenta Aristotelis.*

We may safely regard this title as a mistake of Bale, repeated by later bibliographers. The mistake may have arisen from the presence of Burley's homonymous work in a codex containing a genuine work of Grosseteste.

48. *In Priora Aristotelis.*

A treatise beginning: *Cum omnis sciencia sit veri acquisitiva*... and ending ...*et via que non est inconveniens* is ascribed to Grosseteste by Bale, Pits and Tanner. It is the unpublished work of Robert Kilwardby, and is so ascribed in many early MSS, e.g. Merton 280 (*ca.* 1300) and 289 (XIV^{1}); Bologna Univ. 846 (1626) (XIII^{2}); Erfurt, Amplon. Q. 328 (XIII^{2}), an English MS; Florence, B.N. G. 3 (XIV^{1}), etc. See also Baur, p. 45*.

49. *Prophecia Domini Roberti de Grostest.*

The following twelve lines appear under this rubric in Bodl. Digby MS 196, f. 28 (XV^{m}). It had been noticed by Tanner. Hitherto unpublished.

Externis populis dominabitur aquila fortis,
Alpes transcendet, sulcabit et equora remis;
Jerusalem veniet, infestus erit Sarazenis;
Imperium mundi retinens gaudebit et orbis,
Sub se catholicaque fides vigebit et ille
In superis premium percipiet atque tenebit,
En vagus et primo perdet sed finem resumet.
Multa rapit medio volitans sub fine secundi;
Orbem subvertit reliquo clerumque reducet.
In statum pristini seviens renovet loca sancta,
Hinc terrena spuens sanctus super ethera scandet.
Prophecia de regibus Anglie.

In the right margin has been added:

Prophecia H[enrico] patre defuncto regna.
R[icardus] I, quoque relicto tunc H[enricus] secundus
Edwardus ter regnabit, R[icardus] tunc quoque mira.

I am unfamiliar with this prophecy, nor is it clear to whom it might properly refer during Grosseteste's lifetime. It can hardly refer to Henry III, but possibly to the Emperor, Frederick II.* In that case, however, the *Externis populis* might appear inept. There is also the fact that Grosseteste was not favourably disposed toward the Emperor. The verse is better than any we know Grosseteste to have composed.

50. *Super Exposicione Magistri Sentenciarum.*

An entry in the *Index Bibliothecae Vaticanae* from the time of Sixtus IV (1471–1484) reads: *Linconiensis super exposicione Magistri Sentenciarum ex memb. in albo.* E. Müntz suggested Richard de Lincoln († 1334) as the author.† Pelzer has identified the MS as Vatican lat. 1101, which contains the *Sentences* of Pierre de Poitiers.‡

* T. L. Kington in his *History of Frederick the Second*, I (London, 1862), 448, states that "letters on public affairs certainly passed between them", i.e. Grosseteste and Frederick II. See above, p. 192, n. ‡.

† *La Bibliothèque du Vatican* (Paris, 1887), p. 165.

‡ See his *Codices Vaticani Latini*, pt. I (Vatican City, 1931), *s.n.*

51. *Liber Quadrantis.*

A work on the quadrant, sometimes known as the *Chilinder Oxoniensis*, beginning: *Cum quadrantem componere volueris*... and ending ...*pars virge ad profunditatem putei*, has occasionally been ascribed to Grosseteste in printed catalogues of MSS. The only reason for the ascription would seem to be that it may appear in the same codex with one or more mathematical works by him, such as the *De Sphera* or the *Compotus*. But the fact that this work always remains unascribed when the genuine works are ascribed is actually strong evidence against Grosseteste's authorship. See Baur, p. 142*.

MSS:

Oxford, Digby	98	ff. 162^A–165^b	XIII²
	104	ff. 108^C–109^D	XIV²
London, B.M.			
Add.	25031	ff. 17^a–19^b	XIII²
Egerton	843	ff. 43^a–45^b	XIII², variant expl.
Royal	12. E. XXV	ff. 142^a–145^a	XIII²
Cambridge, Univ.	Ff. vi. 13	ff. 44^a–45^b	XIII², *mut.*

52. *De Officio Quadrantis.*

In Vienna Nationalbibliothek MS 5239–5239*, a paper codex originating probably in Bamberg (XV¹), there is a work which this title would fit, ff. 19^b*–23^a*, beginning: *Sequitur de officio quadrantis prout spectatur ad geometriam per ipsum operari*... and ending, after a *tabula quadrantis* on f. 22^a*–^b*, ...*que area multiplicetur per eius altitudinem et productum dabit capacitatem. Explicit tractatus de quadrante domini lincloniensis* [*sic* !]. The work is based in part on the *Tractatus de Quadrante* of Robertus Anglicus. See next item. The scribe, perhaps influenced by the presence of genuine works of Grosseteste in the codex from which he was copying, or in an earlier part of this same codex, must have hazarded the attribution.

53. *Tractatus de Quadrante.*

The well-known work on the quadrant written by a certain Robertus Anglicus* in Montpellier in 1276–1278, and so described in many early MSS,† beginning: *Geometrie due sunt partes scil. theorica et practica*... and ending ...*dabit capacitatem vasis quadrangularis*, has, at various times, been erroneously ascribed to Grosseteste. P. Tannéry has discussed the MS tradition at some length.‡ There have been several commentaries on this work, adding confusion to the MS cataloguer's problem.§

* Known also as *Perscrutator Eboracensis*.

† It is sometimes ascribed to *Johannes in Monte Pessulano*, e.g. B.M. Royal 12. C. XVII, f. 61^a.

‡ "Le traité du quadrant..." in *Not. et Extraits*..., XXXV, pt. ii (1897), 561 ff. He lists thirty-five MSS. There are probably at least one hundred MSS of the work extant. See also L. Thorndike, *Magic and Experimental Science*, II, 437, and literature there given.

§ E. J. Goodspeed in his *Catalogue of MSS in*... *Univ. of Chicago* (Chicago, 1912), p. 5, MS 3, ff. 7^A–18^D, associates the name of Grosseteste with a fifteenth-century commentary on this work, but the MS ascribes it to Kilwardby.

54. *Salutacio Beate Virgini Marie.*

Inc.: Ave dei genitrix et immaculata
Virgo, celi gaudium, toti mundo nata
Ad salutem, hominum in exemplum data,
Dignare me laudare te, virgo sacrata....

Expl.: ...Tui ergo filii redempti cruore,
Quem in crucis prelio fudit cum liquore,
Hac peruncti gracia, te laudamus ore,
Ut in tuis laudibus simus et amore.

[Twelve stanzas of four lines each.]

Publ. by F. J. Mone, *Lateinische Hymnen des Mittelalters*, II (Freiburg i.Br. 1853–1855), 100–103. The variants given by Mone are considerable. The poem is also listed by U. Chevalier, *Repertorium Hymnologicum*, no. 1761. Mone listed five MSS, all German or South German, and none of the thirteenth century. Only one of these five, Salzburg, St Peter I, 14, XV², bears an ascription: *Sequens salutacio virginis gloriose est composita per magistrum Rudbertum episcopum civitatis linconiensis et Urbanus VI eam confirmavit.* To Mone's one ascribed MS we can add another, Paris, B.N. lat. 10636, from Köln, and also of the late fifteenth century, which contains a copy of the spurious *Disputacio Corporis et Anime*. The Paris ascription reads: *Sequentem salutacionem beate Virgini composuit idem magister Robertus Grossicapitis de Francia episcopus lynchoniensis.* In spite of these suspiciously similar ascriptions the work must be rejected. (*a*) We have no ascription until after *ca.* 1450; (*b*) we have no English copy, nor indeed any English tradition for the composition of any similar poem; (*c*) we have no external evidence of any sort that Grosseteste wrote such a poem; (*d*) the reliability of the German tradition concerning the works of Grosseteste, unlike the Italian, is notoriously low; (*e*) Mone pointed out that many verses were identical with *Carmen* 63 of Peter Damiani.* Those lines are 3, 5–13, 17–18, 21, 25, 27, 29, 33–34, 37, 40, 41. Many others are quite obviously reworked from the original of Damiani.†

MSS:

London, B.M., Royal	8. A. IX	f. 15ᵇ	1305–1317	Unasc. So. Fr.
Mainz, Karth.	No. 380	f. 80	XIV	Unasc. (Mone)
Munich, August. Eccl.	No. 127	last leaf	XIV	Unasc. (Mone)
Paris, B.N.	lat. 10636	ff. 14ᵇ–15ᵃ	XV²	Asc. Köln‡
Salzburg, St Peter	I. 14		XV²	Asc. (Mone)
	IV. 38		XV	Unasc. (Mone)
	VI. 3		XVᵐ	Unasc. (Mone)

* *Patr. Lat.* CXLV, col. 939 f.

† Hauréau, *Not. et Extraits*, VI, 276, describing MS nouv. acq. lat. 1544, f. 78ᵇ, XV, suggests the poem is by a German.

‡ The explicit in this MS reads:

...pium confortamen
Omnes sancte virgines sanctum quoque flamen
Qui regnat per secula seculorum. Amen,

which is very close to the corresponding lines in Damiani's last stanza.

55. *Sentencia Scripturarum.*

Bale, Pits and Tanner list a work under this title beginning: *Abominacio desolacionis quadrupliciter exponitur*... which, so far as I can ascertain, must be the *Index in Pseudo-Chrysostomi Opus Imperfectum*, found, unascribed, in B.M. Royal MS 6. C. v, f. 2ª ff., XVᵐ. There appears to be no reason to ascribe it to Grosseteste, who does not list the *Opus Imperfectum* in his *Concordancia Patrum*. See above, p. 122 ff. This *Concordancia* may be taken as a reliable index of his reading in patristic literature up to the time of its composition, i.e. hardly later than 1240.

56. *Sermones.*

In some printed catalogues of MSS and in a few late MSS, e.g. Trinity Coll. Cambridge R. 8. 16, f. 1ᴬ ff., a collection of sermons beginning: *Convertimini ad me in toto corde vestro. Nota quod quatuor requiruntur*... is ascribed to Grosseteste. It is probably the work of Robert Holcot († 1349), and is so ascribed in B.M. Sloane MS 1616, f. 135ª. In any case these sermons cannot be by Grosseteste. A work of Albertus Magnus, *De Vegetabilibus*, written *ca.* 1260,* is quoted. See B.M. Cotton MS Vitell. C. xiv, f. 142ᴮ. In Trinity Coll., Oxford, MS 19, ff. 122ª–158, *ca.* 1260, there is a collection of about forty sermons beginning: *Convertimini ad me in toto corde vestro. Consilium istud salubre est ad secretum*.... There is no ascription. For a series of sermons by Grosseteste beginning with one on this text see above, p. 182 f. This duplication of text for the initial sermon may explain the rise of an erroneous or vague tradition.

57. *Summa Iusticie.*

Recension I:

Inc.: Summa iusticie Christi fidelium est declinare a malo...

Expl.: ...in tua infirmitate non disperes teipsum sed ora deum.

Recension II:

Inc.: Quia iusticia fidelium est declinare...

Expl.: ...et hec de quinque sensibus sufficiant.

Boston of Bury did not ascribe this unpublished work to Grosseteste, but Pits and Tanner noted the Balliol and Lincoln Coll. MSS; Tanner added the Cambridge Univ. and Peterhouse 89 (now 238) copies, remarking *forsan Joannis Guallensis*. The relative lateness of these MSS may have cast doubt on the genuineness of the work. There is, however, an earlier (*ca.* 1300) MS of the work in Jesus Coll., Cambridge, bearing an ascription to Grosseteste in a second hand of about the middle of the fourteenth century. This makes the rejection of the work more complicated, but none the less imperative. As has been previously noted by Gilson,† there are two versions of the work, a longer and a shorter. He was of the opinion that the longer—"partly plagiarized from this" shorter—was a later work. But the available evidence would seem rather to bear the opposite interpretation. There is no MS of the shorter version (Recension II) that can be dated earlier than the early part of the fifteenth century. There is, on the other hand, one MS of the

* See B. Geyer, *Phil. Jahrbuch* (1917), p. 397 and F. Pelster, *Kritische Studien zum Leben und zu den Schriften Alberts d. Grossen* (1920), p. 133 ff.

† *Catalogue of Royal MSS*, I, 226.

longer version (Recension I) that must be dated *ca.* 1300, and another of the second third of the fourteenth century. As noticed above, p. 252, the longer version is by the author of the *De Lingua*, of which our earliest copy dates from *ca.* 1300. Version I has the same internal characteristics as to style and method of presentment as the *De Lingua*, and particularly so in its copious quotations from Aristotle's *naturalia*. The most frequently cited is the *De Animalibus* in nineteen books, i.e. the Arab-Latin translation of Michael Scot, *ca.* 1230. The author also cites freely from the *Metaphysica*, the *Physica*, the *De Celo et Mundo* in the Arab-Latin translation of Gerard of Cremona, Bks. II and III of the *Meteorologica*, the *De Generacione et Corrupcione*, the *De Vegetabilibus*, the *De Anima*, *De Sensu et Sensato*, *De Memoria et Reminiscencia*, *De Morte et Vita* and the *De Somno et Vigilia*. More interesting to us is the fact that he quotes the *Ethica Nicomachea* in Grosseteste's translation and the *De Fide Orthodoxa* of John Damascene, also in Grosseteste's translation. We may further observe his extensive use of Isidore's *Etymologiae* and *De Summo Bono* for derivations, which would certainly have shocked Grosseteste, who would surely have preferred his own, at least after he had done so much translating from the Greek, as to quote from the *Ethics*, written *ca.* 1243. The author of the long recension knew almost no Greek, and the author of the short recension was perhaps worse off, as he used Hugucius as an authority for etymology, and the *Derivationes* of Hugucius* were about as bad as such compilations could be in the twelfth century. The long recension quotes the Pseudo-Boethius' *De Disciplina Scolarium*, a work of the early thirteenth century.† See Lincoln Coll. MS 105, f. 13A: pt. VII, chap. ii. The *Summa* is, however, the work of an author of great ability and it deserves further study. But we regard it as not by Grosseteste, in summary, for the following reasons:

(*a*) The earlier MSS bear no contemporary ascription.

(*b*) If it were Grosseteste's work it would have to be dated after *ca.* 1243, to account for quotations from his own translations, and if it should have to be dated so late in his life, it would naturally exhibit a knowledge of Greek, which it cannot be said at all to do.

(*c*) Authors are quoted frequently whom Grosseteste carefully avoids in his later years: Isidore and Hugucius.

(*d*) The general approach to questions of theology and the *modus arguendi* are quite un-Grossetestian, in spite of a basic Augustinianism.

Of the shorter recension it need only be said that it is much inferior and obviously a later abridgment, retaining all the un-Grossetestian features, yet without the merit of freshness and balance which marks the longer recension. As Recension I must be placed somewhere after 1250 on internal evidence‡ and before 1300 on paleographical evidence, there seems at the present

* See Haskins, *Mediaeval Science*, p. 150.

† See P. Lehmann, *Die Pseudo-Antike Literatur d. Mittelalters* (Leipzig, 1927), p. 27.

‡ Closer study of the various quotations from the works of Aristotle would possibly show that the *terminus a quo* should be placed *ca.* 1270.

moment no good reason to disregard the old tradition attributing the work to *Joannes Guallensis.**

MSS:

Recension I (in ten parts):

Oxford				
Balliol	320	ff. 57A–149, beg. Pt. VI, c. 8	XV¹	Asc.
Lincoln	105	ff. 1A–32A, beg. Pt. VI, c. 7	XIV²	Asc. XV¹
London, B.M., Harley	632	ff. 168a–247b	XV¹	Unasc. *mut. in fine*
Cambridge				
Univ.	Ff. iii. 24	ff. 1a–116b	XVm	Unasc.
Jesus	36	ff. 1A–218C	*ca.* 1300	Asc. XIVm
Peterhouse	238	ff. 1a–116a	XIV²	Unasc.

Recension II (in nine parts):

Oxford, Univ. Coll.	109	pp. 247a–302b, beg. Pt. II, c. 2	XV¹	Unasc.
London, B.M.				
Harley	1298	ff. 49A–84C	*ca.* 1400	Unasc.
	5369	ff. 101a–196a	XV¹	Unasc.
Royal	8. B. XVII	ff. 1a–52b, beg. Pt. I, c. 8; ends Pt. IX, c. 3	XV¹	Unasc.
Cambridge, St John's	15	ff. 1a–70b	*ca.* 1400	Asc.

58. *Summa Philosophie.*

This work, beginning: *Philosophantes famosi primi fuerunt Caldai*... and ending ...*sicut et colorem eorum pariter mistorum*, has been generally ascribed to Grosseteste from the time of Leland and Bale. The various MSS have been cited by bibliographers, save the Merton copy which seems to have escaped their notice.† There is no ascription in any known MS to any author other than Grosseteste, but it is now recognized as quite impossible that he wrote the work. Baur's edition showed that works of Albertus Magnus were quoted which were not written until after Grosseteste's death, and that there was a reference to the death of Simon de Montfort (1264). There is, furthermore, considerable internal divergence from authentic works of Grosseteste. The earliest known MS must be dated XIVm. Undoubtedly a product of the Oxford School of scientific thought, on evidence thus far available, the work was probably composed in the last quarter of the thirteenth century.‡ Duhem argues that the author was a pupil of Roger Bacon.§

* No. 465 of the MSS of the Earl of Kingston, destroyed by fire at Thoresby, April 4, 1745, bore the title *Joh. Gualensis sive Waleys de Iusticia cc* I.

† Powicke, *Merton Books*, p. 183, note, suggests that an *Isagoge philosophie moralis*, once in Merton MS 43, may have been the *Summa*. It is quite possible. It is notable that the work was there unascribed.

‡ See Baur, p. 140*; Baur's earlier edition of Dominicus Gundissalinus' *De Divisione Philosophiae* (*Beiträge*, Bd. IV, Hefte 2–3, Münster, 1903), p. 152 f.; Ueberweg-Geyer, *Die Patristische und Scholastische Zeit* (Berlin, 1928), p. 408 and literature there given; A. Bertsch, *Studien zur Summa Philosophie d. Pseudo Robert Grosseteste* (Diss.), Braunschweig, 1929.

§ *Système du Monde*, III (Paris, 1915), 460 ff.

MSS:

Oxford				
Digby	220	ff. 1^A–80^D	XV^1	Asc.
Merton	310	ff. 2^A–60^D	XIV^m, ends c. 12	Unasc.
Cambridge				
Univ.	Ii. iii. 19	ff. 1^A–122^B	XV^1	Asc.
Fitzwilliam, McClean	169	ff. 246^a–251^a	XV^1, *frag.*	Asc.

Fr. E. Longpré has kindly told me of having seen another copy of this work in a Spanish library. I was unable to trace it when in Spain in 1935.

59. *Syncategoremata.*

Prantl suggested,* on a basis of Brewer's description† of Digby MS 204, that the work beginning: *Parcium oracionis quedam sunt indeclinabiles*... was a work of Grosseteste. The rubric in the MS says simply *Syncategoreumata fratris Roberti.* Baur (pp. 120*–122*) noticed the error in the old Amplonian catalogue (1412) repeated by Schum in his usually excellent catalogue of the Erfurt MSS, ascribing an early (XIII^2) English copy of this work (MS Q. 328, ff. 74^A–93^D, *mut. in fine*) to Grosseteste. In the Erfurt MS there is now no ascription. The codex contains other works of Kilwardby. Grosseteste is never called *frater Robertus* in MSS. It is, on the other hand, a common designation for Robert Kilwardby, a Dominican friar. The treatise in the Digby MS must be added to the list of the works of Kilwardby.

60. *Testimonia Gentilium de Secta Christiana.*

A MS in the B.M., Add. 34807, of the first half of the fifteenth century, contains, ff. 68^a–78^a, a tractate with this title ascribed to Grosseteste. It begins: *Occasione cuiusdam sermonis quam feceram de adventu Christi*... and ends ...*ad fidei regulam duci ut a veritate non discordet.* It was written in response to a request by a friend that the author cull from the ancient philosophers their statements relative to Christianity. The authorship of this work is disputed. Father F. Delorme ascribed it to Roger Bacon, though most of the MSS bear an ascription to Johannes Parisiensis (Quidort).‡ There are several quotations from Aristotle's *Ethics*, and one reference to Aristotle reads: *dicit translator de greco in latinum.* Cicero, Philo, Alpharabius, Ovid, Eusebius, Trismegistus, Apuleius, the Eritrean Sybil, Mahomet, Orosius and Alcuin are all drawn upon. Since the eternity of the world is admitted, it is difficult to see how Grosseteste can be regarded as the author, particularly as the work is ascribed by copyists writing earlier than the Add. MS to authors whose temper would be more consonant with this sort of compilation. The Latin is rather worse than Grosseteste usually wrote and the lack of organization would, I feel sure, have appalled him. A superficial comparison of this work with others of Jean Quidort suggests that this, the earliest known tradition of authorship, is probably well founded.

* *Gesch. d. Logik im Abendlande*, III (Leipzig, 1867), 121, n. 558.

† R. Bacon, *Op. Ined.* p. lxix. Brewer assumed that the *Roberti* of the MS ascription was a mistake for *Rogeri* and ascribed the work to Bacon.

‡ See *Arch. Franc. Hist.* (April, 1911); *Archiv f. Lit.- und Kirchengesch.* IV, 312–339, and A. G. Little in his list of Roger Bacon's works in *Roger Bacon Essays* (Oxford, 1914), p. 411.

MSS:

Oxford				
Canon., pat. lat.	19	ff. 1^A–14^B	XIV¹	Ital.*
Lincoln	81	ff. 1^A–7^C	*ca.* 1425†	Asc. Joh. Par.
London, B.M., Add.	34807	ff. 68^a–78^a	XV¹	Asc. R.G.
Laon	275		XIV‡	
Paris				
B.N.	lat. 13781	ff. 72^a–95^b	XIV	Asc. Joh. Par.
Arsenal	78	ff. 9^a–28^a	1474§	Asc. Joh. Par.

Leland, *Collectanea*, IV, 66, reported a Balliol MS of *Testimonia gentilium conferentia religioni Christianae autore Rogero Bacon*, with incipit as above. This MS does not now appear among the Balliol MSS.

61. *In Threnos Ieremie.*

This title, listed without incipit by Bale, Pits and Tanner, is most probably the *Glose super Ieremiam* beginning: *Posuit Moyses in occidentali latere tabernaculi*... found in the Pembroke, Cambridge, MS 7, ff. 173^C–192^D. See above, p. 254 f. If, however, as the title strictly speaking indicates, a commentary on Lamentations is meant, it is either a lost work or a false attribution. From what we know of Grosseteste's mind and interests, we need not hesitate to accept the latter alternative. Bale's *Index* (ed. Poole, p. 376) lists an *Expositionem in threnos*, li. 1 with the incipit *Formam primam corporalem, ex catalogo antiquo Nordovicensi.* Bale had obviously made some mistake in compiling his notes. This is the incipit of Grosseteste's *De Luce* (see above, p. 108) and can hardly have any connection with a commentary on Lamentations. Tears and light keep but brief company.

62. *De Septem Viciis Principalibus.*

Under this or a similar title several works have been ascribed to Grosseteste by the bibliographers.

(*a*) Inc.: *Superbia est elacio viciosa que inferiores*..., found in various recensions in the following MSS:

Oxford, Laud Misc.	544	ff. 8^a–15^b	XIII^m	
Cambridge				
Univ.	Ll. i. 15	ff. 194^a–202^a	XIII^m	
C.C.C.	337	ff. 88^B–135^C	XIII^m; the longest text	
Erlangen	221 (Irm. 453)	ff. 151^A–160^A	*ca.* 1300	Ger.

There is no indication of the identity of the compiler in any of the MSS. The work is no more than a collection of sayings from the Bible and the fathers. The Cambridge Univ. MS has a seventeenth-century ascription "Roberti Capito". It has also a section from Robert de Courcon († 1219)

* The rubric reads: *Incipit tractatus mag. Iohannis Parisiensis ord. fratrum predicatorum de incarnacione domini nostri Yhesu Christi.*

† The colophon reads: *Explicit determinacio ffratris Johannis Parys de secta Christiana per testimonia gentilium.*

‡ The colophon reads: *Explicit tractatus patris Johannis Parisiensis de Christo et secta eius.*

§ The colophon reads: *Explicit tractatus patris Johannis Parisiensis de probacione fidei christiane per autoritates paganorum.*

on f. 201ᵇ. Many of the same quotations are found in Cambridge Univ. Ff. i. 14, f. 7ᵃ (*ca.* 1400), but in a different order.

(*b*) Boston of Bury lists as by Grosseteste a *Summa de septem viciis capitalibus secundum quosdam. Pr. Providendi. Fin. Plangit,** which is undoubtedly the work found in B.M. Royal MSS 8. A. x, ff. 54ᵃ–146, *ca.* 1300, and 11. B. III, ff. 226ᵇ–276ᵃ, *ca.* 1300, in both cases unascribed. Both begin *Primo videndum est quid superbia*... and end ...*et quod plangit.* The work also appears in John Rylands Lat. 201, ff. 159ᵃ–212ᵇ, XV¹, unasc. If the original scribe had not been careful, *Primo videndum* might easily be misread *Providendi.* Bale, Pits and Tanner list a *Summa* beginning *Primo videndum* without indicating any MSS. Grosseteste treats the subject of *superbia* in two *Dicta*, 47 and 127. See above, pp. 221 and 230.

(*c*) Tanner mentions Laud MS E. 44 (now Laud Misc. 206, XV¹), which contains, ff. 1ᵇ–55ᵇ, a treatise entitled in the colophon *Lincolniensis de septem viciis*, beginning: *Peccatum est vitandum sextuplici de causa.* See above, p. 253. It is found in two other MSS: Dublin, Trin. Coll. 207 (B. 4. 25), XIV², unasc., and Oxford, Exeter Coll. 7, XV¹, where it is ascribed to *Johannis Wallensis*...*ex parisiensi confectus.* This addition betrays its source. It is modelled after the *Summa de Viciis* of Guillelmus Peraldus, *al.* Parisiensis, employing the same trilogy of *exempla*, *de arte*, *de natura* and *de scriptura*, so characteristic of the *De Lingua* and the *Summa Iusticie.* See above, pp. 252 and 263.

No one of these works, either by reason of a strong tradition or by its internal characteristics, deserves to be long considered as even possibly by Grosseteste.

63. *Theorica Planetarum.*

See above, p. 238 f., for Grosseteste's "correction" of the treatise of Gerard of Sabionetta. Tanner cites Bodley MS NE. F. 10, 11 (=Bodley 300 and 472), in both of which we have the usual work of Gerard, the former (XV¹) ascribed to Grosseteste, the latter (XVᵐ) unascribed. Tanner's error is to be traced to Bernard who, because of the erroneous colophon in one MS, ascribed the work in both cases to Grosseteste.

64. *De Venenis.*

Inc.: Racio veneni potissime convenit peccato prioritate...
Expl.: ...aliis pretermissis et aliis derelictis. [Many variants.]
Publ. 1518 by Stephanus as by Malachias.

The list of MSS given below will show why the bibliographers have ascribed the work to Grosseteste. The majority of the MSS, even those from the middle of the fourteenth century, bear attributions to Grosseteste. M. Esposito argued† for the authorship of Malachias de Hibernia, whom he placed in Oxford (?) in the last quarter of the thirteenth century. None of the three MS ascriptions to Malachias is demonstrably older than the oldest

* See M. R. James, *On the Abbey of S. Edmund at Bury* (Cambridge Antiquarian Soc. 1895), p. 40. Boston records a *Summa de VII Vitiis Capitalibus* in the library at Bury.

† *EHR.* XXXIII (1918), 359–366. See also J. T. Welter, *L'Exemplum dans la Litt. religieuse et didactique du Moyen Âge* (Paris, 1927), p. 173, who refers only to the printed edition, accepting the attribution to Malachias († 1310).

ascription to Grosseteste, so that we cannot reject Grosseteste's authorship on a basis of priority of ascription to another author. But any ascription at all to a relatively obscure person, provided it has intrinsic probability, has great weight. The intrinsic probability in this case lies in the fact that a familiarity with Irish and Scotch legends, not traceable in any of Grosseteste's authentic works, is to be noticed throughout this work. The further fact may be observed that the work often appears in MSS containing the *De Lingua*, the *De Doctrina Cordis* or the *De Oculo Morali*, all of which we have had to reject as spurious. Association, even in MSS, may indicate corruption.

Esposito listed thirty-six MSS. The following list aims at correcting and supplementing his list. An (E) indicates that the MS was mentioned by him. The dates assigned to the MSS and other details are independent of his. J.W. = Johannes Wallensis; Mal. = Malachias. For MSS I have not seen, see *Index codicum manuscriptorum* below, p. 284 ff.

MSS:

Library	Shelfmark	Folios	Date	Ascription
Oxford				
Bodl.	122	ff. 92^{a}–133^{b}	*ca.* 1400	Asc. R.G. (E)
	798	ff. 127^{D}–139^{A}	XIV^{2}	Unasc. (E)
Digby	163	ff. 1^{a}–20^{b}	XV^{1}	Asc. R.G. (E)
Laud Misc.	206	ff. 126^{a}–128^{a}, *frag.*	XV^{1}	Unasc. (E)
	524	ff. 111^{a}–126^{a}	*ca.* 1400	Asc. R.G. *a.m.p.* (E)
	645	ff. 57^{b}–66^{b}	XV^{1}	Asc. R.G. *a.m.* (E)
Lincoln	56	ff. 163^{a}–177^{b}	XV^{1}	Unasc. (E)
Magdalen	6	ff. 133^{b}–159^{a}	1393	Asc. J.W. (E)
	48	ff. 225^{C}–240^{B}	*ca.* 1400	Asc. R.G. (E)
	200	ff. 29^{b}–40^{a}	XV	Unasc. (E)
	202	ff. 220^{C}–233^{D}	*ca.* 1400	Asc. R.G. (E)
Merton	43	ff. 27^{a}–53^{b}	XIV^{2}	Asc. R.G. (E)
	68	ff. 64^{b}–74^{b}	XV^{1}	Asc. R.G. (E)
Univ. Coll.	36	ff. 261^{A}–298^{B}	XIV^{2}	Asc. R.G. (E)
	60	ff. 236^{b}–261^{b}	XV^{1}	Asc. R.G. (E)
London, B.M.				
Cotton	Otho D. x	ff. 22^{a}–28^{b}	XIV^{m}	Unasc. (E)
	Vitell. C. xiv	ff. 57^{A}–65^{B}	XIV^{2}	Asc. Mal. (E)
Royal	7. C. i	ff. 82^{A}–92^{C}	XIV^{2}	Unasc. (E)
	7. F. ii	ff. 1^{A}–9^{D}	XIV^{m}	Unasc. (E)
Sloane	1616	ff. 1^{a}–32^{a}	XV^{1}	Asc. R.G. (E)
London				
Gray's Inn	18	ff. 220^{A}–229^{C}	XV^{1}	Asc. R.G. (E)
	23	ff. 181^{C}–190^{A}	XIV^{1}	Unasc. (E)
Lambeth	483	ff. 77^{a}–111^{a} + 112^{a-b}	XIV^{2}	Unasc. (E)
	523	ff. 88^{a}–113^{a}	*ca.* 1400	Asc. Mal. XV^{1} (E)
Cambridge				
Univ.	Dd. x. 15	ff. 1^{a}–12^{b}	XV^{2}	Unasc. (E)
	Ii. i. 26	ff. 71^{b}–88^{a}	XV^{m}	Asc. R.G. (E)*
Pembroke	239	ff. 240^{a}–254^{b}	XIV^{2}	Asc. R.G. (E)
Peterhouse	237	ff. 122^{A}–131^{B}	XV^{1}	Unasc. (E)
Queens'	10	ff. 62^{b}–67^{b}	XIV^{2}	Asc. R.G. (E)
Sid. Suss.	85	ff. 81^{a}–94^{a}	XIII^{2}	Unasc. (E)
Trinity	B. 15. 35	ff. 251^{a}–256^{a}	XIV^{2}	Unasc. (E)

* Asc. *a. m. coeva: Joh. Grosteste, alii dicunt magistri Joh. Acton canon. lincoln.*

Dublin, Trinity	A. 5. 3	ff. 186^a–196^b	1377	Asc. R.G. (E)
Durham				
Cath.	B. II. 4	ff. 128^C–138^C	*ca.* 1300	Unasc. (E)
	B. III. 18	ff. 233^A–243^A	XV^m	Asc. R.G.
	B. III. 19	ff. 240^A–253^B	*ca.* 1400	Asc. R.G.
Cosin's Lib.	V. ii. 53			Unasc.
Eton Coll.	117, pt. III	pp. 1^a–20^a	XV^1	Asc. R.G.
Lincoln Cath.	49	ff. 129^b–143^a	XV^m	Asc. R.G.
	68	ff. 43^a–58^b	XIV^2	Unasc.
	125	ff. 37^C–50^A	XV^1	Asc. R.G.
	202	ff. 225^A–238^A	XIV^m	Asc. R.G. XV^1 (E)
Bruges	558	ff. 12^b–27^a	XV^1	Asc. R.G. Lowlands
Graz, Univ.	628	ff. 239^C–261^B	1422	Asc. R.G. So. Ger.
Munich, library of J. Halle, dated 1459, Asc. Mal. (E)				
Paris, St Germain	185			
Prague, Nat. Mus.	XIV. C. 9	ff. 173^a–181^a	XIV^2	Unasc. Boh.
Toulouse	230	ff. 156–175	*ca.* 1400	Asc. R.G. (E)
	232	ff. 29–39	XV	Asc. R.G. (E)
Vatican, Pal. lat.	679	ff. 206^a–232^b	XV^1	Unasc. *mut.*

65. *De Virtutibus et Viciis.*

Most of the bibliographers agree that Grosseteste wrote a treatise *De Viciis*, but there is diversity of opinion as to the specific treatise meant. See above, *Spurium* 46, p. 259, and *Spurium* 62, p. 267 f.

LOST OR UNTRACED WORKS

The following works, listed by one or more of the early bibliographers, remain unidentified or untraced. In most cases we may surmise that no such work by Grosseteste ever existed.

1. *De Assiduitate Orandi*, listed by Tanner and, after him, by Pegge, with the incipit *Assidua debet esse oracio*. Such a work was once in Cotton Otho D. x. We have no means of knowing whether it was ascribed to Grosseteste or not. The codex, though containing much Grossetestiana, contains also a number of works by other authors. See above, p. 11.

2. *Super Iobum*. Bale, Pits and Tanner list without incipit from Boston of Bury.

3. *De Lapide Philosophico* and

4. *De Necromancia et Goëcia*. I have nothing to add to Baur's remark, p. 124*, that no such works by Grosseteste exist. He suggests that marginalia in a Prague MS (Univ. 1990) of the *De Artibus Liberalibus* have become separate opuscula. Yet it is barely possible that there may be here some connection with the extracts in Grosseteste's own hand in Savile MS 21. See above, Introd. p. 30 f.

5. *In Lucam*. Listed by Bale, Pits and Tanner without incipit. There may be some remote connection with Laud Misc. MS 291, which contains a *Commentarius in Lucam* with the *Commentarius in Marcum* that appears in Pembroke, Cambridge, MS 7. See above, *Spurium* 32, p. 254.

6. *Exposicio in Epistolas Pauli*. Gascoigne (*Loci e Libro Veritatum*, ed. Rogers, p. 142) tells of having seen Grosseteste's *explanacio* of the epistles of Paul, written *manu sua propria...in margine illius libri*. This may have been a twelfth-century codex containing the text of the epistles and the *glossae interlinearis* and *communis*, a rather common type of text in England, which Grosseteste had annotated in the same way as he had annotated Peter the Lombard's *Commentarius in Psalmos* and the Shrewsbury copy of *Sapiencia* and *Ecclesiasticus* with the two glosses. See above, pp. 72 and 77 f. The copy to which Gascoigne referred, once in the library of the Oxford Franciscans, may yet be found, as also an *exposicio in II Cor.*, which he mentions (*op. cit.* p. 103), though it is probable that the same codex is meant.

7. *Praxis Geometrie*. Bale, Tanner and Wood list a tractate under this title, beginning: *Sciendum est de mensuris communibus*. Wood cites Ashmole MS 76, f. 30. There is no such work in this MS.

8. *De Premiis Apostolorum*. Bale, Pits and Tanner list a treatise with this title beginning: *Misit de summo et accepit me*. The incipit, a scriptural text, does not help much toward a possible identification. I have found no MS of any work corresponding to this description.

9. *In Verba Gabrielis.* Bale, Pits and Tanner list a work under this title beginning: *Ingressus angelus ad eam dixit.* I have found no such work, but there may have been confusion with a hitherto unnoticed work of Richard of Middleton* entitled *Compendium*, beginning *Missus est angelus...in hoc verbo Gabriel...* and ending *...numquam eternaliter deserendo*, found in Prague, Nat. Mus., MS XVI. D. 12 (3688), ff. 69ᵃ–109ᵇ.†

10. *Questio de Originali Peccato.* See above, p. 113 f., under *V Questiones Theologice.*

11. *In Vesperiis Ade.* Bale lists (*Index*, p. 376) *ex Thoma Gascoigne* as a work of Grosseteste the *vesperies* of Adam, probably Adam Marsh.‡ The *vesperies* was the last disputation engaged in by a B.D. before he incepted as a Master. But this disputation at which Grosseteste presided for his friend is either anonymous or lost. No trace of it has been found.

* See E. Hocedez, *Richard de Middleton* (Louvain, 1925). This work seems to have escaped Hocedez's notice.

† F. M. Bartoš, *Soupis Rukopisů Narodního Musea*, II (Prague, 1927), 353 f. The prose *Missus Gabriel* appears in twelfth-century MSS, e.g. Paris, B.N. lat. 1139, of Southern French provenance.

‡ See A. G. Little, "The Franciscan School at Oxford" in *Arch. Franc. Hist.* XIX (1926), 828, and Little and Pelster, *Oxford Theology and Theologians* (Oxford Hist. Soc., vol. XCVI, Oxford, 1934), p. 45.

INDEX NOMINUM

INDEX CODICUM MANUSCRIPTORUM

*An * before a signature indicates that I have not examined the MS. In a few cases the signatures in this list are more complete than in the text.*

INDEX INITIORUM

This index may err on the side of inclusiveness. Single paragraphs and secondary incipits frequently appear, and scriptural texts as well as the beginning of the sermon or dictum proper. If two or more pages are listed, dark figures indicate where the fuller treatment of the work in question is to be found. In several cases one incipit may serve for two separate works.

For EU product safety concerns, contact us at Calle de José Abascal, 56–1°, 28003 Madrid, Spain or eugpsr@cambridge.org.

www.ingramcontent.com/pod-product-compliance
Ingram Content Group UK Ltd.
Pitfield, Milton Keynes, MK11 3LW, UK
UKHW010349140625
459647UK00010B/953

* 9 7 8 1 1 0 7 6 6 8 6 4 5 *